VIOLENCE AND
MENTAL DISORDER

The John D. and Catherine T. MacArthur Foundation
Series on Mental Health and Development

VIOLENCE AND MENTAL DISORDER

Developments in Risk Assessment

Edited by

John Monahan and Henry J. Steadman

THE UNIVERSITY OF CHICAGO PRESS / CHICAGO AND LONDON

The University of Chicago Press, Chicago 60637
The University of Chicago Press, Ltd., London
© 1994 by The University of Chicago
All rights reserved. Published 1994
Printed in the United States of America
Paperback edition 1996

08 07 06 05 04 03 02 01 00 99   3 4 5 6 7 8 9 10

ISBN: 0-226-53406-5 (paperback)

The University of Chicago Press gratefully acknowledges a subvention from the John D. and Catherine T. MacArthur Foundation in partial support of the costs of production of this volume.

Library of Congress Cataloging-in-Publication Data
Violence and mental disorder : developments in risk assessment / edited by John Monahan and Henry J. Steadman.
    p.   cm.—(The John D. and Catherine T. MacArthur Foundation series on mental health and development)
    Includes bibliographical references and index.
    ISBN 0-226-53405-7 (cloth)
    1. Violence—Forecasting. 2. Insane, Criminal and dangerous. 3. Violence—Psychological aspects. I. Monahan, John, 1946– . II. Steadman, Henry J. III. Series
    RC569.5.V55V54   1994
    616.85′82—dc20
                                                                    93-1670
                                                                    CIP

∞ The paper used in this publication meets the minimum requirements of the American National Standard for Information Sciences—Permanence of Paper for Printed Library Materials, ANSI Z39.48-1992.

Contents

Preface

Civil and criminal courts throughout the world increasingly demand that psychiatrists, psychologists, and other mental health professionals offer opinions about the "dangerousness" of mentally disordered persons. Yet research reported in the 1970s dramatically demonstrated the limits of professional expertise: clinicians were consistently found wrong more often than right when they predicted violence. A limited amount of research conducted during the 1980s attempted to improve on this unimpressive record but—with a few notable exceptions—achieved little success.

Perhaps the major reason for the lack of progress in the field is that the risk factors that have been studied have been chosen without reference to any theories of mental disorder or of violent behavior and thus have been poorly conceived. As we indicate in the first chapter, if research in the 1990s is to improve on the unsatisfying results of the 1980s, methodologically sound research designs and theoretically coherent indices of risk must be developed.

The development of such risk indicators is the overriding purpose of this volume. We conceive risk factors for violence as falling into four domains: dispositional, clinical, historical, and contextual factors.

Part 1, chapters 2 through 4, addresses risk factors within the realm of individual dispositional tendencies, specifically the variables of anger, impulsiveness, psychopathy, and personality disorders. Part 2, chapters 5 through 9, deals with clinical or psychopathological factors—diagnoses of mental disorder and substance abuse, psychotic symptoms in patient and community samples, delusions, and hallucinations. Part 3 addresses both historical and contextual factors; chapters 10 and 11 consider case history variables, social networks, and social support. The concluding chapter provides one example of how all of these risk factors can be integrated into a significantly improved risk assessment research methodology.

Many of the chapters in this volume report on risk assessment instruments developed or adapted with the support of the Research Network on Mental Health and the Law of the John D. and Catherine T. MacArthur Foundation.

The Network's hope is that this volume will be of use to our fellow researchers in mental health law, to clinicians who confront questions of violence risk in their daily practice, and to lawyers, judges, and mental health administrators who must resolve issues of both general public policy and specific case disposition in fulfilling their professional roles.

A Risk Working Group, consisting of Henry J. Steadman (project director), Pamela Clark Robbins (project manager), Paul S. Appelbaum, Thomas Grisso, John Monahan (network director), Edward P. Mulvey, and Loren H. Roth, was responsible for planning and implementing the Network's studies of risk.

We are grateful to the staff of the MacArthur Program on Health and Human Development—Denis J. Prager, the program's director, Laurie Garduque, Idy Gitelson, Robert Rose, and Ruth Runeborg—for their vision and for their financial, intellectual, and moral support of the Network's operation. The program of research reported here was designed with the collaboration of the entire Network, including, in addition to members of the Risk Working Group, Shirley S. Abrahamson, Richard J. Bonnie, Pamela S. Hyde, Stephen J. Morse, Paul Slovic, and David B. Wexler. Lynn Daidone has deftly orchestrated the operation of the Network. We are, finally, grateful to the authors of the chapters in this volume for allowing us to produce what is notoriously rare in academic publishing—an edited book completed on schedule.

Contributors

Paul S. Appelbaum, Department of Psychiatry, University of Massachusetts Medical Center, Worcester

Ernest S. Barratt, Department of Psychiatry and Behavioral Sciences, University of Texas Medical Branch, Galveston

Alec Buchanan, Institute of Criminology, Cambridge University, and Institute of Psychiatry, University of London, England

Deidre Klassen, Greater Kansas City Mental Health Foundation, Kansas City, Missouri

Graham Dunn, Institute of Psychiatry, University of London, England

Sue E. Estroff, Department of Social Medicine, University of North Carolina at Chapel Hill

Adelle E. Forth, Department of Psychology, Carleton University, Ottawa, Canada

Philippa Garety, Institute of Psychiatry, University of London, England

Thomas Grisso, Department of Psychiatry, University of Massachusetts Medical Center, Worcester

Don Grubin, Institute of Psychiatry, University of London, England

Robert D. Hare, Department of Psychology, University of British Columbia, Vancouver, Canada

Stephen D. Hart, Mental Health, Law, and Policy Institute, Simon Fraser University, Burnaby, Canada

Bruce G. Link, Epidemiology of Mental Disorders, Columbia University

Dale E. McNiel, Department of Psychiatry, School of Medicine, University of California, San Francisco

John Monahan, University of Virginia School of Law

Edward P. Mulvey, Western Psychiatric Institute and Clinic, University of Pittsburgh

Raymond W. Novaco, Department of Psychology and Social Behavior, School of Social Ecology, University of California, Irvine

William A. O'Connor, Greater Kansas City Mental Health Foundation, Kansas City, Missouri

Katarzyna Ray, Institute of Psychiatry, University of London, England

Alison Reed, Bethlem-Maudsley Hospital, and Special Hospitals Service Authority, London, England

Pamela Clark Robbins, Policy Research Associates, Albany, New York

Loren H. Roth, Western Psychiatric Institute and Clinic, University of Pittsburgh

Henry J. Steadman, Policy Research Associates, Albany, New York

Ann Stueve, Psychiatric Epidemiology, Columbia University

Jeffrey W. Swanson, Department of Psychiatry, Duke University Medical Center

Pamela J. Taylor, Institute of Psychiatry, University of London, and Special Hospitals Service Authority, London, England

Timothy J. Trull, Department of Psychology, University of Missouri

Simon Wessely, King's College Hospital, and Institute of Psychiatry, University of London, England

Thomas A. Widiger, Department of Psychology, University of Kentucky

Catherine Zimmer, Department of Sociology and Anthropology, North Carolina State University

1 Toward a Rejuvenation of Risk Assessment Research

JOHN MONAHAN AND HENRY J. STEADMAN

The concept of risk of harm to others plays a pivotal role in both criminal and civil aspects of mental health law. On the criminal side, for example, the American Bar Association's (1989) Criminal Justice–Mental Health Standards specify in black-letter that a court should commit a person acquitted of a violent crime by reason of insanity to a mental hospital only if the court finds clear and convincing evidence that the person is currently mentally disordered and, as a result, "poses a substantial risk of serious bodily harm to others" (standard 7-7.4).

On the civil side, prior to the late 1960s commitment of the mentally disordered to hospitals was dominated by a paternalistic concern for persons perceived to be "in need of treatment." Beginning with California's Lanterman-Petris-Short Act in 1969, however, paternalism began to yield to the patients' rights movement, and risk of behavior harmful to others—called "dangerousness" in statutes and court decisions (e.g., *Lessard* v. *Schmidt*, 349 F. Supp. 1078 [1972])—attained prominence in civil law. Despite some refocusing of standards in recent years to reemphasize the more diffuse "mental or physical deterioration" that disorder can precipitate (LaFond and Durham 1992), risk of behavioral harm has remained firmly embedded as a standard in modern American mental health law (Appelbaum 1988; Monahan and Shah 1989). The American Psychiatric Association's model state law on civil commitment (American Psychiatric Association 1983), for example, following Roth (1979), explicitly contemplates the commitment of several types of mentally disordered persons, including those "likely to cause harm to others." The guidelines for involuntary civil commitment of the National Center for State Courts urge, in this regard, that

> particularly close attention be paid to predictions of future behavior, especially predictions of violence and assessments of dangerousness. Such predictions have been the bane of clinicians who admit limited competence to offer estimates of the future yet are mandated legally to do so. [However,] such predictions will con-

tinue to provide a basis for involuntary civil commitment, even amid controversy about the scientific and technological shortcomings and the ethical dilemmas that surround them. (National Center for State Courts 1986, commentary to guideline G.1)

The risk that a mentally disordered person will commit harm will therefore remain a core issue in mental health law. In this chapter we offer a framework, derived from the fields of public health and decision theory, for the study of the risk of violence, we survey recent developments in risk assessment research, and we identify methodological obstacles to progress in the field and offer proposals to obviate each of these major difficulties (cf. Monahan 1988).

A Public Health Perspective on Violence

The behavioral sciences traditionally associated with the study of violent behavior have been sociology, criminology, psychology, and psychiatry (see, in general, National Research Council 1993). Each has been heavily influenced by legal conceptions of violent crime and violent or "dangerous" offenders. In recent years, however, in response to rising rates of violent death among many groups in American society—homicide is now the leading cause of death for African Americans aged 15 through 34 (United States Department of Health and Human Services 1991)—a public health perspective on violence and "injury prevention" has arisen. The publications of the Centers for Disease Control's Violence Epidemiology Branch (e.g., Mercy and O'Carroll 1988; Rosenberg and Fenley 1991) and the U.S. Department of Health and Human Service's comprehensive report, *Healthy People 2000: National Health Promotion and Disease Prevention Objectives* (United States Department of Health and Human Services 1991) have brought new insights to bear on the problem of violent behavior by analyzing violence not as a "crime," like burglary or theft, but as a "health problem," like cancer or stroke. The public health perspective has a number of implications for how research on the violent behavior of the mentally disordered (or anyone else) should be conducted (Shepherd and Farrington, in press).

The legal concept of "dangerousness" (Brooks 1978) confounds the variables on which a prediction is based, the type of event being predicted, and the likelihood of the event occurring. For research purposes, "dangerousness" should first be disaggregated into three component parts: "risk factors," the variables that are used to predict violence; "harm," the amount and type of violence being predicted; and "risk level," the probability that harm will occur (National Research Council 1989). Second, the "harm" that is being predicted should be scaled in terms of seriousness, rather than being treated as a dichotomous variable (harm or no harm; Gottfredson and Gottfredson 1988). Third, "risk level" (or simply "risk") should be seen as a continuous probability statement, rather than a dichotomous variable (risk or no risk). Fourth, since risk levels are often not stable but fluctuate over time and context, estimates of risk should be in the form of ongoing "assessments" rather than one-time "predictions." Finally, given that the goal of public health intervention is the prevention, rather than the treatment, of harm, "risk management" as well as "risk assessment" should be a goal of research.

Approaches to the Study of Risk

An essential starting point for exploring how to improve "risk research" is to distinguish the various types of studies that have been covered under this umbrella. In planning the MacArthur Risk Assessment Study (Steadman et al., this volume), the Research Network on Mental Health and the Law of the John D. and Catherine T. MacArthur Foundation found the "lens theory" framework first propounded by Egon Brunswick (1956) to be a valuable heuristic for sorting out approaches to the study of risk (cf. Werner, Rose, and Yesavage 1983; Grisso 1991). As figure 1 makes clear, studies may address three distinct aspects of risk assessment: (*a*) the relationship between *cues* or risk factors (e.g., anger, diagnosis, age) and *judgment* or clinical prediction; (*b*) the relationship between *judgment* or clinical prediction and the *criterion* of violent behavior; and (*c*) the relationship between *cues* or risk factors and the *criterion* of violent behavior. Research exists exploring each of these three relationships. Studies illustrative of each approach are described in the following section.

Cues and Judgment: Clinical Decision Making

Mulvey and Lidz (1984, 1985) have reviewed studies published prior to the mid-1980s of how clinicians go about predicting violence. Here we will dis-

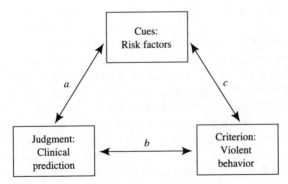

Figure 1.   Approaches to the study of risk.

cuss three more recent investigations of the process by which clinicians use information to form judgments about risk.

Werner et al. (1984) gave experienced psychiatrists information from the files of newly admitted male mental patients. Based on Brief Psychiatric Rating Scale scores and information as to whether violence was a precipitating incident for the current hospitalization, the psychiatrists were asked to estimate the likelihood that the patient would commit a violent act within the first week of hospitalization. They found that "a clinical picture of hostility and agitation, accompanied by paranoid ideation and previous assaultiveness, is viewed as indicating potential for violence in a patient on an acute inpatient unit" (Werner et al. 1984, 264). Cooper and Werner (1990) used a similar methodology to assess the relationship between various factors and clinical judgment of the risk of subsequent violence by psychologists in a federal prison. Positive correlations were found between prediction of violence and type of current offense, severity of the current offense, history of violence, and race.

While Werner et al. studied clinical judgment regarding inpatient violence, Segal et al. (1988a, 1988b) focused on decision making regarding violence in the community. They observed clinicians evaluating 251 cases at several mental hospital emergency rooms in northern California. Observers coded each case according to an 88-item index called Three Ratings of Involuntary Admissability (TRIAD). Global ratings of patient "dangerousness" were also completed by each clinician. TRIAD scores correlated highly with overall clinical ratings of dangerousness (Segal et al. 1988a). They found that "symptoms most strongly related to [clinical judgments of] danger to others in our sample were irritability and impulsivity, but there were also consistent moderate associations with formal thought disorder, thought content disorder, and expansiveness as well as weaker but consistent significant correlations with impaired judgment and behavior and inappropriate affect" (Segal et al. 1988b, 757).

In the ongoing research program of Lidz and Mulvey (e.g., Lidz et al. 1989; Lidz and Mulvey 1990; Lidz et al. 1992; Gondolf, Mulvey, and Lidz 1989, 1990, 1991; Cleveland et al. 1989; and Apperson, Mulvey, and Lidz, in press), research observers trained in speedwriting recorded interviews between clinicians and patients admitted to a hospital's psychiatric emergency room. Clinicians later completed ratings of current and chronic dangerousness in the community and numerous other variables. While a patient's history of violence was the best predictor of clinician ratings, patient hostility and the presence of serious disorder also correlated highly with clinical assessments of current dangerousness, as in the Werner and Segal studies described above. In addition, explicit judgments of the likelihood of future violence were rarely found in actual practice, with this conclusion instead embedded in other decisions about clinical care.

Judgment and Criterion: Clinical Prediction

Research on the accuracy of clinical judgments at predicting the criterion of violent behavior toward others was reviewed in Monahan (1981). Monahan considered five studies available as of 1981 (Kozol, Boucher, and Garofalo 1972; Steadman and Cocozza 1974; Cocozza and Steadman 1976; Steadman 1977; Thornberry and Jacoby 1979) and concluded that "psychiatrists and psychologists are accurate in no more than one out of three predictions of violent behavior over a several-year period among institutionalized populations that had both committed violence in the past (and thus had high base rates for it) and who were diagnosed as mentally ill" (Monahan 1981, 47–49). Remarkably, only one study of the validity of clinicians at predicting violence in the community was published between 1979 and 1993.[1]

Since patients whom clinicians assess as having a very high likelihood of imminent violence are, for that reason, unlikely to be released (and thus are unavailable for community follow-up), research validating actual clinical assessments of high likelihood of community violence can be done only when those predictions are overridden by a judge or other decision maker. This can occur either if the judge substantively disagrees with the clinician's prediction in a given case and orders the person released, or if a court holds that a legal basis for detaining a class of persons is lacking and orders the class released. Kozol, Boucher, and Garofulo (1972) examines the first of these reasons for the availability of subjects; Steadman and Cocozza (1974) study the second. (For a critique of both types of study, see Litwack and Schlesinger 1987.) Either these two contingencies did not occur often after the late 1970s, or they occurred and researchers failed to take advantage of them.

Lidz, Mulvey, and Gardner (1993), in what is surely the most sophisticated study ever done of the clinical prediction of violence, employed a different methodology. Rather than study patients released by a court over clinicians' objections, they took as their subjects patients being examined in the psychiatric emergency room of a large urban hospital. Nurses and psychiatrists were asked to assess potential patient violence to others over the next six-month period. Violence was measured by official records, patient self-report, and the report of a collateral informant in the community. Patients who elicited professional concern regarding future violence were found to be significantly more likely to be violent after release (53%) than were patients who had not elicited such concern (36%). The accuracy of clinical prediction did not vary as a function of the patient's age or race. The accuracy of clinicians' predictions of male violence substantially exceeded chance levels, both for patients

---

1. This was a study conducted in 1978 of court-ordered pretrial mental health assessments (Sepejak et al. 1983). Thirty-nine percent of the defendants rated by clinicians as having a "medium" or "high" likelihood of being dangerous to others were reported to have committed "dangerous" acts during a two-year follow-up (see Sepejak et al. 1983, 181 n. 12).

with and without a prior history of violent behavior. In contrast, the accuracy of clinicians' predictions of female violence did not differ from chance. While the actual rate of violent incidents among released female patients (49%) was higher than the rate among released male patients (42%), the clinicians had predicted that only 22 percent of the women would be violent, compared with predicting that 45 percent of the men would commit a violent act.

While recent studies, with the exception of Lidz et al. (1993), have not focused on validating the clinical prediction of *community* violence, research throughout the 1980s has addressed the prediction of *institutional* violence (Davis 1991). For example, Werner et al. (1984), described above, compared psychiatrists' predictions of patient violence during the first week of hospitalization with the actual occurrence of violence on the ward as indicated by descriptions of assaultive acts in nursing notes. The correlation between clinical predictions and actual violence in the hospital was a nonsignificant .14. McNiel and Binder (1991) also studied clinical predictions that patients would be violent during the first week of hospitalization. Of the patients whom nurses had estimated had a 0% to 33% probability of being violent on the ward, 10% were later rated by the nurses as having committed a violent act; of the patients whom nurses had estimated had a 34% to 66% chance of being violent, 24% were later rated as having committed a violent act; and of the patients whom nurses had estimated had a 67% to 100% chance of being violent, 40% were later rated as having acted violently. Predictions made by staff physicians fared somewhat more poorly.

Cues and Criterion: Actuarial Assessment

A great deal of recent research addresses the relationship between specific cues or risk factors and the occurrence of violent behavior (e.g., Convit et al. 1988; Craig 1982; Tardiff and Sweillam 1982; Rossi et al. 1986). In these studies, patients are assessed according to one or more potential risk factors, such as diagnosis, demographics, or Brief Psychiatric Rating Scale scores, and these measures are correlated with the occurrence of violence either on the hospital ward or in the community. In the latter instance, the subjects—unlike those in the clinical prediction studies described above—have been released with clinical staff concurrence rather than over their objection.

The research program of Dale McNiel and Renée Binder (e.g., Binder and McNiel 1988; McNiel, Binder, and Greenfield 1988; McNiel and Binder 1989, 1991) is an exemplar of actuarial research on the prediction of inpatient violence. For example, McNiel, Binder, and Greenfield (1988) found that gender (female), marital status (married), diagnosis (mania), and prior suicidal behavior (none) were positively associated with violence on the hospital ward.

Actuarial research on the prediction of violence in the community is best reflected in the research program of Deidre Klassen and William O'Connor (e.g., Klassen and O'Connor 1988a, 1988b, 1990). For example, Klassen and O'Connor (1988a) found that a diagnosis of substance abuse, prior arrests for violent crime, and age (young) were significantly associated with arrests for violent crime after release into the community.

Methodological Problems and Proposals

Research on each of these three approaches to the study of the risk of violence among the mentally disordered is certainly needed. To understand better how clinicians reach clinical judgments is of intrinsic scholarly interest and may yield valuable information about the factors clinicians believe to be predictive of violence. Yet, unless actuarial research can independently verify the predictive value of these and other, more theoretically derived factors, their actual as opposed to perceived usefulness in risk assessment will remain unknown. And until clinicians are better informed of the factors that are actuarially associated with the criterion of violent behavior, there is little reason to expect that research on the validity of clinical judgments of risk will produce results superior to those found in the literature of the 1970s. The remainder of this chapter, therefore, will propose methodological strategies to overcome or circumvent impediments to progress in research linking specific cues or risk markers to actual violent behavior. Such an actuarial approach has the greatest potential, we believe, to rejuvenate risk assessment research, to inform clinical practice, and to positively affect the development of mental health law.

Four methodological problems have especially plagued actuarial research on the assessment of the potential of the mentally disordered for violence: inadequacy of cues or factors chosen to forecast whether violence will occur, inability to determine the extent of violence within the population studied, limited applicability of research designs used to validate risk factors, and failure to coordinate research efforts in the field.

Impoverished Predictor Variables

It seems clear that violent behavior among any group of people, let alone people who are seriously mentally disordered, is a complex phenomenon that has many types of social, psychological, and biological antecedents (on the last, see Mednick, Brennan, and Kandel 1988; Tancredi and Volkow 1988; Hodgins, 1993). Despite the multifaceted nature of violence, much of the existing research on risk assessment among the mentally disordered has employed a very narrow range of cues or predictor variables (e.g., the Brief Psychiatric Rating Scale, *or* past history, *or* a psychological test), chosen without conscious regard for any theory of violent behavior or of mental disorder (Klassen and O'Connor, this volume). Studies are only now beginning to include clinical variables derived from basic theories of stress and aggression, such as psychopathy (Hart, Hare, and Forth, this volume), anger control (Novaco, this volume), impulsiveness (Barratt, this volume), delusions (Taylor et al., this volume), hallucinations (McNiel, this volume) or social support (Estroff and Zimmer, this volume). As the National Institute of Mental Health's recent National Plan of Research to Improve Services (National Institute of Mental Health 1991, 44) noted, "Particularly informative would be investigations of the relationship between violence and specific aspects of mental illness—for example, the nature, extent, and effects of delusions."

Perhaps most ironically, given the subject population of the research, many risk assessment studies have relied on woefully inadequate classifications of patients, often lumping them into "psychotic" versus "nonpsychotic" groups or comparing schizophrenia with "all other diagnoses" (see Monahan and Steadman 1983; Cirincione et al., 1992; Swanson, this volume; Widiger and Trull, this volume). Even those studies that do include standard diagnostic information (i.e., DSM III-R diagnoses) among their predictor variables rarely include variations in the course or symptomatology of the disorder, although there is reason to believe that such information has predictive value (Krakowski, Volavka, and Brizer 1986; Link and Stueve, this volume).

A frequent suggestion for improving the validity of clinical risk assessments is to take into account predictor variables reflecting the "environmental" or "situational" context in which violent behavior is likely to occur, in addition to measuring dispositional, historical, or clinical factors (e.g., Monahan and Klassen 1982; Steadman 1982; Felson and Steadman 1983). The few studies that have incorporated situational predictor variables have yielded important and often counterintuitive findings. Klassen and O'Connor (1985), for example, found that the more friends a released patient reported having in the community and the more time he spent with those friends, the more likely he was to commit a violent act. Friends seemed to function more as instigators of violence than as sources of social support.

Finally, what is arguably the most important aspect of the environment of mentally disordered people is routinely neglected in risk assessment research. The extent to which arrangements have been made to provide aftercare to released patients and the extent to which released patients comply with aftercare recommendations (in particular, recommendations to continue taking psychotropic medication) may have a profound effect upon their behavior in the community. For example, Cohen et al. (1986) found that 36% of released insanity acquittees who took their medication regularly were readmitted to the hospital within five years of release, compared with 92% of those who did not comply with medication recommendations.

Research currently in progress by Lidz and Mulvey (e.g., Lidz 1987) is attempting to advance the situational-factors approach to risk assessment by ascertaining the extent to which the occurrence of violence is conditional upon the presence of specific environmental characteristics. The failure of a risk factor to anticipate violence can then be broken down to determine whether the factor is without predictive value or whether its predictive value is contingent upon the presence of situational factors that potentiate its latent relationship to violent behavior. Due to the potential number of interaction effects, the complexity introduced into research designs by disaggregating "personal level" and "situational level" variables is not to be underestimated.

Moving research on risk assessment forward, therefore, requires that an enriched set of cues or predictor variables be studied. Toward that end, researchers should take several steps:

1. Assess risk factors in multiple domains, including dispositional and historical cues.
2. Develop new measures to assess risk factors that appear theoretically relevant to violent behavior but for which no adequate measures currently exist (e.g., anger control).
3. Reflect DSM IV diagnostic criteria, including change in diagnosis and indications of the clinical course of the disorder, as well as descriptions of specific symptom patterns.
4. Assess situational or conditional risk factors, such as the type and availability of aftercare for released patients ànd the extent to which patients comply with clinical recommendations.

Weak Criterion Variables

One of the most persistent criticisms of existing risk assessment studies is that an unknown but perhaps large portion of the criterion—violent behavior—goes undetected. In the context of actuarial research, this would mean that cues that are in fact associated with violence will appear uncorrelated with the criterion (Mulvey and Lidz, in press). The reliance in many community studies solely upon arrest data seems inadequate, given that disordered people who act violently may be returned to a hospital rather than arrested. While Teplin (1985) found that the police were more likely to arrest disordered than nondisordered suspects, Klassen and O'Connor (1988b), found that released schizophrenic patients whose violence in the community evoked an official response were twice as likely to be rehospitalized as they were to be arrested. Reliance upon any type of official records—arrest or hospitalization—will overlook violence that did not precipitate formal intervention by a government agency. In another study, Klassen and O'Connor (1987) found that including patient self-reports of violence increased predictive accuracy by 27.8%. As they note, "more than one quarter of the 'false positives' may not, in fact, be false positives if self-reports are a valid measure of violence" (see also the inpatient study by Convit et al. 1988).

Another recurring problem in risk assessment research is the lack of precision produced by not disaggregating criterion violence into meaningful subtypes. The predictors of one form of violence may be quite different than the predictors of another (Dietz et al. 1991). As the NIMH National Plan of Research to Improve Services (National Institute of Mental Health 1991, 44) states: "In examining dangerous behavior, it would be desirable to examine violence in the family and in public separately, because each implies different strategies for clinical intervention and regulatory policy. There is increasing awareness that patient violence is not a unified phenomenon and that research on patient violence against family members may prove particularly important."

A reinvigorated field of risk assessment research must strengthen the set of criterion variables studied. This requires that researchers do several things:

1. Develop standardized instruments to measure specific types of self-reported violence and, ideally, violence reported by significant others (e.g., family members), which can then be integrated with official agency records.
2. Test new procedures for locating released patients in the community.
3. Assess subjects on all criterion variables repeatedly at specified intervals over an extended period of time.
4. Record rehospitalization precipitated by violent behavior as well as arrest for violent crime.

Constricted Validation Samples

As noted above, existing actuarial risk assessment research employs one of two methodologies. One type of study attempts to identify factors that predict violence *in the hospital,* the other to identify factors that predict violence *in the community.*

One obvious difficulty with trying to predict violence in the hospital is that the structured milieu of the institution and the therapeutic (or at least sedative) effects of medication seriously suppress the base rate of violence. As Werner, Rose, and Yesavage (1983) have stated:

> To the extent that hostile, excited, suspicious, and recent assaultive behavior is viewed by ward staffing as presaging imminent violence, it is the patient manifesting such behavior who is singled out for special treatment (e.g., additional medications, more psychotherapy); such selection may reduce the likelihood of engaging in violence. Thus, paradoxically, if the patient who

"looks" imminently violent in this setting is given effective treatments that forestall violent behavior, he will not in fact engage in violence as predicted, and the initial forecast. . . will be shown to be inaccurate.

The NIMH National Plan of Research to Improve Services (National Institute of Mental Health 1991, 44) endorses research on inpatient violence, but with an important annotation: "It is much easier and cheaper to do research on inpatient violence than on violence by mental patients in the community. It should, however, be undertaken with certain goals in mind. Its highest priority should be on discerning types of interaction that are likely to be present in patient violence in the community as well." Validating risk assessments in the community presents different issues than validating risk assessments in the hospital. As noted, actuarial research on community violence uses as subjects patients released from the hospital with staff concurrence (e.g., Klassen and O'Connor 1988a). Since staff are unlikely to recommend someone for release that they view as likely to be imminently violent, the association that is found between valid predictors and violence will, to the extent that clinicians base their release decisions on those cues, be attentuated (Quinsey and Maguire 1986). Under these conditions, in order to obtain a sufficient level of violence during the follow-up, researchers often limit themselves to enrolling only subjects with a high base rate of violence (e.g., males with a prior history of violence). While assuring a base rate of follow-up violence sufficient to permit statistical validation of the predictor variables is indeed a necessity, restricting the sample to only one gender obviously eliminates any chance of uncovering associations between risk factors and violence in the other, and therefore also eliminates the possibility of discovering interactions between gender and the risk factors being studied. Given that several recent studies (e.g., Swanson et al. 1990; Steadman et al. 1993) have reported that, among acutely disordered populations, the level of violence committed by women is at least as high as that committed by men, the restriction of actuarial risk research to male samples seems ill advised. And given that the predictors of violence among persons who have already committed a violent act—that is, the predictors of repeat violence—may be different than the predictors of initial violence (see Mulvey, Blumstein, and Cohen [1986] on the distinction between predicting the prevalence and predicting the incidence of violence), making prior violence a criterion for inclusion in actuarial risk assessment research may yield findings inapplicable to persons who have not yet been violent. The use of large sample sizes would allow fewer constraints to be placed on subject recruitment while providing a sufficient amount of follow-up violence to permit the statistical validation of risk factors. By obtaining basic descriptive data on subjects *not* selected for the research, one could extrapolate results from the study sample back to the entire population from which the sample was drawn.

For the field to progress, future research on risk assessment must follow certain standards:

1. Enroll a broadly representative sample of patients—males and females, with and without prior violence.
2. Employ large sample sizes.

Unsynchronized Research Efforts

Lack of communication among researchers and lack of coordination among research programs are problems in many areas, but appear to be particularly acute in research on the risk of violence by the mentally disordered. It is unusual in this field to find two studies that have even defined actuarial predictor variables in the same manner. Given the retrospective nature of much of the research investigators often have had to rely for predictor variables upon whatever information happened to be in the patients' records (e.g., Steadman and Cocozza 1974). Follow-up periods vary widely. Only after one study from one site on one subject group is published does a second research group undertake a validation study of a conceptually (although often not operationally) similar set of predictor variables (for notable programmatic exceptions see Klassen and O'Connor 1988a, 1988b, 1990; Binder and McNiel 1988; McNiel and Binder 1989, 1991). This fragmentation of research efforts has seriously hindered the development of knowledge of the actuarial correlates of violence. The fact that each research site idiosyncratically defines its predictor and criterion variables and rarely replicates the measures used by others drastically reduces the confidence with which findings can be generalized and impedes the cumulative development of knowledge. It also means that data from several sites can rarely be pooled into larger samples for more powerful statistical analyses with more specific and informative subgroups.

Research is typically uncoordinated not only across sites but across disciplines. Psychiatrists favor one set of predictor variables, psychologists a second set, and sociologists a third. Yet insights in an area as complex as violence among the mentally disordered are unlikely to derive from research in any one discipline. A wide variety of clinical, theoretical (both basic and applied), statistical, and operational skills are required to conceptualize, operationalize, design, conduct, and analyze the kind of research that would give new life to the field of actuarial risk assessment. A diversity of disciplinary backgrounds among the research participants is conducive to accomplishing such multifaceted tasks.

For the largest payoffs, future research on risk assessment should

1. be launched simultaneously in several sites using common predictors and criterion variables and a common research design, and
2. be planned and managed by an interdisciplinary team.

Conclusion

To overcome the problems that have so far hobbled the scientific study of violence among the mentally disordered, we must enrich our predictor variables, strengthen our criterion variables, broaden our subject sampling strategy, and synchronize our research efforts. If we do, the rejuvenated field of risk assessment may yield results quite different than those to which we have become inured. If an actuarially valid array of risk markers for violence could be reliably identified, clinicians could be trained to incorporate these factors into their routine practice, and the accuracy of clinical predictions of violence among the mentally disordered would be commensurately increased. Such an increase in predictive accuracy would not obviate the profound questions of social policy (Monahan 1984) or of professional ethics (Grisso and Appelbaum 1992) that attend any preventive use of the state's police power. It would, however, mean that relatively fewer people would be erroneously institutionalized as "dangerous," and that relatively fewer people in the community would be victimized by patients erroneously released—or left untreated—as "nondangerous." This would be no small thing.

References

American Bar Association. 1989. ABA criminal justice mental health standards. Washington, D.C.: American Bar Association.

American Psychiatric Association. 1983. Guidelines for legislation on the psychiatric hospitalization of adults. *American Journal of Psychiatry* 140:672–79.

Appelbaum, P. 1988. The new preventive detention: Psychiatry's problematic responsibility for the control of violence. *American Journal of Psychiatry* 145:779–85.

Apperson, L., E. Mulvey, and C. Lidz. In press. Clinical prediction of assaultive behavior: Artifacts of research methods. *American Journal of Psychiatry*.

Binder, R. and D. McNiel. 1988. Effects of diagnosis and context on dangerousness. *American Journal of Psychiatry* 145:728–32.

Brooks, A. 1978. Notes on defining the dangerousness of the mentally ill. In C. Frederick, ed., *Dangerous behavior: A problem in law and mental health*. Washington, D.C.: Government Printing Office.

Brunswick, E. 1956. *Perception and the representative design of psychological experiments*. Berkeley: University of California Press.

Cirincione, C., H. Steadman, P. Robbins, and J. Monahan. 1992. Schizophrenia as a contingent risk factor for criminal violence. *International Journal of Law and Psychiatry* 15:347–58.

Cleveland, S., E. Mulvey, P. Appelbaum, and C. Lidz. 1989. Do dangerousness-oriented commitment laws restrict hospitalization of patients who need treatment? A test. *Hospital and Community Psychiatry* 40:266–71.

Cocozza, J., and H. Steadman. 1976. The failure of psychiatric predictions of dangerousness: Clear and convincing evidence. *Rutgers Law Review* 29:1084–1101.

Cohen, M., J. McEwen, K. Williams, S. Silver, and M. Spodak. 1986. *A base expec-*

tancy model for forensic release decisions. Alexandria: Research Management Associates.

Convit, A., D. Isay, R. Gadioma, and J. Volavka. 1988. Underreporting of physical assaults in schizophrenic inpatients. *Journal of Nervous and Mental Disease* 176:507–9.

Convit, A., J. Jaeger, S. Lin, M. Meisner, and J. Volavka. 1988. Predicting assaultiveness in psychiatric inpatients: A pilot study. *Hospital and Community Psychiatry* 39:429–34.

Cooper, R., and P. Werner. 1990. Predicting violence in newly admitted inmates: A lens model of staff decision making. *Criminal Justice and Behavior* 17:431–47.

Craig, T. J. 1982. An epidemiologic study of problems associated with violence among psychiatric inpatients. *American Journal of Psychiatry* 139:1262–66.

Davis, S. 1991. Violence by psychiatric inpatients: A review. *Hospital and Community Psychiatry* 42:585–90.

Dietz, P., D. Matthews, C. Duyne, J. Warren, T. Stewart, D. Martell, and J. Crowder. 1991. Threatening and otherwise inappropriate letters to Hollywood celebrities. *Journal of Forensic Sciences* 36:185–206.

Felson, R. B., and H. J. Steadman. 1983. Situational factors in disputes leading to criminal violence. *Criminology* 21:59–74.

Gondolf, E., E. Mulvey, and C. Lidz. 1989. Family violence reported in a psychiatric emergency room. *Journal of Family Violence* 4:249–58.

———. 1990. Characteristics of perpetrators of family and nonfamily assaults. *Hospital and Community Psychiatry* 41:191–93.

———. 1991. Psychiatric admission of family violent versus nonfamily violent patients. *International Journal of Law and Psychiatry* 14:245–54.

Gottfredson, D., and S. Gottfredson. 1988. Stakes and risks in the prediction of violent criminal behavior. *Violence and Victims* 3:247–62.

Grisso, T. 1991. Clinical assessments for legal decisionmaking: Research recommendations. In S. Shah and B. Sales, eds., *Law and mental health: Major developments and research needs.* Washington, D.C.: Government Printing Office.

Grisso, T., and P. Appelbaum. 1992. Is it unethical to offer predictions of future violence? *Law and Human Behavior* 16:621–33.

Hodgins, S., ed. 1993. *Crime and mental disorder.* Newbury Park, Calif.: Sage Publications.

Klassen, D., and W. O'Connor. 1985. Predicting violence among ex-mental patients: Preliminary research results. Paper presented at the annual meeting of the American Society of Criminology.

———. 1987. Predicting violence in mental patients: Cross-validation of an actuarial scale. Paper presented at the annual meeting of the American Public Health Association.

———. 1988a. A prospective study of predictors of violence in adult male mental patients. *Law and Human Behavior* 12:143–58.

———. 1988b. Crime, inpatient admissions, and violence among male mental patients. *International Journal of Law and Psychiatry* 11:305–12.

———. 1990. Assessing the risk of violence in released mental patients: A cross-validation study. *Psychological Assessment: A Journal of Consulting and Clinical Psychology* 1:75–81.

Kozol, H., R. Boucher, and R. Garofalo. 1972. The diagnosis and treatment of dangerousness. *Crime and Delinquency* 18:371–92.

Krakowski, M., J. Volavka, and D. Brizer. 1986. Psychopathology and violence: A review of the literature. *Comprehensive Psychiatry* 27:131–48.

LaFond, J., and M. Durham. 1992. *Back to the asylum: The future of mental health law and policy in the United States.* New York: Oxford University Press.

Lidz, C. 1987. Conditional prediction and the management of dangerousness. Grant no. MH 40030-07. Antisocial and Violent Behavior Branch, National Institute of Mental Health.

Lidz, C., and E. Mulvey. 1990. Institutional factors affecting psychiatric admission and commitment decisions. In G. Weisz, ed., *Social Science Perspectives on Medical Ethics,* 83–96. Philadelphia: University of Pennsylvania Press.

Lidz, C., E. Mulvey, P. Appelbaum, and S. Cleveland. 1989. Commitment: The consistency of clinicians and the use of legal standards. *American Journal of Psychiatry* 146:176–81.

Lidz, C., E. Mulvey, L. Apperson, K. Evanczuk, and S. Shea. 1992. Sources of disagreement among clinicians' assessments of dangerousness in a psychiatric emergency room. *International Journal of Law and Psychiatry* 15:237–50.

Lidz, C., E. Mulvey, and W. Gardner. 1993. The accuracy of predictions of violence to others. *Journal of the American Medical Association* 269:1007–11.

Litwack, T., and L. Schlesinger. 1987. Assessing and predicting violence: Research, law, and applications. In I. Weiner and A. Hess, eds., *Handbook of forensic psychology.* New York: Wiley-Interscience.

McNiel, D. E., and R. L. Binder. 1987. Predictive validity of judgments of dangerousness in emergency civil commitment. *American Journal of Psychiatry* 144:197–200.

———. 1989. Relationship between preadmission threats and later violent behavior by acute psychiatric inpatients. *Hospital and Community Psychiatry* 40:605–8.

———. 1991. Clinical assessment of the risk of violence among psychiatric inpatients. *American Journal of Psychiatry* 148:1317–21.

McNiel, D., R. Binder, and T. Greenfield. 1988. Predictors of violence in civilly committed acute psychiatric patients. *American Journal of Psychiatry* 145:965–70.

Mednick, S., P. Brennan, and E. Kandel. 1988. Predisposition to violence. *Aggressive Behavior* 14:25–33.

Mercy, J. A., and P. W. O'Carroll. 1988. New directions in violence prediction: The public health arena. *Violence and Victims* 3:285–301.

Monahan, J. 1981. *The clinical prediction of violent behavior.* Washington, D.C.: Government Printing Office.

———. 1984. The prediction of violent behavior: Toward a second generation of theory and policy. *American Journal of Psychiatry* 141:10–15.

———. 1988. Risk assessment of violence among the mentally disordered: Generating useful knowledge. *International Journal of Law and Psychiatry* 11:249–57.

Monahan, J., and D. Klassen. 1982. Situational approaches to understanding and predicting individual violent behavior. In M. Wolfgang and N. Weiner, eds., *Criminal violence.* Beverly Hills, Calif.: Sage Publications.

Monahan, J., and S. Shah. 1989. Dangerousness and commitment of the mentally disordered in the United States. *Schizophrenia Bulletin* 15:541–53.

Monahan, J., and H. Steadman. 1983. Crime and mental disorder: An epidemiological approach. In N. Morris and M. Tonry, eds., *Crime and justice: An annual review of research.* Chicago: University of Chicago Press.

Mulvey, E., A. Blumstein, and J. Cohen. 1986. Reframing the research question of mental patient criminality. *International Journal of Law and Psychiatry* 9:57–65.

Mulvey, E., and C. Lidz. 1984. Clinical considerations in the prediction of dangerousness in mental patients. *Clinical Psychology Review* 4:379–401.

———. 1985. Back to basics: A critical analysis of dangerousness research in a new legal environment. *Law and Human Behavior* 9:209–18.

———. In press. Measuring patient violence in dangerousness research. *Law and Human Behavior.*

National Center for State Courts. 1986. Guidelines for involuntary commitment. *Mental and Physical Disability Law Reporter* 10:409–514.

National Institute of Mental Health. 1991. *Caring for people with severe mental disorders: A national plan of research to improve services.* Washington, D.C.: Government Printing Office.

National Research Council. 1989. *Improving risk communication.* Washington, D.C.: National Academy Press.

———. 1993. *Understanding and preventing violence.* Washington, D.C.: National Academy Press.

Quinsey, V., and A. Maguire. 1986. Maximum security psychiatric patients: Actuarial and clinical prediction of dangerousness. *Journal of Interpersonal Violence* 1:143–71.

Rosenberg, M., and M. Fenley, eds. 1991. *Violence in America: A public health approach.* New York: Oxford University Press.

Rossi, A., M. Jacobs, M. Monteleone, R. Olsen, R. Surber, E. Winkler, and A. Wommack. 1986. Characteristics of psychiatric patients who engage in assaultive or other fear-inducing behaviors. *The Journal of Nervous and Mental Disease* 174:154–60.

Roth, L. 1979. A commitment law for patients, doctors, and lawyers. *American Journal of Psychiatry* 136:1121–27.

Segal, S. P., M. A. Watson, S. M. Goldfinger, and D. S. Averbuck. 1988a. Civil commitment in the psychiatric emergency room. I: The assessment of dangerousness by emergency room clinicians. *Archives of General Psychiatry* 45:748–52.

———. 1988b. Civil commitment in the psychiatric emergency room. II: Mental disorder indicators and three dangerousness criteria. *Archives of General Psychiatry* 45:753–58.

Sepejak, D., R. Menzies, C. Webster, and F. Jensen. 1983. Clinical predictions of dangerousness: Two-year follow-up of 408 pre-trial forensic cases. *Bulletin of the American Academy of Psychiatry and the Law* 11:171–81.

Shepherd, J., and D. Farrington. In press. Assault as a public health problem. *Journal of the Royal Society of Medicine.*

Steadman, H. 1977. A new look at recidivism among Patuxent inmates. *The Bulletin on the American Academy of Psychiatry and the Law* 5:200–209.

———. 1982. A situational approach to violence. *International Journal of Law and Psychiatry* 5:171–86.

Steadman, H., and J. Cocozza. 1974. *Careers of the criminally insane.* Lexington, Mass.: Lexington Books.

Steadman, H., J. Monahan, P. Robbins, P. Appelbaum, T. Grisso, D. Klassen, E. Mulvey, and L. Roth. 1993. From dangerousness to risk assessment: Implications for appropriate research strategies, 39–62. In S. Hodgins, ed., *Crime and mental disorder.* Newbury Park, Calif.: Sage Publications.

Steadman, H., and S. Ribner. 1982. Life stress and violence among ex-mental patients. *Social Science in Medicine* 16:1641–47.

Swanson, J., C. Holzer, V. Ganju, and R. Jono. 1990. Violence and psychiatric disorder in the community: Evidence from the Epidemiologic Catchment Area surveys. *Hospital and Community Psychiatry* 41:761–70.

Tancredi, L., and N. Volkow. 1988. Neural substrates of violent behavior: Implications for law and public policy. *International Journal of Law and Psychiatry* 11:13–49.

Tardiff, K., and A. Sweillam. 1982. Assaultive behavior among chronic inpatients. *American Journal of Psychiatry* 139:212–15.

Thornberry, T., and J. Jacoby. 1979. *The criminally insane: A community follow-up of mentally ill offenders.* Chicago: University of Chicago Press.

Teplin, L. 1985. The criminality of the mentally ill: A dangerous misconception. *American Journal of Psychiatry* 142:676–77.

United States Department of Health and Human Services. 1991. *Healthy people 2000: National health promotion and disease prevention objectives.* Washington, D.C.: Government Printing Office.

Werner, P., T. Rose, and J. Yesavage. 1983. Reliability, accuracy, and decision-making strategy in clinical predictions of imminent dangerousness. *Journal of Consulting and Clinical Psychology* 51:815–25.

Werner, P., T. Rose, J. Yesavage, and K. Seeman. 1984. Psychiatrists' judgments of dangerousness in patients on an acute care unit. *American Journal of Psychiatry* 141:263–66.

Part I
Dispositional Factors

"Dispositional" risk factors for violence are those that reflect the individual person's predispositions, traits, tendencies, or styles. Within the dispositional domain lie many relatively enduring characteristics of persons that have been nominated as risk factors for violence. The following three chapters focus on what we believe are the most promising candidates for dispositional markers of risk—anger, impulsivity, and psychopathy.

Raymond Novaco begins by considering anger and the individual's ability to control its expression as risk factors for violence. In a large study of violence on mental hospital wards, he finds anger problems closely linked to violent behavior. He presents the rationale for a new instrument for assessing anger proneness and the first data on the instrument's psychometric properties.

Ernest Barratt deals with impulsivity, another prime candidate for a dispositional precursor of violence. Barratt describes how impulsivity fits into personality theory more generally, and the specific role it may play in the genesis of aggression. He also reviews the large body of research that has been conducted using the Barratt Impulsivity Scale.

Stephen Hart, Robert Hare, and Adelle Forth address psychopathy, a third dispositional risk factor for violence. They survey the existing research literature on the relationship between psychopathy and violence in criminal justice populations and describe the difficult problem of reliably and efficiently assessing psychopathy. A new instrument for use in clinical evaluations of psychopathy is described and data validating the instrument is presented.

2 Anger as a Risk Factor for Violence among the Mentally Disordered

RAYMOND W. NOVACO

The prediction of violent behavior is a perplexing problem presenting multiple difficulties (Monahan 1981), but the neglect of anger has been a conspicuous shortcoming. Given its role as a central determinant of individual and collective violence and as a significant component of many psychiatric syndromes (Novaco 1986), anger is hypothetically a key element of the risk assessment equation. However, understanding anger as a marker for risk of harm-doing behavior calls for an assessment procedure different from those presently available, which predominantly address anger as an everyday experience. Since anger is a normal emotion serving many adaptive functions, it is not surprising that existing anger assessment procedures have been developed primarily with nonclinical populations. As a consequence of the "normality" of anger and the absence of a theoretical base, current instruments do not provide a differentiated assessment of the dysfunctional elements of anger. In this regard, dimensions of cognitive, arousal, and behavioral systems reciprocally related to anger and aggression ought to be assessed. While much contemporary interest in anger has a health psychology focus, attention to its links with aggression have been neglected in the assessment realm.

Anger, even strong anger, is not inherently dysfunctional. Its mobilizing and self-assertive qualities are distinctively adaptive. Our psychosocial metaphors for anger reflects its duality, depicting the emotion alternately as eruptive, destructive, savage, burning, or poisonous and as energizing, empowering, correcting, or relieving. One set of metaphors suggests that anger is something to be expressed and utilized, but the other implies that anger should be contained and controlled.[1]

Conceptions of anger as a dysfunctional emotional state are rooted in historical notions about anger as a passion. Themes of insanity and destructive-

---

1. An elaborated discussion of anger in terms of psychosocial imagery is given in Novaco (in press). A linguistic metaphorical analysis can be found in Lakoff and Kovecses (1987), although their account is predicated exclusively on anger as a negative emotion.

ness associated with arousal of anger spring from a perspective that separated anger from rationality. This view originated with Plato and Aristotle and continued with the Stoics, the Scholastics of the Middle Ages, and the philosophers of the Renaissance and Enlightenment periods (Novaco and Welsh 1989). Anger is the prototype of the emotions, understood as passions, by which the personality is "gripped," "seized," or "torn" (Averill 1974, 1982). Becoming angry commonly signifies that one is out of control, being driven by uncivilized forces that ultimately must be checked. Dramatic characters, from Shakespeare's King Lear and Othello to Howard Beale in *Network* and Travis Bickle in *Taxi Driver,* embody the association of anger with mental disorder and resulting violence.

The links between mental imbalances, anger, and aggression have been part of our thinking for at least two millennia, and there is emerging evidence of the prevalence of anger among psychiatric patients and of its association with violence (Craig 1982; Kay, Wolkenfeld, and Murrill 1988; Segal et al. 1988). Researchers concerned with violence risk need to give attention to the assessment of anger, but this effort must contend with two nonisomorphic aspects of the relation between anger and aggression: since anger is a normal emotion with adaptive functions, the presence of anger, even intense anger, can only be partially predictive of violence; similarly, the absence of anger does not guarantee that violence will not occur. This chapter reports on the development and evaluation of an anger scale suitable for use with both mentally disordered and normal populations. It sought to improve upon existing measures by being grounded in theory and designed for applicability to clinical treatment. Before presenting its systematic development, I will discuss the clinical context.

Anger and Violence among Psychiatric Patients

Violence in psychiatric hospitals is acknowledged as a serious problem in the United States and Europe (Drinkwater and Gudjonsson 1989; Larkin, Murtagh, and Jones 1988; Lion and Reid 1983). Assaultive behavior by psychiatric patients in both public and private facilities presents an enormous challenge for hospital staff who must not only provide treatment to remedy such behavior but must guard against physical harm to themselves. In their review of studies of assaults on psychiatric staff, Haller and Deluty (1988) speculate that the frequency of assaults by inpatients has increased substantially over the past decade. Carmel and Hunter (1989), for example, found that, in 1986, 121 staff members sustained 135 injuries from patient violence at Atascadero State Hospital, one of California's two primarily forensic facilities. This included 16% of the ward nursing staff, 5.7% of the psychiatric technicians, and 1.9% of the clinical professionals, yet I will show below that assaultive behavior is even more prevalent at California state hospitals that are predominantly civil commitment institutions. Even in a university hospital, Conn and Lion (1983) found that, during their 18-month study period, there were 25 assaults on the 54-bed psychiatric facility, which represented 41% of the assaults in the entire 800-bed general hospital.

The study of violent behavior among psychiatric hospital patients is a relatively recent research field, which began with studies by Ekblom (1970), Depp (1976), and Fottrell (1980). Gathering data on the entire Swedish mental hospital population, Ekblom (1970) reported that 8% of the patients were categorized ("stamped") as dangerous based on assaultive behavior before or after admission. However, he found only 25 reports of assaultive incidents by patients in the hospital in a ten-year period during which the census averaged about 28,000 patients and the reporting of assaults was mandatory. He concluded that there was "only a small risk" for violence in mental hospitals. Depp (1976) conducted his study at Saint Elizabeth's Hospital in Washington, D.C., investigating the personological and contextual characteristics of 238 patient assaults over a 20-month period, but he did not provide prevalence data. The notion that violence among psychiatric patients is a serious problem emerged with the study by Fottrell (1980) of the incidence of violence among inpatients at three British hospitals (two large psychiatric hospitals and one psychiatric wing of a general hospital). In the one large hospital that he studied for a full year, he found that 10% of the patients had been violent; this rate was also obtained in the other large hospital, where he studied four wards over a four-month period. Schizophrenia was the most common diagnosis for the violent patients, although this might simply reflect the proportion of such patients on the census, which Fottrell did not provide. Subsequently, in a more systematic study involving two large state hospitals, Tardiff (1983) found that 7.8% of male patients and 7.1% of female patients had been assaultive within the three months prior to his survey. He also found that nonparanoid schizophrenics, psychotic organic brain syndrome patients, and those with mental retardation were overrepresented in the assaultive category, which he explained by stating that these groups were "less amenable to treatment" (Tardiff 1983, 16). Tardiff and Deane (1980) had previously found that approximately 20% to 30% of both male and female patients between the ages of 16 and 35 had been judged to be dangerous to others in the month prior to their survey of 9,559 patients in four state hospitals. Perhaps the highest prevalence rate for hospital patient violence is reported in Larkin, Murtagh, and Jones (1988) for one of the British Special Hospitals (Rampton), where 36.6% of the patients were found to be assaultive in a six-month interval.

Recent epidemiological studies with psychiatric patients point strongly to the importance of anger as a risk factor for violence among the mentally disordered. Craig (1982) examined the cases of 1,033 patients (virtually all of the admissions in one county for one year) and found that 11% had engaged in assaultive behavior before admission and that anger was the factor most strongly associated with assaultiveness. The association of anger with assaultiveness was significant for schizophrenics, organic brain syndrome patients, and alcoholics. Dangerousness to others, in a study of psychiatric emergency commitments, was found by Segal et al. (1988) to be strongly associated with irritability. Anger was found by Kay, Wolkenfeld, and Murrill (1988) to be the strongest predictor of physical aggression in the clinical and diagnostic profiles of their cohort of 208 psychiatric inpatients. In contemporaneously distinguishing aggressive from nonaggressive patients, anger had the strongest effect, followed by a set of other anger-related factors. The predictive effects for anger on physical aggression were assessed by Kay, Wolkenfeld, and Murrill in a three-month follow-up analysis of behavior on psychiatric wards. Their aggression outcome ratings, however, were *ratings by clinicians,* a step removed from the behavioral event archival data used in many studies of patient violence, although it is now well known that such archival measures underreport the true incidence of assault (Brizer et al. 1988; Larkin, Murtagh, and Jones 1988; Lion, Snyder, and Merrill 1981).

To be sure, the physical and social environment of the hospital itself is relevant to patient violence. In their review of violence in psychiatric facilities in the United States and Europe, Edwards and Reid (1983) point to anger and irritability as staff characteristics that can provoke assaults by patients. Various studies (e.g., Madden, Lion, and Penna 1976; Ruben, Wolkon, and Yamamoto 1980) have found that clinical staff who are victims of assault subsequently report that they had behaved in a provocative way. Staff members certainly become angry after having been assaulted (Aiken 1984; Ryan and Poster 1989). Hypothetically, the expectation of being assaulted by patients or the inclination towards coercive styles of controlling patients may potentiate a disposition to anger in some staff which, when situationally activated by perceived threat, can provoke attack. However, the nonisomorphism between anger and aggression leaves much to be explained with regard to violence prediction and much to be protected with regard to the human right to self-determination, for which anger can be beneficial. Regarding the latter, one should consider the 1908 autobiography of Clifford Beers, as anger was central to his recovery from a debilitating disorder while in a psychiatric hospital. Nevertheless, while anger may indeed be a justified response to aspects of institutionalization, its manifestation as aggressive behavior typically has problematic consequences; a good perspective on this issue for clinical practice and research is given by Howells and Hollin (1989).

Anger in the Institutional Context of the Present Study

The development of the new measure for anger involved a number of procedural steps (detailed later), including extensive interviews with clinicians and patients in California state hospitals, where the project was conducted. However, the first step was the gathering of archival data on anger and assaultiveness among this hospital population. The data were obtained from the Level of Care Survey (LOCS), which had been administered almost yearly since 1980 by the California Department of Mental Health. All patients 18 years of age and older who were on the hospital census on a designated date (usually in May) are included in the LOCS, which is completed by hospital unit staff. Originally developed by the New York State Department of Mental Health, the LOCS is a two-sided, legal-sized questionnaire, and it has special value for the present project because it records data regarding documented aggressive behavior and clinically rated anger. A systematic study of the full data set concerning the anger-aggression relationship, involving internal validity assessments and replicated panel analyses with multiple covariates, is reported in Novaco and Thacker (1993). Here I will give some descriptive and simple inferential statistics that are pertinent to the present project's development.

Among the data obtained by the LOCS are (a) physical assaults in the 30-day period prior to the survey, given as a dichotomous item based on information in the patient's chart, and (b) anger ratings, seven items rated on a five-point scale by the patient's primary clinician as part of a 36-item rating scale. An *anger rating index* was constructed from these seven items, based on a prior factor analysis by the California Department of Mental Health. The items are "gets angry or annoyed easily," "is impatient," "is irritable or grouchy," "quick to fly off the handle," "easily upset if something doesn't suit him," "verbally abuses other," and "is disruptive." We found that the internal consistency of this index averaged .95 over four survey years.

Table 1 presents descriptive data on assaultiveness, homicide attempt history, and the *single item* "gets angry or annoyed easily" for the five California state hospitals in 1988, the year prior to beginning development of the anger scale. Across hospitals, 13.9% of the patients had been physically assaultive in the 30 days prior to the survey, 28.2% have at some time tried to kill someone, and 35.2% were given ratings of "often," "very often," or "always" on the item "gets angry or annoyed easily." While a history of homicide attempts was more prevalent among patients in the two forensic hospitals, the anger and assault rates were higher for patients in the predominantly civil commitment hospitals. This is consistent with other studies of forensic facilities that also have civil commitment patients which have found the latter class to be more dangerous (Stokman and Heiber 1980).

The association of anger with physical assault is presented in table 2 where the *anger rating index* is trichotomized in cross-tabulations with assault for concurrent year and prospective year analyses. In the concurrent analysis (both anger and assault in 1988), 3.8% of the "low anger" patients were assaultive, while the rate was 28.5%, more than seven times greater, for the "high anger" patients. In the prospective analysis (1987 anger with 1988

Table 1. Anger and assaultiveness among psychiatric patients at California state hospitals in 1988

Variable	Hospital					
	A	B	C	D	E	Total
Physically assaultive in last 30 days	64 6.8%	61 6.4%	133 25.9%	152 19.2%	187 17.3%	597 13.9%
Has ever tried to kill someone	420 44.9%	454 47.4%	48 9.4%	90 11.4%	198 18.5%	1210 28.2%
Gets angry or annoyed easily	258 27.5%	279 29.2%	207 40.4%	311 39.2%	453 42.0%	1508 35.2%

Note: The data were obtained from the 1988 Level of Care Survey, as explained in the text. Hospitals A and B are primarily forensic facilities, whereas C, D, and E are primarily civil commitment facilities. The data on physical assault and attempted homicide are based on hospital chart recordings. The anger data are patients for whom their primary clinicians gave ratings of "often," "very often," or "always" for the attribute "gets angry or annoyed easily."

Table 2. Association of anger level with physical assault in concurrent and prospective analyses

Concurrent year

Physical assault (1988)	Anger rating index (1988)			
	Low	*Middle*	*High*	*Total*
No	1450 96.2%	1304 88.5%	933 71.5%	3687 86.1%
Yes	57 3.8%	169 11.5%	371 28.5%	597 13.9%

Prospective years

Physical assault (1988)	Anger rating index (1987)			
	Low	*Middle*	*High*	*Total*
No	589 93.9%	502 87.6%	690 79.2%	1781 86.0%
Yes	38 6.1%	71 12.4%	181 20.8%	290 14.0%

Note: The anger rating index is a summary score of seven items rated on five-point scales by each patient's primary clinician. The summary index has an alpha coefficient of .95 in each year and is here trichotomized for the cross-tabulation. The physical assault variable represents a recorded event in a period 30 days prior to the survey. Both cross-tabulations are highly significant. For the 1988 concurrent analysis, chi-square $(2, N = 4,284) = 366.1$, $p < .0001$. For the 1987–1988 prospective analysis, chi-square $(2, N = 2,071) = 67.3$, $p < .0001$.

assault), the "low anger" assault rate was 6.1%, compared to 20.8% for the "high anger" patients. While the differential between groups was not as great in the prospective analysis, patients who are rated high in anger in 1987 were still more than three times more likely to be assaultive in 1988 than are those rated low in anger. Both analyses produced highly significant chi-square effects. If patients who have been assaultive in 1987 are removed from the prospective analysis (to control for prior assault), the 1987 high-anger tertile is still nearly three times more likely to be assaultive in 1988 than is the low-anger tertile (15.6% vs. 5.3%), chi-square $(1, N = 1088) = 28.8, p < .0001$.

These analyses demonstrate that anger and violence were prevalent problems among the patients in the clinical institutional setting in which the new anger instrument would be developed and that anger was significantly related to assaultive behavior. Whereas existing psychiatric epidemiological research on violence has lacked a theoretical foundation, the present research is, on the other hand, explicitly guided by a theory of anger and aggression, and it seeks to interface such aggregate data with individual patient testing and ultimately with treatment outcome research.

Overview of Existing Anger Assessment Instruments

The neglect of theory in the development of existing anger assessment instruments, including one previously developed by me (Novaco 1975, 1988), is puzzling. The instruments have been developed ad hoc, "empirically" generated from interviews with convenience samples, or produced in a form parallel to instruments previously developed to measure other constructs. Because anger is a rich theoretical construct, linked not only to aggression but to many physical and psychological disorders, an anger assessment instrument should first seek to operationalize the construct. Assessment data could then, hypothetically, be more readily utilized in treatment and would be more applicable to research questions pertaining to anger determinants, mediational processes, and consequences. On the other hand, success in operationalizing construct complexity in one mode of measurement, such as a self-report scale, may be outweighed by the inability of that form of measurement to assess relevant variables (due to limitations of conscious awareness or subjective bias, for example) or by matters of parsimony—selecting the most simple method that is efficacious.

Since anger is a subjective emotion, it is appropriate that anger has primarily been studied by self-report measures. The normative study of anger based on subjects' reports began with G. Stanley Hall (1899) and continued sporadically to the exemplary studies by Averill (1982). This body of research has concerned anger as a normal emotion, and its procedures have ranged from introspection to daily diaries with rating scales to questionnaires and inventories. Recent studies have involved autobiographical narrative (Baumeister, Stillwell, and Wotman 1990) and imagined scenarios (Ben-Zur and Breznitz 1991). Experimental laboratory methodologies have entailed combinations of self-report, behavioral, and physiological measures, but this genre of research has almost exclusively involved college student samples and been concerned with anger as a precondition to inducing aggression. Anger measures, therefore, have typically been manipulation check assessments to establish the internal validity of procedures designed to provoke aggression (e.g., Baron 1971, 1984). The exceptions to this generalization have been some studies on "catharsis" (e.g., Konecni 1975b); studies in the field of psychosomatic medicine, both classic (e.g., Ax 1953) and contemporary (Armstead et al. 1989; Engebretson, Mathews, and Scheier 1989); and recent research by Berkowitz (1990). However, only contemporary research on cardiovascular disorders has given explicit attention to anger assessment, although aggressive behavior has remained outside its scope of its concern with physical health.

A number of systematized self-report measures of anger have been developed, although none has been developed in conjunction with a theory of anger. Only a few of the 18 self-report measures of anger that were located in the literature have been utilized in research concerned with aggressive behavior. Perhaps the most widely known is the Buss-Durkee Hostility Inventory (Buss and Durkee 1957) which has 75 true-false items composing eight subscales (physical assault, indirect hostility, irritability, negativism, resentment, suspicion, verbal hostility, and guilt). The Buss-Durkee measure pertains to what people do when they become angry rather than the events that provoke anger or the degree of anger experienced. The instrument has been found to have good internal and test-retest reliability (from .70 to .80), but various validity studies have produced mixed results. Aside from college student studies, typically involving concurrent validity assessments with other instruments, significant but inconsistent relationships have been found between Buss-Durkee scores and ratings of patients' aggressiveness by doctors and nurses. This measure has been found to discriminate violent from nonviolent alcohol abusers (Renson, Adams, and Tinklenberg 1978) and criminals (Selby 1984). The Selby study compared the effectiveness of instruments in discriminating violent male felons. However, a set of studies by Edmunds and Kendrick (1980), abounding in factor analytic methodology, consistently disconfirmed the Buss-Durkee inventory in regard to the discrimination of violent samples and predictions of laboratory aggressive behavior.

Subsequent to his attempt to validate the Buss-Durkee inventory as applied to an Italian population, Caprara constructed several scales which he found to be related to aggressive behavior in psychological laboratory studies (Caprara et al. 1985; Caprara 1986). These scales of Irritability, Emotional Susceptibility, and Dissipation-Rumination involve 20 to 40 items rated on six-point scales, with responses ranging from "completely true for me" to "completely false for me." Although the validational analyses have been performed on student samples in laboratory aggression experiments, the scale constructs are theoretically relevant to the present research.

In the 1950s a number of Minnesota Multiphasic Personality Inventory scales of hostility and control were developed, but a cross-validational study of 12 such scales, conducted by Megargee and Mendelsohn (1962) found that these assorted scales did poorly in predictively discriminating violent criminals from nonviolent criminals and other noncriminal groups. In fact, it was found that extremely assaultive offenders were "overcontrolled" (rigid inhibitions), which led Megargee (1966) to develop an MMPI-derived overcontrolled hostility scale. This measure successfully discriminated extremely assaultive from less assaultive groups. The idea of overcontrolled hostility was buttressed by research by Blackburn (1968) with psychiatric offenders. Megargee did not articulate the psychological mechanisms involved in the overcontrol phenomenon but did refer to psychodynamic concepts—repression, denial, displacement, and sublimation. There are, however, more parsimonious interpretations than these to account for why someone not previously aggressive suddenly becomes a murderer, and these include anger, rumination, and disinhibition (cf. Novaco 1986). Selby (1984) indeed found that violent groups had significantly higher anger scores than did nonviolent felons.

One of the MMPI scales examined by Megargee and Mendelsohn which did poorly in discriminating assaultiveness was the Cook-Medley Hostility Scale (Cook and Medley 1954). This scale was originally developed with samples of teachers and, curiously, came to be used in studies of type A behavior and heart disease (e.g., Barefoot, Dahlstrom, and Williams 1983). Cook-Medley hostility scores have been found to be predictive of the incidence of heart disease and mortality in retrospective longitudinal studies. The scale has been found to have high test-retest reliability and good concurrent validity with other anger-hostility instruments. Selby (1984) did find this scale to significantly differentiate violent from nonviolent groups.

Currently, one of the most commonly used anger measures is the Spielberger State-Trait Anger Scale (Spielberger et al. 1983). Developed from Buss-Durkee items and other anger measures, the state-anger and trait-anger scales each initially consisted of fifteen items rated on four-point scales. The instrument was designed in parallel to Spielberger's State-Trait Anxiety measures; ten-item state-anger and trait-anger scales were subsequently produced by eliminating items highly correlated with the anxiety measures. Normative data were gathered on students, military recruits, and other working adults. For trait anger, Spielberg et al. (1983) obtained high internal reliability (.88 to .92), and modest test-retest reliability has been found (.54; Stauder et al. 1983). The trait scale has significant concurrent validity with other self-report anger-hostility measures, but its predictive value for violence is unexamined.

The trait-anger scale has been found to be related to blood pressure and hypertension.

Other inventory measures have included the Reaction Inventory (Evans and Strangeland 1971), the Anger Self-Report Inventory (Zelin, Adler, and Myerson 1972), the S-R Inventory of Hostility (Endler and Hunt 1968), the Novaco Provocation Inventory (Novaco 1975, 1988), and the Multidimensional Anger Inventory (Siegel 1986). These measures inventory the anger-arousing potential of various situations. Most were developed with college students, and they typically have not been used with either violent or clinical populations. Siegel's measure is the most recent and attempts to build on previous inventories, including the Buss-Durkee; her Multidimensional Anger Inventory seeks to assess aspects of anger relevant to cardiovascular disease. This measure gauges anger across the response dimensions previously specified by the present author (Novaco 1985), plus hostile outlook and "range of anger-eliciting situations" (her rationale for and operationalization of the latter category are unclear). Developed on two samples of college students and factory workers, relatively small for the factor analysis conducted, this 30-item measure has good internal and test-retest reliabilities and modest to poor concurrent validities. Siegel's extraction of five factors (anger arousal, range of situations, hostile outlook, anger-in, and anger-out) is puzzling and is weakly supported by her validational measures.

The Novaco Provocation Inventory (NPI), first reported in Novaco (1975), is an 80-item self-report instrument for assessing anger responsiveness. The inventory consists of brief descriptions of provocative situations, for each of which the respondent indicates a degree of anger on a five-point scale of arousal. The items were intuitively derived and based partly on interviews with subjects about situations of anger arousal. The instrument was found to have internal consistency ($r = .95$), but several items were replaced to incorporate more situations of home life. The resulting 80-item measure was then administered to a variety of clinical and nonclinical samples, including university students, industrial workers, police officers, military personnel, mental health workers, psychiatric patients, child abusers, and prison hospital inmates. Designed to gauge the range and intensity of anger responses, the NPI does not assess the frequency, duration, or mode-of-response parameters of anger problems (Novaco 1985), nor does it differentially assess theoretically relevant psychological components of anger and aggression. It was developed for three purposes: (a) to provide a general index of anger responsiveness across a wide range of situations, (b) to serve as a guide for interview assessments, and (c) to generate an empirical basis for the content of laboratory provocation procedures reported in Novaco (1975). The inventory provides information about the types of situations most likely to arouse anger and the overall magnitude of a respondent's proneness to provocation.

The principal index for the inventory is the total score, computed by summing the item intensity ratings. The mean for normal samples ranges from 230 to 255, which approximates endorsing the midpoint of the scale across the 80 items. The standard deviation is consistently about 45. Internal reliability coefficients are consistently high across samples (above $r = .93$). Test-retest reliabilities with university student samples have ranged from $r = .83$ ($N = 34$) for a one-month interval to $r = .89$ ($N = 39$) and $r = .90$ ($N = 69$) for one-week intervals. In Selby's (1984) study of 204 male felons, the NPI had a test-retest reliability of .74 over a one-month interval. Correlations with the Buss-Durkee Hostility Inventory range from .41 to .50.

The provocation items in the NPI were categorized intuitively. Seven primary categories were identified: annoying behavior of others, humiliation-verbal insult, personal injustice, social injustice, frustration, personal clumsiness, and physical assault. Items were sorted into these categories with a 94% rate of agreement between judges (Novaco and Robinson 1984). Factor analysis of the inventory has been performed with undergraduate, industrial worker, military, and child abuser samples by means of principal axis analysis rotated to a Varimax solution. The factor solution was selected by the "scree" method. Across samples, three factors emerge consistently: injustice-unfairness, frustration-clumsiness, and physical affronts. One departure from this pattern is that for female undergraduates humiliation-verbal insult emerges as the first factor. However, since the items were generated from intuitive categories, factor analysis here bears similarities to looking for Easter eggs that one hid oneself.

Validational studies on the inventory have found it to be significantly related to laboratory self-report measures of anger (Novaco 1975). Studies with military samples have found significant associations with the Jenkins Activity Survey measure of type A behavior ($r = .34$, $N = 59$) and inverse relationships to job performance evaluations ($r = -.32$, $N = 59$). Selby (1984) found that a 25-item subset of the NPI discriminated between violent and nonviolent criminal offenders with 90% accuracy, which far exceeded that for several alternative instruments. Regarding physiological arousal, Katz and Toben (1986) found that the NPI was significantly associated with blood pressure and heart rate reactivity to experimental challenge conditions. In contrast, they found that the Jenkins measure of type A behavior, was significantly related to the NPI ($r = .42$) but was unrelated to cardiovascular reactivity.

A recent anger measure to appear in the literature is the Brief Anger-Aggression Questionnaire developed by Maiuro, Vitaliano, and Cahn (1987). The BAAQ is indeed brief, consisting of six items judged to be representative of six Buss-Durkee subscales (assault, indirect hostility, irritability, negativism, resentment, and verbal hostility). Maiuro and his colleagues conducted analyses with separate samples, finding an internal consistency of .82, one-week test-retest reliability of .84, strong concurrent validity with the Buss-

Durkee (.78), and modest criterion validity in discriminating assaultive psychiatric outpatients from nonviolent (dental clinic) cases. While this measure appears to have value for certain mental health screening decisions, such as might occur in outpatient intake procedures, its scope and brevity limit its potential for assessing psychological deficits associated with anger problems and providing information for therapeutic intervention.

The Guiding Conceptual Framework and Anger Scale Design

The development of the new anger scale was guided by a set of empirical generalizations having considerable consensus in the field of human aggression. The simple conceptual framework is represented by figure 1. Within that framework's specified cognitive, arousal, and behavioral domains, subsets of component dimensions were designated as pertinent to psychological deficits regarding anger as a clinical problem. The rationale for these domains and dimensions is elaborated in the following section.

The basic conception is that anger is a subjective emotional state, entailing the presence of physiological arousal and cognitions of antagonism, and is a causal determinant of aggression. The "subjective affect" element of anger is a cognitive labeling of the emotional state as "angry" or something semantically proximate, such as "annoyed," "irritated," "enraged," or "provoked." This cognitive labeling is a highly automatic process, neither deliberate nor necessarily in tandem to the arousal. Associated with this cognitive labeling process is an inclination to act in an antagonistic or confrontational manner toward the source of the provocation. This action impulse is regulated by inhibitory mechanisms (internal and external controls) which may be overridden by disinhibitory influences (such as heightened arousal, aggressive modeling, low probability of punishment, biochemical agents, and contextual

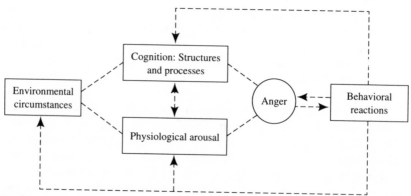

Figure 1.   Determinants and consequences of anger.

cues for aggression). Although provoking events are typically aversive (something the person would choose to avoid), people may engineer their own anger experiences by deliberate exposure to either internal or external stimuli; the arousal of anger may be satisfying as well as being functional.

The relationship of anger to aggressive behavior is that it is a significant activator of and has a mutually influenced relationship with aggression, but it is neither necessary nor sufficient for aggression to occur. The "mutually influenced" idea postulates a bidirectional causality (Konecni 1975a, 1975b), asserting that level of anger influences level of aggression and vice versa. Aggressive behavior can produce anger reduction by cathartic effects, as Konecni's meticulously performed experiments have demonstrated, but one can also speculate that anger might be intensified by aggressive behavior which has not yet redressed the provocation. In the latter case, acting aggressively pulls for the cognitive label "anger" and thereby serves to define one's emotional state as anger, which in turn serves to justify acting aggressively. That anger is "neither necessary nor sufficient" means simply that aggression can occur in the absence of anger and that it takes more than anger to produce aggression. Whether or not aggression occurs following provocation is a function of a number of social learning factors, such as reinforcement contingencies, expected outcomes, modeling influences, disinhibitory factors, and self-control capabilities (Bandura 1983). When the infliction of injury or damage is expected to produce personal gain or when the aggressive act is a well-learned behavior, aggression may occur without anger. Elsewhere, I have elaborated this "neither necessary nor sufficient" postulate for both individual and collective violence (Novaco 1986).

A full theoretical exposition of the anger construct is beyond the scope of this chapter; the focus here is on anger as a clinical problem, with emphasis on the personal or individual level of analysis. The account of anger determinants, moderators, mediational processes, and consequences is thereby restricted, more or less, to the phenomenological experience of the individual. A contextual perspective has emerged in the field of psychology (Stokols 1987, 1988), and the study of anger has much to gain from it and from research on human stress. A contextual perspective on anger must consider (*a*) anger's embeddedness within physical and social environments; (*b*) the reciprocal influences between the determinants, experience, and sequelae of anger within and across life domains; and (*c*) anger's transformational potential with regard to life in social systems (Novaco, 1992). By giving nearly exclusive attention to intrapsychic variables, clinical models impose unnecessary boundaries on our understanding of anger. While it is difficult to import physical and social milieux into the therapy room, we ought to give greater attention to the enduring contextual factors that shape anger experiences even inside of hospitals, as Depp's (1976) analysis of psychiatric inpatient assaults would suggest.

This broader view of anger is quite compatible with Averill's (1982) "constructivist" viewpoint, a major advance in theory about anger though not fully appreciated by behavioristically minded psychologists. Averill views anger as a socially constituted syndrome, a transitory social role governed by social rules. His perspective emphasizes the idea that the meaning and function of emotions are primarily determined by the social systems in which they occur and of which they are an integral part. Thus, anger is a rule-governed syndrome, an idea consistent with my functional analysis of anger (Novaco 1976), especially with regard to the dramaturgical or promotional dimension. Averill's exceedingly complex analysis has, however, been restricted to anger as a normal emotion. Because he does not address anger as a psychological disturbance, it is not clear how his perspective would extend to the clinical arena, and therapeutic interventions lie outside its scope.

Anger Scale Design

The assessment of anger follows from this general conception of cognitive, arousal, and behavioral domains linked by feedback mechanisms. Each of these domains is construed as having component dimensions relevant to anger as a clinical problem. The Novaco Anger Scale (NAS) separately assesses these dimensions, then sums the results to generate aggregate scores for each domain.

The NAS is constructed in two parts. Part A contains the clinically oriented scales (three domains, each with four subscales); the response scaling ("never true," "sometimes true," "always true") is newly developed, designed to have the simplicity of true-false endorsements while providing greater variation than dichotomous responses. Part B is an abbreviated improvement of the NPI, intended to provide an index of anger intensity and generality across a range of potentially provocative situations (five subscales); the five-point scaling used by the NPI and other anger intensity measures is reduced to four points to simplify response for mentally disordered persons (Spielberger's scales also use four-point ratings).

Because the scale was intended for use with mentally disordered persons, item construction required particular attention to statement clarity. Double negatives were avoided, and no more than two chunks of information were contained in a item.[2] Guided by the theoretical framework, the construction

2. An emphasis was placed on clarity and simplicity in item construction. Existing instruments often contain items that are overly complicated and lack clarity, sometimes to the point of being obscure. The Cook-Medley scale is especially problematic in this regard. For example, the following are some Cook-Medley scale items: "I prefer to pass by school friends, or people I know but have not seen for a long time, unless they speak to me first"; "I have sometimes stayed away from another person because I feared doing or saying something that I might regret otherwise"; "I have frequently worked under people who seem to have things arranged so that they

of items involved scrutiny of existing instruments, extensive interviews with clinical staff and patients, pilot testing, and formal reliability and concurrent validity testing with hospital patients. These procedural steps are detailed below, following the theoretical rationale for the scale's structural components.

NAS Part A Components

Cognitive Domain

The arousal of anger is cognitively mediated. This premise has been axiomatic for many aggression theorists (Novaco 1979). Much psychological theorizing is now cognitively based, but the viewpoint is ancient, having received a full exposition in Lucius Seneca's ([41] 1917) first-century treatise on morals, and it was generally accepted by classical period Stoic philosophers. The central proposition, from both the classical and contemporary cognitivist perspective (e.g., Ortony, Clore, and Collins 1988), is that there is no direct relationship between external events and anger. The arousal and maintenance of anger is a function of our perceptions and the way in which we process information. Indeed, the cognitive mediation of anger heightens the relevance of mental disorder with regard to occurrences of anger that exceed the parameters of normal functioning.

The notion of cognitive mediation is often misunderstood. The idea does not necessarily refer to an intermediary process interposed between exposure to stimulus and the resulting physiological and behavioral reactions. Cognitive mediation should be understood as an automatic and intrinsic part of the perceptual process and not simply as explicit thinking or otherwise conscious operations that might be involved in an event-thought-reaction sequence. Cognitive mediational processes, such as appraisal, are intrinsic to perception. Philosophers of science, such as Wittgenstein (1953) and Hanson (1969), have made this point in elaborate and elegant accounts of the perceptual process. In the field of human aggression, Berkowitz (1983) has criticized the cognitive mediation view, but he fails to treat cognitive appraisal as anything other than an operation tandem to observing (i.e., the event is observed then cognitively processed). Berkowitz's (1990) proposed "cognitive neo-associationist" model, which posits what could be called a "fight or flight" network of associations and reactions generated by negative affect, ironically incorporates tandem sequence premises about cognitive operations pertaining

---

get credit for good work but are able to pass off mistakes onto those under them"; "There are certain people whom I dislike so much that I am inwardly pleased when they are catching it for something they have done." These and other items have multiple chunks of information, are worded ambiguously, and are improperly punctuated. Several Buss-Durkee items (especially on the suspicion subscale) also appear to be too complex for mental patients.

to the generation of anger. My position here is that cognitive appraisal of provocation is often a highly automatized process and that an intervening "negative affect" state is an unnecessary hypothetical condition. Furthermore, the selection of what receives attention and ultimately functions as a provocation is very much influenced by cognitive dispositions known as expectations, schemas, and scripts. An elaborate model of cognitive scripts for aggression has been developed by Huesmann (1988).

The cognitive domain is operationalized by four subscales in the NAS: attentional focus, suspicion, rumination, and hostile attitude. They are intended as refinements of the appraisal and expectation constructs that I previously proposed as representing cognitive mediation structures for anger (Novaco 1979). Distillation of these dimensions occurred through consideration of theory, existing measures, interviews with patients and clinicians, and pilot testing of a preliminary instrument. They are here conjectured to be the most pertinent to anger as a clinical problem; a rationale is given below.

Attentional focus. In order to get angry about something, you must pay attention to it. I attribute this idea to William James; attentional processes are also emphasized by Bandura's (1983) social learning formulation of aggression. It seems evident that becoming angry about something can result from selective attention to cues having high provocation value. This cue salience may involve a negativity bias in processing information or in prioritizing focus. The subscale attempts to assess the tendency to lock onto provoking cues, which then dominate attentional space.

Suspicion. Perceived threat is a central activator of anger and aggressive behavior. Although these responses have biologically based survival value, this is more than offset by the customary need for adaptive response, which is precluded by excessive threat perceptions. Suspicion is linked to expectations of mistreatment by others, predisposing a person to appraise situations antagonistically. Previous anger measures have often incorporated suspicion and mistrust items.

Rumination. Once anger has been activated, it can be prolonged, intensified, or revivified by continued attention to the provocation. The tendency to be preoccupied with provoking experiences has been a neglected topic in anger-aggression research (Novaco 1986), but Caprara (1986) has found that his rumination measure is significantly related to aggressive behavior in laboratory studies. Anger rumination has important implications both for duration and intensity in the arousal domain and for the rehearsal of aggressive behavior scripts in the behavioral domain. This subscale assesses the person's tendency to dwell on anger experiences or to keep their memory ever-present.

Hostile attitude. The recurrently angry disposition takes the form of a "combat orientation"—a hyperreadiness to respond antagonistically. "Hostility" is an attitude or mental set, whereby prepotent antagonistic appraisals are overgeneralized. The appraisal here connotes the inclination to act aggressively (whereas suspicion or threat appraisals might not). This subscale was composed with items that pull for a disposition toward harm-doing, rather than merely negativity.

Arousal Domain

The physiological arousal component of anger is generally acknowledged by aggression researchers, as well as by those in the field of psychosomatic medicine. Early writings in the field of psychosomatic medicine (Alexander 1939; Saul 1939) and numerous important laboratory studies (Ax 1953; Funkenstein, King, and Drolette 1957; Oken 1960; and Schachter 1957) called attention to the physiological correlates of anger. Contemporary research on stress and cardiovascular disorders (e.g., Chesney and Rosenman 1985) has brought about a resurgence of interest in the physiology and sequelae of anger. Anger arousal is marked by physiological activation in the cardiovascular, endocrine, and limbic systems, as well as other autonomic and central nervous system areas, and by tension in the skeletal musculature.

In the field of aggression, assessment of anger physiology was prominent in research on catharsis, best exemplified by the work of Hokanson and his colleagues (Hokanson and Burgess 1962a, 1962b; Hokanson and Shelter 1961), and also in studies by Zillmann on "excitation transfer" (Zillmann 1971, 1983; Zillmann and Bryant 1974). Zillmann's experiments showed that excitation residues from prior arousal can combine with excitatory responses evoked by some present event. This transfer of excitation, when it is cognitively guided by cues for anger or aggression, enhances or intensifies the experience of anger and thus aggressive behavior in the immediate situation. Transfer effects are not hypothesized to occur when residual arousal is attributed to nonprovocative sources. This concept is important because it provides a theoretical and empirical basis for understanding how exposure to stressors, either acute or ambient, can predispose the person to respond angrily when faced with a minor provocation.

Previous anger self-report measures have not systematically measured arousal features. The NAS arousal domain is operationalized by four dimensions: intensity, duration, tension, and irritability. They were generated from the theoretical background and through such scale development procedures as consideration of existing instruments and clinical interviews. Their rationale is given below.

Intensity. Many existing anger instruments do measure intensity but only as a by-product of their response scaling—i.e., by incorporating a Likert-type response scale on which degree of anger is endorsed (part B of the present scale has this format). It is here assumed that high-intensity anger reactions are problematic. The capacity to process information efficiently and to act prudently is diminished under conditions of high arousal. This subscale assesses "hot responding" or the tendency for anger reactions to exceed regulatory capacity. This dimension should be related to impulsive aggression.

Duration. The prolongation of anger and its accompanying cognitions produces wear and tear on the body, interferes with task functioning, and increases the risk for aggressive behavior. The duration dimension has been neglected in previous anger assessment procedures, although some diary self-report studies have obtained duration data (cf. Averill 1982). This subscale is intended to measure whether anger responses are prolonged as opposed to momentary. It is expected that this dimension will be related to rumination and to planned aggression.

Somatic tension. The presence of physical tension is predisposing for anger and aggression. This idea is embedded in the anger treatment model (Novaco 1975, 1977) which incorporates relaxation counterconditioning procedures. The research by Zillmann (1971, 1983) has also shown that residues of arousal can increase the probability of anger and aggression. This subscale is concerned with somatic residues that can be predisposing for anger reactions, which may then be triggered by an otherwise minor provocation.

Irritability. The affective propensity to respond with anger to perceived annoyances is understood here as an arousal readiness dimension. Although irritability is not known to have distinct physiological arousal characteristics, hypothetically, it is inversely related to response latency. Irritabilitiy has otherwise been assessed by previous instruments (Buss and Durkee 1957; Caprara 1985). Here, items referring to being bothered or annoyed by minor events are intended to assess this anger readiness dimension.

Behavioral Domain

Behavioral responses and response inclinations play an important role in shaping and indeed defining anger. Implicit in the cognitive labeling of anger is an inclination to act in an antagonistic or confrontative manner towards the source of the provocation. Such action impulses partly define the emotional state as anger as opposed to some other state or emotion. Also, anger is often a product of behavioral exchanges involving an escalation of aversive events (e.g., Toch 1969), so the behavioral manifestations of anger are critical dimensions for assessment and treatment. In stressful situations, anger can also result from an absence of behavioral, problem-solving skills.

The NAS behavioral domain is operationalized by four dimensions: impulsive reaction, verbal aggression, physical confrontation, and indirect expression. An avoidance-withdrawal dimension was initially included in the preliminary scale but could not be successfully operationalized. The rationale for the subscales is given below.

Impulsive reaction. The tendency to respond impulsively is thought to be a dimension of anger that is related to aggressive behavior. The analysis by

Berkowitz (1986) of impulsive aggression clearly implicates anger. Impulsive reaction implies the absence of inhibitory controls. Items on this subscale concern rapid responses and the absence of reflective, moderating processes. This dimension is expected to be related to intensity.

Verbal aggression. Verbal antagonism is perhaps the most common manifestation of anger, as it stops short of behavior that will incur legal sanctions but allows one to assert dominance or control. It is the human form of the stereotyped threat displays that occur elsewhere in the animal kingdom. Because it has provoking as well as expressive functions, it is a problem dimension that can escalate conflict and leave a residue of bad feelings. This subscale assesses verbal behavior that is distinctly aggressive. It is expected to be related to hostile attitude, intensity, irritability, and duration.

Physical confrontation. The inclination to do physical harm to others is the most consequential problem feature of anger. It is oddly neglected in many anger self-report measures. Because of the reciprocal relationship between anger and aggression, this dimension is doubly important. The items on the subscale are concerned with physically coercive style and retaliatory behavior as personal dispositions. It is expected that this subscale will be related to hostile attitude, rumination, and intensity.

Indirect expression. The presence of external controlling factors, such as anticipated punishment, may inhibit the expression of anger or aggression toward the provoking source. The displacement of anger to substitute targets can be an adaptive alternative, but it is often problematic because it leaves the problem situation unchanged. It can also involve attacks on vulnerable others who present a lower risk of retaliation. Displacement and ventilation may provide temporary relief but have low problem-solving effectiveness. The subscale is expected to be related to rumination, intensity, duration, and somatic tension.

NAS Part B Components

This part of the NAS is intended to provide an index of anger intensity and generality across a range of provocations. The items assess degree of anger experienced with regard to various situations of provocation. Since the occurrence of anger is assumed to be a function of the person's cognitions (appraisals and expectations), items are constructed with cognitive mediation in mind. The subscales consist of five provocation categories, determined by previous research with the Novaco Provocation Inventory (Novaco 1988) and selected here for their applicability to clinical as well as normal populations. Their grouping was determined by conceptual criteria (theoretical and semantic meaning) and empirical criteria (internal consistency correlations). The five subscales, each with five items on four-point scaling, allow a maximum score of 100, thus providing a convenient index.

Disrespectful treatment. Perceived disrespect having ego-treat implications is a main source of anger reactions. The subscale items concern occurrences that pull for appraisals of demeaning criticism, effrontery, intrusive behavior, and mockery.

Unfairness/injustice. Situations of inequity commonly elicit anger which is seen to be a justified response to the unfairness. Anger is often linked with themes of justification. The items describe bullying, being slighted, discrimination, manipulation, and false accusation.

Frustration/interruption. The blocking of goal-directed behavior can elicit anger, particularly when the thwarting is seen to be arbitrary, repetitive, or inconsiderate. Interruption itself has arousal activating effects. The theme of personally invested action that is derailed without proper cause is reflected in the subscale items.

Annoying traits. Attributions of external blame commonly occur in anger reactions. Finding fault with others, attributing one's malaise to their shortcomings, is a recurrent theme. Items on this subscale pertain to the appraised characteristics of others to which anger responses can be attributed, such as haughtiness, self-centeredness, and insensitivity.

Irritations. Sensitization to incidental annoyances and aggravations is part of chronic anger patterns. Being bothered by nuisances involves exaggeration of event significance and a hyperreactance to things going wrong. Subscale items concern miscues, disappointment, and abrasive occurrences.

Scale Development Procedures

The new anger scale was developed through a sequence of hierarchical procedures: (1) categorization and codification of all existing anger measures found in a literature search; (2) acquisition and analysis of archival data on hospitalized patients in the state of California from 1980 through 1988; (3) interviews with hospital treatment staff about anger as a clinical problem; (4) preliminary scale construction and pilot testing with students; (5) interviews with hospital patients having very serious anger problems; (6) scale reconstruction; (7) reliability and concurrent validity testing with hospital patients; (8) final scale reconstruction and development of validity testing measures; and (9) predictive validity testing with hospital patients, involving retrospective and prospective analyses. Throughout the project, there were elaborate human subject reviews at the state, individual hospital, and campus levels.

Collection and codification of existing anger measures. A total of 18 self-report measures were gathered from the research literature and classified according to their focus, composition, and assessed dimensions. Most importantly, each item was coded for semantic-thematic content and for repetition across scales. This facilitated retrieval of items for potential use in the scale to be constructed and provided a basis for item content analysis and interscale comparisons. In its final form, 14 of the 44 items in part A and 15 of the 25 in part B of the NAS were preexisting instrument items or modifications of them.

Analysis of archival data on hospital patients.[3] The Level of Care Survey data, gathered on an approximately annual basis since 1980 by the California Division of State Hospitals, was downloaded from Department of Mental Health information system files. Project staff constructed the file for analysis and generated unique identifiers for the 21,904 cases, in order to allow cross-sectional and panel analyses. This data set had several uses: (1) it provided descriptive information about all hospital patients in the state's five institutions, which was ideal for comparing the characteristics of the samples used in the reliability and validity phases of the anger scale testings; (2) it guided procedural decisions in the recruitment of participants and enabled me to be highly informed in discussions with hospital administrators, hospital staff, and human subject review committees; (3) it provided valuable ideas about criterion measures, such as staff rating scales and the incidence of assaultive behavior; and (4) it constituted a strong data set for examining the epidemiology of anger and aggression among hospitalized patients and for testing hypotheses about anger as a risk factor for violence among the mentally disordered, as was illustrated earlier.

Regarding the internal validity of the Level of Care Survey, I conducted structured interviews with all 23 unit supervisors at Metropolitan State Hospital immediately after the LOCS was conducted in 1989. The analysis of the interview data indicated that the LOCS has considerable validity, although there is some qualification with regard to the time frame for the behavior-rating component, at least for the anger-related items; the raters do not adhere to the instructions "last 3 days only," hence their ratings should be understood as being general characterizations of the patient.

Interviews with hospital treatment staff.[4] Interviews were conducted with 12 to 15 treatment staff at each of the three hospital sites. The interviews concerned how the clinician conceptualized anger; characteristics of patients who have anger problems; anger-related precursors of assaultive behavior; hospital situations associated with anger and aggression; cognitive and arousal determinants; functions of anger in the hospital setting; the role of impulsivity, delusions, and rumination; family involvement in provocative and sup-

3. I would like to thank Dr. Bill DeRisi and his staff at the Program Development and Evaluation Branch of the Division of State Hospitals, California Department of Mental Health, for their gracious assistance concerning the LOCS data and other aspects of the project.

4. I am deeply appreciative of the great many occasions of assistance provided by administrators and clinical staff at Atascadero, Metropolitan, and Napa state hospitals. While I should properly name dozens who conscientiously gave me assistance, space here only permits me to give special thanks to Dr. Harold Carmel, Dr. Beth Hahn, and Mr. Dave Graziani. I beg the forgiveness of those unnamed, whom I have not forgotten.

portive roles; and anger control dimensions. In addition, information was obtained about the hospital ecology and about the various units at each hospital where angry or aggressive patients are located. The interviews were transcribed and were instrumental in generating a preliminary anger scale.

Information was also obtained about the capabilities of patients to take self-report scales; clinicians estimated about two-thirds of the patients to be capable, which proved to be accurate. Thus, the patient testing sample cannot be expected to be representative of the entire hospital population. A plan for providing incentives (payment) for patient participation was also developed from these interviews.

Preliminary scale construction and pilot testing with students. A preliminary 101-item version of the self-report scale was constructed, based on theoretically specified dimensions. The catalogue of codified items from the literature search and the interviews with clinical treatment staff were used to generate the preliminary instrument. Approximately half of the items were adopted or modified from previously developed measures.

Reliability and concurrent validity testings were conducted with university student samples, as it was thought that items and subscales that were unreliable with this population would surely be unstable with mental patients. The results of the pilot testings were most encouraging. Internal reliabilities ($N = 171$) of the scale components were .92 for part A, .92 for part B, and .94 for the total. Cognitive, arousal, and behavioral domain components had internal reliabilities of .78, .84, and .81, respectively. Test-retest reliabilities (two weeks, $N = 69$) were also quite high: .78, .87, and .83 for the cognitive, arousal, and behavioral domains; .86, .72, and .84 for part A, part B, and total. Each of these reliabilities were improved by scale revisions, as determined in the testings with hospital patients.

Concurrent validity analyses were also done, using the Buss-Durkee, Spielberger, and Caprara scales. Many coefficients were in the .60 to .80 range. Using these existing scales as criterion measures has limitations, especially since they were not developed from clinical populations, but they have great relevance to discriminate validity questions (see below), and the concurrent validity and reliability findings in the college student testing, along with concurrent hospital patient interviews, guided the reconstruction of the NAS.

Interviews with state hospital patients. Forty-five patients, 15 at each of the three hospital sites (Atascadero, Metropolitan, and Napa) were interviewed with regard to their anger experiences. These patients were nominated by hospital staff as having very serious problems with anger and violence. The interviews were conducted by the author with the patients individually in a private room on their hospital unit. Notes were handwritten, and the patients were given the opportunity to ask questions throughout the interview. Determinants of anger inside and outside the hospital were discussed, as well as their ways of responding to anger situations. The interviews were used to develop new items and to refine the instrument. For example, the interviews with forensic patients generated the Hostile Attitude item, "If someone cheats me, I'll make them feel sorry"; the demeanor of many patients suggested the Somatic Tension item, "I feel agitated and unable to relax"; repeated observations of edgy reactiveness prompted the Irritability item, "A lot of little things bug me"; recognition of the patients' diminished domain of privacy produced the Disrespectful Treatment item, "Someone looks through your things without your permission"; and the unmistakable sense of assaultive behavior at the edge of fragile controls which could easily be overridden suggested the Physical Confrontation item, "When I get mad, I can easily hit someone."

Some pilot testing of the preliminary scale was also done at this time to gauge comprehensibility and ease of response. During this patient interview phase, many essential hospital contacts were developed at the unit level. Practical information was also obtained about how to conduct the formal testing of patients at each hospital and on particular units.

Reconstruction of the anger scale. The reconstruction of the scale involved the elimination of items having poor test-retest reliabilities or poor internal consistencies within designated subscales. The scale was reduced from 101 items to 88. One subscale (Resentment) and a variety of items were removed for redundancy, lack of clarity, or inapplicability to hospital patients. Several items suggested by the patient interviews were added. These modifications were efficacious, as indicated by the subsequent reliability data from patient testing with the reconstructed scale. Indeed, the internal reliability and test-retest reliability coefficients for the patient testing were higher than those achieved with the student samples, as reported below.

Reliability and Concurrent Validity Testing with Patients

The revised NAS was administered twice, two weeks apart, for test-retest reliability and internal reliability evaluation. The two-week interval was selected in consideration of the hospital treatment context. The concurrent validity testing involved the administration of six other scales: the Buss-Durkee Hostility Inventory, the Spielberger Trait Anger Scale, the Cook-Medley Hostility Scale, the Caprara Irritability Scale, the Caprara Rumination Scale, and the Barratt Impulsivity Scale (Barratt 1965). The last (BIS-11 revision) was incorporated because of the relevance of impulsivity to aggressive behavior by mentally disordered persons (e.g., Segal et al. 1988). Half of the six alternative scales were given with the NAS on the first testing and half on the second, administered in a counterbalanced order. A total of 142 patients completed the first testing, and 126 of them completed the second testing. Only one patient declined to be tested a second time (he was too annoyed); the others had been discharged before the retest.

Patients were recruited with the assistance of the unit psychology staffs and the unit supervisors. Participants were judged by their primary clinician to be able to give informed consent. Their demographic and psychological characteristics were similar to those of the patients in the validity phase, described later in comparison with the hospital population. Typically, the patient candidates on a particular unit were assembled as a group and informed about the project by project staff (myself or the project manager). They were told that they would be given $20, deposited into their trust accounts, for their participation. Research assistants then met with them individually, obtained written consent, and arranged for private testing in a room on the patient's unit.

Analyses of internal reliability, test-retest, and validity coefficients with the comparison scales were supplemented by item analyses in reconstructing the instrument. The reconstructed NAS reliability coefficients are presented in table 3. In fact, the reconstruction had the effect of lowering test-retest reliability, because it removed items with skewed distributions.

The internal reliability of part A, part B, and total were .95, .95, and .97, respectively. These can be compared with the alpha coefficients for the alternative scales used in the concurrent validity testing: Buss-Durkee (.91), Spielberger Trait (.90), Cook-Medley (.89), Caprara Irritability (.89), Caprara Rumination (.80), and Barratt Impulsivity (.81). The reliabilities for the separate NAS subscales are also given in table 3. The small number of items (four or five) per subscale affects the magnitude of the coefficients.

The test-retest reliabilities of part A, part B, and total were .84, .86, and .86, respectively. This is a higher overall degree of consistency than had been obtained with the college student testing on the preliminary instrument, reflecting the improvements made in scale reconstruction and the feasibility of its use in the testing of mentally disordered patients. The test-retest coefficients for the separate subscales are also given in table 3.

The concurrent validity coefficients for the subscales are obviously too numerous to summarize in text or tables here. Most centrally, the NAS total correlates .82 with the Buss-Durkee total, .84 with the Spielberger Trait scale, .68 with Cook-Medley, .78 with Caprara Irritability, .69 with Caprara Rumination, and .47 with the Barratt Impulsivity total. These correlations are given in table 4 along with the other interscale relationships.

Regarding discriminate validity, the NAS subscales were examined for their relationship to the scales or subscales of other measures with regard to their particular focus. The overall pattern was one of good discriminate validity. For example, the NAS Suspicion subscale was more strongly correlated with the Buss-Durkee Suspicion subscale (.61) than with any other Buss-Durkee scale, and it was also correlated with the Cook-Medley scale (.60) which is an MMPI derivative with suspicion content. The Intensity subscale was more strongly correlated with the Spielberger Trait scale (.73) than any other criterion measure and more than was any other NAS subscale; it was

Table 3. Reliability coefficients for Novaco Anger Scale (January 1990)

Scale component	Internal reliability	Test-retest reliability
Part A	**.947**	**.841**
Cognitive domain	.820	.744
Attentional focus	.440	.547
Rumination	.655	.697
Hostile attitude	.655	.644
Suspicion	.452	.557
Arousal domain	.889	.840
Intensity	.723	.762
Duration	.739	.715
Tension	.714	.749
Irritability	.576	.677
Behavioral domain	.894	.833
Impulsive reaction	.791	.765
Verbal aggression	.637	.731
Physical confrontation	.752	.737
Indirect expression	.674	.722
Part B	**.953**	**.861**
Disrespect	.722	.771
Unfairness	.728	.753
Frustration	.827	.768
Annoying traits	.836	.780
Irritations	.842	.799
TOTAL	**.966**	**.861**

Note: The test-retest procedure involved a two-week interval. A total of 142 patients were involved in the first testing, and 126 of these were present for the second testing.

also the NAS subscale most strongly correlated with the Barratt Impulsivity total. The Physical Confrontation subscale was most strongly correlated with the Buss-Durkee Assault subscale (.73), and none of the other criterion measures correlated higher than .58 with that Buss-Durkee subscale. This NAS subscale was also correlated .63 with the Spielberger Trait measure. The Irritability subscale was strongly correlated with Caprara Irritability (.66), although less with that subscale on Buss-Durkee (.56). The Irritations subscale also correlated more strongly with the Caprara Irritability scale (.63) than with any other criterion measure. The Ruminations subscale was nicely associated with the Caprara Rumination scale (.65), and its .62 correlation with the Buss-Durkee Resentment was the highest relationship with that instrument's subscales (next highest was .52). The Impulsivity subscale correlated only modestly with the Barratt Impulsivity Total (.40) but more strongly with Spielberger Trait (.73). The Indirect Expression subscale correlated more

Table 4. Intercorrelations among Caprara, Buss-Durkee, Spielberger, Cook-Medley, Barratt, and Novaco Scales

	Caprara		Buss-Durkee	Spielberger Trait	Cook-Medley	Barratt total	Novaco total
	Rumination	Irritability					
Caprara							
Rumination	1.0		.73	.61	.63	.40	.69
Irritability	.58	1.0	.76	.71	.59	.55	.78
Buss-Durkee	.73	.76	1.0	.76	.73	.58	.82
Spielberger Trait	.61	.71	.76	1.0	.52	.49	.84
Cook-Medley	.63	.59	.73	.52	1.0	.38	.68
Barratt Total	.40	.55	.58	.49	.38	1.0	.47
Novaco Total	.69	.78	.82	.84	.68	.47	1.0

N = 141

strongly with the Buss-Durkee Indirect Expression subscale (.71) than with any other subscale from that instrument (next highest was .47).

Intrascale and interscale relationships. With respect to the interrelationships among the NAS subscales, the issue of overlap or redundancy arises. One question concerns the degree to which the new scale is too highly correlated with other anger measures, such as the Buss-Durkee and Spielberger scales. Although its correlation with each of these was indeed high (.82 and .84, respectively), it correlated with both of these scales more strongly than they did with each other (.76). The intercorrelations among the various instruments (synchronous testings) are given in table 4.

Within the NAS, the intercorrelations of subscales with other subscales were mostly in the .35 to .55 range. Even at .70, the shared variance is 49%. The overall set of subscale-to-subscale relationships indicated that redundancy was not a problem. As the foregoing theoretical section indicated, certain subscales should be related to other particular subscales, and indeed this occurs: Rumination correlated strongly with Duration (.72) and Irritability (.64); Impulsivity correlated strongly with Intensity (.73), Verbal Aggression (.69), and Physical Confrontation (.67); and Intensity correlated strongly (.68) with both Rumination and Physical Confrontation.

Scale revisions. While the NAS subscales were found to have good discriminate validity with the criteria and very good overall reliability, there were some problematic elements. As indicated previously, individual item analyses were conducted, examining the response distributions. Those items that were highly skewed were removed, unless the low frequency scores were predictive. One entire subscale, Avoidance and Withdrawal, was removed due to poor reliability and validity. Two subscales, Attentional Focus and Suspicion, were found to have low internal consistency (below .50) and low test-retest reliability (below .60). Item changes were made in those subscales before the predictive validity testing with the new sample of patients. In addition to item substitutions and deletions based on statistical results, the extensive testing of individual patients provided information about item quality or suitability, and so several wording modifications were made.

Predictive Validity Testing

Retrospective Analyses

For the 142 patients who participated in the reliability and concurrent validity testing phase, archival data were obtained regarding Special Incident Reports and the occurrence of Seclusion and Restraints for each patient, as well as PRN medications. The SIR and S&R data were tallied from individual forms at two of the hospitals and from computerized records at the third.

The NAS indices and the alternative scales were correlated with a set of aggressive behavior criteria: the number of criminal convictions for violence against persons, violence against property, and sex crimes; Axis 5 diagnosis (Global Assessment of Functioning Scale, partly defined on the low end by violent behavior); and the use of emergency procedures in the hospital to control violent behavior (restraints, seclusion, restraints and seclusion, and PRN medication) during the six months prior to testing.

With regard to these criteria, coded from the retrospective analysis of patients' hospital charts, the NAS indices had a greater range of significant ($p < .01$) coefficients than any other measure. That is, while one of the alternative measures may have had a coefficient of comparable magnitude on some particular criterion, NAS indices were significantly related to a greater number of criteria. For the correlations reported below, those that are above .20 are significant at $p < .01$, and those above .27 are significant at $p < .001$.

Perhaps the most important criterion in the retrospective analysis was the patient's number of convictions for violent crimes against persons. The correlation of that criterion is .34 with the NAS part A measure, .36 with Hostile Attitude, .37 with Duration, and above .30 with a number of other NAS indices. Of the alternative scales, only the Caprara Rumination Scale (.33) correlates above .30. The correlation is .27 for both Spielberger Trait and Buss-Durkee and .21 for Cook-Medley. Similarly, for Axis 5 diagnosis, the part A index is correlated $-.36$; this relationship is $-.35$ for both the Total and the Arousal Domain, and is above $-.30$ for a number of other NAS indices. Of the others, only the Caprara Irritability scale ($-.35$) had a coefficient above .30; the correlation is $-.24$ for Spielberger Trait, $-.18$ for Buss-Durkee, and $-.24$ for Cook-Medley.

On the other retrospective criteria, the NAS was neither better nor worse than any other measure. The Intensity subscale had the strongest relationship (.34) to the use of seclusion and to restraint and seclusion (three- or five-point restraints plus room seclusion), but no other index had a coefficient of similar magnitude. Tension (.34), Intensity (.30), and Rumination (.30) have noteworthy correlations with PRNs, but these are not strongly distinguished from the alternative scales. The best predictor of property violence was the Barratt Impulsivity Total (.33), and the Spielberger Trait Anger measure was the best predictor of sex crimes at .25, compared to .20 for the NAS total. Curiously, the scale that did the least well across criterion measures is the Cook-Medley scale, a measure containing items from the Minnesota Multiphasic Personality Inventory, which had been generated for use with clinical populations. Although first developed from the MMPI with samples of teacher education students, the Cook-Medley scale is now widely used in psychosomatic research regarding heart disease; however, of all the instruments used, it presented the greatest difficulty for patients because of the complex wording of its items.

Prospective Analyses

The prospective analyses involved 158 patients, approximately 50 patients each from Atascadero, Metropolitan, and Napa state hospitals. The validity testing procedure entailed a two-week ($N = 158$), a one-month ($N = 155$), and a two-month ($N = 151$) follow-up testing. Sixty-eight of the patients tested in this phase of the project had participated in the previous patient testing phase, which concerned test-retest reliability, concurrent validity, and retrospective validity assessments. The criterion for patient participation was that they be able to give informed consent, and they were paid $10 for their participation. Patient participants were recruited on their units with the assistance of unit clinical staff.

In comparison to the state hospital population, as reflected in the 1990 LOCS data, the testing sample was younger (31.6 vs. 37.9 years), had more years of education (11.2 vs. 10.4), and was more likely to be divorced or separated (22.2% vs. 14.4%). The racial characteristics of the testing sample were 63.6% white, 20.8% black, and 11.0% Hispanic, whereas the state hospital population was 55.6% white, 24.2% black, and 14.9% Hispanic. Their psychological characteristics vary from the overall population, as might be expected, given participation in an anger self-report testing. They were higher on the Novaco and Thacker (1993) LOCS anger rating index (16.5 vs. 15.1), higher on our depression index (6.4 vs. 5.5), and lower on our psychotic symptoms index (9.9 vs. 11.6), although the latter difference is entirely due to male participants (the female means are identical at 11.98). The sample was 30.1% female, compared to 18.9% in the population. Females were oversampled to allow for gender group analyses.

Instruments and Procedure

All patients were administered the July 1990 version of the NAS and the Spielberger Trait Anger Scale at the start of this phase. For each of the follow-up testings, the Spielberger State Anger Scale was administered, this being the main validity criterion measure. The Spielberger Trait scale thus serves as an alternative measure of anger, against which the NAS can be compared for its relationship to subsequent state anger. It should be noted that the similarity of the Spielberger trait-anger and state-anger scales makes the comparison of predictive validity coefficients a challenging one for the NAS.

No other self-report instruments were used in the follow-up testings because of project logistics in getting the target number of patients tested. However, we did obtain hospital chart data pertaining to anger and aggression on a weekly basis over the two-month period, as well as clinician behavior ratings performed on a newly developed rating scale. The chart coding instrument was developed to record patient history and pertinent hospital record data concerning patient behavior. The patients' hospital charts were also coded by project staff for weekly behavioral data. A weekly behavior rating form was also developed to be completed by hospital unit staff. Numerous meeting were held with clinical staff at each hospital to establish the procedure for obtaining the behavior ratings and to obtain staff cooperation. Behavior ratings by hospital unit staff were systematically collected each week. The patient testings were conducted on 24 units at the three hospitals, and the behavior ratings were done by 57 staff members across those units.

Revised NAS: Descriptive Statistics and Internal Reliability

The means, medians, and standard deviations of the NAS subscales and total score are given in table 5, along with the values for the internal reliability analysis of the revised instrument. Part A, which contains 48 items rated on three-point scales, has a mean of 90.1 and a standard deviation of 18.2, that

Table 5. Descriptive statistics for NAS subscales (July 1990 version)

Subscale	Alpha	Mean	Median	SD
Part A	**.946**	90.05	89.00	18.17
Cognitive domain	.814	31.00	31.00	5.82
Attentional focus	.376	8.38	8.00	1.67
Rumination	.636	7.88	8.00	1.99
Hostile attitude	.682	7.04	7.00	2.09
Suspicion	.396	7.71	8.00	1.61
Arousal domain	.879	30.50	31.00	6.80
Intensity	.683	7.61	8.00	2.09
Duration	.744	7.65	8.00	2.21
Tension	.666	7.33	7.00	2.05
Irritability	.593	7.91	8.00	1.78
Behavioral domain	.897	28.55	28.00	7.10
Impulsive reaction	.761	7.27	8.00	2.23
Verbal aggression	.690	7.71	8.00	2.03
Physical confrontation	.730	7.24	7.00	2.13
Indirect expression	.660	6.33	6.00	1.92
Part B	**.948**	65.25	65.00	17.46
Disrespect	.774	13.01	13.00	3.76
Unfairness	.739	13.89	14.00	3.67
Frustration	.779	13.45	14.00	3.64
Annoying traits	.851	12.6	13.00	4.28
Irritations	.803	12.22	12.00	3.95
Total	**.967**	**155.30**	**152.42**	**33.47**

Note: N = 158, California state hospital patients from 3 hospitals.

is, patients' ratings across items average slightly below the midpoint of the response scale ("sometimes"). Part B, which has 25 items rated on four-point scales, has a mean of 65.3 and a standard deviation of 17.5, indicating that on average patients' ratings of these anger situation fall between "a little angry" and "fairly angry." The mean for the NAS total was 155.3, with a standard deviation of 33.5. With regard to the sample composition, there were no significant differences in these means between the 68 patients who had been previously tested and the 90 newly tested patients.

The internal reliabilities of part A, part B, and total are .95, .95, and .97. These coefficients are virtually the same as those generated in the reliability study with the initial version, which had 15 more items. They are also higher than the alpha coefficients obtained for the Spielberger Trait Anger Scale at the previous testing (.90) and at this present testing (.93). All of the other comparison anger scales used in the reliability and concurrent validity phase study had lower alpha coefficients. The reliabilities of the various NAS sub-scales are also shown in table 5. Overall, there were relatively small changes in the individual subscale alpha coefficients, as seven subscales increased, while ten subscales decreased. The alpha decreases are not surprising since the number of items was reduced. This had a particular impact on the sub-scales which had been reduced from five and six items to four items.

The two subscales with the lowest alphas in the initial version were again problematic. Both Attentional Focus (.38) and Suspicion (.39) had low inter-nal reliabilities. One Suspicion item was particularly poor ("Most people will do what they say they will do," which has subsequently been reworded as, "People can be trusted to do what they say"). The Suspicion scale is an important one theoretically, and it was found to have good discriminant va-lidity with the Buss-Durkee subscales (it correlated .61 with Buss-Durkee Suspicion, which was higher than it did with any other Buss-Durkee sub-scale), and it also correlated .60 with the Cook-Medley scale, which many investigators in health psychology field regard as a suspicion measure. An Impulsive Reaction scale item ("If someone crosses me, I get back at them") having low internal reliability has now been changed to "If someone bothers me, I react first and think later." These modifications and a few minor word-ing changes have resulted in the current version of the NAS.[5]

Concurrent and Prospective Validity

Concurrent validity was examined by correlational analyses with the 1990 LOCS clinical ratings for those patients ($N = 108$) on the hospital census

5. The instrument form has been given the title Reactions to Provocations (NAS) and can be obtained from the author. Other scale revisions await results from the testing of other populations.

Table 6. Predictive validity correlations of NAS components with
Spielberger State Anger scale testing

NAS components and Spielberger Trait Anger	Spielberger State Anger Scale testing		
	2 weeks (N = 158)	1 month (N = 155)	2 months (N = 151)
Cognitive domain	.28	.35	.37
Arousal domain	.38	.50	.47
Behavioral domain	.33	.33	.42
Part A	.36	.43	.46
Part B	.33	.37	.43
NAS total	.37	.42	.47
Spielberger Trait Anger	.32	.44	.50

Note: For comparison, the Spielberger Trait Anger Scale was given at the same time as the NAS. All of the above correlations are statistically significant at $p < .001$.

when the LOCS was conducted. The correlations are too numerous to present here, but some central findings can be briefly reported. Significant correlations with LOCS ratings of "gets angry or annoyed easily" and the anger rating index were found for the NAS total ranging from $r = .21$ to .24. The strongest relationship with these criteria occurred for the behavioral domain score ($r = .26$ and .27), and its Impulsivity subscale was the only predictor that was significantly (alpha $= .01$) related to assault ($r = .26$, $p < .004$). The Physical Confrontation subscale was significantly related to the anger ratings (.22 and .24) but was only marginal for assault ($p < .05$). The Hostile Attitude subscale, which had been found to be a significant predictor of violence (number of convictions for violent crimes against persons) in the patient history analyses, was not significant in the 1990 LOCS data; however, analyzing the 1989 LOCS data, it is significantly correlated with assault ($r = .34$, $p < .01$).

The central prospective validity analysis involved the contemporaneous administration of the NAS and the Spielberger Trait Anger Scale (counterbalanced in order) and the subsequent administration of the Spielberger State Anger Scale at two-week, one-month, and two-month follow-up intervals. The results of the predictive validity for state anger are given in table 6. It can be seen that each of the NAS component indices are significantly related to the criteria at greater than $p < .001$, and that the magnitude of the correlations increases with time (from the two-week to the two-month testings). It can also be seen that the correlations with the Spielberger state-anger criterion for the NAS total (.37, .42, and .47) are very similar to those for the Spielberger Trait Anger Scale (.32, .44, and .50). Given the great similarity in scale structure and item wording between the trait and state versions of the Spielberger scales, the results for the NAS are quite strong.

Implications for Risk Assessment

The epidemiological findings from the Level of Care Survey establish that anger and aggressive behavior are frequent and serious problems for psychiatric patients and that patient anger as rated by their primary clinicians is significantly related to assaultive behavior by the patients in both the current and the subsequent year. The subsequent year effects are important not only because of the prospective relationship but because the recording of the occasions of physical assault are very likely made in the patient's hospital charts by different staff members (unit supervisors) than the ones doing the anger ratings (therapists).

To be sure, hospital and community environments, both physical and social, are relevant to patient violence. In their review of violence in psychiatric facilities in the United States and Europe, Edwards and Reid (1983) point to anger and irritability as staff characteristics that can provoke assault by patients, and of course staff members become angry after having been assaulted (Aiken 1984; Ryan and Poster 1989); such bidirectionally causal transactions are abundant in community episodes of violence. Anger is very much a contextual phenomenon. Anger experiences are embedded in physical and social contexts and are reciprocally related to the elements of those contexts (Novaco 1992).

The degree to which anger constitutes a risk factor for violence hinges on its operation as a mediator of the relationship between aversive events (occurrences the person would choose to avoid) and harm-doing behavior. However, as it is conjectured that anger is neither necessary nor sufficient for aggression, violence can occur in the absence of anger, and it takes more than anger to produce violent behavior. Because the occurrence of harm-doing behavior is also regulated by inhibitory mechanisms, the determination of violence risk can be gauged only partly from the assessment of anger. Nevertheless, the role of anger as a potent activator of aggressive behavior and its involvement in a wide range of clinical disorders have beckoned for refinements in its measurement.

To say that the occurrence of violence is a function of inhibitory control mechanisms, of course, begs the question of what psychological and psychobiological processes contribute to the capacity to regulate anger and aggression. While the new anger scale seeks to improve assessment by partitioning anger in terms of cognitive, arousal, and behavioral domains and of subsidiary dimensions within them, much remains to be addressed with regard to psychological deficits in anger control. Considerably more research is needed to understand the dynamics of the perception of threat or offense, the experience of anger, and the inhibition of aggression.

By basing scale development on a conception of anger as a theoretical construct and by systematically generating the scale through a hierarchical procedure that emphasized applicability to mentally disordered persons and to violence, this new anger scale sought to remedy shortcomings in existing instruments. It is hoped that the NAS will be useful not only for the understanding of violence risk but also for guiding and evaluating clinical treatment of anger and aggression. Through the identification of a patient's salient anger dimensions, treatment might fruitfully be targeted and orchestrated. Additionally, for research investigations, the new instrument should have value in screening patients for treatment research and in evaluating treatment effectiveness in a more differentiated manner than has been possible with previous measures. The reliability and validity results for the new scale support its prospective use.

Acknowledgments

This research was supported by the John D. and Catherine T. MacArthur Foundation Research Network on Mental Health and Law. The author wishes to thank Stacy Thacker for her able assistance with this research.

References

Aiken, G. 1984. Assaults on staff in a locked ward: Prediction and consequences. *Medicine, Science and the Law* 24:199–207.

Alexander, F. 1939. Emotional factors in essential hypertension. *Psychosomatic Medicine* 1:173–79.

Armstead, C. A., K. A. Lawler, G. Gordon, J. Cross, and J. Gibbons. 1989. Rationship of racial stressors to blood pressure responses and anger expression in black college students. *Health Psychology* 8:541–56.

Averill, J. R. 1974. An analysis of psychophysiological symbolism and its influence on theories of emotion. *Journal for the Theory of Social Behaviour* 4:147–90.

———. 1982. *Anger and aggression: An essay on emotion.* New York: Springer-Verlag.

Ax, A. F. 1953. The physiological differentiation between fear and anger in humans. *Psychosomatic Medicine* 15:433–42.

Bandura, A. 1983. Psychological mechanisms of aggression. In R. G. Green and E. I. Donnerstein, eds., *Aggression: Theoretical and empirical reviews.* Vol. 1. New York: Academic Press.

Barefoot, J. C., G. Dahlstrom, and R. B. Williams. 1982. Hostility, CHD incidence, and total mortality: A 25-year follow-up of 255 physicians. *Psychosomatic Medicine* 55:59–64.

Baron, R. A. 1971. Magnitude of victim's pain cues and level of prior anger arousal as determinants of adult aggressive behavior. *Journal of Personality and Social Psychology* 17:236–43.

———. 1984. Reducing organizational conflict: An incompatible response approach. *Journal of Applied Psychology* 69:272–79.

Barratt, E. 1965. Factor analyses of some psychometric measures of impulsiveness and anxiety. *Psychological Reports* 16:544–47.

Baumeister, R. F., A. Stillwell, and S. R. Wotman. 1990. Victim and perpetrator accounts of interpersonal conflict: Auto-biographical narratives about anger. *Journal of Personality and Social Psychology* 59:994–1005.

Beers, C. W. 1908. *A mind that found itself.* Garden City, N.Y.: Doubleday.

Ben-Zur, H. and S. Breznitz. 1991. What makes people angry: Dimensions of anger-provoking events. *Journal of Research in Personality* 25:1–22.

Berkowitz, L. 1983. The experience of anger as a parallel process in the display of impulsive, "angry" aggression. In R. G. Geen and E. I. Donnerstein, eds., *Aggression: Theoretical and empirical reviews.* Vol. 1. New York: Academic Press.

———. 1986. Some varieties of human aggression: Criminal violence as coercion, rule-following, impression management and impulsive behavior. In A. Campbell and J. J. Gibbs, eds., *Violent transactions.* Oxford: Basil Blackwell.

———. 1990. On the formation and regulation of anger and aggression: A cognitive-neoassociationistic analysis. *American Psychologist* 45:494–503.

Blackburn, R. 1968. Personality in relation to extreme aggression in psychiatric offenders. *British Journal of Psychiatry.* 114:821–28.

Brizer, D. A., M. L. Crowner, A. Convit, and J. Volavka. 1988. Videotape recording of inpatient assaults: A pilot study. *American Journal of Psychiatry* 145:751–52.

Buss, A. 1961. *The psychology of aggression.* New York: John Wiley and Sons.

Buss, A., and A. Durkee. 1957. An inventory for assessing different kinds of hostility. *Journal of Counseling Psychology* 21:342–49.

Caprara, G. V. 1986. Indicators of aggression: The dissipation-rumination scale. *Personality and Individual Differences* 7:763–69.

Caprara, G. V., V. Cinanni, G. D'Imperio, S. Passerini, P. Renzi, and G. Travaglia. 1985. Indicators of impulsive aggression: Present status of research on irritability and emotional susceptibility scales. *Personality and Individual Differences* 6:665–74.

Carmel, H., and M. Hunter. 1989. Staff injuries from inpatient violence. *Hospital and Community Psychiatry* 40:41–46.

Chesney, M., and R. Rosenman. 1985. *Anger and hostility in cardiovascular and behavioral disorders.* Washington: Hemisphere Publishing.

Conn, L. M., and J. R. Lion. 1983. Assaults in a university hospital. In J. R. Lion and W. H. Reid, eds., *Assaults within psychiatric facilities,* 61–69. New York: Grune and Stratton.

Cook, W. W., and D. M. Medley. 1954. Proposed hostility and pharisaic-virtue scores for the MMPI. *Journal of Applied Psychology* 38:414–18.

Craig, T. J. 1982. An epidemiological study of problems associated with violence among psychiatric inpatients. *American Journal of Psychiatry* 139:1262–66.

Depp, F. C. 1976. Violent behavior patterns on psychiatric wards. *Aggressive Behavior* 2:295–306.

Drinkwater, J., and G. Gudjonsson. 1989. The nature of violence in psychiatric hospitals. In K. Howells and C. Hollin, eds., *Clinical approaches to violence*. London: John Wiley.

Edmunds, G., and D. C. Kendrick. 1980. *The measurement of human aggressiveness*. New York: John Wiley.

Edwards, J. G., and W. H. Reid. 1983. Violence in psychiatric facilities in Europe and the United States. In J. R. Lion and W. H. Reid, eds., *Assaults within psychiatric facilities*, 131–42. New York: Grune and Stratton.

Ekblom, B. 1970. *Acts of violence by patients in mental hospitals*. Uppsala: Svenska Bokforlaget.

Endler, N. S., and J. McV. Hunt. 1968. S-R inventories of hostility and comparisons of the proportion of variance from persons, responses, and situations for hostility and anxiousness. *Journal of Personality and Social Psychology* 9:309–15.

Engebretson, T. O., K. A. Mathews, and M. F. Scheier. 1989. Relations between anger expression and cardiovascular reactivity: Reconciling inconsistent findings through a matching hypothesis. *Journal of Personality and Social Psychology* 57:513–21.

Evans D. R. and M. Strangeland. 1971. Development of the reaction inventory to measure anger. *Psychological Reports* 29:412–14.

Fottrell, E. 1980. A study of violent behavior among patients in psychiatric hospitals. *British Journal of Psychiatry* 136:216–21.

Funkenstein, D. H., S. H. King, and M. E. Drolette. 1957. *Mastery of stress*. Cambridge: Harvard University Press.

Hall, G. S. 1899. A study of anger. *American Journal of Psychology* 10:516–91.

Haller, R. M., and R. H. Deluty. 1988. Assaults on staff by psychiatric in-patients: A critical review. *British Journal of Psychiatry* 152:174–79.

Hanson, N. R. 1969. *Perception and discovery*. San Francisco: Freeman.

Hokanson, J. E., and M. Burgess. 1962a. The effects of three types of aggression on vascular processes. *Journal of Abnormal and Social Psychology* 64:446–48.

———. 1962b. The effects of status, type of frustration, and aggression on vascular processes. *Journal of Abnormal and Social Psychology* 65:232–37.

Hokanson, J. E., and S. Shelter. 1961. The effects of overt aggression on physiological arousal level. *Journal of Abnormal and Social Psychology* 63:446–48.

Howells, K., and C. Hollin. 1989. *Clinical approaches to violence*. London: John Wiley.

Huesmann, R. 1988. An information processing model for the development of aggression. *Aggressive Behavior* 14:13–24.

Katz, R. C., and T. Toben. 1986. The Novaco Anger Scale and Jenkins Activity Survey as predictors of cardiovascular reactivity. *Journal of Psychopathology and Behavioral Assessment* 8:149–55.

Kay, S. R., F. Wolkenfeld, and L. M. Murrill. 1988. Profiles of aggression among psychiatric inpatients. II: Covariates and predictors. *The Journal of Nervous and Mental Disease* 176:547–57.

Konečni, V. J. 1975a. Annoyance, type and duration of post-annoyance activity, and aggression: The "cathartic effect." *Journal of Experimental Psychology: General*. 104:76–102.

————. 1975b. The mediation of aggressive behavior: Arousal level versus anger and cognitive labeling. *Journal of Personality and Social Psychology* 32:706–12.

Lakoff, G., and Z. Kovecses. 1987. The cognitive model of anger inherent in American English. In D. Holland and N. Quinn, eds., *Cultural models in language and thought,* 195–221. Cambridge: Cambridge University Press.

Larkin, E., S. Murtagh, and S. Jones. 1988. A preliminary study of violent incidents in a special hospital (Rampton). *British Journal of Psychiatry* 153:226–31.

Lion, J. R., and W. H. Reid. 1983. *Assaults within psychiatric facilities.* New York: Grune and Stratton.

Lion, J. R., W. Snyder, and G. L. Merrill. 1981. Under-reporting of assaults on staff in a state hospital. *Hospital and Community Psychiatry* 32:497–98.

Madden, D., J. Lion, and M. Penna. 1976. Assaults on psychiatrists by patients. *American Journal of Psychiatry* 133:422–25.

Maiuro, R. D., P. P. Vitaliano, and T. S. Cahn. 1987. A brief measure for the assessment of anger and aggression. *Journal of Interpersonal Violence* 2:166–78.

Megargee, E. I. 1966. Undercontrolled and overcontrolled personality types in extreme antisocial aggression. *Psychological Monographs,* no. 611.

Megargee, E. I., and G. A. Mendelsohn. 1962. A cross-validation of 12 MMPI scales of hostility and control. *Journal of Abnormal and Social Psychology* 65:431–38.

Monahan, J. 1981. *The clinical prediction of violent behavior.* Washington, D.C.: Government Printing Office.

Novaco, R. W. 1975. *Anger control: The development and evaluation of an experimental treatment.* Lexington, Mass.: D. C. Heath.

————. 1976. The function and regulation of the arousal of anger. *American Journal of Psychiatry* 133:1124–28.

————. 1977. Stress inoculation: A cognitive therapy for anger and its application to a case of depression. *Journal of Consulting and Clinical Psychology* 45:600–608.

————. 1979. The cognitive regulation of anger and stress. In P. Kendall and S. Hollon, eds., *Cognitive-behavioral interventions.* New York: Academic Press.

————. 1985. Anger and its therapeutic regulation. In M. Chesney and R. Rosenman, eds., *Anger and hostility in cardiovascular and behavioral disorders.* Washington: Hemisphere Publications.

————. 1986. Anger as a clinical and social problem. In R. Blanchard and C. Blanchard, eds., *Advances in the study of aggression.* Vol. 2. New York: Academic Press.

————. 1988. Novaco Provocation Inventory. In M. Hersen and A. Bellack, eds., *Dictionary of behavior assessment techniques.* New York: Pergamon Press.

————. 1992. A contextual perspective on anger with relevance to blood pressure. In E. Johnson, D. Gentry, and S. Julius, eds., *Personality, elevated blood pressure, and essential hypertension,* 113–32. New York: Hemisphere Publishing.

Novaco, R. W., and G. L. Robinson. 1984. Anger and aggression among military personnel. In R. M. Kaplan, V. J. Konečni, and R. W. Novaco, eds., *Aggression in children and youth.* The Hague: Martinus Nijhoff.

Novaco, R. W., and S. L. Thacker. 1993. *Anger and assaultive behavior among psychiatric hospital patients.* Unpublished manuscript.

Novaco, R. W., and W. Welsh. 1989. Anger disturbances: Cognitive mediation and clinical prescriptions. In K. Howells and C. Hollin, eds., *Clinical approaches to violence*. London: John Wiley.

Oken, D. 1960. Experimental study of suppressed anger and blood pressure. *Archives of General Psychiatry* 2:441–56.

Ortony, A., G. L. Clore, and A. Collins. 1988. *The cognitive structure of emotions*. Cambridge: Cambridge University Press.

Renson, G., J. Adams, and J. Tinklenberg. 1978. Buss-Durkee assessment and validation with violent versus nonviolent chronic alcohol abusers. *Journal of Consulting and Clinical Psychology* 46:360–61.

Ruben, I., G. Wolkon, and J. Yamamoto. 1980. Physical attacks on psychiatric residents by patients. *Journal of Nervous and Mental Disease* 168:243–45.

Ryan, J. A., and E. C. Poster. 1989. The assaulted nurse: Short-term and long-term responses. *Archives of Psychiatric Nursing* 3:323–31.

Saul, L. 1939. Hostility in cases of essential hypertension. *Psychosomatic Medicine* 1:153–61.

Schachter, J. 1957. Pain, fear, and anger in hypertensives and normotensives. *Psychosomatic Medicine* 19:17–29.

Segal, S. P., M. A. Watson, S. M. Goldfinger, and D. S. Averbuck. 1988. Civil commitment in the psychiatric emergency room. II: Mental disorder indicators and three dangerousness criteria. *Archives of General Psychiatry* 45:753–58.

Selby, M. J. 1984. Assessment of violence potential using measures of anger, hostility, and social desirability. *Journal of Personality Assessment* 48:531–44.

Seneca, L. [41] 1917. *Seneca's morals*. New York: Harper.

Siegel, J. M. 1986. The multidimensional anger inventory. *Journal of Personality and Social Psychology* 51:191–200.

Spielberger, C., G. Jacobs, S. Russell, and R. S. Crane. 1983. Assessment of anger: The State-Trait Anger Scale. In J. N. Butcher and C. D. Spielberger, eds., *Advances in personality assessment*. Vol. 2. Hillsdale, N.J.: Erlbaum.

Stauder, L. J., K. A. Holroyd, M. A. Appel, L. Gorkin, U. K. Upole, and P. G. Saab. 1983. Anger and essential hypertension: A factor analysis of measures used in recent research. Paper presented at the meeting of the Society of Behavioral Medicine, Baltimore.

Stokman, C., and P. Heiber. 1980. Incidents in hospitalized forensic patients. *Victimology* 5:175–92.

Stokols, D. 1987. Conceptual strategies of environmental psychology. In D. Stokols and I. Altman, eds., *Handbook of environmental psychology*. New York: John Wiley and Sons.

———. 1988. Transformational processes in people-environment relations. In J. E. McGrath, ed., *The social psychology of time*. Newbury Park, Calif.: Sage Publications.

Swanson, J. W., C. Z. Holzer, V. K. Ganju, and R. T. Jono. 1990. Violence and psychiatric disorder in the community: Evidence from the Epidemiologic Catchment Area surveys. *Hospital and Community Psychiatry* 41:761–70.

Tardiff, K. 1983. A survey of assault by chronic patients in a state hospital system. In J. R. Lion and W. H. Reid, eds., *Assaults within psychiatric facilities*, 3–19. New York: Grune and Stratton.

Tardiff, K., and K. Deane. 1980. The psychological and physical status of chronic psychiatric inpatients. *Comprehensive Psychiatry* 21:91–97.

Toch, H. 1969. *Violent men.* Chicago: Aldine.

Williams, R. B., J. C. Barefoot, and R. B. Shekelle. 1985. The health consequences of hostility. In M. Chesney and R. Rosenman, eds., *Anger and hostility in cardiovascular and behavioral disorders.* Washington: Hemisphere Publishing.

Williams, R. B., T. Haney, K. Lee, Y. Kong, J. Blumenthal, and R. Whalen. 1980. Type A behavior, hostility, and coronary atherosclerosis. *Psychosomatic Medicine* 42:539–49.

Wittgenstein, L. 1953. *Philosophical investigations.* New York: MacMillan.

Zelin, M., G. Adler, and P. Myerson. 1972. Anger self-report: An objective questionnaire for the measurement of aggression. *Journal of Consulting and Clinical Psychology* 39:340.

Zillmann, D. 1971. Excitation transfer in communication-mediated aggressive behavior. *Journal of Experimental Social Psychology* 7:419–34.

———. 1983. Arousal and aggression. In R. G. Geen and E. I. Donnerstein, eds., *Aggression: Theoretical and empirical reviews.* New York: Academic Press.

Zillmann, D., and J. Bryant. 1974. Effect of residual excitation on the emotional response to provocation and delayed aggressive behavior. *Journal of Personality and Social Psychology* 30:782–91.

3 Impulsiveness and Aggression

ERNEST S. BARRATT

Impulsiveness, however defined, is essentially related to the *control* of thoughts and behavior (Barratt 1972). Hence, the historical and philosophical underpinnings of the social sciences, theology, jurisprudence, and the mental and behavioral sciences are replete with relevant concepts—self-control, free will, volition, inhibition, executive functions in the brain, and social control to name but a few. These concepts usually emphasize internal control of behavioral acts, and they are not new concepts. Early psychologists, for example, discussed facets of internal control in ways that are still relevant to our understanding of impulsiveness. The work of William James is one example.

Within his overall discussion of *will,* James ([1890] 1950) discusses at length voluntary versus involuntary movements and the role of mental antecedents to movements. Is it necessary to have a "volitional mandate" before movements occur? He answers that there are voluntary acts that do not require a cognitive antecedent, noting that some voluntary actions can occur because "consciousness is in its very nature impulsive" (James [1890] 1950, 526). James explains what he means by consciousness being impulsive as follows:

> I abstract here from the fact that a certain *intensity* of the consciousness is required for its impulsiveness to be effective in a complete degree. There is an inertia in the motor processes as in all natural things. In certain individuals, and at certain times (disease, fatigue) the inertia is unusually great and we have ideas of action which produce no visible act, but discharge themselves into merely nascent predispositions to activity or into emotional expression. (James [1890] 1950, 526)

James draws a clear distinction between thought and action. He proposes a dimensional approach to impulsiveness by noting that the relationship of "impulses" to the "control of impulses" represents a balance which ranges from normal to abnormal states, especially with regard to biological drives (e.g.,

61

sex and hunger). James further proposes a concept of "effort" and a "concern about the future" as part of the impulsiveness of thought:

> Compared with these various objects, all far-off considerations, all highly abstract conceptions, unaccustomed reasons, and motives foreign to the instinctive history of the race, have little or no impulsive power. They prevail, when they ever do prevail, *with effort; and the normal,* as distinguished from the pathological, *sphere of effort is thus found wherever non-instinctive motives to behavior are to rule the day.* (James [1890] 1950, 536)

Again, James alludes to a dimensional approach to impulsiveness, as well as a subtrait of future considerations ("all far-off considerations"). A *control* system separate from an *impulse* system is suggested and is related to a concept of effort. The concept of separate control and impulse systems has more recently been endorsed by Gray (1987) who proposes a behavioral activating system and a behavioral inhibition system. The former relates to impulsiveness while the latter relates to emotions such as anxiety or anger.

James also alludes to possible genetic and social learning components in impulsiveness:

> There is a normal type of character, for example, in which impulses seem to discharge so promptly into movements that inhibitions get no time to rise. These are "dare-devil" and "mercurial" temperaments, overflowing with animation and sizzling talk which are so common in Latin and Celtic races, and with which the cold-blooded and long-headed English character forms so marked a contrast. (James [1890] 1950, 537)

In addition to suggesting a partially genetic basis for impulsiveness, James describes rather well the impulsive aspect of "losing one's temper" or the "hair trigger" ("inhibitions get no time to rise"). James concludes his discussion of will or volition in terms of the interplay between sensory-motor and neural correlates. He notes that there may be special properties of the nervous system (e.g., reflexes) that may be related to the impulsive nature of thought.

The control of actions and their voluntary versus involuntary nature have been the object of both extensive theoretical and experimental studies in recent years. For example, Logan and Cowan (1984) propose that there is a "stopping process" that is set in motion by external stimuli or performance errors. Specific areas of the brain have been proposed as bases for controlling these cognitive and behavioral processes (Gray 1987; Gorenstein and Newman 1980). And in social learning theory, as another example, independent variables consist of the relative values of reinforcers in terms of both size and delay measurements. Everything else being equal, one would predict that long delays for rewards would have less of an influence on behavior than more immediate rewards. Likewise a large reward would have more influence than a small one. Logue notes:

> A choice of a large, more delayed reinforcer over a smaller, less delayed reinforcer has frequently been termed self-control . . . while the choice of a smaller, less delayed reinforcer over a larger, more delayed reinforcer is impulsiveness. (Logue 1988, 655)

Barratt Impulsiveness Scale

Our attempts to develop a scale to measure impulsiveness date from the late 1950s. The Barratt Impulsiveness Scale (BIS) (Barratt 1959) contained original items plus items rewritten from impulsiveness subscales on other inventories (Cattell 1945). It was noted that the variously named impulsiveness and anxiety subscales of self-report inventories like the Thurstone Temperament Schedule (Thurstone 1953) and the Guilford-Zimmerman Temperament Survey (Guilford and Zimmerman 1949) had low (usually insignificant) correlations with each other. Since anxiety, as measured by the Taylor Manifest Anxiety Scale (Taylor 1953), was being used as a measurement of habit strength in the Hull-Spence learning theory tradition, I speculated that impulsiveness might relate to the concept of "oscillation" of behavior in the same theory (Spence 1956; Hull 1943). In order to develop a measure of impulsiveness that would have a low correlation with measures of anxiety, the BIS went through a number of unpublished revisions.

In 1965, a factor analysis of the BIS-5 produced four orthogonal factors: (1) speed of cognitive response—items included "I make up my mind quickly" and "I make up my mind easily"; (2) lack of impulse control—"I like work requiring patience and carefulness" and "I like detailed work"; (3) adventure-seeking or extroversion—"I like being where there is something going on all the time" and "I like work that has lots of excitement"; and (4) risk taking—"As a youngster I rarely took part in risky stunts" and "I like to take a chance just for the excitement."

As data accumulated from the overall research program on impulsiveness, different views of the concept of impulsiveness as a personality trait evolved. The general goal of our research became three-fold: (1) to describe impulsiveness in "normal" persons, (2) to arrive at the role of impulsiveness in psychopathology, and (3) to develop a personality framework within which impulsiveness as a personality trait could be related to other traits. In pursuing these goals we realized the shortcomings of relying solely upon self-report personality inventories to measure impulsiveness (Barratt 1972; Barratt and Patton 1983), a caution that was shared by others (Nicholls, Licht, and Pearl 1982). Parenthetically, Shooster (1974) discusses the use of tests as predictors using a systems analysis approach with many of the characteristics of our model (Barratt 1985a). Within the above contexts, the BIS was continually being revised. Only the more recent revisions will be discussed here.

Our research (Barratt 1965a) and that of others (Twain 1957; Eysenck and Eysenck 1977; Schalling, Edmon, and Asberg 1983; Gerbing, Ahdi, and Patton 1987) indicate that impulsiveness is not a unitary dimension. In 1983, after reviewing many studies and relying on our clinical experience, I concluded on an a priori basis that there were three subfactors of impulsiveness: (1) *motor* impulsiveness, which involved acting without thinking; (2) *cognitive* impulsiveness, which involved making quick cognitive decisions; and (3) *nonplanning* impulsiveness, which involved a lack of concern for the future. On the basis of both psychometric and clinical studies, we revised the BIS (now BIS-10) to include these three factors. The original analyses (Barratt 1985b) of the BIS-10 substantiated these three factors empirically. Later, Gerbing, Ahdi, and Patton (1987) identified fifteen impulsiveness subtraits; each of the three BIS-10 factors were evident in their analyses.

Some typical scores of the BIS-10 for selected populations are presented in table 1. Several observations are important. First, population sampling is a critical issue. For example, the college students score almost a standard deviation higher on motor impulsiveness than do the general adult sample. On

Table 1. Barratt Impulsiveness Scale (BIS-10) scores for selected populations

	Motor impulsiveness (Im)		Cognitive impulsiveness (Ic)		Nonplanning impulsiveness (Inp)		
	Score	SD	Score	SD	Score	SD	N
Mixed adult population ("normal")	15.0	4.2	16.3	5.3	17.8	4.9	300
College students (freshmen)	19.6	5.1	10.3	6.1	16.8	5.1	379
Felons (halfway house)	16.5	6.7	20.6	6.7	23.2	7.4	40
Unwed mothers	20.4	6.7	20.4	8.2	19.9	8.4	40
Cocaine abusers	21.0	8.0	20.0	7.0	24.0	7.0	81
Psychiatric inpatients	18.0	7.0	19.0	7.0	22.0	9.0	135
Substance abusers (other than cocaine)	19.0	6.0	20.0	6.0	22.0	7.0	239
College students (Spanish university)	18.0	6.8	18.6	5.4	20.8	7.2	303
Medical students	14.0	4.6	14.7	4.7	14.7	5.5	20
Adult matched controls for prisoner study	17.8	6.0	18.8	4.1	17.4	5.3	20
Prisoners (impulsive aggressive)	22.9	6.9	21.9	6.2	25.0	7.7	74

cognitive impulsiveness, they score about a standard deviation lower. One could offer many conjectures about these differences. The important point is the need for caution in using self-report questionnaires to define impulsiveness. What is a relevant sample to develop "norms"? It is also important in relating impulsiveness to aggression to note that "impulsive aggressive" prisoners in our current research score consistently higher than the other groups on all subtests and significantly higher than the mixed adult sample. These prisoners were selected for the study because they have high levels of overt aggression, not on the basis of personality traits. It was predicted that they would score high on impulsiveness and, in general, they did. The mixed psychiatric patients appear to score highest on nonplanning impulsiveness compared to the other groups.

As we continued to use the BIS-10, the results of the original analyses did not hold up, especially the alpha coefficients for the cognitive subfactor. Cognitive functions are difficult to measure with self-report questionnaires because cognition is always inferential. We proceeded then to revise the BIS-10 and to develop the BIS-11 with an emphasis on the "cognitive" items.

Analyses to date of the BIS-11 indicate that there are three well-defined factors in analyses using college students (table 2). The alpha coefficients for these three factors are: factor 1, .72; factor 2, .73; and factor 3, .50. Factor 1 combines items from the BIS-10 cognitive and motor factors. In line with William James's writings about motor impulsivity, this appears to be an "ideo-motor" factor. The items include both motor (e.g., "I do things without thinking") and cognitive items (e.g., "I am a careful thinker"). Factor 2 is a "careful planning" factor. Factor 3 combines future orientation with stability of everyday life coping; we tentatively labeled this "coping stability."

The BIS-11 factors for psychiatric inpatients (table 2) appear to separate the motor and cognitive items more clearly. Factor 1, for example, has primarily cognitive items combined with "planning ahead" and "stability" of life items. Factor 2, again, appears to be an ideo-motor factor. Factor 3 is probably a doublet that factors out because of some peculiarity of the patient population; this is interesting but its interpretation is not clear at this time.

Comparing the factor analyses for college students and patients, it is clear that there are differences in personality structure between "normals" and persons with psychopathology. It is this difference in overall structure that relates to the patient's "personality system" and inability to maintain stability in coping with everyday life events.

In summary, our current data suggest that there are three subtraits in the BIS-11 item pool: an "ideo-motor" impulsiveness subtrait, a "careful planning" (attention to details) subtrait, and a future-oriented "coping stability" subtrait. The cognitive and motor distinction that has been made in the development of the BIS-10 appears to be combined empirically in the BIS-11 into

Table 2. Factor analyses of BIS-11 items for college student and psychiatric inpatient populations

Item	College students (N = 151)			Psychiatric inpatients (N = 92)		
	Factor 1	Factor 2	Factor 3	Factor 1	Factor 2	Factor 3
9. I find it hard to sit still for long periods of time.	.58				.40	
2. I do things without thinking.	.56			.44		
29. I am restless at lectures or talks.	.53				.44	
27. I have outside thoughts when thinking.	.49				.55	
10. I am a careful thinker.	−.47			.79		
7. I concentrate easily.	−.45			.58		
4. I have racing thoughts.	.44				.51	
12. I say things without thinking.	.44				.58	
23. I walk and move fast.	.40					.68
19. I am a steady thinker.	−.37			.63		
26. I talk fast.	.36					
21. I buy things on impulse.	.35				.49	
5. I plan trips well ahead of time.		.75		.39		.76

Item				
1. I plan tasks carefully.	.72		.72	
18. I act on the spur of the moment.	−.64		.40	.57
8. I save regularly.	.58			
15. I act "on impulse."	−.53			.70
11. I plan for job security.		.59	.64	
30. I plan for the future.		.53	.51	
17. I have regular medical/dental check ups.		.52	.43	
20. I change where I live.		.46		
13. I like to think about complex problems.		.46		
16. I get easily bored when solving thought problems.		.44		.51
22. I finish what I start.		.43	.50	
25. I spend or charge more than I earn.		.37		.38
24. I solve problems by trial-and-error.				.42
6. I am self-controlled.			.59	
28. I am more interested in the present than the future.				−.37
3. I am happy-go-lucky.				
14. I change jobs.			.35	

Note: This research is being coordinated by Dr. Jim Patton, Baylor University, Waco, Texas.

a cognitive-motor trait and an attention-to-detail trait—the latter probably being related to "cognitive style." The BIS-11 is still being developed and these results may change as standardization progresses.

Is impulsiveness a well-defined personality factor from a psychometric viewpoint? Malle and Neubauer (1991) conclude that it is not, but they appear to miss the point in their assessment of our research. We reported that "scales that are labeled 'impulsiveness' do not always significantly correlate with each other." For example, in our current aggression research, the NEO personality inventory facet score of impulsiveness (Costa and McCrae 1985) does not correlate significantly with our impulsiveness measures. Further, we do not think that the Matching Familiar Figures Test (Kagan 1966) measures impulsivity among adults (Barratt and Patton 1983). We propose that impulsiveness is part of an action-oriented second-order trait similar to extroversion (Barratt and Patton 1983).

Luengo, Carrillo-de-la-Pena, and Otero (1991) recently found a high correlation between the BIS-10 and the 1.7 impulsiveness scale developed by Eysenck and Eysenck (1977). They have found that the BIS-10 cognitive subscale did not emerge as a separate factor and suggested that it be redefined. Their suggestion is consistent with our current research results with the BIS-11 as previously discussed. However, from a clinical viewpoint, we still think that there is a cognitive impulsiveness factor. The reason that it is difficult to measure relates to the inferential nature of cognition. A basic question involves the extent to which persons can assess *their own* cognitive functions, especially if they are impulsive.

Behavioral Description: Laboratory Studies

The overt behavioral characteristics of impulsiveness among persons selected using self-report personality questionnaires have been previously reviewed (Barratt 1972, 1985a; Barratt and Patton 1983) and will be briefly summarized here. In laboratory studies, high-impulsiveness subjects, when compared with low-impulsiveness subjects, perform less efficiently on a wide range of perceptual motor tasks (pursuit rotor, selected reaction time tasks, mazes, visual tracking, paced tapping). They are also more variable in their performance (Barratt 1983). In general, the relationship between impulsiveness and perceptual-motor or psychomotor performance is complex in itself. This can be demonstrated by considering the relationship of impulsiveness to reaction time (Barratt 1985a). In reaction time tasks with the time between the warning signal and the signal to respond (imperative signal) varying from 3 to 9 seconds, high-impulsive subjects have slower "release" reaction times than do low-impulsive subjects. Further, the higher the amount of information to be processed (imperative signal), the greater the discrepancy between the two groups. If there is no warning signal, the high-impulsive subjects in general respond faster.

Why do high-impulsive subjects tend to respond less efficiently and with greater variability than low-impulsive subjects? The current cognitive psychophysiological studies (as discussed below) suggest that impulsiveness is related to frontal lobe executive functions along with parietal lobe sensory integration functions during perceptual motor performance. Impulsiveness may also relate to the efficiency of functioning of the motor system.

It should be noted that our past research has found an interaction effect between impulsiveness and anxiety in perceptual motor performance (Barratt 1959, 1967). It is logical to assume that within a systems model, impulsiveness interacts with other personality traits.

Behavioral Descriptors: Clinical and Social

We have studied impulsiveness, especially in relationship to anxiety, in a wide variety of everyday life situations (Barratt 1965b, 1966). In general, high-impulsive subjects are more unreliable in keeping appointments, make good first impressions but do not develop stable long-lasting interpersonal relationships, and tend to develop more psychiatric problems, especially when anxiety is also high. Among clinical populations, patients with substance abuse problems, antisocial personality disorders, and impulsive aggressive tendencies tend to score high on impulsiveness in general, although the subtrait relationships with clinically related problems are less clear. In our current research, impulsive aggressive prisoners score significantly higher than matched controls on all three BIS-10 subtraits (table 1).

To determine the role of impulsiveness in psychopathology is not easy because of the wide range of interactions that are possible with other personality traits. From a systems viewpoint, that is why it is so important to determine the least number of traits that are necessary to define personality. One would not expect impulsiveness to be related to all psychopathological disorders.

Biological Descriptors

Psychometric impulsiveness measures have been related to a wide range of biological measures (Barratt 1987, 1972, 1985b, 1963; Barratt et al. 1987). The general findings suggest: (1) frontal lobe functions are related to impulsivity, (2) high-impulsive subjects tend to be augmenters in visual tasks (Barratt et al. 1987), and (3) serotonin levels are inversely related to impulsiveness scores (Brown et al. 1989; Kent et al. 1988). There is also evidence that impulsiveness is partially genetically determined (Pedersen et al. 1988; Martin, Eaves, and Fulker 1979). Serotonin levels have been shown to be partially genetically controlled (Meltzer and Arora 1988), which may partially account for the genetic predisposition toward impulsiveness.

Autonomic measures have been related to motor impulsivity (Barratt 1963; Boyle, Dykman, and Ackerman 1965), with more labile subjects generally being more impulsive. High levels of impulsivity have been negatively correlated with low plasma cortisol levels (King et al. 1990) and low MAO levels (Von Knorring, Oreland, and Winblad 1984; Schalling et al. 1988) but these relationships have not been consistent in all studies.

One of the main problems in relating biological correlates to impulsiveness is the lack of research relating profiles of the biological measures to profiles of personality measures (Barratt and Pritchard 1986). There are complex interrelationships among both sets of measurements, which indicate further the need for a general personality model in explicating these interrelationships.

Cognition

Our research (Barratt and Patton 1983) has documented several cognitive characteristics of high-impulsive subjects. First, they are present-oriented in terms of "time-zone" thinking. Past and future commitments are not as important as satisfying immediate needs. Second, they report rapid subjective experiences of thought processing. This is confirmed in experiments involving estimating the passage of time. High-impulsive subjects judge time to pass quickly. When asked to indicate when one minute has passed, they will indicate, on the average, that a minute passes in thirty-five seconds. These cognitive attributes are important in coping with everyday life problems. Clinically, they often describe themselves as being "cognitively driven."

Environmental Descriptors

Within our general systems model, environment is a separate category. The importance of this category can be appreciated if one considers that all personality variance beyond that which is genetically determined is environmentally determined. In our aggression research, we compare the expression of impulsive aggression with the stimuli which provoke it to determine the appropriateness of the behavior. In both laboratory studies of impulsiveness and in everyday life, we look at impulsiveness across a wide range of environments. As noted earlier in discussing the relationship between reaction time and impulsiveness, the properties of the stimuli determine in part the response pattern. In a three-year study of medical students, we found that their expression of impulsive behaviors varied with different social situations (Barratt and White 1969).

Aggression: Definitions and Measurements

The problems inherent in measuring and defining impulsiveness are also present in aggression research. Early in our research, a need for a nosology of aggression to provide a basis for criterion measurement became obvious. Where does aggression "fit" in our general systems model (Barratt 1991) and how do we distinguish among different types of aggression?

There have been many techniques developed to measure and classify human aggression. Some of these techniques are aimed primarily at describing aggressive acts and emphasize different facets of overt aggression. Within our model, we consider aggression to be overt *behavior*. This behavior may be influenced by personality traits, but aggression is not itself a personality trait. Most personality theorists propose that aggression is related to a particular profile of personality traits. Buss and Plomin (1975), for example, noted that "a person high in activity, emotionality, and impulsivity is likely to be aggressive." Some scales are aimed at describing overt violent or aggressive acts (Yudofsky et al. 1986) while others measure a wider range of aggression, including mild or moderate aggression (Wistedt et al. 1990). Eichelman and Hartwig (1990) have developed an in-depth multiaxial approach to classifying destructive behavior; it includes a medical diagnosis axis, psychological correlates, biological correlates, and moral-cultural correlates. We will not review the many nosologies of aggression and related measurement techniques that have been developed but will discuss briefly our own approach.

We classify aggression broadly into three categories: (1) premeditated or learned aggression, (2) medically related aggression, and (3) impulsive aggression (Barratt 1991). Premeditated aggression is learned within a social context over time. It varies with social groups and cultures. Some examples are war, some sports (e.g., football or boxing), and planned homicides. In some instances, persons are encouraged to become more aggressive and will take assertiveness training.

Medically related aggression covers a wide range of aggression which may be secondary to illness, including psychopathology. Closed head injuries, panic attacks, thought disorders, and certain neurological disorders are often accompanied by aggression. Lion (1981) discusses the medical treatment of violent individuals and lists the wide range of disorders that can have aggression as a symptom. One of the major problems in aggression research has been failure to distinguish between aggression as a symptom and aggression that is not related to a medical disorder.

Impulsive aggression is characterized by a "hair-trigger" temper. That is, the impulsive aggressive person usually "responds" aggressively without thinking and, following the aggressive act, often expresses guilt and remorse, vows not to commit the act again, but lacks the self-control to refrain from doing it again. During the act of aggression, incoming stimuli are not processed logically. A person who is the target of the aggression can apologize but usually to no avail. Incoming stimuli of any type appear to reinforce the aggressive behaviors, which build to a crescendo and then subside. We propose that the personality traits of impulsiveness and anger-hostility are related to most impulsive aggressive acts. The act itself has many of the properties of a subthreshold seizure (Barratt, in press b).

A person may be subject to all three types of aggression. It is probable that many aggressive persons exhibit at least two types, which we propose is why aggression research and clinical interventions are difficult. One might argue that impulsive aggression is really part of medically related aggression. We feel that it is distinct enough to be classified separately. From a therapeutic viewpoint, one would treat a person differently if they were diagnosed as having impulsive aggressive tendencies, per se, versus having a combination of impulsive aggressive tendencies and another medically related basis for aggression. Within DSM III-R (American Psychiatric Association 1987) there are no syndromes similar to "impulsive aggression." Within ICD-10 (World Health Organization 1992), the emotionally unstable personality disorder impulsive type (F60.3) is somewhat similar to impulsive aggression. Several recent theories also have described aggressive disorders similarly to impulsive aggression as we have defined it.

Lewis and Pincus (1989) have proposed a neuropsychotic-aggressive syndrome that includes a "constellation of certain kinds of neurological impairment, cognitive deficits, and psychotic symptoms (especially episodic paranoid misperceptions), and a history of an abusive and violent upbringing which was most strongly associated with ongoing repetitive violent criminality in adults." Elliot (1990) places an emphasis on the neurological subtraits of aggression in the episodic dyscontrol syndrome. This syndrome involves a "rage response to minimal provocation and is often completely out of character." In the course of developing their theories, both Lewis and Pincus and Elliot allude to "soft signs" of brain dysfunctioning which are often present in persons with aggression.

From a biological viewpoint, a number of studies have related low serotonin levels to aggression of various types and have suggested that it relates more specifically to impulsive aggression (Linnoila et al. 1983; Coccaro et al. 1989; Coccaro 1989, 1992). Roy and Linnoila (1988) have reviewed much of this research and suggest that there is a "need for further studies of possible peripheral markers for suicidal and impulsive behavior." The basic question in this research is whether the low serotonin levels relate to impulsiveness, per se, or to impulsive aggression.

In addition to serotonin, testosterone and cortisol have been related to aggression (Salvador et al. 1986; Christiansen and Knussman 1987). It is important to note, however, that socioeconomic status (SES) is a moderating variable in these relationships, with less of a relationship between testosterone and aggression being noted in the higher SES levels (Dabbs and Morris 1990). Overall, the relationship of hormones to aggression has been less consistent than the relationship of low serotonin levels to impulsive aggression. Part of the inconsistencies relate to the wide range of criterion measures used in aggression research, including confusion between measures of antisocial behaviors per se in general aggression. There is also evidence of a genetic component of aggression (Mattes and Fink 1987).

Impulsiveness and Aggression: A Hypothesized Relationship

We propose that the personality trait of impulsiveness is significantly related to one form of aggression which we have labeled "impulsive aggression," a term that has also been used by others (Coccaro 1989). This is based upon common descriptive characteristics of impulsiveness and selected forms of aggression. These common characteristics include a genetic predisposition, acting without thinking, low serotonin levels, and an inability to control certain behaviors even though one vows to do so. There is evidence that serotonin levels are partially genetically determined, which could account, in part, for the genetic predisposition noted for both.

In addition to the above bases for relating impulsiveness to aggression, there are other less direct reasons. Impulsive aggressive persons often have problems with learning and have conduct disorders in school. "Soft" neurological signs have been related to both learning disorders and conduct disorders, and the frontal lobes are usually implicated in both. We have proposed that the frontal lobes are involved in impulsiveness. In our current research on impulsive aggression among prisoners there is a positive significant relationship between attention deficit disorders and level of aggression.

As noted previously, we propose that the personality trait of anger-hostility is related to impulsive aggression. Anger has been related to a behavioral inhibition system, along with anxiety and other emotions. We propose that there is a learned underlying predisposition in many adults to respond to selected stimuli or classes of stimuli with "feelings of anger." When a person is confronted by these stimuli, especially as a surprise, they tend to respond aggressively. The higher the level of impulsivity, the less control they have over their aggressive response.

It is important to define aggression objectively in research and in clinical interventions. As noted previously, learned or premeditated aggression and aggression as a symptom in a medical disorder often occur independent of impulsive aggression. When impulsive aggression occurs along with another form, it is difficult to identify or differentiate.

Impulsiveness and Aggression: Research Evidence

We are studying the effects of phenytoin in impulsive aggression among prisoners in a maximum security prison. In a pilot study (Barratt et al. 1991), phenytoin significantly reduced the frequency of impulsive aggressive acts. In a more extensive study in progress, the results to date confirm the results of the exploratory study, with seven out of ten persons having fewer impulsive aggressive acts when taking phenytoin in comparison to the placebo condition. These studies involve a double-blind, placebo-controlled design. Criteria for entry require that subjects (1) have no psychiatric or neurological disorders, (2) have an IQ above 80, and (3) not be on any other medications. All acts of aggression are documented and the written reports can be appealed if the prisoner feels that they are not valid. These are objective measures of aggression in a "real life" situation.

In addition to the effects of phenytoin on aggression, there are other important findings relevant to the hypothesized relationships between impulsiveness and aggression. As noted in table 1, the impulsive aggressive prisoners scored significantly higher than all others on the BIS-10. They also scored significantly higher as a class on self-report measures of anger, although not all subjects had high impulsiveness or anger scores. However, the higher the level of impulsiveness, the wider was the *range* of criminal acts performed by the prisoners (Stanford and Barratt 1992).

Our subjects in this research performed poorly on a number of neuropsychology measures and were significantly poorer in reading skills than matched controls. They had difficulties with learning and dropped out of school early. Related to their learning problems, the cognitive psychophysiological results indicate that the prisoners process "surprise," or new, stimuli differently than do matched controls. There are several psychophysiological results that are significant. First, the prisoners had much slower event related potentials (ERP) in the parietal areas near the supramarginal angular gyrus bilaterally. This is a sensory integration area and has been related to learning disorders. Prisoners showed significantly less independent cortical functioning in the frontal-parietal relationships than did controls during cognitive processing of visual tests in the 250 ms to 600 ms time window during information processing in oddball tasks. The components of the late positive portion of the ERPs also developed sequentially in quantitatively different ways, with the initial source of positive electrophysiological activity being in the frontal lobes for prisoners but not for controls. The overall psychophysiological results suggest two brain-related problems, both affecting the frontal lobe but in different ways. One problem involves the relationship of the frontal lobes to central parietal lobe functions and is probably related to the learning disorders that the prisoners experienced early in life. The inefficient and more variable performance of high-impulsive subjects discussed here may be related to these brain functions. Another problem involves frontal lobe functioning, per se. Impulsiveness probably relates primarily to the frontal lobe functioning, and is common to both the learning problems and the impulse control problems.

The above discussion is not meant to suggest that psychosocial factors are not involved in impulsive aggression. In our current research, the prisoners score low on conscientiousness, a learned social trait (Costa, McCrae, and Dye 1991). Within our general personality model, we would not expect anger or impulsiveness to be completely biologically determined. Actually, many of our prisoners were from unstable families as children—environments that were less than supportive. A possible scenario for these prisoners could have been the presence of a learning disorder (attention deficit disorder), lack of support from the family in learning as a child, and the development of a conduct disorder. They did not want to go to school because they were not being rewarded, and the schools did not want them as students because they were disruptive. They learned a set of stimuli related to anger which were incorporated into their memory and which ultimately became triggers for impulsive aggression. But, there are also some impulsive aggressive prisoners who came from "stable" families. It is our hunch that the impulsive aggression in these latter instances has a more inclusive biological basis. This has been confirmed in our data to date.

References

American Psychiatric Association. 1987. *Diagnostic and statistical manual of mental disorders*. 3d ed., rev. (DSM III-R). Washington, D.C.: American Psychiatric Association.

Barratt, E. 1959. Anxiety and impulsiveness related to psychomotor efficiency. *Perceptual and Motor Skills* 9:191–98.

———. 1963. Intraindividual variability of performance: ANS and psychometric correlates. *Texas Reports on Biology and Medicine* 21:496–504.

———. 1965a. Factor analysis of some psychometric measures of impulsiveness and anxiety. *Psychological Reports* 16:547–54.

———. 1965b. Psychophysiological correlates of impulsiveness and risk taking: Cross sectional and longitudinal correlates. Annual report submitted to the Office of Naval Research, Washington, D.C.

———. 1966. Psychophysiological correlates of impulsiveness and risk taking: Cross sectional and longitudinal correlates. Annual report submitted to the Office of Naval Research, Washington, D.C.

———. 1967. Perceptual-motor performance related to impulsiveness and anxiety. *Perceptual and Motor Skills* 25:485–92.

———. 1972. Anxiety and impulsiveness: Toward a neuropsychological model. In C. Spielberger, ed., *Anxiety: Current trends in theory and research*. New York: Academic Press.

———. 1983. The biological basis of impulsiveness: The significance of timing and rhythm disorders. *Personality and Individual Differences* 4:387–91.

————. 1985a. Impulsiveness defined within a systems model of personality. In C. Spielberger and J. Butcher, eds., *Advances in personality assessment.* Vol. 5. Hillsdale, N.J.: Earlbaum.

————. 1985b. Impulsiveness subtraits: Arousal and information processing. In J. Spence and C. Izard, eds., *Motivation, emotion, and personality.* Amsterdam: Elsevier.

————. 1987. Impulsiveness and anxiety: Information processing and electroencephalograph topography. *Journal of Research in Personality* 21:453–63.

————. 1991. Measuring and predicting aggression within the context of a personality theory. *Journal of Neuropsychiatry* 3:535–39.

————. In press a. Aggression/impulsivity: Neurobiological correlates. In B. Smith and G. Adelman, eds., *Neuroscience year:* supplement 3 to the *Encyclopedia of neural science.* New York: Spectrum.

————. In press b. The use of anticonvulsants in aggression and violence. *Psychopharmacology Bulletin.*

Barratt, E., T. Kent, S. Bryant, and A. Felthous. 1991. A controlled study of phenytoin in impulsive aggression. *Journal of Clinical Psychopharmacology* 11:388–89.

Barratt, E., and J. Patton. 1983. Impulsivity: Cognitive, behavioral, and psychophysiological correlates. In M. Zukerman, ed., *Biological bases of sensation seeking, impulsivity, and anxiety.* Hillsdale, N.J.: Earlbaum.

Barratt, E., and W. Pritchard. 1986. Personality traits and neurotransmitters: complexity vis-a-vis complexity. *Behavioral and Brain Sciences* 9:336.

Barratt, E., W. Pritchard, D. Faulk, and M. Brandt. 1987. The relationship between impulsiveness subtraits, trait anxiety, and visual N100 augmenting/reducing: A biographic analysis. *Personality and Individual Differences* 8:43–51.

Barratt, E., and R. White. 1969. Impulsiveness and anxiety related to medical student's performance and attitudes. *Journal of Medical Education* 44:604–7.

Boyle, R., R. Dykman, and P. Ackerman. 1965. Relationships of resting autonomic activity, motor impulsivity, and EEG tracings in children. *Archives of General Psychiatry* 12:314–23.

Brown, C., T. Kent, S. Bryant, R. Gevedon, J. Campbell, A. Felthous, E. Barratt, and R. Rose. 1989. Blood platelet uptake of serotonin in episodic aggression. *Psychiatry Research* 27:5–12.

Buss, A., and R. Plomin. 1975. *A temperament theory of personality development.* London: Wiley-Interscience.

Cattell, R. 1945. The description of personality: Principles and findings in factor analysis. *American Journal of Psychology* 58:69–70.

Christiansen, K., and R. Knussman. 1987. Androgen levels and components of aggressive behavior in men. *Hormones and Behavior* 21:170–80.

Coccaro, E. 1989. Central serotonin and impulsive aggression. *British Journal of Psychiatry* 155:52–62.

————. 1992. Impulsive aggression and central serotonergic system function in humans: An example of dimensional brain-behavior relationship. *International Clinical Psychopharmacology* 7:3–12.

Coccaro, E., L. Seiver, H. Klar, G. Maurer, K. Cochrane, T. Cooper, R. Mohs, and

K. Davis. 1989. Serotonergic studies in patients with affective and personality disorders. *Archives General Psychiatry* 46:587–99.

Costa, P., and McCrae, R. 1985. *The NEO personality inventory manual.* Odessa, Fla.: Psychological Assessment Resources.

Costa, P., R. McCrae and D. Dye. 1991. Facete scales for aggreeableness and conscientiousness: A revision of the NEO personality inventory. *Personality and Individual Differences* 12:887–98.

Dabbs, J., and R. Morris. 1990. Testosterone, social class, and antisocial behavior in a sample of 4,462 men. *Psychological Science* 1:209–11.

Eichelman, B., and A. Hartwig. 1990. The Caroline nosology of destructive behavior. *Journal of Neuropsychiatry* 2:288–96.

Elliot, F. 1990. Neurology of aggression and episodic dyscontrol. *Seminars in Neurology* 10:303–12.

Eysenck, S., and H. Eysenck. 1977. The place of impulsiveness in a dimensional system of personality description. *British Journal of Social Clinical Psychology* 16:57–68.

Gerbing, D., S. Ahdi, and J. Patton. 1987. Toward a conception of impulsivity: Components across the behavioral and self report domains. *Multivariate Behavioral Research* 22:357–80.

Gorenstein, E., and J. Newman. 1980. Disinhibitory psychopathology: A new perspective and a model for research. *Psychological Review* 87:301–15.

Gray, J. 1987. *The psychology of fear and stress.* New York: Cambridge.

Guilford, J., and W. Zimmerman. 1949. *The Guilford-Zimmerman Temperament Survey: Manual of instructions and interpretations.* Beverly Hills, Calif.: Sheridan.

Hull, C. 1943. *Principles of behavior.* New York: Appleton-Century.

James, W. [1890] 1950. *The principles of psychology.* New York: Dover.

Kagan, J. 1966. Reflection-impulsivity: The generality and dynamics of conceptual tempo. *Journal of Abnormal Psychology* 1:17–24.

Kent, T., C. Brown, S. Bryant, E. Barratt, A. Felthous, and R. Rose. 1988. Blood platelet uptake of serotonin in episodic aggression: Correlation with red blood cell proton T1 and impulsivity. *Psychopharmacology Bulletin* 24:454–57.

King, R., J. Jones, J. Scheuer, D. Curtis, and V. Zargone. 1990. Plasma cortisol correlates of impulsivity and substance abuse. *Personality and Individual Differences* 11:287–91.

Lewis, D., and J. Pincus. 1989. Epilepsy and violence: Evidence for a neuropsychotic-aggressive syndrome. *Journal of Neuropsychiatry* 1:413–18.

Linnoila, M., M. Virkkunen, M. Scheinin, A. Nuutile, R. Rimon, and F. Goodwin. 1983. Low cerebrospinal fluid 5-hydroxyindoleacetic acid concentration differentiates impulsive from nonimpulsive violent behavior. *Life Sciences* 33:2609–14.

Lion, J. 1981. Medical treatment of violent individuals. In J. Hays and K. Solway, eds., *Violence and the violent individual.* New York: SP Medical and Scientific.

Logan, G., and W. Cowan. 1984. On the ability to inhibit thought and action: A theory of an act of control. *Psychological Review.* 91:295–327.

Logue, A. 1988. Research on self-control: An integrating framework. *Behavioral and Brain Sciences* 11:665–709.

Luengo, M., M. Carrillo-de-la-Pena, and J. Otero. 1991. The components of impulsiveness: A comparison of the 1.7 Impulsiveness Questionnaire and the Barratt Impulsiveness Scale. *Personality and Individual Differences* 12:656–67.

Malle, B., and A. Neubauer. 1991. Impulsivity, reflection, and questionnaire response latencies: No evidence for a broad impulsivity trait. *Personality and Individual Differences* 12:865–67.

Martin, N., L. Eaves, and D. Fulker. 1979. The genetical relationship of impulsiveness and sensation seeking to Eyesenck's personality dimensions. *Acta Geneticae Medicae et Gemellologiae* 28:197–210.

Mattes, J., and M. Fink. 1987. A family study of patients with outbursts. *Journal of Psychiatric Research* 21:249–55.

Meltzer, H., and R. Arora. 1988. Genetic control of serotonin uptake in blood platelets: a twin study. *Psychiatry Research* 24:263–69.

Nicholls, J., B. Licht, and R. Pearl. 1982. Some dangers of using personality questionnaires to study personality. *Psychological Bulletin* 92:572–80.

Pedersen, N., R. Plomin, G. McLearn, and L. Friberg. 1988. Neuroticism, extroversion, and related traits in adult twins reared apart and reared together. *Journal of Personality and Social Psychology* 55:950–57.

Roy, A., and M. Linnoila. 1988. Suicidal behavior, impulsiveness and serotonin. *Acta Psychiatrica Scandinavica* 78:529–35.

Salvador, A., V. Simon, F. Suay, and L. Llorens. 1986. Testosterone and cortisol responses to competitive fighting in human males: A pilot study. *Aggressive Behavior* 13:943.

Schalling, D., G. Edmon, and M. Asberg. 1983. Impulsive cognitive style and inability to tolerate boredom: Psychobiological studies of temperamental vulnerability. In M. Zuckerman, ed., *Biological bases of sensation seeking, impulsivity, and anxiety.* Hillsdale, N.J.: Earlbaum.

Schalling, D., G. Edmon, J. Asbert, and L. Oreland. 1988. Platelet MAO activity associated with impulsivity and aggressivity. *Personality and Individual Differences* 9:597–605.

Shooster, C. 1974. Tests and prediction: A systems analysis approach. *Behavioral Sciences* 19:111–18.

Spence, K. 1956. *Behavioral theory and conditioning.* New Haven: Yale University Press.

Stanford, M. S., and E. S. Barratt. 1992. Impulsivity and the multiimpulsive personality disorder. *Personality and Individual Differences* 13:831–34.

Taylor, J. 1953. A personality scale of manifest anxiety. *Journal of Abnormal and Social Psychology* 48:285–90.

Thurstone, L. 1953. *Examiner manual for the Thurstone Temperament Schedule.* Chicago: Science Research Associates.

Twain, D. 1957. Factor analysis for particular aspects of behavioral control: Impulsivity. *Journal of Clinical Psychology* 13:133–36.

Von Knorring, L., L. Oreland, and B. Winblad. 1984. Personality traits related to monoamine oxidase activity in platelets. *Psychiatry Research* 12:11–76.

Wistedt, B., A. Rasmussen, L. Pedersen, U. Malm, L. Traskman-Bendz, J. Wakelin, and P. Bech. 1990. The development of an observer-scale for measuring social dysfunction and aggression. *Pharmacopsychiatry* 23:249–52.

World Health Organization (WHO). 1992. *The ICD-10 classification of mental and behavioral disorders*. Geneva: World Health Organization.

Yudofsky, S., J. Silver, W. Jackson, J. Endicott, and D. Williams. 1986. The overt aggression scale for the objective rating of verbal and physical aggression. *American Journal of Psychiatry* 143:35–39.

4 Psychopathy as a Risk Marker for Violence: Development and Validation of a Screening Version of the Revised Psychopathy Checklist

STEPHEN D. HART, ROBERT D. HARE, AND ADELLE E. FORTH

Observers of human behavior have long argued that people can be classified into "types" on the basis of their personality and, furthermore, that certain personality types are more likely than others to engage in antisocial and aggressive behavior (see Pichot 1978; Tyrer and Ferguson 1988). In modern clinical psychology and psychiatry, we refer to these personality types as *personality disorders:* characteristic ways of perceiving and relating to the world, first evident at an early age and persisting across the lifespan, that result in social dysfunction or disability (e.g., American Psychiatric Association 1987; Millon 1981).

Psychopathy can be differentiated from other personality disorders on the basis of its characteristic pattern of interpersonal, affective, and behavioral symptoms (e.g., Cleckley 1976; Hare 1991; McCord and McCord 1964). Interpersonally, psychopaths are grandiose, egocentric, manipulative, dominant, forceful, and coldhearted. Affectively, they display shallow and labile emotions, are unable to form long-lasting bonds to people, principles, or goals, and are lacking in empathy, anxiety, and genuine guilt or remorse. Behaviorally, psychopaths are impulsive and sensation-seeking, and tend to violate social norms; the most obvious expressions of these predispositions involve criminality, substance abuse, and a failure to fulfill social obligations and responsibilities.

Despite the link between psychopathy and crime apparent in clinical descriptions, researchers generally have been rather pessimistic about the value of diagnoses of psychopathy in the *prediction* of criminal or violent behavior. However, it is important to note that this pessimism stems from a literature that historically was beset by methodological problems, not the least of which was the use of inadequate diagnostic procedures. We have spent the last decade developing improved methods to assess psychopathy, culminating in the publication of the Psychopathy Checklist and its revision (PCL and PCL-R; Hare 1991). Recent research conducted using the PCL and PCL-R, some of

81

which is discussed below, suggests that the construct of psychopathy may indeed have predictive validity.

The primary theme of this chapter is the development and validation of the Psychopathy Checklist: Screening Version (PCL:SV; Hare, Cox, and Hart, in press). The PCL:SV is a brief, easily-administered scale for the assessment of psychopathy in civil and forensic settings. It was designed as a screening tool for use by clinicians and researchers with limited time and case history information. We begin the chapter with an abbreviated history of the PCL-R, which was the basis for development of the PCL:SV. Next, we review key research on psychopathy and violence. Finally, we provide our analyses of the PCL:SV.

The PCL-R

Due to space limitations, it is not possible to review the substantial body of evidence attesting to the reliability and validity of the PCL-R. Detailed information is presented in the PCL-R manual (Hare 1991); for a brief overview, see Hart, Hare, and Harpur (1992). The PCL-R was based on traditional conceptions of psychopathy (Cleckley 1976). It consists of 20 items designed to assess a range of relevant personality traits and behaviors. Each item is scored on a three-point scale according to the degree to which it applies to the individual: 0 = does not apply; 1 = uncertain, applies to a certain extent; 2 = applies. The total score can range from 0 to 40, and represents the degree to which an individual resembles the prototypical psychopath. For diagnostic purposes, a score of 30 or above is considered to be indicative of psychopathy.

Over the last decade, the PCL-R has become a common metric for forensic researchers and clinicians interested in psychopathy. Now in wide use, it has substantially reduced method variance and, as a result, has brought a semblance of order—theoretically meaningful and replicable findings—to an area long plagued by a bewildering variety of diagnostic procedures, most with inadequate psychometric properties and little conceptual or empirical relation to one another. The PCL-R is the basis for one of the criterion sets for antisocial personality disorder (APD) currently being field-tested by the American Psychiatric Association for possible inclusion in the fourth edition of the association's *Diagnostic and Statistical Manual of Mental Disorders* (see Hare et al. 1991).

One important characteristic of the PCL-R is its factor structure. The PCL-R meets statistical criteria for a homogeneous measure of a unidimensional construct, yet research indicates that two stable factors underlie it (Hare et al. 1990; Harpur, Hakstian, and Hare 1988). Though correlated about .5 on average, the factors have different patterns of correlations with external variables (Harpur, Hare, and Hakstian 1989). Factor 1 reflects interpersonal and affective characteristics, such as egocentricity, manipulativeness, callousness, and lack of remorse. It is positively correlated with prototypical ratings for psychopathy, narcissistic personality disorder, and self-report measures of narcissism, and negatively correlated with self-report measures of empathy and anxiety. Factor 2 reflects those characteristics of psychopathy associated with an impulsive, antisocial, and unstable lifestyle, or social deviance. It is most strongly correlated with diagnoses of antisocial personality disorder, criminal behaviors, substance abuse, and various self-report measures of psychopathy.

The scoring procedures for the PCL-R require the administration of a lengthy, semistructured interview (90 to 120 minutes), as well as access to extensive and detailed case-history information. Not surprisingly, a full assessment usually takes two or three hours. This of course reduces the value of the PCL-R for assessors with limited time and resources. What was needed, we felt, was a screening instrument for psychopathy, an assessment procedure that required less time to administer and score and that could predict PCL-R diagnoses of psychopathy with a reasonable degree of accuracy. Our expectation was that the screening instrument could be used on its own, as a rough index of psychopathy, or in conjunction with the PCL-R, with diagnoses made using the screening version confirmed by subsequent administration of the PCL-R.

The PCL-R and Risk for Violence

A number of studies have looked at the association between psychopathy, assessed using the PCL or PCL-R, and violent behavior both inside and outside of prison (e.g., Hare and McPherson 1984; Kosson, Smith, and Newman 1990; Wong 1984). Only a few key studies are described here; for more complete reviews, see Hare (1991) or Hare and Hart (1993).

Hart, Kropp, and Hare (1988) administered the PCL to 231 male inmates prior to their conditional release from prison. Regression analysis demonstrated that the PCL made a significant contribution to the prediction of outcome over and beyond that made by relevant criminal-history and demographic variables. Following release, offenders in the top third of the PCL distribution were almost three times more likely to violate the conditions of release, and almost four times more likely to commit a violent crime, than were those in the bottom third. Similar results were obtained by Serin, Peters, and Barbaree (1990) and Serin (1991a) who found a strong association between the PCL-R and outcome following release from prison on unescorted temporary absence and parole. The PCL-R predicted both violent and nonviolent outcome better than did a combination of criminal-history and demographic variables, and several standard actuarial risk instruments, including the Base Expectancy Scale (Gottfredson and Bonds 1961), the Recidivism

Prediction Scale (Nuffield 1982), and the Salient Factor Score (Hoffman and Beck 1974).

Psychopathy also predicts violent recidivism in male young offenders. Forth, Hart, and Hare (1990) found that PCL-R scores in a sample of 75 young offenders were significantly correlated with the number of charges or convictions for violent offenses after release.

In a long-term (10 years on average) follow-up study of 169 male patients released from a maximum security psychiatric hospital, Harris, Rice, and Cormier (1991) found that PCL-R scores were strongly correlated ($r = .42$) with violent recidivism. The violent recidivism rate of the psychopaths (77%) was almost four times that of the other releasees (21%); 78% of the predictions were accurate, with a relative improvement over chance (RIOC) of 62%. The addition of the PCL-R to a combination of criminal-history variables raised the multiple correlation with violent outcome from .31 to .45.

Rice and Harris (1992) looked at recidivism rates in 96 male schizophrenics who had been found not guilty by reason of insanity and remanded to a forensic psychiatric facility. A control group consisted of 96 nonschizophrenic male forensic patients who had been remanded for brief pretrial psychiatric assessments, and who were matched on a number of variables that included age, index offense, and criminal history. Schizophrenics had lower rates of general and violent recidivism, although only the rate for general recidivism was significantly lower. Despite these differences, psychopathy predicted general recidivism equally well in both groups: the correlation between the PCL-R and general recidivism was $r = .33$ in schizophrenics and $r = .30$ in nonschizophrenics. PCL-R scores were also predictive of violent recidivism in schizophrenics ($r = .20$).

Heilbrun et al. (1993) looked at the association between psychopathy, schizophrenia, and violence in a sample of 218 men, consecutive admissions to a state forensic psychiatric hospital in Florida. Inpatient violence was indexed by verbal and physical assaults during the first three and last three months of hospitalization. For the 183 patients who were subsequently released from hospital, Heilbrun et al. (1992) also coded violent recidivism—that is, any arrest for a violent offense that appeared on the patients FBI criminal record during the follow-up period. All variables were coded dichotomously (0 = no, 1 = yes). The PCL-R was correlated $r = .30$ with assaults during the first three months of hospitalization, but only $r = .03$ with assaults in the last three months. The PCL-R was also correlated with violent recidivism ($r = .16$).

Rice, Harris, and Quinsey (1990) administered the PCL-R to 54 rapists before their release from a maximum security psychiatric hospital. The correlation between the PCL-R and violent recidivism during the follow-up period, which averaged 46 months, was $r = .35$. A combination of PCL-R scores and a phallometric measure of sexual arousal was as effective at predicting sexual offenses as was a large battery of demographic, psychological, and criminal-history variables. These two variables alone correctly predicted the postrelease outcome of 77% of the rapists, with a RIOC of 44%.

We should emphasize that it is not only the social deviance components of psychopathy (as measured by PCL-R factor 2) that are related to risk for violence. In most cases, the affective-interpersonal components (factor 1) are as predictive, in some cases more so, of violence as is social deviance.

The PCL:SV

Development

The PCL:SV was designed with several key requirements in mind. First, it must be conceptually and empirically related to the PCL-R, in order to tap into the latter's extensive research literature. Second, it must be psychometrically sound, with good reliability and validity. Third, it must be suitable for use with clinical populations, including the mentally disordered, in both forensic and civil settings. And finally, it should require minimal time, effort, and training to administer and score.

In order to meet the first two requirements, the new scale retained the format that had proven successful with the PCL-R—namely, a symptom-construct rating scale. This was consistent with our belief that behavioral checklists and self-report scales are poorly suited to assessing psychopathy because of their susceptibility to a variety of response biases and because they have difficulty measuring the interpersonal and affective symptoms of the disorder (e.g., Hare, Forth, and Hart 1989; Hart, Forth, and Hare 1991). Like the PCL-R, the new scale would yield both dimensional and categorical indexes of psychopathy.

Fulfilling the third requirement did not appear to be problematic, as previous research had indicated that psychopathy, as defined by the PCL-R, could be measured reliably in forensic psychiatric patients (e.g., Harris, Rice, and Cormier 1991; Hart and Hare 1989; Heilbrun et al. 1992). This research also suggested that psychopathy tends to have a low rate of comorbidity with acute mental disorders (excluding substance use disorders). One concern was that all our previous research on psychopathy had been conducted in forensic settings; we needed to revise the content of some items to make them appropriate for use with noncriminals.

Finally, we believed that it would be relatively easy to fulfill at least part of the fourth requirement—brevity—merely by decreasing the number of items in the new scale, as the high internal consistency of the PCL-R suggested that there was a degree of redundancy among the original items. Our main concern here was that decreasing the number of items would decrease interrater reliability. We did not perceive the issue of training to be a problem, as our experience suggested that even undergraduates could be taught to make reliable PCL-R assessments of psychopathy.

Our optimism about the new scale was not unreasonable, given that we had some previous experience with a similar scale, referred to here as the Clinical Version of the PCL (CV; Cox, Hart, and Hare 1989; Roesch 1992; Roy 1988). The CV contained only six items: Superficial, Grandiose, Manipulative, Lacks Remorse, Lacks Empathy, and Doesn't Accept Responsibility. The content of these items was derived directly from the PCL-R, but the item descriptions were short, presented in point form, and scored on the basis of a brief interview (about 20 minutes). Like the PCL-R, a three-point scale was used for each item; total scores ranged from 0 to 12. The CV was tested in a sample of 50 male federal inmates (Roy 1988) and in two samples of men awaiting trial, 100 in one sample and 700 in the other (Cox, Hart, and Hare 1989; Roesch 1992). The results were encouraging. Both the interrater reliability and internal consistency of the CV were high, averaging about .85. Two problems were apparent with the CV, however. First, its reliability and validity suffered significantly in the absence of at least minimal collateral information, such as a criminal record or an institutional progress log (Roy 1988). Second, subsequent factor analyses of the PCL and PCL-R (Harpur, Hakstian, and Hare 1988; Hare et al. 1990) revealed that all six CV items tapped only the interpersonal and affective symptoms of psychopathy (Factor 1).

Rather than develop a scale de novo, we decided to revise and expand the CV. First, the six CV items were labeled "part 1," analogous to factor 1 of the PCL-R. Second, we added six new items to tap factor 2 symptoms: Impulse, Poor Behavior Controls, Lacks Goals, Irresponsible, Adolescent Antisocial Behavior, and Adult Antisocial Behavior. These new items were labeled "part 2." In order to make them more suitable for nonforensic settings, the content of the last two items—adolescent and adult antisocial behavior—was altered from the original PCL-R descriptions to include actions that did not result in formal contact with the criminal justice system. Third, we decided to make access to some form of collateral information a requirement for CV ratings. Although it has been our experience that, in some cases, the availability of collateral information results in only minor increases in psychopathy ratings, there are occasional instances where the lack of this information results in a gross underestimate of psychopathy (i.e., a false negative diagnostic error). The result of these efforts was a 12-item screening scale, the PCL:SV, summarized in table 1.

Complete scoring details are available in the forthcoming PCL:SV manual (Hare et al., in press). Briefly, items are scored using the same three-point scale as the PCL-R. Raters have the option of omitting items if they feel there is insufficient information with which to score it; scores are prorated to adjust for the missing items. The PCL:SV yields three dimensional scores. *Total* scores (the sum of items 1 through 12) can range from 0 to 24, and

Table 1. Items in the PCL:SV

Part 1	Part 2
1. Superficial	7. Impsulsive
2. Grandiose	8. Poor behavior controls
3. Manipulative	9. Lacks goals
4. Lacks remorse	10. Irresponsible
5. Lacks empathy	11. Adolescent antisocial behavior
6. Doesn't accept responsibility	12. Adult antisocial behavior

reflect the degree of overall psychopathic symptomatology exhibited by the individual. *Part 1* scores (sum of items 1 through 6) can range from 0 to 12, and reflect the severity of the interpersonal and affective symptoms of psychopathy (i.e., PCL-R factor 1). *Part 2* scores (sum of items 7 through 12) can also range from 0 to 12, and reflect the severity of the social deviance symptoms of psychopathy (i.e., PCL-R factor 2). A total score of at least 18 (equivalent to a score of at least 30 on the PCL-R) is considered indicative of psychopathy.

With respect to ease of administration, scoring, and training, the 12-item PCL:SV is 40% shorter than the 20-item PCL-R and excludes a number of PCL-R items that are scored on the basis of detailed, highly specific, or difficult-to-confirm information (e.g., items tapping marital or sexual history). Pilot testing revealed that the PCL:SV interview could be completed in 30 to 60 minutes, with the collateral review and scoring requiring a further 30 minutes—a 50% reduction in administration time relative to the PCL-R. Finally, we were able to train raters with varied educational and professional backgrounds—from undergraduates to clinical psychologists—with a program consisting of a 3-hour lecture and ten practice ratings.

Overview of Validation Research on the PCL:SV

In validating the PCL:SV for research use, we focused on several specific issues, not all of which were investigated in each sample.

First, with respect to the psychometric properties of the PCL:SV, we determined its internal consistency and interrater reliability. (We chose not to examine test-retest directly, as previous research has indicated that the construct of psychopathy, as measured by the PCL-R, has high temporal stability; see Hare 1991). To determine interrater reliability, interviews with subjects were videotaped; an independent rater than completed the PCL:SV on the basis of the videotaped interview and collateral information. We calculated intraclass correlations (ICC; Bartko 1976) between the independent ratings (ICC_1), and also estimated the reliability of averaged ratings (ICC_2).

Second, we looked at the factor structure of the PCL:SV. Because it was derived from the PCL-R, which has two underlying factors correlated about $r = .5$, we expected that the PCL:SV would have a parallel structure. We also examined the internal consistency and interrater reliability of the PCL:SV subscales (parts 1 and 2).

Third, we examined the concurrent validity of the PCL:SV with respect to PCL-R total scores and the number of adult APD symptoms, as listed in the revised third edition of the *Diagnostic and Statistical Manual of Mental Disorders* (DSM III-R; American Psychiatric Association 1987). We expected the correlations among these measures to be high. In order to keep the PCL:SV ratings independent from the PCL-R and APD, different raters assessed them in different sessions, separated by a break of 2 to 7 days. In these analyses, only PCL-R data from forensic settings were used in order to avoid ambiguity in the interpretation of the results. (Because the PCL-R was not designed for use in civil settings, a low correlation with the PCL:SV might well reflect problems with the PCL-R rather than with the PCL:SV). We also examined concurrent validity with respect to self-report questionnaires related to psychopathy; however, based on past research (e.g., Hare 1985; Hart, Forth, and Hare 1991) we expected that self-reports would be only moderately correlated with the PCL:SV.

Finally, we examined the convergent and discriminant validity of the PCL:SV. In different samples, we calculated the correlation between the PCL:SV and scores on interview-based and self-report measures of DSM III-R Axis I and II disorders. Based on previous research (e.g., Hart and Hare 1989; Smith and Newman 1990), we expected moderate, positive correlations between the PCL:SV and measures of narcissistic, histrionic, and borderline personality disorder, as well as with measures of substance use. Correlations with measures of other disorders were predicted to be low, and possibly negative in direction. We also calculated correlations between the PCL:SV and state measures of psychological distress at the time of assessment; we expected these correlations to be near zero in magnitude.

Samples

At this time, we have data concerning the reliability and validity of the PCL:SV in ten samples from four different settings—forensic/nonpsychiatric, forensic/psychiatric, civil/psychiatric, and civil/nonpsychiatric—with a total N of 520. The samples were as follows: (1) inmates at Matsqui Institution, a federal prison in British Columbia; (2) inmates at the Burnaby Women's Correctional Centre (BWCC), a provincial prison in British Columbia; (3) inmates at various federal prisons in British Columbia who were part of a larger study looking at the correlates of family violence in offenders (Dutton and Hart 1992); (4) patients attending the Forensic Psychiatric Outpatient Clinic (FPOC), operated by the Forensic Psychiatric Services Commission in

Table 2. Demographic characteristics of subjects

Setting and sample	N^a			Age (yrs.)		Race
	M	F	Total	M	SD	(% White)
Forensic/nonpsychiatric						
1. Federal inmates	50	—	50	29.8	(7.7)	92.0
2. Provincial inmates	—	32	32	30.0	(9.1)	81.3
3. Federal inmates	67	—	67	33.7	(7.6)	90.9
Forensic/psychiatric						
4. Outpatients	67	4	71	37.4	(10.0)	90.1
5. Inpatients	49	—	49	33.9	(8.2)	16.3
Civil/psychiatric						
6. Vancouver, B.C.	15	17	32	30.7	(13.9)	90.6
7. Pittsburgh, Penn.	20	20	40	34.0	(9.9)	63.5
8. Kansas City, Mo.	54	26	80	31.2	(8.8)	66.3
9. Worcester, Mass.	26	23	49	32.6	(8.9)	91.8
Civil/nonpsychiatric						
10. University students	25	25	50	24.8	(6.7)	66.0

[a] M = male; F = female.

Vancouver; (5) inpatients at the Kirby Forensic Psychiatric Center in New York, New York (data collected under the supervision of Drs. R. Wack and D. Martel); (6) patients at the psychiatric unit of the University Hospital in Vancouver, British Columbia; (7) patients attending the Western Psychiatric Institute and Clinic, Pittsburgh, Pennsylvania (data collected under the supervision of Dr. E. Mulvey); (8) patients at the Greater Kansas City Mental Health Center, Kansas City, Missouri (data collected under the supervision of Dr. D. Klassen); (9) patients at the Worcester State Hospital in Worcester, Massachusetts (data collected under the supervision of Drs. P. Appelbaum and T. Grisso); and (10) undergraduate students attending the University of British Columbia. Table 2 presents the sex, age, and race of subjects in each sample.

Results

Table 3 presents the mean and standard deviation of PCL:SV total scores in the ten samples. Also shown is the base rate of psychopathy (i.e., percentage of subjects with total scores of 18 or higher).

There was considerable variability in mean PCL:SV scores, both within and among the four types of setting. As expected, total scores were higher in forensic than in civil settings. Also, in civil settings, scores were higher among psychiatric patients than among nonpatients. In forensic settings, the

Table 3. PCL:SV total scores and base rate of psychopathy

Setting and sample	Descriptive Statistics		Base rate[a] of psychopathy (%)
	M	SD	
Forensic/nonpsychiatric			
1. Federal inmates	15.77	4.34	34.0
2. Provincial inmates	16.41	3.49	37.5
3. Federal inmates	12.97	4.92	17.9
Forensic/psychiatric			
4. Outpatients	13.72	4.05	19.7
5. Inpatients	16.56	3.28	34.7
Civil/psychiatric			
6. Vancouver, B.C.	4.92	4.29	3.1
7. Pittsburgh, Penn.	8.68	5.92	10.0
8. Kansas City, Mo.	13.14	5.71	23.8
9. Worcester, Mass.	9.63	4.90	6.1
10. University students	3.09	3.43	0.0

[a]Base rate = percentage of subjects with PCL:SV scores ≥ 18.

base rate for psychopathy diagnoses was similar to, although slightly higher than, that obtained using the PCL-R. The base rate in civil settings was generally quite low, except for sample 8.

With respect to demographic characteristics, older subjects tended to receive slightly lower PCL:SV scores than younger subjects, but this association was only significant in sample 2; the average correlation with age was −.10. White subjects tended to get slightly higher scores than those of other racial backgrounds, although this association did not achieve significance in any of the samples; the average correlation between race and PCL:SV scores was .07. Women tended to receive lower ratings than men in those studies that included both sexes; this difference was statistically significant in samples 6 and 8. The average correlation between sex (dummy-coded; male = 0, female = 1) and PCL:SV scores was −.22.

Reliability

The internal consistency and interrater reliability of PCL:SV total scores are presented in table 4. The alpha and ICC values were generally adequate and consistent across samples, with the exception of ICC_1 in samples 2 and 5. The reasons for this are unclear, but may include the unusual demographic characteristics of subjects (see table 2) or inadequate training of some raters at these sites. Even in these samples, however, the interrater reliability of averaged PCL:SV ratings was adequate, as the ICC_2 results reveal.

Table 4. Internal consistency (IC) and interrater reliability (IR) of PCL:SV total scores

Setting and sample	IC	IR[b]	
	Alpha[a]	ICC$_1$	ICC$_2$
Forensic/nonpsychiatric			
1. Federal inmates	.88	.89	.94
2. Provincial inmates	.77	.70	.85
3. Federal inmates	.81	—	—
Forensic/psychiatric			
4. Outpatients	.83	.81	.91
5. Inpatients	.72	.67	.83
Civil/psychiatric			
6. Vancouver, B.C.	.90	.83	.92
7. Pittsburgh, Penn.	.87	—	—
8. Kansas City, Mo.	.88	—	—
9. Worcester, Mass.	.83	—	—
Civil/nonpsychiatric			
10. University students	.91	.92	.96

[a] Alpha = Cronbach's alpha.
[b] ICC = intraclass correlation; ICC$_1$ = ICC for single ratings; ICC$_2$ = ICC for averaged ratings; — = data not available. Ns for the calculation of ICCs were as follows: sample 1, 50; sample 2, 32; sample 4, 59; sample 5, 26; sample 6, 24; and sample 10, 50.

In sum, the PCL:SV appears to have acceptable reliability. Indeed, despite a 40% reduction in length, its internal consistency and interrater reliability are very similar to those of the PCL-R. Any problems with low interrater reliability may be overcome by averaging the results of two independent raters. The use of two raters is also recommended for the longer scale. Thus the relative saving in administration costs remains even when the PCL:SV is used with two raters.

Factor Structure

We performed factor analyses of the 12 PCL:SV items in each sample using a variety of extraction and rotation techniques. Detailed results of these analyses are presented in Hare et al. (in press); briefly, as expected, the single best solution consisted of two oblique factors.

Table 5 presents the internal consistency and interrater reliability of the two PCL:SV subscales, part 1 and part 2. For the sake of brevity, we have collapsed across samples within each of the four settings. The correlation between parts 1 and 2 in each setting is also presented in table 5.

**Table 5. PCL:SV subscales: Internal consistency,
interrater reliability, and intercorrelation**

Setting[a]	Part 1			Part 2			r^d
	Alpha[b]	ICC_1[c]	ICC_2	Alpha	ICC_1	ICC_2	
Forensic/nonpsychiatric (samples 1–3)	.84	.77	.89	.78	.79	.90	.45
Forensic/psychiatric (samples 4, 5)	.80	.77	.88	.67	.74	.87	.53
Civil/psychiatric (samples 6–9)	.84	.78	.89	.83	.87	.93	.68
Civil/nonpsychiatric	.84	.67	.83	.81	.82	.91	.73

[a] See text for full description of settings. Ns for the calculation of ICCs were as follows: sample 1, 50; sample 2, 32; sample 4, 59; sample 5, 26; sample 6, 24; and sample 10, 50.
[b] Alpha = Chronbach's alpha.
[c] ICC = intraclass correlation; ICC_1 = ICC for single ratings; ICC_2 = ICC for averaged ratings.
[d] r = correlation between parts 1 and 2.

The internal consistency of the subscales was reasonably high, despite their brevity and despite the homogeneity of the full scale. Interrater reliability of the subscales was lower than for the entire scale, although the ICC_2 values indicate that averaged ratings are sufficiently reliable for most purposes. The correlation between parts 1 and 2 averaged about .55 to .60 across samples. These results paralleled those obtained with the PCL-R.

Concurrent Validity

Table 6 presents the correlation of the PCL:SV with PCL-R total scores and the number of APD adult symptoms. The results have been collapsed across the four settings; more complete results are available in Hare, Cox, and Hart (in press).

On average, the PCL:SV correlated about .80 with the PCL-R. This is about the maximum r we would expect between the two scales, as it is disattenuated by variance due to raters, time, and the unreliability of the individual scales.

We also looked at another aspect of the PCL:SV's concurrent validity, namely, its predictive efficiency with respect to PCL-R diagnoses of psychopathy. We pooled all subjects who had been assessed using both scales and then calculated various indexes of predictive efficiency. Kappa was .48, indicating fair overall diagnostic agreement beyond chance levels. Sensitivity of the PCL:SV was .81, specificity was .85, positive predictive power was .44, and negative predictive power was .97. These results indicate that the PCL:SV overdiagnosed psychopathy relative to the PCL-R (i.e., made false

Table 6. Concurrent validity of the PCL:SV:
Correlation with PCL-R and APD

Setting[a]	r with PCL-R[b]	r with APD[c]
Forensic/nonpsychiatric (samples 1–3)	.79	.61
Forensic/psychiatric (samples 4, 5)	.78	.58
Civil/psychiatric (samples 6–9)	—[d]	.85
Civil/nonpsychiatric (sample 10)	.81	.67

[a]*N*s were as follows: sample 1, 50; sample 2, 32; sample 4, 71; sample 5, 49; sample 6, 27; and sample 10, 50.
[b]PCL-R = Revised Psychopathy Checklist (Hare 1991).
[c]APD = Subjects with adult antisocial personality disorder symptoms.
[d]— = data not available.

positive errors), but made virtually no false negative errors. (This assumes that the PCL-R is the "gold standard" of psychopathy; it could be argued, of course, that the PCL-R underdiagnosed psychopathy.)

Table 6 also presents the correlation between PCL:SV ratings and number of adult APD symptoms. The average across the sites was about .65, a value very similar to that obtained in research using the PCL-R (Hare 1991; Hart and Hare 1989).

Self-report measures related to psychopathy were available for several samples. For example, the correlation between the Socialization scale (Gough 1969) and PCL:SV scores was − .22 in sample 2 and − .47 in sample 10; and the Antisocial scale of the Million Clinical Multiaxial Inventory-II (MCMI-II; Millon 1987) correlated .68 with PCL:SV ratings in sample 3 (see below). These values are similar to those obtained in research looking at the correlation between the Socialization and MCMI-II scales and the PCL-R (see Hare 1991; Hart, Forth, and Hare 1991).

Convergent and Discriminant Validity

We computed the correlations of the PCL:SV with interview and self-report measures of DSM III-R personality disorders. The interview measure was the Personality Disorder Examination (PDE; Loranger 1988), a structured diagnostic interview designed to assess all 13 DSM III-R personality disorders (including the two disorders in the appendix of the DSM III-R). It was administered to 27 nonpsychotic subjects in sample 6 by clinicians different from those who completed the PCL:SV; we analyzed PDE dimensional scores. The self-report measure was the MCMI-II (Millon 1987), an inventory that assesses various Axis I and II disorders. We administered the MCMI-II to 40 subjects in sample 3, and analyzed base-rate scores for the personality disorders.

As table 7 indicates, there was considerable consistency in the pattern of correlations obtained from interview and self-report methods. Consistent with the analyses of concurrent validity, presented above, the PCL:SV correlated highly with interview and self-report measures of antisocial personality disorder. It also correlated moderately with both measures of borderline, narcissistic, sadistic, and passive-aggressive personality disorder. Correlations with schizotypal, paranoid, and histrionic personality were smaller in magnitude, and were not consistent across methods. Overall, the results were in line with our predictions and with the results of previous research with the PCL-R (Hart, Forth, and Hare 1991).

We administered the Michigan Alcoholism Screening Test (MAST; Selzer 1971) and the Drug Abuse Screening Test (DAST; Skinner 1982) to subjects in samples 3 and 10. Correlations between the PCL:SV and the MAST were .35 and .38 in samples 3 and 10, respectively; correlations with the DAST were .37 and .62, respectively. These results are consistent with research looking at the association between the PCL-R and substance use (Hart and Hare 1989; Smith and Newman 1990).

To obtain data on psychological distress, we administered the State form of the State-Trait Anxiety Inventory (STAI; Spielberger, Gorsuch, and Lushene

Table 7. Convergent and discriminant validity of the PCL:SV:
Correlation with interview and self-report measures
of DSM III-R personality disorder

Personality disorder	Interview (PDE)[a]	Self-report (MCMI-II)[b]
Paranoid	.11	.40*
Schizoid	.12	.23
Schizotypal	.12	.50*
Antisocial	.83*	.68*
Borderline	.68*	.45*
Histrionic	.68*	.16
Narcissistic	.68*	.44*
Avoidant	.33	.22
Dependent	.37	−.23
Obsessive-compulsive	−.03	.08
Passive-aggressive	.46*	.48*
Sadistic	.60*	.44*
Self-defeating	.38	.28

[a]PDE = Personality Disorder Examination (Loranger 1988; $N = 27$).
[b]MCMI-II = Millon Clinical Multiaxial Inventory-II (Millon 1987; $N = 40$).
*$p < .05$.

1970) and the Beck Depression Inventory (BDI; Beck et al. 1961) to subjects in samples 2, 4, 6, and 10 on the day that they completed the PCL:SV interview. Correlations between the PCL:SV and these scales were all small (ranging from − .22 to .14) and nonsignificant. Thus, the subject's emotional state at the time of assessment does not appear to unduly influence PCL:SV ratings.

Conclusions

The basic requirements we set for the development of a screening tool for the assessment of psychopathy appear to have been met. The PCL:SV is conceptually and empirically related to the PCL-R; it is reliable and valid; it can be used with both civil and forensic populations, including the mentally disordered; and it requires relatively little time, effort, and training to administer and score. Despite our optimism, however, we caution readers that the PCL-R remains the method of choice for assessing psychopathy in forensic settings at the present time due to the extensive body of evidence supporting its validity.

Traditionally, psychopathy has been of interest only those who work in the criminal justice system. We hope that this situation will change with the publication of the PCL:SV. The PCL:SV appears to be well-suited for research on civil psychiatric patients, including treatment outcome, adoption, and family history studies. In addition, the PCL:SV may allow us to examine the utility of the concept of psychopathy in normal populations (i.e., community residents). For example, do psychopathic traits predict poor occupational performance in employees, such as police recruits or prison guards? Or, are the cognitive and psychophysiological correlates of psychopathy in community residents the same as those in criminals? Research on questions of this sort will help us to more fully appreciate the consequences of psychopathy, both for the individual and for society at large.

Acknowledgments

This chapter and the research it describes were generously supported by the Research Network on Mental Health and the Law of the John D. and Catherine T. MacArthur Foundation. We are grateful to John Monahan for his encouragement and advice on the project and to Dr. Henry Steadman and Pamela Clark Robbins of Policy Research Associates for making their data available to us. We also acknowledge the contributions of Dr. David Cox to the development of the PCL:SV.

Correspondence should be addressed to Stephen D. Hart at the Mental Health, Law, and Policy Institute, Simon Fraser University, Burnaby, British Columbia, Canada, V5A 1S6.

References

American Psychiatric Association. 1987. *Diagnostic and statistical manual of mental disorders.* 3d ed., rev. (DSM III-R) Washington, D.C.: American Psychiatric Association.

Bartko, J. J. 1976. On various intraclass correlation reliability coefficients. *Psychological Bulletin* 83:762–65.

Beck, A. T., C. H. Ward, M. Mendelson, J. Mock, and J. K. Erbaugh. 1961. An inventory for measuring depression. *Archives of General Psychiatry* 4:561–71.

Cleckley, H. R. 1976. *The mask of sanity.* Saint Louis: Mosby.

Cox, D. N., S. D. Hart, and R. D. Hare. 1989. *A Clinical Version of the Psychopathy Checklist.* Unpublished manuscript.

Dutton, D. G., and S. D. Hart. 1992. Risk markers for family violence in a federally incarcerated population. *International Journal of Law and Psychiatry* 15:101–12.

Forth, A. E., S. D. Hart, and R. D. Hare. 1990. Assessment of psychopathy in male young offenders. *Psychological Assessment: A Journal of Consulting and Clinical Psychology* 2:342–44.

Gottfredson, D. M., and J. A. Bonds. 1961. *A manual for intake base expectancy scoring.* San Francisco: California Department of Corrections, Research Division.

Gough, H. 1969. *Manual for the California Psychological Inventory.* Palo Alto: Consulting Psychologists Press.

Hare, R. D. 1985. Comparison of procedures for the assessment of psychopathy. *Journal of Consulting and Clinical Psychology* 53:7–16.

———. 1991. *Manual for the Hare Psychopathy Checklist-Revised.* Toronto: Multi-Health Systems.

Hare, R. D., and D. N. Cox. 1978. Clinical and empirical conceptions of psychopathy, and the selection of subjects for research. In R. D. Hare and D. Schalling, eds., *Psychopathic behavior: Approaches to research.* Chichester, England: Wiley.

Hare, R. D., D. N. Cox, and S. D. Hart. In press. *Manual for the Screening Version of the Hare Psychopathy Checklist-Revised (PCL:SV).* Toronto: Multi-Health Systems.

Hare, R. D., A. E. Forth, and S. D. Hart. 1989. The psychopath as prototype for pathological lying and deception. In J. C. Yuille, ed., *Credibility assessment.* Dordrecht, The Netherlands: Kluwer.

Hare, R. D., T. J. Harpur, A. R. Hakstian, A. E. Forth, S. D. Hart, and J. P. Newman. 1990. The Revised Psychopathy Checklist: Descriptive statistics, reliability, and factor structure. *Psychological Assessment: A Journal of Consulting and Clinical Psychology* 2:338–41.

Hare, R. D., and S. D. Hart. 1993. Psychopathy, mental disorder, and crime. In S. Hodgins, ed., *Mental disorder and crime.* Newbury Part, Calif.: Sage.

Hare, R. D., S. D. Hart, and T. J. Harpur. 1991. Psychopathy and the proposed DSM-IV criteria for antisocial personality disorder. *Journal of Abnormal Psychology* 100:391–98.

Hare, R. D., and L. M. McPherson. 1984. Violent and aggressive behavior by criminal psychopaths. *International Journal of Law and Psychiatry* 7:35–50.

Harpur, T. J., A. R. Hakstian, and R. D. Hare. 1988. Factor structure of the Psychopathy Checklist. *Journal of Consulting and Clinical Psychology* 56:741–47.

Harpur, T. J., R. D. Hare, and A. R. Hakstian. 1989. Two-factor conceptualization of psychopathy: Construct validity and assessment implications. *Psychological Assessment: A Journal of Consulting and Clinical Psychology* 1:6–17.

Harris, G. T., M. E. Rice, and C. A. Cormier. 1991. Psychopathy and violent recidivism. *Law and Human Behavior* 15:625–37.

Hart, S. D., A. E. Forth, and R. D. Hare. 1991. The MCMI-II as a measure of psychopathy. *Journal of Personality Disorders* 5:318–27.

Hart, S. D., and R. D. Hare. 1989. Discriminant validity of the Psychopathy Checklist in a forensic psychiatric population. *Psychological Assessment: A Journal of Consulting and Clinical Psychology* 1:211–18.

Hart, S. D., R. D. Hare, and T. J. Harpur. 1992. The Psychopathy Checklist: An overview for researchers and clinicians. In J. Rosen and P. McReynolds, eds., *Advances in psychological assessment*. Vol. 8. New York: Plenum.

Hart, S. D., P. R. Kropp, and R. D. Hare. 1988. Performance of male psychopaths following conditional release from prison. *Journal of Consulting and Clinical Psychology* 56:227–32.

Heilbrun, K., S. D. Hart, R. D. Hare, D. Gustafson, C. Nunez, and A. J. White. 1993. *Inpatient and post-discharge aggression in mentally disordered offenders: The role of psychopathy.* Unpublished manuscript.

Hoffman, P., and J. L. Beck. 1974. Parole decision-making: A Salient Factor Score. *Journal of Criminal Justice* 2:195–206.

Kosson, D. S., S. S. Smith, and J. P. Newman. 1990. Evaluating the construct validity of psychopathy in black and white male inmates: Three preliminary studies. *Journal of Abnormal Psychology* 99:250–59.

Loranger, A. 1988. *Personality Disorder Examination (PDE) manual.* Yonkers, N.Y.: DV Communications.

McCord, W., and J. McCord. 1964. *The psychopath: An essay on the criminal mind.* Princeton, N.J.: Van Nostrand.

Millon, T. 1981. *Disorders of personality: DSM-III Axis II.* New York: Wiley.

———. 1987. *Millon Clinical Multiaxial Inventory-II Manual.* Minneapolis: National Computer Systems.

Nuffield, J. 1982. *Parole decision-making in Canada: Research towards decision guidelines.* Ottawa: Ministry of Supply and Services.

Pichot, P. 1978. Psychopathic behavior: An historical review. In R. D. Hare and D. Schalling, eds., *Psychopathic behavior: Approaches to research.* Chichester, England: Wiley.

Rice, M., and G. T. Harris. 1992. A comparison of criminal recidivism among schizophrenic and nonschizophrenic offenders. *International Journal of Law and Psychiatry* 15:397–408.

Rice, M. E., G. T. Harris, and V. L. Quinsey. 1990. A follow-up of rapists assessed in a maximum security psychiatric facility. *Journal of Interpersonal Violence* 4:435–48.

Roesch, R. 1992. *Mental health interventions in jails.* Keynote address at the Third European Conference of Law and Psychology, Oxford, England, September.

Roy, R. 1988. *A criterion-based evaluation of an instrument for the assessment of psychopathy.* Unpublished thesis, Department of Psychology, Simon Fraser University, Burnaby, British Columbia, Canada.

Selzer, M. 1971. The Michigan Alcoholism Screening Test: The quest for a new diagnostic instrument. *American Journal of Psychiatry* 127:1653–58.

Serin, R. C. 1991a. Psychopathy and violence in criminals. *Journal of Interpersonal Violence* 6:423–31.

———. 1991b. *Violence and recidivism in criminal psychopaths.* Unpublished manuscript.

Serin, R. C., R. D. Peters, and H. E. Barbaree. 1990. Predictors of psychopathy and release outcome in a criminal population. *Psychological Assessment: A Journal of Consulting and Clinical Psychology* 2:419–22.

Skinner, H. A. 1982. The drug abuse screening test. *Addictive Behavior* 7:363–71.

Smith, S. S., and J. P. Newman. 1990. Alcohol and drug abuse/dependence disorders in psychopathic and nonpsychopathic criminal offenders. *Journal of Abnormal Psychology* 99:430–39.

Spielberger, C. D., R. L. Gorsuch, and R. E. Lushene. 1970. *Manual for the State-Trait Anxiety Inventory.* Palo Alto: Consulting Psychologist Press.

Steadman, H., J. Monahan, P. Applebaum, T. Grisso, E. Mulvey, L. Roth, P. Clark Robbins, and D. Klassen. In press. Designing a new generation of risk assessment research. This volume.

Tyrer, P., and B. Ferguson. 1988. Development of the concept of abnormal personality. In P. Tyrer, ed., *Personality disorders: Diagnosis, management, and course.* London: Wright.

Wong, S. 1984. *Criminal and institutional behaviours of psychopaths.* Ottawa: Ministry of the Solicitor-General of Canada.

Part II
Clinical Factors

"Clinical" risk factors for violence reflect the various types and symptoms of mental disorder. Chapters 5 and 6 concern the epidemiology of mental disorder; chapters 7 and 8 address special symptom patterns; and chapter 9 considers disorders of personality.

Jeffrey Swanson focuses on the relationship between mental disorder and violence in his analysis of data from the well-known Epidemiologic Catchment Area (ECA) study. No matter what indices of violence he uses, Swanson finds a significant, albeit modest, effect for mental disorder as a risk factor for violence. Substance abuse and violence, however, bear a much stronger association.

Bruce Link and Charlotte Ann Stueve take Swanson's ECA data a large step forward. They analyze data from the Washington Heights section of New York City, where community respondents were administered the Psychiatric Epidemiology Research Interview (PERI). Link and Stueve find that only a subset of psychotic symptoms—called by the researchers "threat/control-override" symptoms—are related to violence. Further, these symptoms are associated with violence not only among former mental patients, but among members of the general population who have never been treated for mental disorder.

The British research team of Pamela Taylor, Philippa Garety, Alec Buchanan, Alison Reed, Simon Wessely, Katarzyna Ray, Graham Dunn, and Don Grubin address the poorly understood and rarely researched issue of delusions and violence. Despite clinical indications that delusions precipitate violence in some offenders, a reliable and valid way to assess the existence and content of delusional beliefs has proven elusive. Taylor and her colleagues report on the development of the Maudsley Assessment of Delusions Schedule (MADS) and present data on the relationship between delusions, as measured by the MADS, and violent behavior.

Dale McNiel explores the literature relating hallucinations to violence. He finds evidence for a positive relationship, but one affected by many other factors, such as the course of the disorder of which hallucinations are symptomatic. Given that hallucinations tend to respond to treatment with anti-psychotic medication, predictors of noncompliance with medication among hallucinating patients may be predictors of violence among people experiencing hallucinations.

Finally, Thomas Widiger and Timothy Trull discuss disorders of personality. Despite the apparent relevance of personality disorder for violent behavior, they find that only two disorders, antisocial personality and borderline personality, have received research attention. An alternative framework for conceptualizing precursors of violence as dimensional factors of personality, rather than as categorical "disorders" of personality, is presented.

5 Mental Disorder, Substance Abuse, and Community Violence: An Epidemiological Approach

JEFFREY W. SWANSON

There is a dearth of general population data for examining the relationships among diagnosable mental disorders, substance abuse, and violence. Uncertainty about these matters characterizes the posture of the American Psychiatric Association (APA), as reflected in its 1987 diagnostic manual. Among the "associated features" of psychoactive substance use disorders, the manual notes the common occurrence of "mood liability and suspiciousness, both of which can contribute to violent behavior" (American Psychiatric Association 1987, 171). Concerning the linkage of violence with schizophrenia, however, the APA officially remains agnostic:

> Although violent acts performed by people with this disorder often attract public attention, whether their frequency is actually greater than in the general population is not known. (American Psychiatric Association 1987, 191)

Similarly, Monahan and Steadman noted in 1983:

> An exhaustive search of the epidemiological literature, including correspondence with the leading researchers in the field, has revealed no study of the prevalence of true mental disorder in the general population that has inquired whether the individuals identified as mentally ill were ever arrested for, or admit to ever having committed, criminal acts. (Monahan and Steadman 1983, 153)

In the early 1980s, however, the National Institute of Mental Health (NIMH) funded a series of parallel surveys in New Haven, Baltimore, Saint Louis, Durham, and Los Angeles, for the primary purpose of determining the prevalence of untreated psychiatric disorders in community populations. The data from these surveys also provide the first large-sample estimates of the general prevalence of assaultive behavior among persons with and without diagnosable mental disorders in the community.

In the first wave of the Epidemiological Catchment Area (ECA) project, university-based research teams conducted structured diagnostic interviews

101

with about 3,000 to 5,000 household-resident adults at each of the five sites, resulting in a combined total of 17,803 community respondents in the pooled data base. Additional interviews were conducted with 1,379 residents of nursing homes, prisons, and psychiatric hospitals. The design and substantive findings of the ECA project concerning psychiatric disorders in the community have been discussed in detail elsewhere (Eaton and Kessler 1985; Robins and Regier 1991).

The findings presented in this chapter result from recent secondary analysis of the ECA community data for a purpose not intended or anticipated by the original investigators. That is to say, the ECA project was not designed to provide a general epidemiologic assessment of violent behavior in the community. However, a limited amount of information on violence was gathered fortuitously in the course of interviews designed to assess the presence of symptom criteria for psychiatric disorders. The diagnostic criteria for two disorders in particular—antisocial personality disorder and alcohol abuse—included violent behavior.

At the outset, it must be said that in order to examine the occurrence of violence as a separate, generalizable phenomenon in the ECA data, one must overcome a number of methodological challenges and make some potentially problematic assumptions. A number of the methodological difficulties stem from the fact that, during the three-year period when the various ECA sites were collecting their data, several modifications were made in the interview which produced some lack of uniformity across sites in the information that is now available to identify recent violent behavior among all adult respondents. For this reason, not all five sites could be used for the analyses presented in this chapter. The number of sites that may be pooled depends, in part, on which items from the interview are included in the index of violence, and on what assumptions are made about respondents who were not asked all of the violence questions.

In what follows, the initial descriptive analysis and comparisons between alternative indices of violence are based on data from Durham and Los Angeles only, with a pooled sample size of about 7,000. These were the only two sites whose surveys uniformly included all of the variables used to construct all six of the indices that will be compared. For the multivariate analyses to be presented subsequently, data from a third site—Baltimore—were pooled with the other two samples for a combined total of about 10,000 respondents. As will be discussed in more detail below, the inclusion of the Baltimore sample required the use of a somewhat controversial index of violent behavior, as well as a potentially problematic assumption about missing data.

To take into account the selection biases inherent in the ECA project's multistage stratified sampling design, the data for each respondent were assigned a weight coefficient based on the respondent's probability of having been selected. Since these samples were selected in several stages (geographic clusters, households, individual respondents), the pooled data base by design provides a larger sampling variance than would have occurred with simple random selection (Holzer et al. 1985). This means that, without a correction, the precision of estimates would be exaggerated and the statistical significance of most effects would be overstated. Leaf, Myers, and McEvoy (1991) describe a correction that effectively reduces the ECA sample size by about one half, for the purpose of statistical analysis on the equivalent of a simple random sample. Similarly, for analyses comparable to those presented here, Holzer et al. (1986) estimated average ECA design effects to be in the range of 1.4 to 1.8. In this chapter, a uniform correction was introduced prior to all statistical significance tests in order to account for an average design effect of 1.8. Accordingly, for example, a chi-square value of 12 would be reduced to 6.7; with one degree of freedom, this would adjust the significance of the test statistic from $p < .001$ to $p < .01$.

Measurement

Psychiatric disorder. All ECA site teams administered the NIMH Diagnostic Interview Schedule (DIS; Robins et al. 1981), which uses a lengthy series of preset questions with structured follow-up probing to assess the presence of psychiatric diagnostic criteria in adult respondents. The DIS was designed to be administered by trained lay interviewers and to generate DSM III diagnoses (American Psychiatric Association 1980) comparable to clinicians' formal assessments. The diagnostic categories to be considered here include: schizophrenia and schizophreniform disorder, major affective disorders (major depression, mania, and bipolar disorder), anxiety disorders (obsessive-compulsive disorder, panic, and phobias), and substance abuse (alcohol and other drug abuse and dependence disorder). With the exception of antisocial personality disorders (ASP), the ECA surveys did not assess disorders classified on Axis II of DSM III (personality disorders). Due to the obvious confounding of the ASP diagnosis with the dependent measures of this study, the analyses in this chapter exclude ASP from all operational definitions of mental disorder.

This DIS "recency probes" allowed prevalence rates to be calculated for several alternative time intervals in addition to the respondent's entire lifetime. The interval chosen for this analysis was one year. To count as a positive case, the respondent had to meet DSM III lifetime criteria for a given disorder and report that some symptoms of the disorder were present during the 12-month period preceding interview. A hierarchical coding scheme was used to classify respondents who met criteria for more than one disorder. The aggregation and coding of disorders will be described in detail in the results section to follow.

Violence. As a precise quantitative measure of violence, the ECA self-report data on assaultive behavior leave much to be desired. Although the items cover a wide range of assaultive behavior, they overlap and do not assess the severity or frequency of specific violent acts. In an earlier analysis (Swanson et al. 1990), the number of positive items was counted as a rough indicator of severity and frequency. This measure left some gaps: for example, a person with a positive response to three items—using a weapon, hitting a spouse, and fighting while drinking—might be reporting only a single episode that was characterized by all three features. Conversely, a respondent who committed multiple acts of assault (even homicide) might be positive on only one item. For the present analyses, no attempts are made to approximate indicators of the severity and frequency of violence, since the data do not directly provide such an indicator. Instead, what is available is a general (and rather blunt) index of the presence or absence of *any* violent behavior that includes certain features.

Four of the five DIS items pertaining to assaultive behavior occurred in a section designed to identify antisocial personality disorder (ASP). The prevailing psychiatric view of the nature of ASP guided the way in which the DIS was designed to assess its presence. Specifically, psychiatrists construe ASP as a disorder that emerges developmentally, i.e., in the early formation of an individual's personality rather than as an illness that may have an acute onset in adults (Robins, Tipp, and Przybeck 1991). According to the DSM III criteria underlying the ECA study, the diagnosis of ASP could not be given unless its symptoms were manifested during childhood or adolescence (e.g., playing hooky from school, telling lies, getting in fights at school, running away from home over night).

Applying these criteria straightforwardly, the DIS originally instructed interviewers to skip the violence questions altogether unless at least three childhood symptoms of ASP had been reported. This made sense, since the reason for asking about violent behavior was to identify ASP. As a result, however, in the ECA sites where the skip-out rule was applied, there is no obvious way to assess the general prevalence of violent behavior; the denominator for these items excludes a large number of respondents ostensibly at low risk for being assaultive.

However, in Saint Louis, Durham and Los Angeles, the DIS was modified so that all adults were asked some of the violence questions. At these sites, the following questions were asked of all respondents with reference to their adult lifetime:

1. Have you ever used a weapon like a stick, knife, or gun, in a fight since you were 18? [excludes the use of weapons as a legitimate occupational duty, such as by a police officer, security guard, or soldier in battle]

2. Since age 18, have you been in more than one fight that came to swapping blows, other than fights with your (husband/wife/partner)?
3. Have you ever spanked or hit a child (yours or anyone else's) hard enough so that he or she had bruises, or had to stay in bed or see a doctor?

Respondents who had been married, or lived with someone as though married, were also asked the following questions:

4. Did you ever hit or throw things at your (wife/husband/partner)?
   A. Were you ever the one who threw things first, regardless of who started the argument?
   B. Did you hit or throw things first on more than one occasion?

A fifth item pertaining to violence was asked in the diagnostic section for alcohol abuse and dependence disorder:

5. Have you ever gotten into physical fights while drinking?

These five items may be combined in various ways to form alternative indices of violence, i.e., alternative criteria by which to count a given respondent as violent or not. Table 1 shows the three combinations of items that were used to form the alternative indices for this analysis. The two-item index includes only those questions asked of all respondents, and those for which the opportunity to commit the violent acts in question would not be conditioned by one's marital status or parental role. The four-item index adds two questions that ostensibly identify domestic violence, i.e., spouse battering and child abuse. The five-item index adds fighting while drinking. The rationale, assumptions, and implications of these various indices will be discussed further in the context of showing the prevalence rates yielded by each.

In order to calculate estimates of *current* prevalence from the answers to these questions, what was required in addition was a way to determine how recently these types of violent acts or incidents occurred. Clearly, many respondents could have been violent only in their distant past; without information on recency, they would still be identified as violent on the basis of these questions alone. Unfortunately, for the first four items (those taken from the ASP section), the DIS did not ask how recently each kind of violent incident had occurred. Rather, a general probe question was asked at the end of the ASP diagnostic section: "When is the last time you did any of these things, such as . . . [interviewer mentions all of the individual violence items and other symptoms that were reported]?" Thus, it would be possible to misclassify someone as recently violent who had been violent only in the past, but recently had other antisocial symptoms.

The potential for introducing error by applying a global recency probe to the specific domain of violence is diminished, however, in light of the fact

Table 1. Indices of violent behavior in the ECA data

DIS items	Adult lifetime index			One-year index		
	Two-item	Four-item	Five-item	Two-item	Four-item	Five-item
Behavior						
Used weapon in fight	*	*	*	*	*	*
[or]						
Hit others (not spouse)	*	*	*	*	*	*
[or]						
Hit spouse or partner		*	*		*	*
[or]						
Hit child		*	*		*	*
[or]						
Fought while drinking			*			*
[and]						
Recency						
Violent behavior and/ or other antisocial symptoms in the last year				*	*	*
[or]						
Fought while drinking in the last year						*

Note: Derived from Epidemiologic Catchment Area data from Durham, N.C., and Los Angeles.

that violence, while rare in general, is very common in the context of antisocial symptomatology. In fact, in the ECA data, violence occurs several times more frequently than the diagnosis of ASP itself. While only 17% of the respondents who reported violent behavior met criteria for antisocial personality disorder, nine out of ten who were positive on ASP reported at least one of the violence items. Thus, it appears likely that recent violence would be identified most of the time by the section level recency probe. That is to say, most people who (a) admitted to violent behavior and, (b) admitted to committing violent acts or other antisocial behavior *during the past year* were, indeed, violent during the past year. With this assumption in mind, indicators of "recent violence" were constructed for these analyses. Comparable to the DIS diagnoses, one year was chosen as the time frame for the indicators of recent violence.

With the fifth item (fights while drinking), a specific recency question was asked in Durham, Los Angeles, and Baltimore. Hence, adding the fifth item to the index further lessened the chance of misclassifying someone as recently violent who had been violent only in the past. It also meant that a third site—Baltimore—could be added. This was done by identifying the population that provided information on item 5 (getting in fights while drinking), and using this population as the Baltimore denominator for the overall index. This had the effect of slightly lowering the estimate of the general prevalence of violence, since it counted people as not violent in general if they were not violent while drinking. However, when the adjusted Baltimore estimate was compared to the rates from the other two sites (those with no missing data due to the skip-out), the three rates differed only slightly; they fell within a range of 1.6 percentage points, with Baltimore in the middle.

Socioeconomic status. SES was measured by a census-based ranking that combined the respondent's educational level, occupational status, and household income. Holzer et al. (1986) have described these procedures for calculating SES in the ECA data, using a modified version of techniques developed by Nam and Powers (1983). Dohrenwend (1990) has provided a recent instructive overview of past debates and the current state of research—including the major ECA findings—on issues surrounding socioeconomic status and psychiatric disorders.

Methods of Analysis

Simple frequency analyses were conducted to describe and compare the prevalence of self-reported violence in different subpopulations, as identified by the alternative indices. The importance of differences in rates of violence among various demographic and diagnostic subsamples was assessed statistically in several ways. First, chi-square statistics and associated probabilities were calculated to determine whether given differences could reasonably have occurred by chance alone. As mentioned, these statistics were adjusted to account for the increased sampling variance due to the ECA project's selection design.

Second, odds ratios were calculated to illustrate the relative magnitude of rate differences between groups, according the following formula given in Fleiss et al. (1986):

$$OR = P_r (1 - P_c)/[P_c (1 - P_r)]$$

where P_r is the prevalence (or probability) of violence in the risk group, and P_c is the prevalence (or probability) of violence in the comparison group.

Third, attributable risk rates were calculated to illustrate the effect that a given risk factor may have on overall violence in the population taking into account the relative size of the group with the risk factor. Attributable risk was calculated by the following formula:

$$AR = (P_r - P_c)N_r/N_t$$

where P_r is the prevalence (or probability) of violence in the risk group, P_c is the prevalence (or probability) of violence in the comparison group (i.e., those without the risk factor), N_r is the number of people in the risk group, and N_t is the number of violent persons in the total population.

Finally, multivariate categorical models of the predictors of violent behavior were developed. Logistic regression was used to analyze the pattern of rates of violence by gender, age group, marital status, socioeconomic status, race-ethnicity, presence of mental disorders and substance abuse, history of psychiatric hospitalization, and history of arrest. This technique included chi-square tests for the statistical significance of each variable controlling for the others. It also assessed the fit between the observed rates in the ECA data and the values predicted by a relative risk model based on the relationships among these variables. The model's predicted values for individual respondents were aggregated and analyzed descriptively for several subgroups of interest. Adjusted odds ratios and attributable risk coefficients were calculated using these predicted probabilities for small subsamples.

Results

General prevalence of violent behavior. How prevalent is violent behavior generally in the ECA data? The answer varies according to which index is used to identify violence. The measure that provides the most conservative, uniform assessment, with the least problematic assumptions, is the two-item adult-lifetime index. In the pooled data from Durham and Los Angeles, there were 615 respondents (weighted N = 654) out of 6,911 (weighted N = 6,947) who, by their own report, had at some time in their adult lives used a weapon "like a stick, knife, or gun" in a fight or engaged in repeated incidents of "swapping blows" with a person or persons other than a spouse or partner. These two questions were asked of all respondents in the Durham and Los Angeles surveys, irrespective of their past or present status as marriage partners or parents. (The Saint Louis survey also asked these two questions of all respondents, but since it omitted one of the questions for the five-item one-year index to be examined later, it was excluded in order to allow a comparison of rates on the same data across all six of the indices shown in table 1.) Less than two percent of the data were missing on these variables. By this measure, then, about 9% of the population were ever violent.

This percentage represents a conservative estimate of the adult lifetime prevalence of serious violence, i.e., of the kind that the public is most likely to fear in association with mental illness: violence committed using weapons or committed against someone other than an immediate family member. However, since this two-item index specifically omitted the DIS questions on hitting a spouse or partner, hitting a child, and getting in fights while drinking, it undoubtedly *underestimated* the true prevalence of all assaultive behavior in the community. In fact, except for situations in which a weapon was used against a spouse or child, or in which the victim was some other family member, the two-item index misses the sphere of domestic violence altogether.

Alternatively, the four-item index added questions that refer specifically to assaultive acts directed toward a spouse, partner, or child. Using this expanded measure, 16% of the ECA respondents reported that they had committed violent acts at some time in their adult lives. In turn, the five-item index added the question on fighting while drinking, which resulted in a further increase in the estimated prevalence of violence to 18%. Thus, the inclusion of domestic violence and alcohol-related fighting doubled the 9% prevalence estimate derived using the minimal two-item set.

Each of these three indices of violent behavior yields an estimate of current (one-year) prevalence when available information on the recency of violent behavior is taken into account. Thus, the estimates of the general population prevalence of recent violence in the pooled Durham and Los Angeles samples are as follows: two-item measure, 1.9%; four-item measure, 2.8%; five-item measure, 3.5%.

The five-item measure allows the addition of a third ECA site—Baltimore—which brings the weighted sample size up to 10,059 respondents who provided some information on violence. Of these, 3.7% reported committing at least one of the five kinds of violent acts during the one-year period preceding the interview, based either on the item recency probe for fighting while drinking or on the section recency probe for antisocial symptomatology including violence. The rates and weighted sample sizes for the individual sites were: Baltimore, 3.9% ($N = 3,102$); Durham, 3.08% ($N = 3,845$); and Los Angeles, 4.14% ($N = 3,113$).

Prevalence of psychiatric disorder among violent and not-violent subgroups. Do people who commit violent acts tend to be mentally ill? Again, the answer depends partly on how inclusive a criterion is used to identify violence on the one hand and mental disorder on the other. Tables 2 and 3 display various estimates of the prevalence of psychiatric disorder among violent and nonviolent subgroups, as defined by alternative indices of violence in the two sites (Durham and Los Angeles) where all of the component variables were uniformly available.

Several important findings emerge here. First, people who assaulted others were indeed significantly more likely to have psychiatric disorders, with odds ratios typically in the range of 2.5 to 4.0. This pattern held up irrespective of which index was used to identify violence or mental illness.

Second, however, while a fairly high percentage of respondents in the violent subgroups (up to 50%) met criteria for at least one diagnosis on Axis I of DSM III, the rates of disorder dropped considerably when a more restrictive definition of mental illness was employed—especially one that excluded persons who only had substance abuse disorders with no accompanying psycho-

Table 2. Current-year psychiatric disorder among nonviolent and violent subgroups

Violence group		Weighted N	Any disorder[a]	Major disorder[b]	Major mental disorder[c]
			Current-year diagnosis (%)		
Lifetime index					
2-item:	no	6293	17.40[d]	7.41	3.43
	yes	654	40.17	29.78	9.23
4-item:	no	5869	16.66	6.76	2.99
	yes	1080	35.20	24.49	9.30
5-item:	no	5718	15.87	5.95	2.93
	yes	1239	36.57	26.09	8.91
One-year index					
2-item:	no	6812	18.88	8.87	3.81
	yes	135	52.91	42.41	12.36
4-item:	no	6751	18.75	8.68	3.71
	yes	198	46.59	38.02	12.90
5-item:	no	6710	18.45	8.34	3.72
	yes	247	49.46	42.23	11.48

Source: Epidemiologic Catchment Area data from Durham, N.C., and Los Angeles.
[a] Includes schizophrenia spectrum, affective disorders, psychoactive substance use disorders, and anxiety disorders.
[b] Includes schizophrenia spectrum, affective disorders, and psychoactive substance use disorders.
[c] Includes schizophrenia spectrum and affective disorders only.
[d] Differences between rates in all pairs shown were statistically significant at $p < .0001$.

pathology (see column 4 in table 2). By this criterion, at least 85% of people in the violent group *could not* be considered to be mentally ill.

Third, table 2 shows that recent violence, rather than violence committed at any time in the past, was most strongly associated with current mental illness. That is to say, the violence measures that include recency criteria (the one-year estimates) tended to define a group of violent individuals who were more likely to be mentally ill than those defined by the adult-lifetime measures. For example, the prevalence of any major disorder was 42.4% among those defined as recently violent on the two-item one-year index, and considerably lower—29.8%—among those defined as violent on the corresponding two-item lifetime measure.

Fourth, it is apparent that the choice of violence index within the lifetime or one-year sets makes little or no difference in the estimated prevalence of psychiatric disorder. While the size of the identified violent group increased with a more inclusive definition of violence, the proportion of a given violent group defined as mentally ill remained fairly stable.

Table 3 displays the prevalence of disorder in the violent and nonviolent

Table 3. Current-year major mental disorder, substance abuse, and dual diagnoses among nonviolent and violent subgroups

		Current-year diagnosis (%)		
Violence group	Weighted N	Mental disorder only[a]	Substance abuse only[b]	Mental disorder and substance abuse[c]
Lifetime index				
2-item: no	6293	2.91	3.98	0.52
yes	654	5.39**	20.55****	3.84****
4-item: no	5869	2.58	3.77	0.41
yes	1080	6.21****	15.19****	3.09****
5-item: no	5718	2.56	3.02	0.38
yes	1239	5.84****	17.18****	3.07****
One-year index				
2-item: no	6812	3.09	5.06	0.72
yes	135	6.17[ns]	30.05****	6.19****
4-item no	6751	3.02	4.97	0.70
yes	198	7.48**	25.12****	5.41****
5-item: no	6710	3.03	4.61	0.69
yes	247	6.17*	30.75****	5.31****

Source: Epidemiolic Catchment Area data from Durham, N.C., and Los Angeles.

[a] Schizophrenia spectrum or major affective disorders only.

[b] Alcohol or other drug abuse or dependence disorders only.

[c] Schizophrenia spectrum or affective disorders combined with alcohol or other drug abuse or dependence disorders.

$* p < .05.$ $** p < .01.$ $*** p < .001.$ $**** p < .0001.$

subgroups controlling for substance abuse comorbidity. In general, mental illness alone was about twice as prevalent in the subgroups identified as violent, while substance abuse alone and comorbidity were about five times more prevalent among those who reported violence than among those who did not.

Major mental disorder without alcohol or drug abuse complications emerged as a quite rare condition in the community, yet one that was significantly more common among persons who reported that they had committed assaultive acts. The only case under which this finding did not achieve statistical significance was when the most restrictive definition of violence (two-item one-year) was paired with the most restrictive definition of mental illness (current-year schizophrenia or major affective disorder only). Yet even here, the odds ratio for mental illness in the violent group exceeded 3.5; while the rate differences in this comparison were similar to those in the other indices, the number of cases was smaller, requiring a larger rate difference to pass muster as a finding not reasonably explained by chance variation.

Table 3 also makes it apparent that the higher prevalence of "any disorder" observed with recent versus lifetime measures of violence had mainly to do with the association of violence with substance abuse. When the criterion was major mental disorder only, the prevalence rates remained about the same (about 6%) in the violent subgroups whether defined by recent or lifetime measures. Clearly, since violence is a relatively rare feature of "pure" mental illness but a much more common feature of substance abuse, the rate of current mental illness was less affected than was the rate of current alcohol or drug abuse disorders by whether people were included in the reference population who were violent only in the past.

In the three-site ECA analysis reported elsewhere (Swanson et al. 1990), it was shown that the rate of any alcohol or drug abuse or dependence disorder was 41.64% among the violent (defined by the five-item one-year index), compared to only 4.93% among the nonviolent. The prevalence of any affective disorder was three times higher in the violent subgroup (9.37% vs. 2.95%) while the prevalence of schizophrenia or schizophreniform disorder was similarly increased (3.92% vs. 1.03%). The prevalence of anxiety disorders was 20.13% among the violent, compared to 14.13% among the nonviolent.

Prevalence of violence by psychiatric diagnosis. To what extent do persons in the community with mental illness pose a higher risk for engaging in assaultive behavior than do persons who are demonstrably free of mental illness? As a general answer to this central question, figures 1 and 2 portray the lifetime and one-year estimated prevalence rates of self-reported violence toward others, among community respondents in four subgroups: (1) those with no major psychiatric disorder in the past year; (2) those with a current-year diagnosis of schizophrenia, schizophreniform, or major affective disorder only; (3) those with a current-year diagnosis of alcohol or drug abuse or dependence disorder only; and (4) those with a current-year dual diagnosis of mental illness combined with substance abuse. Ultimately, the magnitude of the observed relationship between psychiatric diagnosis and violent behavior is influenced a great deal by whether persons with substance abuse and dependence and dual diagnoses are to be counted among those with mental disorders.

On the one hand, to be sure, having a major mental disorder even without substance abuse was associated with a significant increase in the prevalence of violence. However, it is important to note that since violence itself was a statistically rare event, the *absolute risk* of violence in the presence of mental illness remained low—about 7% in the course of a year—even while the *relative risk* was about three times as high as in the nondisordered population. On the other hand, having a substance abuse diagnosis was associated with a much higher risk of violence in both absolute and relative terms. Considering the adult lifetime index of violence that included fighting while drinking, the self-reported prevalence of violent behavior was as high as 55.2% among single-diagnosis substance abusers and 63.89% among those with dual diagnosis. For recent violence, the risk among substance abusers

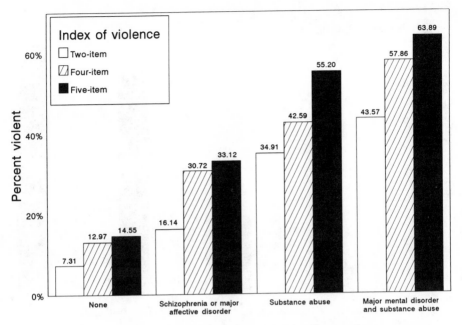

Figure 1. Lifetime prevalence of violent behavior by current-year major psychiatric diagnosis (%). Source: ECA data from Durham, N.C., and Los Angeles.

was generally more than twice as high as that observed in the group with only mental disorder and several times higher than the rate for those with no major disorder.

The group with dual diagnoses was of particular interest given the common notion that the combination of psychopathology with alcohol and drugs may be especially volatile, and might be associated with a much higher likelihood of violent behavior than is either condition alone. Indeed, the ECA findings showed the group with comorbidity to be more violence-prone than either group with single diagnoses—but in a pattern that suggested additive rather than truly synergistic effects (Swanson and Holzer 1991). While respondents with dual diagnoses had a much greater risk of violence than those with mental disorder alone, they had by comparison only a slightly (and in the one-year measures not significantly) greater risk than those with substance abuse alone. That is to say, substance abuse itself was associated with a very high relative risk for assaultive behavior, whether or not it occurred in the presence of other major psychopathology. Because of this "ceiling effect" with substance abuse alone, the addition of the relatively small risk attributable to other mental illness did not produce the magnitude of increase in risk that an interaction model would have predicted.

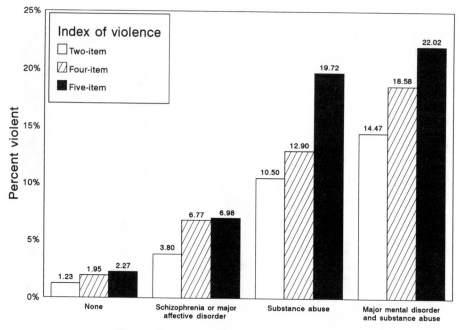

Current-year major psychiatric diagnosis

Figure 2.   One-year prevalence of violent behavior by major psychiatric diagnosis (%). Source: ECA data from Durham, N.C., and Los Angeles.

These patterns of increased rates by diagnosis varied little across the various indices of violence, though the prevalence of violence tended to increase rather uniformly in all categories with lifetime measures and those that included domestic violence and fighting while drinking. An exception to this pattern was noted in the subgroups with no major disorder and with mental disorder only, insofar as the addition of fighting while drinking (in the five-item index) identified very few respondents as violent who were not already coded as such by the four-item measure. This was likely due to the fact that controlling for comorbidity ahead of time in the summary classification of these disorders removed from the mentally ill group those who were violent *only* when drinking, i.e., those who denied committing violent acts in response to all of the other questions.

By contrast, among respondents with substance abuse problems—especially those with single diagnoses and no other psychopathology—the addition of the drinking and fighting item brought about a notable increase in the estimated prevalence of violence: from 42.5% to 55.2% reporting lifetime violence, and from 12.9% to 19.7% reporting recent violence. This finding is noteworthy because it suggests that these respondents perceived fighting while drinking to be in a separate category from other violent behavior about which

Table 4. Psychiatric disorder and indices of adult lifetime violent behavior

One-year major psychiatric diagnoses	Index of adult lifetime violent behavior		
	Two-item	Four-item	Five-item
No major disorder[a]			
Unweighted N	6297	6301	6307
Weighted N	6285.40	6287.60	6293.70
Prevalence of violence (%)	7.31	12.97	14.55
Schizophrenia spectrum or major affective disorder only			
Unweighted N	223	223	223
Weighted N	218.51	218.51	218.51
Prevalence of violence (%)	16.14	30.72	33.12
Odds ratio	2.44	2.97	2.91
Atributable risk	2.95	3.59	3.27
Chi-square (adjusted)[b]	13.03*	31.51**	31.42**
Substance abuse or dependence only			
Unweighted N	342	342	343
Weighted N	385.17	385.17	385.67
Prevalence of violence (%)	34.91	42.59	55.20
Odds ratio	6.80	5.00	7.26
Attributable risk	16.25	10.56	12.65
Chi-square (adjusted)	189.39**	141.22**	237.47**
Major mental disorder and substance abuse			
Unweighted N	49	49	50
Weighted N	57.63	57.63	59.64
Prevalence of violence (%)	43.57	57.86	63.89
Odds ratio	9.78	9.21	10.40
Attributable risk	3.19	2.40	2.37
Chi-square (adjusted)	59.13**	55.18**	62.61**

Note: Based on Epidemiologic Catchment Area data from Durham, N.C., and Los Angeles.

[a]Comparison category for odds ratios, attributable risks, and chi-square tests shown in the other three categories.

[b]Chi-square statistics have been divided by an average estimated design effect of 1.8 (see Holzer et al. 1986).

* $p < .001$.   ** $p < .0001$.

they had been asked without reference to alcohol use. Indeed, if substance-abusing respondents had not made this mental distinction, then the observed difference could not logically have occurred, since the other questions did not prima facie exclude violence while drinking. In other words, there should have been a complete overlap between assaultiveness in general and assaultiveness while drinking.

Tables 4 and 5 summarize various aspects of the association between psy-

Table 5. Psychiatric disorder and indices of recent violent behavior

One-year major psychiatric diagnoses	Index of violent behavior in one year		
	Two-item	Four-item	Five-item
No major disorder[a]			
Unweighted N	6297	6301	6307
Weighted N	6285.40	6287.60	6293.70
Prevalence of violence (%)	1.23	1.95	2.27
Schizophrenia spectrum or major affective disorder only			
Unweighted N	223	223	223
Weighted N	218.51	218.51	218.51
Prevalence of violence (%)	3.80	6.77	6.98
Odds ratio	3.18	3.64	3.23
Attributable risk	4.17	5.33	4.16
Chi-square (adjusted)[b]	5.93*	13.21**	11.00**
Substance abuse or dependence only			
Unweighted N	342	342	343
Weighted N	385.17	385.17	385.67
Prevalence of violence (%)	10.50	12.90	19.72
Odds ratio	9.43	7.44	10.59
Attributable risk	26.53	21.33	27.21
Chi-square (adjusted)	99.69***	96.14***	193.91***
Major mental disorder and substance abuse			
Unweighted N	49	49	50
Weighted N	57.63	57.63	59.64
Prevalence of violence (%)	14.47	18.58	22.02
Odds ratio	13.59	11.16	12.16
Attributable risk	5.67	4.85	4.76
Chi-square (adjusted)	41.61***	42.65***	53.44***

Note: Based on Epidemiologic Catchment Area data from Durham, N.C., and Los Angeles.

[a]Comparison category for odds ratios, attributable risks, and chi-square tests shown in the other three categories.

[b]Chi-square statistics have been divided by an average estimated design effect of 1.8 (see Holzer et al. 1986).

* $p < .05$.   ** $p < .001$.   *** $p < .0001$.

chiatric disorder and violent behavior, measured by alternative indices in two ECA sites. For each summary category of disorder, the bottom line shows a statistically significant positive association with self-reported violent behavior—irrespective of which index of violence was used, or which prevalence period. However, one must keep in mind that a data base as large as the ECA (even with only two sites) provides sufficient power to detect differences in rates which, while significant by the "greater than chance" criteria of statistics, might matter little in substantive or theoretical terms.

Odds ratios give a second perspective on the magnitude of increase in rates of violence observed in subgroups with psychiatric disorder. Epidemiologists typically consider an odds ratio of 2.5 to be the lower limit of strong association between two binary variables (Fleiss 1986). In these data, the odds for violence in the group with only major mental disorder versus no major disorder ranged from 2.4 to 2.9 in the lifetime indices, and from 3.1 to 3.6 in the one-year indices. The one odds ratio that fell slightly below the 2.5 cutoff was that with the two-item lifetime index, which excluded not only fighting while drinking but domestic violence. With this exception, the choice of index had little effect on the odds ratios; that is to say, the relative differences in the prevalence of violence between mentally ill and non-mentally ill groups held fairly constant, irrespective of the way violence was measured.

In the group with substance abuse only and the group with dual diagnoses, the odds for violence tended to be of much greater magnitude—ranging from 5.0 to 13.6—and more sensitive to differences in the indices of violence. In particular, the inclusion of the item on fighting while drinking in the five-item index produced not only a higher prevalence rate but a higher odds ratio. In other words, among people without alcohol or drug problems, whatever assaultive propensities may be manifested tended to be determined by factors other than drinking, so that the exclusion of this item from the index had little effect on the assessment of the prevalence of violence. In contrast, people whose only disorder was substance abuse or dependence were most often violent while drinking, so that an index lacking the drinking and fighting question tended to underestimate the prevalence of violence in the group. Thus, the alcohol-related item tended to heighten the difference in violence rates observed between the substance-abuse-only group and the no disorder group. Specifically, moving from the four-item to the five-item measure brought about an increase from 5.0 to 7.3 in the lifetime violence odds ratio in this group, and from 7.4 to 10.6 in the current-year ratio.

Attributable risk rates provide a way to place these odds in a broader context by addressing the question of whether or not mental disorder accounts for a sizable proportion of the total violence that occurs in the community. The attributable risk rates presented in tables 4 and 5 are affected by three components: (1) the total number of violent respondents in the sample; (2) the prevalence of violence in a given risk group; and (3) the size of that risk group relative to the total population. If the risk of violence associated with a given condition is very high, but the condition is extremely rare, then the presence of that condition in the community may still account only for a very small proportion of the total amount of violence that occurs. Conversely, if a risk condition is extremely common, it may account for a large proportion of events—even if the odds of violence occurring in any given case of the risk condition are relatively low. Both of these situations are, in turn, affected by the general prevalence of violence in the community. For example, if the predicted event is itself rare, then a rare risk factor may account for a greater proportion of events since there are fewer events to account for.

Attributable risk rates in these tables may be interpreted as the percentage reduction in the violent population that would occur if the group with a given risk factor (e.g., mental disorder) had a rate of violence as low as that observed in the comparison group without the risk factor (e.g., no disorder). Thus, given that mental disorder is associated with an increase in violence, the attributable risk statistic allows us to consider the hypothetical impact on violence that would be expected if mental disorder were eliminated or if people with mental disorders were no more violent than anyone else. Also, the attributable risk values for mutually exclusive categories of a given variable can be added together, yielding a sum which amounts to the proportion of total events accounted for by having any one of those aggregated conditions. The relationship of violence to mental disorder and substance abuse is very much the sort of phenomenon that should be interpreted in the light of attributable risk, as well as prevalence rates and odds ratios.

Consider table 5: In the category of mental disorder only, the one-year prevalence of violence and the attributable risk rates happen to be about the same. That is to say, in the course of one year 4% to 7% of people with only mental disorder were violent (depending on how measured), while their particular risk for being violent accounted for about 4% to 5% of the total violence in the population. In contrast, in the group with only substance abuse, the attributable risks were considerably higher (26.5% to 27.2%), for two reasons: Violence was more prevalent among alcohol and drug abusers (as high as 20%), and there were more people with substance abuse problems in the community than there were with major mental illness only. Finally, however, the group with dual diagnoses had rather low attributable risks (4.8% to 5.7%) even though their violence prevalence rates were the highest of all, since there were relatively few such people in the community to commit assaultive acts.

To sum up, the alternative indices of violence allow (or require) different assumptions and yield different conclusions. The lifetime measures identified several times more violent people than the one-year measures did; clearly, most people who reported committing assaultive acts at some time in their adult lives did not do so within the year preceding their ECA interview. One-year measures thus seem to offer a more realistic assessment of the proximal risk of violence that may be associated with current mental illness. Yet, because of certain ECA-DIS idiosyncrasies, these current-interval measures require the assumption that a global recency probe for violence *or other antisocial symptoms* did, in fact, almost always correctly identify the recency of the violence that the respondent reported. Lifetime measures circumvent this inherent methodological problem by answering a different, entirely retrospective question about risk: given a population that *currently* meets criteria for having serious mental illness, what is the chance that they have *ever* been violent since age 18? But while this information is interesting, it does not allow us to infer a temporal connection between mental illness and violence, nor to estimate future risk within a practical time frame.

Within each of these intervals, the choice of how many items to include—two, four, or five—also affects the estimation of the prevalence of violence among the mentally ill. The minimal two-item index offers the advantage of including only those questions asked of all respondents, irrespective of marital status. Yet it carries the disadvantage of excluding domestic violence unless a weapon was used and, thus, underestimates the true extent of dangerousness.

The four-item index offers the advantage of including only those items which are independent of the diagnostic criteria for alcohol abuse or dependence disorder. Yet by excluding the question about fighting while drinking, it results in an underestimate of the prevalence of assaultive behavior among people with substance abuse or comorbidity.

In spite of these irregularities, all of the indices analyzed herein support the following basic findings:

- While most mentally ill people do not commit assaultive acts, nevertheless serious mental disorder by itself is quite significantly associated with violence—as shown by odds ratios in the range of about 2.4 to 3.6

- Since serious mental illness by itself is quite rare, the attributable risk for violence associated with it is not very high—in the range of about 3.0% to 5.3%

- Mentally disordered individuals with substance abuse comorbidity are significantly more likely to be violent than those with mental disorder alone—as shown by odds ratios ranging from about 3.1 to 4.3

These findings will be examined more specifically in the context of multivariate models presented below.

Sociodemographic relationships, diagnosis and violence. The findings presented in the remainder of this chapter are based on analysis using an original index reported in a previously published study (Swanson et al. 1990)—the five-item one-year estimate. Several reasons justify this choice. First, a one-year estimate provides a more practical indication of the risk for violence represented by people with current mental disorder. Second, given the prominent role that alcohol abuse and domestic relationships play in violence in the community, an index should both identify violence directed at spouses and children and explicitly include violence while drinking—especially, given our focus on mental illness, since persons with mental illness are at risk for substance abuse problems as well. As argued elsewhere (Swanson and Holzer 1991), a person with a psychiatric disorder who engages in fighting while drinking should not be excluded as a false positive for violence associated with mental illness. Such a person may or may not meet criteria for alcohol abuse or dependence, but is nonetheless mentally ill (by DSM-DIS standards) and violent. Third, the five-item index allows us to add a third site—Baltimore—and several thousand cases to the data set, which considerably enhances the statistical power of these data to examine violence in a multivariate context.

To what extent are the effects of mental illness on violence conditioned by sociodemographic variables? In bivariate analyses it was found that several characteristics—being young, male, of low socioeconomic status, nonwhite (black or Hispanic), or single, separated, or divorced—were significantly associated with committing assaultive acts. With the exception of marital status, the association of each of these demographic variables with violence in the ECA data has been presented elsewhere (Swanson et al. 1990). As a summary of these earlier findings, table 6 displays the prevalence of violence by gender, age group and socioeconomic status—without consideration of psychiatric diagnosis. Race was not included as a relevant category in table 6 because (as will be shown later) when SES was held constant, race was not found to be significantly associated with violent behavior.

The complexities of the linkage between race and ethnicity, socioeconomic status, psychiatric disorder, and violence may be illustrated by the following findings. Among respondents with no major psychiatric disorder, 2.7% of nonwhites versus 1.7% of whites were identified as violent—a trivial difference in substantive terms, since both rates were very low. By contrast, among respondents with major mental disorder or substance abuse—where rates of violence were generally higher—the relationship of violence to race and ethnicity stands out more sharply. For example, in the dual diagnosis group, 34.6% of nonwhites versus 14.1% of whites were violent. Similarly, among respondents with a history of both psychiatric hospitalization and arrest, nonwhites were twice as likely to be violent as whites (41.9% vs. 19.1%). Yet these differences may be attributed largely to the prior association between socioeconomic status and race and ethnicity. In general, nonwhites were more than twice as likely as whites to be in the lowest SES group (33% vs. 14%). In the group with mental disorders and substance abuse, nearly 80% of the nonwhite respondents were in the lowest two SES ranks. And as will be shown in multivariate models to follow, while SES emerged as a significant predictor of violent behavior when controlling for other variables, race and ethnicity did not.

The interpretation of findings regarding marital status and violence proved

Table 6. Current-year prevalence of violent behavior by gender, age group, and socioeconomic status

	Age group			
	18–29	30–44	45–64	65+
Males				
SES	N^a = (1600)	(1278)	(1272)	(567)
0–25	16.09	7.65	3.34	0.20
26–50	11.68	6.23	2.00	0.30
51–75	8.06	4.57	2.14	0.00
76–100	6.05	2.56	0.29	0.00
Females				
SES	N^a = (1635)	(1377)	(1472)	(822)
0–25	9.11	3.92	0.93	0.00
26–50	5.01	3.47	0.25	0.00
51–75	2.46	1.77	0.54	0.00
76–100	3.27	1.17	1.01	0.00

Note: The information in this table was previously published in Swanson et al. 1990. Violence and psychiatric disorder in the community: Evidence from the Epidemiologic Catchment Area surveys. *Hospital and Community Psychiatry* 41:761–70. Reprinted with permission.

[a] Weighted Ns are rounded; percentages may not correspond to whole numbers.

equally problematic. As with race, marital status tended to be confounded with other variables that were significant correlates of violence. For example, widows had much lower rates of violence than did the incumbents of any other marital status, but this was due mostly to the fact that widows were disproportionately elderly and female.

As shown previously (Swanson et al. 1990), a significant proportion of assaultive acts identified in these data were directed against spouses, cohabitants, or children. Respondents who had never been married, and had never lived with someone as though married, were not asked about hitting a spouse or partner since they had never had the opportunity to do so. Moreover, never-coupled respondents typically had little opportunity to engage in child abuse; most of them had never become parents or played a parental role. In sum, two of the five items on the full index of violence in the ECA were less applicable to people of a particular marital status (never married). Rates of violence by marital status thus need to be interpreted in a manner similar to the comparison of different indices shown in tables 3 and 4.

In bivariate analyses, the never-married subgroup had the highest one-year rates of assaultive behavior—6.43%, compared with 2.5% among married people ($p < .0001$)—notwithstanding the fact that these respondents typically had fewer ways of being identified as violent by the DIS. It is important to note, however, that the never-married category was more likely to include violence-prone respondents, as defined by other risk factors. In particular, younger adults, males, and those with substance abuse and major mental illnesses were all significantly more likely to be in the never-married group: 60.4% of respondents aged 18 to 29 years had never been married versus only 14.5% of those aged 30 to 45 years ($p < .0001$); 42.8% of respondents with major mental disorder and substance abuse had never been married versus only 24.2% of those with no major disorder ($p < .0001$). These relationships suggest that the observed effect of marital status on violence may be somewhat spurious, as it masks the underlying effects of age, gender, psychiatric disorder and substance abuse. Moreover, it suggests that the five-item index (which asks about spouse battering and child abuse) may contain a bias in the direction of *underestimating* the prevalence of violence among the mentally ill (who are less likely to be married), relative to those who are not mentally ill.

Regarding the confounding of marital status with age in particular, when age category was held constant the effect of never having been married was found not to be significantly associated with violence. Moreover, adult *lifetime* rates of violence—presumably less sensitive to the age effect—were the same in the single and married groups—15.9% and 16.2%. In the presence of controls for other demographic variables, only one current marital status proved to be significantly associated with violence: being separated or divorced.

A causal interpretation of the linkage between divorce and violence remains largely opaque to these cross-sectional data. On the one hand, to conceptualize divorce as a risk factor or predictor of violence begs the question of whether, in any given case, domestic violence came first and broke up the marriage in question. A third factor such as alcoholism may have precipitated both violence and divorce. On the other hand, from a risk-assessment point of view, it is simply the case that people with a history of divorce are more likely than never-divorced people to be violent.

Multivariate models. Logistic regression analysis was used to examine simultaneously the relative effects on violence of selected sociodemographic variables, substance abuse, and major mental illness. Table 7 presents a model that included only sociodemographic variables. All predictors were coded as dichotomous dummy variables, excluding the following as reference categories: female, over 65 years of age, upper socioeconomic status, married, and white non-Hispanic. Chi-square values were adjusted for average design effects of 1.8 (Holzer et al. 1986). This model shows that the most significant demographic predictors of violence were the following: being male, aged 18 to 29 years, of lower socioeconomic status, and separated or divorced. In the presence of controls for demographic covariation, the effects of being in the upper-middle SES category, single, widowed, or black or Hispanic were *not* significantly associated with violent behavior.

Table 8 presents a model that includes only the significant demographic

Table 7. Logistic regression model of predictors of violent behavior in the last year: demographic variables only

Variable	Parameter estimate	Standard error	Adjusted chi-square
Intercept	−8.6179	0.9912	41.99****
Male	0.9495	0.1180	36.01****
Age 18–29	4.7765	0.9742	13.36***
Age 30–44	4.0497	0.9749	9.59**
Age 45–64	2.8421	0.9780	4.69*
Lower SES	1.1904	0.2275	15.21****
Lower middle SES	0.8051	0.2075	8.36**
Upper middle SES	0.3572	0.2097	1.61^{ns}
Single	0.1555	0.1352	0.72^{ns}
Separated/divorced	0.7682	0.1612	12.56***
Widowed	0.0728	0.5134	0.01^{ns}
Black	−0.2389	0.1354	1.73^{ns}
Hispanic	0.0301	0.1508	0.02^{ns}

Note: Weighted N = 10,024. Weighted N violent = 368. Chi-square for covariates: 380.818 with 12 DF ($p < 0.0001$). Association of predicted probabilities and observed responses:

Concordant = 78.9%	Somers' D = 0.596	
Discordant = 19.4%	Gamma = 0.606	
Tied = 1.7%	c = 0.798	

* $p < .05$.   ** $p < .01$.   *** $p < .001$.   **** $p < .0001$.

variables from the first model, with effects of the DIS psychiatric diagnoses and comorbidity added in. These were examined by coding respondents into six categories: (1) no disorder; (2) anxiety disorder; (3) affective disorder; (4) schizophrenia or schizophreniform disorder; (5) alcohol or drug abuse or dependence only; (6) dual diagnosis of mental disorder combined with substance abuse. Categories 2 through 6 were included in the model as dichotomous dummy variables, with group 1 (no disorder) as the excluded (reference) category.

Categories 2 through 4 were coded hierarchically, i.e., respondents were assigned to the diagnostic group with the highest number for which they met criteria: anxiety plus affective disorder was coded as affective disorder; affective disorder plus schizophrenia was coded as schizophrenia. Category 5 was coded if the respondent met criteria for any psychoactive substance use disorder *without* having one of the diagnoses in groups 2 through 4. Category 6 was coded if the respondent had substance abuse combined with at least one of the disorders in groups 2 through 4. Category 1 was a residual group composed of respondents who did not have any disorder coded in groups 2 through 6.

The model shown in table 8 demonstrates that, except for anxiety disorders, all of the diagnostic categories were significantly associated with violence. Among these diagnostic variables, substance abuse and comorbidity were by

124   JEFFREY W. SWANSON

Table 8. Logistic regression model of predictors of violent behavior in the last year: demographic variables and psychiatric diagnoses

Variable	Parameter estimate	Standard error	Adjusted chi-square
Intercept	−5.9257	0.2221	395.47****
Male	0.6203	0.1268	13.29***
Age 18–29	2.1837	0.1909	72.71****
Age 30–44	1.3606	0.2072	23.97****
Lower SES	0.6918	0.1539	11.22***
Lower middle SES	0.3395	0.1293	3.83*
Separated/divorced	0.5061	0.1590	5.62*
Diagnosis			
Anxiety disorder only	0.1872	0.2155	0.42ns
Affective disorder only	1.2209	0.2800	10.57****
Schizophrenia only	1.2133	0.4029	5.04*
Substance abuse only	2.1249	0.1401	127.72****
Mental disorder and substance abuse	2.1001	0.1990	61.87****

Note: Weighted N = 10,024. Weighted N violent = 368. Chi-square for covariates: 617.564 with 11 DF ($p < 0.0001$). Association of predicted probabilities and observed responses:
Concordant = 83.3% Somers' D = 0.687
Discordant = 14.6% Gamma = 0.701
Tied = 2.1% c = 0.843
* $p < .05$. ** $p < .01$. *** $p < .001$. **** $p < .0001$.

far the strongest predictors of violence. Note that the size of chi-square values and associated probabilities are affected both by the magnitude of prevalence rate differences between groups (or difference in violence probabilities, adjusting for covariation) and by the size of the groups; thus, while respondents with schizophrenia had a somewhat higher probability of violence than those with affective disorders (see figure 3), as a variable in the model schizophrenia appeared less significant because there were fewer people with this disorder than with affective illness.

Figure 3 portrays the probabilities of violence predicted by the model for males and females by psychiatric diagnosis. It is clear from these probabilities that anxiety disorder by itself added virtually nothing to the risk of violence. As mentioned, those with schizophrenia were somewhat more violence-prone than those with affective disorders, according to the model. Those with substance abuse and dual diagnoses had the highest probability of violence. The addition of mental disorder to substance abuse did not increase the risk predicted by the model for those with substance abuse alone.

Figure 3 shows that in every diagnostic category, the predicted probabilities of violence for males were higher than for females. This finding contrasts with unadjusted prevalence rates previously published (Swanson et al. 1990), which showed that among respondents with major mental disorders and substance abuse diagnoses, males and females had virtually equal rates of vio-

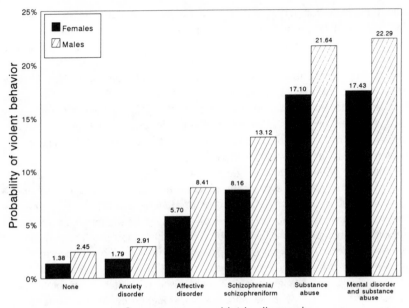

Current-year psychiatric diagnosis

Figure 3.   Predicted one-year probability of violent behavior by psychiatric diagnosis and gender (%). Estimates predicted by logistic regression model specifying covariates of gender, age, marital status, and SES (see table 8). Source: ECA data from Durham, N.C., Los Angeles, and Baltimore.

lence—a pattern also found in a recent study of acutely disturbed psychiatric patients undergoing short-term hospitalization (Binder and McNiel 1990).

The difference between these two analyses of the effect of gender on violence using the ECA data may be explained by the covariation of gender with other demographic variables that contribute to violence and disorder. First, female substance abusers were significantly more likely than male substance abusers to be in the younger (higher risk for violence) age groups. Conversely, the group of male substance abusers included a greater proportion of older persons, suggesting that males tend to drink and abuse drugs for more of their adult life than do females with the same problem. These older male substance abusers were, in turn, less likely to be currently violent, which brought down the one-year rate for males relative to females with substance abuse.

Second, females with psychiatric disorders were more likely than their male counterparts to have been married, borne children, separated, and divorced—which, for reasons already discussed, added further to their risk not only of committing assaultive acts in a domestic context but of being identified as violent on the DIS in particular.

Third, for reasons not unrelated to their increased divorce rate, females with alcohol or drug problems or major mental disorders were more likely than their male counterparts to be in the lower socioeconomic strata, which, in turn, significantly increased their risk for violence. Thus, adjustments for age, marital status, and socioeconomic status in the multivariate model tended to highlight the underlying effect of gender on violence (shown in figure 3), which was masked in the unadjusted prevalence rates among those with substance abuse and mental disorders.

One of the most remarkable findings of the ECA surveys was that fairly large numbers of persons met formal diagnostic criteria for major mental disorders, yet had never been identified or treated by the mental health care system. Inpatient treatment was particularly rare; only 16% of community respondents with one-year single diagnoses of major affective disorder or schizophrenia reported ever being admitted to a hospital for a mental health problem. People with single diagnoses of alcohol or other drug dependence were even less likely to have received inpatient treatment: only about 8% reported a hospitalization for a problem with their substance abuse or mental health. However, having a major psychiatric illness with a concurrent substance abuse diagnosis increased the likelihood of hospitalization to 38%.

Dual diagnosis also increased the likelihood of contact with the criminal justice system: 27% of those who had major mental disorder combined with alcohol or drug dependence had a history of arrest, compared to 13% of those with only mental health diagnoses. Moreover, those with dual diagnoses were about three times more likely than those with single diagnoses of either type to have been labeled by both criminal justice and mental health systems (about 14% vs. 4%).

Clearly, societal response to violent behavior falls at the interface between the criminal justice and mental health systems. While personal assaultiveness may, on the one hand, be a feature of psychiatric illness it is also, of course, a criminal infraction that may receive legal sanctions including the loss of personal liberty. The ECA data demonstrate that respondents with dual diagnoses are more likely to be violent; in turn, those who are violent increase their chances of both psychiatric hospitalization and arrest.

For the present analysis, respondents were sorted into four groups: (1) those who had neither been hospitalized for a mental health problem nor been arrested; (2) those with at least one psychiatric hospitalization but no arrests; (3) those who had been arrested but never hospitalized; and (4) those whose history included both psychiatric hospitalization and arrest. While there exist a variety of reasons for arrest and psychiatric hospitalization, and a range of other societal responses to deviant behavior, the juxtaposition of these two particular variables provided at least a general way to delineate and compare subgroups of ECA respondents who have had serious contact with the mental health system only, the criminal justice system only, or both. Such a classification then allows at least some assessment of the extent to which institutional contact and labeling was associated with violent behavior by persons with psychiatric disorder. In a sense, one can use these ECA variables to approximate a comparison between community populations and selected clinical or institutional populations.

Table 9 presents a logistic regression model that includes three groups of predictors of violence: demographic, diagnostic, and institutional contact indicators. The adequacy of the model's overall fit is shown at the foot of the table, in the association of predicted probabilities and observed responses.

In the presence of these additional variables theoretically linked to violence, some of the demographic effects were in fact diminished, as would be expected. In particular, only the lowest of the SES categories remained a significant predictor of violence. Also, the effect attributable to being divorced or separated became nonsignificant.

For the model shown in table 9, the psychiatric diagnostic variables were aggregated into four mutually exclusive categories: (1) no major disorder; (2) major mental illness only; (3) substance abuse only; and (4) mental disorder and substance abuse combined. Groups 2 through 4 were included in the model as dichotomous dummy variables, with group 1 (no major disorder) as the excluded (reference) category. The results show that, after controlling for covariation with the demographic and institutional variables, all three diagnostic categories remained significantly associated with recent violence at sig-

Table 9. Logistic regression model of predictors of violent behavior in the last year: demographics, psychiatric diagnoses, history of mental hospitalization and arrest

Variable	Parameter estimate	Standard error	Adjusted chi-square
Intercept	−5.9204	0.2218	395.68****
Male	0.4633	0.1289	7.17**
Age 18–29	2.2559	0.1938	75.24****
Age 30–44	1.3548	0.2094	23.26****
Lower SES	0.6125	0.1553	8.64**
Lower middle SES	0.2636	0.1305	2.27ns
Separated/divorced	0.4200	0.1611	3.77ns
MH diagnosis only	0.9760	0.2448	8.83**
Substance abuse only	1.8575	0.1341	106.56****
MH and substance abuse	1.8671	0.3060	20.68****
Psych hosp only	0.5308	0.3062	1.67ns
Arrest only	0.8667	0.1463	19.49****
Psych hosp and arrest	1.6062	0.2982	16.12****

Note: Weighted $N = 10,024$. Weighted N violent $= 368$. Chi-square for covariates: 668.509 with 12 DF ($p < 0.0001$). Association of predicted probabilities and observed responses:

Concordant = 84.4%   Somers' D = 0.710
Discordant = 13.4%   Gamma   = 0.726
Tied   = 2.2%   c   = 0.855
* $p < .05$.   ** $p < .01$.   *** $p < .001$.   **** $p < .0001$.

nificance levels of $p < .001$ or better. Clearly, once again, substance abuse and dual diagnoses were much more strongly related to violence than was major mental disorder alone.

Among the categories of institutional contact, a history of arrest and a combined history of arrest and psychiatric hospitalization were highly significant predictors of recent violent behavior. However, a history of mental hospitalization without arrest was *not* significant in the presence of controls for diagnosis. That is to say, among people who had never been arrested and were not currently mentally ill, merely being a former mental patient was not a significant risk factor for violent behavior in the community.

This finding is illustrated in figure 4, which presents the model's predicted probabilities of violent behavior by major psychiatric diagnosis and history of mental hospitalization and arrest. Among people who were not assessed by the DIS to have a major disorder in the year preceding interview, the subgroup with no institutional contact had a predicted violence rate of 1.63%, while the subgroup of never-arrested former patients had a slightly (but not significantly) higher rate of 2.30%.

Figure 4 also suggests that for the group with major mental disorders only, the combination of arrest and hospitalization produces a much higher relative

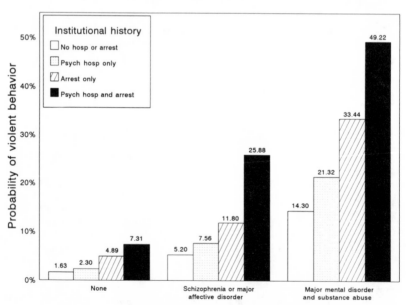

Current-year major psychiatric diagnosis

Figure 4.   Predicted one-year probability of violent behavior by major psychiatric diagnosis, history of psychiatric hospitalization, and arrest (%). Estimates predicted by logistic regression model specifying covariates of gender, age, marital status, and SES (see table 9). Source: ECA data from Durham, N.C., Los Angeles, and Baltimore.

risk of violence than does either condition alone. Specifically, in this diagnostic category the violence odds ratio for mental hospitalization alone was 1.5, while for arrest alone it was 2.6. However, for hospitalization combined with arrest, the violence odds ratio was 6.4—greater than the product of the odds for the single conditions alone.

The most plausible interpretation for this finding is that the (relatively small) subgroup of violence-prone individuals among all those with serious mental illness in the community were the least likely to escape notice both by the criminal justice system and by the mental health system. Therefore, the subgroup of mentally disordered persons who had been identified by both of these systems had been selected, in effect, for violent behavior, which indirectly indicates the severity of their disorder or deviance.

Figure 5 demonstrates the single and combined effects of all three categories of risk factors. The rates shown are predicted probabilities of violent behavior in the same categories defined in figure 4, now limited to a high-risk demographic subpopulation: males aged 18 to 44 years, of low to low-middle socioeconomic status. The predicted risk values for violence in this sociodemographic group range from 5.41% (no major diagnosis, no history of arrest or psychiatric hospitalization) to 64.45% (major mental illness with substance abuse, history of both arrest and hospitalization).

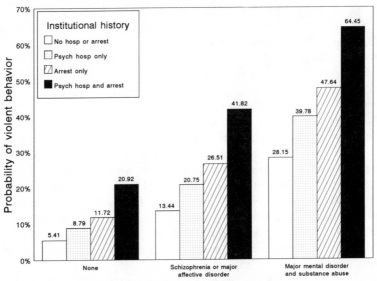

Figure 5.   Predicted one-year probability of violent behavior by major psychiatric diagnosis, history of psychiatric hospitalization, and arrest: Lower-SES males aged 18–44 years (%). Estimates predicted by logistic regression model specifying covariates of gender, age, marital status, and SES (see table 9). Source: ECA data from Durham, Los Angeles, N.C., and Baltimore.

Table 10. Effects of major psychiatric disorder on probability of violent behavior
controlling for covariates in logistic regression model (shown in table 8)

	No major disorder[a]	Major MH disorder only	Substance abuse only	Major MH and substance abuse
Unweighted N	8941	340	562	78
Weighted N	8965.10	319.07	654.87	85.30
Prevalence of violent behavior (%)	2.10	7.29	21.01	22.82
Predicted probability of violent behavior (%)	1.87	6.85	20.85	23.97
Odds ratio (adjusted)	—	3.94	13.67	16.79
Attributable risk (adjusted)	—	4.35	33.97	4.89
Chi-square (adjusted)	—	8.83*	106.56**	20.68**

[a]Comparison category.
* $p < .01$.   ** $p < .0001$.

Table 10 summarizes the association between the major psychiatric diagnoses and violent behavior, with controls for the covariates shown in table 9. Of note, once again, are the differences between the odds ratios and attributable risk rates where substance abuse is concerned. The odds, calculated on the basis of predicted probabilities, were highest in the dual diagnosis group (16.79), but not a great deal higher than in the substance-abuse-only group (13.67). Both of these contrasted with the much lower (but still significant) odds ratio found for mental disorder only (3.94).

A somewhat different picture emerged from the attributable risk analysis. In these terms, it was found that the risk for violence among those with mental disorder only and among those with dual diagnoses accounted for about equal proportions of the total population of violent respondents—4.35% and 4.89%, respectively. This shows that the relatively high risk associated with substance abuse comorbidity (predicted probability = 23.97%) was balanced by the small number of persons in this category (weighted N = 85). Conversely, the relatively low risk among persons with only mental disorders (predicted probability = 6.85%) was balanced by the larger number of persons in this category (weighted N = 319). However, in the category of persons with only alcohol or drug abuse or dependence disorder, the attributable risk for violence was higher—33.97%—because both the probability of violence and the number of people in the category were relatively high (20.85%, weighted N = 655).

Table 11 shows a regression model that was specified identically to the model presented in table 9, except that the independent variable was the four-item, two-site index of violence that excluded fighting while drinking. While the effects were generally comparable in the two models, it is noteworthy that the effect of male gender was reduced to nonsignificance in table 11. The

Table 11. Logistic regression model of violent behavior using alternative four-item index of violent behavior

Variable	Parameter estimate	Standard error	Adjusted chi-square
Intercept	−5.5752	0.2630	249.63****
Male	0.2369	0.1657	1.13ns
Age 18–29	1.9490	0.2385	37.09****
Age 30–44	1.0949	0.2608	9.79**
Lower SES	0.6086	0.1985	5.22*
Lower middle SES	0.1074	0.1738	0.21ns
Separated/divorced	0.4976	0.2159	2.95ns
MH diagnosis only	0.9485	0.3066	5.32*
Substance abuse only	1.3309	0.1967	25.42****
MH and substance abuse	1.7324	0.4030	10.27***
Psych hosp only	0.7289	0.3837	2.01ns
Arrest only	1.1010	0.2045	16.09****
Psych hosp and arrest	1.7203	0.4493	8.14**

Note: Weighted N = 6,926. Weighted N violent = 198. Chi-square for covariates: 261.169 with 12 DF ($p < 0.0001$). Association of predicted probabilities and observed responses:

Concordant = 80.3%	Somers' D = 0.634
Discordant = 16.8%	Gamma = 0.653
Tied = 2.9%	c = 0.817

* $p < .05$.   ** $p < .01$.   *** $p < .001$.   **** $p < .0001$.

most plausible reason for this finding has to do with the higher prevalence of alcohol abuse and associated violence among males. Specifically, without the item about fighting while drinking, the index underidentified violent males, so that in the pared down "violent" group males did not significantly outnumber females.

Implications for Research

The ECA surveys have provided the first large-sample estimates of the general prevalence of assaultive behavior among persons with (and without) diagnosable mental disorders in the community. They have also provided the first estimates of the "true prevalence" of mental disorders among those with (and without) a self-reported history of violence in the community. Now that the basic findings from these large general samples are available, what is their significance for the current state of research, and for future investigations, in the area of mental disorders and violence?

These findings supply a context—a broad sense of perspective—for interpreting other research on the linkage of violent behavior to psychiatric illness and substance abuse. On the one hand, we now have some hard numbers to back up the notion that persons with serious and persistent mental illnesses are on average more violent than the rest of the population. Even those mentally ill persons who are not substance abusers, and have not been selected into treatment settings, bear a two- to threefold increase in risk for assaultive behavior, compared to their counterparts without psychiatric illness. On the other hand, we now have compelling evidence that the mentally ill, as a group, do not pose a high risk in absolute terms. Only about 7% of all those with major mental disorder (but without substance abuse) engage in any assaultive behavior in a given year.

Researchers have known all along that studies of violent behavior and mental illness in selected populations—treated patients, prisoners, and the like—tend to produce a biased view of the association between these phenomena. However, it has been difficult to estimate the magnitude of such a bias. The ECA data speak to this issue directly by allowing a comparison of the prevalence of violence among mentally ill persons with (and without) a history of psychiatric hospitalization and arrest. Specifically, for example, these findings suggest that studies of mentally ill persons sampled from populations of previously hospitalized and arrested individuals would tend to overestimate the prevalence of violence by a factor greater than three for those with mental disorder only (26% vs. 7%) and a factor greater than two for those with dual diagnoses (49% vs. 22%).

At the same time, the ECA findings clearly implicate active psychiatric symptomatology—and not merely a history of mental hospitalization—in the association of mental illness with assaultive behavior. Otherwise it would be difficult to explain the relative absence of current violent behavior in the ECA's group of former inpatients (with no arrests) who were free from psychopathology in the past year: only 2.3% of this group were estimated to be violent by the ECA model, not significantly more than the rate of 1.6% among their counterparts without a history of psychiatric hospitalization.

Moreover, the ECA analysis underscores the importance of multivariate, contextualized, and life-course approaches to the study of violence and mental illness. While serious mental disorder emerges as one significant factor that helps to explain (or statistically predict) violence, it is only one (and probably not the most important) determinant. Variables such as age, gender, marital history, economic status, education, and position in social strata all define conditions under which mental disorder may be more or less likely to engender assaultive behavior.

As a general epidemiologic survey, the ECA project might seem on the surface to offer little to the fields of basic and clinical research concerned with the psychobiological processes underlying the etiology of violence. Indirectly, however, these findings do contribute to the fundamental understanding of violent behavior. For one thing, the ECA study highlights important questions about why and how different variables interact in the occurrence of violent acts—questions that should be pursued further at various levels of scientific inquiry. Such questions may include the following: How might the occurrence of major mental disorder attentuate male-female differences in the predisposition to violence? Do certain patterns of psychopathology interact "synergistically" with substance abuse to produce violent behavior? Why do rates of violent behavior fall off so dramatically with age?

Furthermore, the ECA might suggest likely target groups for the most productive investigations of the mechanisms linking psychopathology to aggressive behavior—such as young males with schizophrenia, with and without substance abuse comorbidity. For their part, psychosocial researchers may be interested in examining the occurrence of violence in specific subpopulations defined both by sociodemographic and diagnostic characteristics—such as young married females with major depression. They may look to the ECA to provide a general comparative epidemiologic profile of violence in such populations and their natural "control groups" in the community.

The ECA project also teaches some lessons by negative example, making it clear that future epidemiologic research on the topic should be done somewhat differently. Most importantly, a future mental health survey in the community should gather much more detailed information on specific episodes of violent behavior, independent of psychiatric diagnostic assessments. Ideally, dimensions to be measured should include the following: severity, frequency, timing, and recency of assaultive behavior; precipitating life events, targets, location, context, and consequences; presence of active psychiatric symptoms, medication, or psychoactive substance intoxication at the time violent behavior occurs; and subject's interpretation of violent episodes. This sort of research should be done longitudinally and should supplement self-report assessments with other sources of information. Finally, it should take a life-historical approach in attempting to reconstruct, insofar as possible, the key influences on the identity formation and development of persons who later commit violent acts toward others.

Of course, such a community survey of violent behavior on the scale of the ECA project would be enormously expensive and difficult to justify in light of other research priorities. Meanwhile, however, there is more to be gleaned from further analysis of the existing data. The study presented herein conceptualized mental disorder only in terms of diagnoses and groups of diagnoses. However, the ECA also includes data on individual symptoms and groups of symptoms reported by respondents who may or may not have met criteria for a given diagnostic category. It would be possible to examine the linkage of violent behavior to various symptom patterns—for example, paranoia and delusions combined with anxiety. It is also possible to approximate an assessment of chronicity with the ECA data by considering the age of onset of symptoms for people who meet criteria for a disorder. Comparisons on the violence indices could be made between respondents with early versus late onset of psychiatric illness.

Thus, more could be done to unpack the effects of specific types of psychiatric malfunctioning related to violence, such as impairment in the capacity to control aggressive impulses, to correctly perceive and evaluate threatening versus nonthreatening situations, to anticipate the consequences of actions, and to empathize and interact successfully with others. In this light, the ECA data may contribute to ongoing debates regarding the place of violence in psychiatric nosology: When should violence be construed as a primary manifestation—or *symptom*—of psychiatric illness? When it is better viewed as an *associated feature,* not formally part of an illness itself but commonly to be expected in the presence of the illness? And when is violence to be seen only as a rare *complication* for the treatment of a psychiatric illness?

Other promising analyses include a more detailed look at the institutional history of ECA respondents in connection to violence. The analyses conducted so far have examined only one variable related to criminal justice history (ever arrested) and one variable related to mental health services utilization (ever hospitalized for a mental health problem). Obviously, more information exists in the ECA to examine these two important domains in relation to violence. Variables that may be relevant include, for example, history of felony convictions, recent use of outpatient mental health services, and dependency on public financial entitlements.

In addition to the core items in the five-site ECA data, some of the individual site data sets include variables that could shed more light on the violence–mental disorder relationship. For example, the Durham site included additional items on social support, and assessments of the history of childhood traumatic events and abuse—both of which may correlate in significant ways to adult violent behavior. Finally, it might prove productive to analyze the violence data in the ECA institutional samples and in the second wave of community data.

In conclusion it should be noted that the ECA study—for all its faults that stand out when viewed through our current "retrospectoscope"—represents a major advance in the study of violence and mental disorder. It both confirms and corrects previous understanding and suggests new avenues for future research. And there is surely more to come, especially now that the core ECA data are available in the public domain.

Acknowledgments

Some of the findings that appear in this chapter have been described previously in Swanson et al. (1990). The data analysis presented herein was supported in part by a contract from the National Institute of Mental Health and by additional funding from the John D. and Catherine T. MacArthur Foundation Research Network on Mental Health and the Law. The Epidemiologic Catchment Area program was supported in part by grants from the National

Institute of Mental Health. Principal collaborators at the NIMH were Darrel
A. Regier, Ben Z. Locke, and William W. Eaton; the NIMH project officer
was Carl A. Taube. The principal investigators and coinvestigators from the
five sites were: Jerome K. Myers, Myrna M. Weissman, and Gary L. Tischler
(Yale University); Morton Kramer, Ernest Gruenberg, and Sam Shapiro
(Johns Hopkins University); Lee N. Robins and John Helzer (Washington
University, Saint Louis); Dan Blazer and Linda George (Duke University);
Richard L. Hough, Marvin Karno, Javier I. Escobar, M. Audrey Burnam,
and Dianne M. Timbers (University of California, Los Angeles). The author
is indebted to Charles E. Holzer III, whose collaboration on earlier analyses
of the ECA violence data greatly facilitated the present study. Richard Lan-
derman provided additional technical assistance. Responsibility for the findings described in this chapter rests with the author alone and not with the
original ECA investigators or the National Institute of Mental Health.

References

American Psychiatric Association. 1980. *Diagnostic and statistical manual of mental
    disorders.* 3d ed. (DSM III). Washington, D.C.: American Psychiatric Association.
American Psychiatric Association. 1987. *Diagnostic and statistical manual of mental
    disorders.* 3d ed., rev. (DSM III-R). Washington, D.C.: American Psychiatric
    Association.
Binder, R. L., and D. E. McNiel. 1990. The relationship of gender to violent behav-
    ior in acutely disturbed psychiatric patients. *Journal of Clinical Psychiatry* 51:
    110–14.
Dohrenwend, B. P. 1990. Socioeconomic status (SES) and psychiatric disorders: Are
    the issues still compelling? *Hospital and Community Psychiatry* 25:41–47.
Eaton, W. W., and L. G. Kessler, eds. 198.*. *Epidemiological field methods in psy-
    chiatry: The NIMH Epidemiologic Catchment Area study.* New York: Academic
    Press.
Fleiss, J., J. B. Williams, and A. F. Dubro. 1986. The logistic regression analysis of
    psychiatric data. *Journal of Psychiatric Research* 20:145–209.
Holzer, C. E., B. M. Shea, J. W. Swanson, P. J. Leaf, J. K. Myers, L. K. George,
    and P. M. Bednarski. 1986. The increased risk for specific psychiatric disorders
    among persons of low socioeconomic status: Evidence from the NIMH Epidemio-
    logic Catchment Area study. *American Journal of Social Psychiatry* 6:259–71.
Holzer, C. E., E. Spitznagel, K. B. Jordan, D. M. Timbers, L. G. Kessler, and J. C.
    Anthony. 1985. Sampling the household population. In W. W. Eaton and L. G.
    Kessler, eds. 1985. *Epidemiological field methods in psychiatry: The NIMH Epi-
    demiologic Catchment Area study.* New York: Academic Press.
Leaf, P. J., J. K. Myers, and L. T. McEvoy. 1991. Procedures used in the Epidemio-
    logic Catchment Area study. In L. N. Robins and D. A. Regier, eds. 1991. *Psychi-
    atric disorders in America: The Epidemiologic Catchment Area study,* 11–32. New
    York: Free Press.
Monahan, J., and H. J. Steadman. 1983. In M. Tonry and N. Morris, eds. *Crime and

justice: An annual review of research, 4:153. Chicago: University of Chicago Press.

Nam, C. B., and M. G. Powers. 1983. *The socioeconomic approach to status measurement.* Houston: Cap and Gown Press.

Robins, L. N., J. E. Helzer, J. Croughan, and K. Ratcliffe. 1981. National Institute of Mental Health Diagnostic Interview Schedule: Its history, characteristics and validity. *Archives of General Psychiatry* 38:381–89.

Robins, L. N., and D. A. Regier, eds. 1991. *Psychiatric disorders in America: The Epidemiologic Catchment Area study.* New York: Free Press.

Robins, L. N., J. Tipp, and T. Przybeck. 1991. Antisocial personality. In L. N. Robins and D. A. Regier, eds. *Psychiatric disorders in America: The Epidemiologic Catchment Area study,* 258–90. New York: Free Press.

Swanson, J. W., and C. E. Holzer. 1991. Violence and ECA data (letter to the editor). *Hospital and Community Psychiatry* 42:954–55.

Swanson, J. W., C. E. Holzer, V. K. Ganju, and R. T. Jono. 1990. Violence and psychiatric disorder in the community: Evidence from the Epidemiologic Catchment Area surveys. *Hospital and Community Psychiatry* 41:761–70.

6 Psychotic Symptoms and the Violent/Illegal Behavior of Mental Patients Compared to Community Controls

BRUCE G. LINK AND ANN STUEVE

People often assume that mental patients, current and former, are more dangerous on average than other people and more likely to commit violent or illegal acts. Results from a 1990 nationwide telephone survey indicate, for example, that a third (36%) of the American public believe that mentally ill people are more likely to commit violent crimes than other people; almost half (45%) report that it's natural to be afraid of someone who is mentally ill; half (52%) claim it is important to remember that former mental patients may be dangerous; and a large majority (80%) endorse at least one of the above (Link et al., 1992). At the same time some advocates of the mentally ill contend that such beliefs are unfounded, that psychiatric patients are inappropriately stigmatized as dangerous and violent. A National Mental Health Association pamphlet (1987) claims, for example: "People with mental illness pose no more of a crime threat than do other members of the general population."

Are current and former psychiatric patients—and persons with a mental illness generally—more likely to commit violent or illegal acts than other people? Are they more dangerous on average than the so-called normal person next door? Is the likelihood of engaging in violent or illegal acts greater among psychiatric patients regardless of symptom profile or diagnosis or only among individuals with a discrete and identifiable subset of signs and symptoms? While research to date tends to show an elevated rate of violent or illegal acts among current and former mental patients, and some studies point to psychotic symptoms as the critical variable (Link, Andrews, and Cullen 1992), the results of most investigations are open to conflicting interpretations.

Determining whether there is a causal relationship between mental illness or patient status on the one hand and violent or illegal behavior on the other is critical, however, not only to understanding the extent and direction of stigmatizing processes but also for how our conclusion informs a broad range of educational, treatment, and research concerns. For example, can available

137

evidence legitimize campaigns to "educate" the public that former mental patients are no more dangerous than their nonpatient peers? Are early detection and control of some symptoms of mental illness important for ensuring public safety, and, if so, which ones? Should research funds be allocated to investigate the connection between violence and the signs and symptoms of mental illness, or would such expenditures be misguided in light of existing evidence?

This paper examines the relationship between psychotic symptoms and violent behavior. Specifically, we investigate which psychotic symptoms, if any, explain the elevated rates of violent behavior previously observed among current and former mental patients as compared with community controls (Link, Andrews, and Cullen 1992). The rationale for this inquiry stems from our consideration of previous research on the links between violent or illegal behavior and mental illness.

Previous Research

Two classes of studies address the association between mental illness and violent or illegal behavior. Following Monahan (1992), we call these "arrest rate" and "epidemiological" studies. The designs, strengths, and limitations of the two approaches complement one another in such a way that their results, when combined, suggest a coherent picture.

Arrest Rate Studies

Arrest rate studies share a common design. Arrest records of patients discharged from mental hospitals or public clinics are examined and rates of violent or illegal behavior are generated and compared with those for the general population. While arrest rate studies have been criticized both for their reliance on official arrest records and for certain design limitations (see below), two strengths of this approach should be highlighted. First, because the outcome measure is based on official data, it is not subject to the kinds of reporting biases found in studies that rely on self-reports about socially undesirable behavior. Second, arrest rate studies are prospective in the sense that patients are followed after being discharged from treatment; thus the time order of some of the critical events at issue (i.e., treatment for mental illness and subsequent arrests) is known.

In an early and influential review of arrest rate studies, Rabkin (1979) observed that whereas investigations conducted prior to 1965 showed no elevated rates for former mental patients, studies between 1965 and 1979 consistently showed that discharged mental patients were arrested more often than the general public. Rabkin observed that the excess was "particularly pronounced in the category of felonies, and specifically, of violent crimes or crimes against people" (Rabkin 1979, 24). Combining seven studies reported in Rabkin's article with six more recent investigations, Link et al. (1992) calculated a median patient-to-public arrest ratio of greater than 3 to 1. The strength and consistency of this association have led some to assert that it is causal (Sosowsky 1986, 1325) and others to express grave policy concerns. For example, Torrey (1988) contends that "if the public ever becomes fully aware of how often mentally ill individuals with a history of violent behavior are released from jails and hospitals with no mandatory continuing treatment, there will be a mass outcry directed toward the lawyers, judges and psychiatrists who are responsible for this state of affairs" (Torrey 1988, 16).

While their results are impressive, arrest rate studies have been criticized on three important grounds. The first criticism—investigated under the rubric of the "criminalization of mental illness"—is that arrest rate differentials may tell us less about the association between mental illness and criminal behavior than about the association between mental illness and the arrest process. For example, based on observations of police-citizen encounters, Teplin (1983, 1984, 1985) reports that mentally disordered citizens were more likely to be arrested than citizens who were seemingly free of mental disorder even when the offending behaviors were the same. Higher arrest rates among patients may therefore have little to do with underlying rates of violent or illegal behavior.

The second criticism suggests a different filtering process, what some have called "the medicalization of deviance" or the "psychiatrization of criminal behavior" (Monahan 1973; Melick, Steadman, and Cocozza 1979; Steadman, Cocozza, and Melick 1978). According to this view greater numbers of behaviors, including violent and illegal behaviors, are coming under the purview of psychiatrists. Consequently more people prone to violent or illegal behavior are drawn into patient populations. As a result, elevated arrest rates among patients may not be due to a close connection between mental illness and violent or illegal behavior but to the medicalization of these acts.

The final limitation stems from arrest rate studies' use of general population arrest rates for comparison purposes. The patients studied are typically drawn from public mental hospitals or clinics that serve people from disadvantaged circumstances among whom rates of violent or illegal behavior are higher even for people who are not mentally ill. Thus the higher arrest rates of former mental patients in these studies may have less to do with mental illness than with failure to control for the community conditions with which the patients must contend.

Given these limitations, it would be risky to base any broad conclusions about the connection between mental patient status or mental illness and violent or illegal behavior on arrest rate studies. However, two "epidemiological" studies have taken a different approach to the question.

Epidemiological Studies

The two epidemiological studies share two important properties. First, unlike arrest rate studies, each of the epidemiological investigations collects information about people who have mental disorders ("cases") and people who do not ("controls"). Second, both studies use indicators of violent or illegal behavior other than official arrest.

The first investigation, reported in Swanson et al. (1990), is based on the large-scale Epidemiological Catchment Area (ECA) survey conducted in five communities in the United States. Within each community probability samples were drawn and respondents were interviewed using the lay-administered Diagnostic Interview Schedule (DIS), an instrument yielding DSM III psychiatric diagnoses. As part of the interview, respondents were asked to report on their violent behaviors (e.g., hitting, fighting, using a weapon) during the previous year. Swanson and colleagues found elevated rates of violent behavior for respondents meeting criteria for one or more psychiatric disorders even when controlling for sex, age, and socioeconomic status.

The second study, conducted by Link, Andrews, and Cullen (1992), is based on data from an epidemiological study of psychiatric patients and community residents from the Washington Heights section of New York City using the fully structured Psychiatric Epidemiology Research Interview (PERI; Dohrenwend et al. 1980). The instrument contains reliable symptom scales and measures of violent or illegal behaviors and self-reported arrests. Measures of officially recorded arrests were also obtained from the New York State Department of Criminal Justice Services.

Using the patient and community samples, Link, Andrews, and Cullen (1992) compared community residents with no history of mental health treatment with three distinct patient groups: those having their first contact with mental health professionals during the year prior to interview ("first-treatment contact"), those who were in treatment during the year prior to interview and had a prior treatment history ("repeat-treatment contact"), and former patients identified in the community sample who were not in treatment during the previous year ("former patients"). Compared with never-treated community residents, the patient groups had substantially higher rates of official arrest (ever), self-reported arrest (ever), hitting (past month orpast year), fighting (past five years), weapon use (past five years) and hurting someone badly in a fight (ever). Of the 18 potential differences between the three patient groups and never-treated community residents, 16 showed elevated patient rates and 10 were statistically significant. Moreover, these differences remained despite extensive controls for respondents' sociodemographic characteristics, the socioeconomic level and homicide rate of the community of residence, and the Crowne-Marlowe need for approval scale. Briefly put, the study's attempts to explain patient-community differences in violent or illegal behavior as artifactual consistently failed.

Instead Link and colleagues found that psychotic symptoms are related to patient-community differences in violent or illegal acts; differences in relatively recent violent behaviors were substantially reduced when a 13-item PERI scale of psychotic symptoms (Dohrenwend et al. 1980) was entered as a control. Given the attention to possible alternative explanations, such a finding suggests that elevated rates of violent behaviors among patients are directly tied to their experience of psychotic symptomatology and supports the thesis that differences between patients and nonpatients are not artifactual but real.

In addition to corroborating the connection between violence and mental illness or patient status, the epidemiological studies address some of the ambiguities surrounding arrest rate results. Consider first the concept of "criminalization." While elevated arrest rates among mental patients may be explained by a filtering process that disproportionately directs individuals with mental illnesses into the criminal justice system, such an explanation cannot account for the higher rates of self-reported violence not involving arrest found by both Swanson et al. (1990) and Link, Andrews, and Cullen (1992).

Similarly, while is it possible to explain higher arrest rates among patient groups in terms of processes that direct people displaying violent behaviors into mental health treatment (and thus increasing the prevalence of violent acts among mental patient populations), such a "medicalization of violence" argument cannot account for results reported by Swanson and colleagues, which were based on samples of community residents. Moreover, the argument is inconsistent with Link and colleagues' finding that psychotic symptoms explain patient-community differences in violence. If medicalization processes were operating, violent people would be selected into treatment whether or not they had psychotic symptoms; there would be no reason to expect that psychotic symptoms would explain the association between mental patient status and violent behavior.

Finally, each of the epidemiological studies addresses the possibility that arrest rates are higher among patients because state hospital and public clinic patients are more likely to come from poor, violence-prone segments of society. Link, Andrews, and Cullen (1992) control for most of the sociodemographic and community context variables alleged to explain patient-community differences. Swanson et al. (1990) eschew patient samples altogether in addition to controlling for sociodemographic differences between diagnostic groups. Such steps diminish the possibility that selection from violence-prone neighborhoods explains higher rates of violent behavior among mentally ill or patient populations.

In short, the epidemiological investigations replicate the association between violence and mental illness or patient status found in the arrest rate studies while casting doubt on three explanations—criminalization, medicalization, and social selection—often thought to account for higher arrest rates. However, while clarifying potentially ambiguous aspects of the arrest rate studies, the epidemiological investigations have two important weaknesses. First, they rely on retrospective data that render unclear the time ordering of violence and mental illness. It is possible that violence and contextual factors associated with it predate and cause mental disorder rather than mental disorder causing violence. Second, the epidemiological studies rely heavily or exclusively on self-report measures. Given that both violence and symptoms of mental illness are socially undesirable, their robust association may be due to individual differences in willingness to report socially undesirable behavior, although Link and colleagues control for social desirability using the Marlowe-Crowne scale.

Conclusions Based on Past Literature

To summarize, while both arrest-rate and epidemiological investigations document an association between violence and mental illness or patient status, no single study or type of study conducted thus far definitively demonstrates a causal connection. Yet when the range of studies are considered together, it becomes difficult to dismiss the connection between violence and mental illness as simply artifactual. Not only has the association been remarkably consistent across studies and approaches, but each type of investigation tends to clarify issues left ambiguous or open to challenge in the other. Whereas results from arrest rate studies are open to alternative explanations based on criminalization, medicalization, or social selection processes, results from the epidemiological studies tend to discount these competing interpretations. Similarly, whereas heavy reliance on self-report and retrospective data raise questions about results from the epidemiological studies, arrest rate investigations are uniformly prospective and based on official records that while flawed are subject to biases different from those of self-report. In short, alternative explanations that appear compelling when applied to one study or type of investigation fail when applied across the full range of research.

The robust pattern of findings across studies using different designs, samples, and measures tips us in favor of the conclusion that there is a causal connection between some types of mental illness and violence. The words "tips in favor" are chosen carefully since our conclusion is based not on a definitive study but on a weighing of the evidence. New evidence could change the balance, making us more or less confident in our conclusion. The most compelling evidence will eventually come from prospective epidemiological studies. Here we undertake a more modest investigation and elaborate on work begun by Link, Andrews, and Cullen (1992). Specifically, we investigate whether specific symptoms chosen according to the principle of "rationality-within-irrationality" can account for patient-community differences in violent behavior.

Psychotic Symptoms and Violent Behavior: The Principle of Rationality-within-Irrationality

The principle of rationality-within-irrationality posits that once one suspends concern about the irrationality of psychotic symptoms and accepts that they are experienced as real, violence unfolds in a "rational" fashion. By rational we do not mean reasonable or justified but rather understandable. Specifically, we suggest that when a person fears personal harm or feels threatened by others interpersonal violence becomes more likely. In addition we argue that violence is more likely when internal controls that might otherwise block the expression of violence break down. From this perspective the nature and content of the psychotic experience become important. If the psychotic experience involves the removal of self-control through, for example, thought insertion or having one's mind dominated by outside forces, routine, self-imposed constraints on behavior are more likely to be overridden, and violence becomes a greater possibility. Further, if the afflicted person believes that he or she is gravely threatened by someone who intends to cause harm, violence is again more likely. In contrast, if the psychotic episode involves odd experiences such as hearing voices, seeing visions, or having one's thoughts taken away, without the intrusion of external, uncontrollable, and threatening forces, violence is less likely.

If the principle of rationality-within-irrationality is operative, it should help specify which psychotic symptoms are most likely to explain patient-community differences in recently occuring violence. Table 1 divides the 13 PERI psychotic symptoms into two groups. The first group includes three symptoms that either involve the overriding of internal self-controls by "external" factors (items 1 and 2) or imply a specific threat of harm from others (item 3). We call these three items threat/control-override items and predict that they will account for elevated rates of recent violence among patient groups. The second group of symptoms (e.g., feeling that one does not exist, having one's thoughts taken away or broadcast), while equally severe in suggesting the presence of psychosis, directly imply neither threat from others nor the override of internal controls. We refer to this second group simply as "other psychotic symptoms" and predict that except for their association with threat/control-override symptoms, they will be unrelated to violent behavior.

Method

The data for this investigation are drawn from a methods study conducted by Dohrenwend and colleagues to compare one-month and one-year versions of

Table 1. Psychotic symptoms scale separated into threat/control-overide and other psychotic symptoms subscales

Threat/control-overide symptoms

During the past year . . .

1. how often have you felt that your mind was dominated by forces beyond your control?
2. how often have you felt that thoughts were put into your head that were not your own?
3. how often have you felt that there were people who wished to do you harm?

Other psychotic symptoms

During the past year . . .

1. how often have you felt that you do not exist at all, that you are dead, dissolved?
2. how often have you heard things that other people say they can't hear?
3. how often have you felt that your unspoken thoughts were being broadcast or transmitted, so that everyone knows what you are thinking?
4. how often have you thought that you were possessed by a spirit or a devil?
5. how often have you had visions or seen things that other people say they cannot see?
6. how often have you felt you have special powers?
7. how often have you thought something odd was going on?
8. how often have you felt your thoughts were taken away from you by some external force?
9. how often have you had ideas or thoughts that nobody else would understand if you talked about them?
10. how often have you seemed to hear your thoughts spoken aloud—almost as if someone standing nearby could hear them?

the Psychiatric Epidemiology Research Interview (PERI; Dohrenwend et al. 1986; Shrout et al. 1988). Samples of psychiatric patients and community residents, randomly assigned to either a one-month or a one-year time frame for questions, were interviewed in person using the PERI schedule between 1979 and 1982 (Dohrenwend et al. 1980). Given the design of the original study, approximately half of the respondents were queried about symptoms occurring in the year prior to interview while the rest were asked about symptoms occurring in the past month. Questions eliciting self-reports of violent or illegal behaviors, with the exception of "hitting someone," were asked in the one-year version only, thus limiting all analyses involving these variables to a random half of our patient and community samples as described below.

Study Samples

Community sample. To obtain a community sample of individuals between 19 and 59 years of age, households in the Washington Heights section of New York City were enumerated and contacted to determine whether an eligible respondent lived there. Information about ethnic background was used to sample roughly equal proportions of non-Hispanic blacks, Hispanics, and non-Hispanic whites from this predominantly Hispanic urban neighborhood. Screening information was provided by 93% of the households; 68% contained one or more potential respondents. Of the 943 eligible individuals, 541 (57%) were interviewed successfully. Twenty of these individuals, however, either had moved away from Washington Heights ($N = 7$) or provided inadequate information to identify their census tract ($N = 13$); they are excluded from the following analyses since our study requires that psychiatric patients be compared to nonpatients from the same neighborhoods. Of the 521 respondents available for analysis, 255 were interviewed with the one-year version of the PERI, while 266 were interviewed with the one-month version.

To check on the representativeness of the community sample we first compared respondents' sociodemographic characteristics with 1980 census data for the same area. While differences in gender and age (within the 19–59 range) are minimal, there are differences on educational level and ethnicity that can be attributed largely to efforts to stratify. The Hispanic majority, which tends to have less education than either blacks or non-Hispanic whites in the Washington Heights area, was purposely undersampled. Thus the sampling decision contributed to the underrepresentation of lower-educated respondents in the community sample.

As a further check on the representativeness of the community sample, we compared "hard to schedule" respondents with individuals who were more easily interviewed. We reasoned that hard to schedule respondents would be more like the larger pool of nonrespondents than the more easily obtained individuals since without extensive efforts they would not have been interviewed. Forty-eight of the 541 respondents were identified as "hard to schedule" because they (*a*) initially refused but later agreed to participate ($N = 33$), (*b*) failed to keep two appointments (the usual cutoff as a lost case) but were obtained on a subsequent attempt ($N = 12$), or (*c*) could not be reached after eight attempts at telephone contact (the usual cutoff as a lost cause) but were obtained on a subsequent attempt ($N = 3$). We found no significant differences between hard to schedule respondents and other community respondents on any of the six indicators of violent or illegal behavior, the variables of key interest to us.

Patient Samples. Psychiatric patients used in this analysis were recruited by Dohrenwend et al. (1986) from the outpatient clinic and an inpatient community service at Columbia-Presbyterian Medical Center, both of which are centrally located in the Washington Heights community. In all, 375 patients from these two settings were interviewed. Although both settings are community-based services, 101 of the 375 patients lived outside the Washington Heights community and thus are excluded from our analysis. An additional 42 patients are excluded because there is insufficient information to identify their census tract. Thus the number of patients included in this analysis is

232, 46 of whom were inpatients. Of these 232, 127 were interviewed with the one-year PERI; 105 received the one-month version.

DSM III diagnoses of patients were either made or supervised by members of the Biometrics Unit at New York State Psychiatric Institute, using clinical records and unstructured interviews. In this study, we use diagnosis only for descriptive purposes, because our main objective is to compare patients with nonpatients and diagnoses are not available for nonpatients. Of the 232 patients included in this study, 33.6% ($N = 78$) were diagnosed with major depression, 19.4% ($N = 45$) with schizophrenia, and 10.3% ($N = 24$) with a psychotic disorder other than schizophrenia. The remaining 36.6% ($N = 85$) had diagnoses other than major depression or a disorder characterized by psychotic symptomatology.

Formation of Study Groups

In earlier work, Link, Andrews, and Cullen (1992) combined respondents from the patient and community samples and created four subgroups for analysis: first-treatment contact patients ($N = 83$), repeat-treatment contact patients ($N = 173$), former patients ($N = 111$), and never-treated community residents ($N = 386$). In this study we highlight analyses that combine first-contact, repeat-contact, and former patients into one group both because each patient group tended to be higher on indicators of violence than never-treated community controls in the Link, Andrews, and Cullen (1992) analysis and because combining patient groups simplifies presentation of the data. We report results that use the more-detailed treatment groups in the text of this paper.

Measures of Violent/Illegal Behavior

We use three measures of violent or illegal behavior—hitting, fighting, and weapon use. We do not examine the three lifetime assessments (official arrest, self-reported arrest, and self-reported ever hurting another person badly) used by Link, Andrews, and Cullen (1992) because relevant theory suggests that it is only when a person is actively psychotic that he or she is at risk of violent or illegal behavior. Lifetime assessments tap events which may have occurred too long ago to be influenced by current psychotic symptomatology. The time frame of two of the violence measures, fighting and weapon use, is five years—a longer period than we would like. However, given that our goal is to determine whether psychotic symptoms explain the association between mental patient status and violence, using a five-year time period actually biases against finding that symptoms explain patient-community differences in fighting and weapon use. If relatively recent psychotic symptoms fail to explain such differences it could be because the psychotic symptoms did not occur in the same time period. However, if patient-community differences in fighting and weapon use are explained by psychotic symptoms the inference that the differences between patients and community residents are due to psychotic symptoms would be strongly supported.

Hitting. This measure was constructed from the following question, asked in both the one-month and one-year versions of the PERI: "When you have gotten angry in the past year (month), how often have you hit someone?" Response categories were "very often, fairly often, sometimes, almost never, never." To make this measure parallel the categorical nature of the other two outcomes, we dichotomized responses, with respondents answering "very often," "fairly often," or "sometimes" scored 1 and those answering "almost never" or "never" scored 0. In this analysis, we combine subjects interviewed with the one-month and one-year time frames to enhance statistical power and enter a dummy variable reflecting the different time frames as a control.

Fighting. This measure was constructed from two questions present only in the one-year version of the PERI. The first reads: "Since the time you were about 12 years old, have you been in a physical fight with anyone?" Respondents who answered yes were then asked: "Have you been in a physical fight in the last five years?" Using these two questions, our measure of fighting indicates whether respondents were involved in a physical fight in the past five years.

Weapon use in a fight. This measure was also constructed from two questions available only in the one-year version of the PERI. The first reads: "Have you ever had anything in your hands like a knife or a stick or a gun during a fight?" Respondents answering yes were then asked: "How old were you the last time you fought with something in your hands?" Using respondents' answers to these questions and their age, we constructed a measure of weapon use during the past five years. We used a five-year period because shorter intervals (e.g., one year) produced very few cases.

Psychotic Symptoms

The PERI psychotic symptoms are listed in table 1 (see above). Each symptom is responded to on a frequency continuum ranging from very often (4) to never (0). We divided these symptoms into two scales, one with three items, the threat/control-override scale, which we believe will be strongly associated with our indicators of violence and another with 10 items, the other psychotic symptoms scale, that we believe will be related to violence only because it is correlated with the threat/control-override scale. Each scale was constructed by summing the relevant symptoms. Thus the threat/control-override scale can vary from 0 to 12, whereas the scale of other psychotic symptoms can vary from 0 to 40.

Measures of Control Variables

We use the same control variables used in the earlier Link, Andrews, and Cullen (1992) analysis. The controls were selected in that study to evaluate the plausibility of alternative explanations for the association between mental patient status and indicators of violent or illegal behavior. Most of the control variables test whether the elevated rates among mental patients are due to their sociodemographic characteristics and social context rather than their mental illness.

Sociodemographic characteristics. Based on data collected from both patients and community residents, we control for age (in years), sex (female = 1, male = 0), education (in years), and ethnicity (black, Hispanic, and white or other).

Homicide rates. We measure level of community violence using homicide data collected by the New York City Department of Health for the same four-year time period in which the Dohrenwend study took place (1979–82). These data record the address of each homicide victim in New York City along with the date the homicide occurred. We used a geocoding program to locate each homicide victim in a census tract. To create a homicide rate for each census tract included in the Dohrenwend study, we divided the number of homicide victims living in a given tract during the four-year period by four and then divided by the total population of the tract in 1980. Homicide rates varied from 3.51 to 168.69 per 100,000 persons per year in the census tracts inhabited by our respondents. This wide variation in rates underscores the importance of comparing patients with residents from similar areas when seeking to assess whether patients are more violent than their peers.

Need for approval. We use a 15-item version of the Crowne-Marlowe need-for-approval scale (Crowne and Marlowe 1960) to control for social desirability response biases. The items ask respondents to admit to things that are very common but socially undesirable (e.g., "You are sometimes irritated by people who ask favors of you") or to deny things that are uncommon but socially desirable (e.g., "You never resent being asked to return a favor"). The scale is the sum of the fifteen true-false items coded so that a high score indicates a strong "need for approval."

Results

Recall that the main purpose of this analysis is to determine which of the 13 psychotic symptoms explain the association between mental patient status and indicators of violence. We begin by considering the bivariate associations between mental patient status and violence and then incorporate the psychotic symptoms scales to test our specific hypotheses. As noted above, analyses of hitting combine data from both the one-month and one-year subsamples

Table 2. Associations between mental patient status and
hitting, fighting, and weapon use

	Percent hitting, past month/year (Patient $N = 385$; Community $N = 365$)	Percent fighting, past 5 years (Patient $N = 191$; Community $N = 185$)*	Percent using a weapon, past 5 years (Patient $N = 195$; Community $N = 186$)**
Patients/former patients	12.3	25.7	9.7
Never-treated community controls	5.2	15.1	2.7

*p < .05.   **p < .01.   ***p < .001.

whereas analyses of fighting and weapon use are based only on cases interviewed with the one-year version. Excluding cases with missing information on the violence measures (hitting, 3; fighting, 6; weapon use, 1), the number of respondents are 750 for hitting, 376 for fighting, and 381 for weapon use.

Mental Patient Status and Violence

As table 2 shows, current and former patients are significantly more likely to have engaged in hitting, fighting, and weapon use than never-treated community controls. Link and colleagues (1992) report this same association using more detailed treatment groups (first-contact, repeat-contact, and former patients). They then entered numerous potentially confounding variables that might explain the association between mental patient status and violence. Specifically they controlled for sociodemographic variables, Crowne-Marlowe need-for-approval, and levels of community violence. None of these variables, however, reduced the association between mental patient status and violence to nonsignificance. It was only when the 13-item psychotic symptom scale was controlled that the patient status variables became nonsignificant.

Controlling for Types of Psychotic Symptoms

The threat/control-override scale. Table 3 shows the percentages of current or former patients and never-treated community controls who have engaged in hitting, fighting, and weapon use by levels of the threat/control-override psychotic symptom scale. We categorized the symptoms scale into four levels, low (0), medium-low (1,2), medium-high (3–5), and high (6–12), in order to display these associations in contingency table format.

First, note the strong "dose-response" effects of the threat/control-override psychotic symptoms on violent behaviors. Both fighting and hitting show consistent dose-response effects with persons at the high end of the symptom

Table 3. Associations between mental patient status and violence controlling for
threat/control-override psychotic symptoms

Level of threat/control-override psychotic symptoms	Percent hitting, past month/year (number of cases in parentheses)		Percent fighting, past 5 years (numbr of cases in parentheses)		Percent using a weapon past 5 years (number of cases in parentheses)	
Low (scale score = 0)						
Patients/former patients	3.6	(137)	14.7	(68)	2.9	(69)
Never-treated community controls	1.7	(229)	10.3	(107)	0.9	(107)
Medium–low (scale score = 1–2)						
Patients/former patients	11.5	(87)	18.8	(48)	9.8	(51)
Never-treated community controls	9.1	(99)	18.0	(50)	2.0	(51)
Medium–high (scale score = 3–5)						
Patients/former patients	15.7	(70)	27.3	(44)	6.8	(44)
Never-treated community controls	10.6	(47)	21.7	(23)	13.0	(23)
High (scale score = 6–12)						
Patients/former patients	27.1	(70)	58.1	(31)	29.0	(31)
Never-treated community controls	20.0	(10)	60.0	(5)	0.0	(5)

scale reporting much higher rates of violence than those at the low end. The only exception occurs for weapon use, which is very rare. The percentages for weapon use are based on very small numbers of cases and are somewhat unstable as a consequence. Even here the dose-response effect is evident if one collapses the two highest categories; the percentages reporting weapon use at the low, medium-low, and combined high levels are 2.9, 9.8, and 16.0, for patients and 0.9, 2.0, and 10.8 for community respondents.

Second, differences in violent behaviors between current or former patients and never-treated community controls are sharply reduced when we stratify by levels of the threat/control-override scale. While patients still tend to have higher rates of violent behaviors, even controlling for these symptoms, the differences are small and not statistically significant. Thus, to a large extent, the threat/control-override symptom scale explains the association between patient status and violence.

The other-psychotic-symptoms scale. Table 4 shows the percentages of current or former patients and never-treated community residents who have engaged in violent behaviors by levels of the other-psychotic-symptoms scale. Again we categorized the symptoms scale into four levels: low (0–2), medium-low (3–7), medium-high (8–15), and high (16–40). As with the threat/control-override symptoms, there is a strong association between violent behaviors and the scale of other psychotic symptoms, and, as in table 3, differences between current or former patients and community respondents are substantially smaller, although perhaps not as strikingly so, when con-

Table 4. **Associations between mental patient status and violence controlling for other psychotic symptoms**

Level of other psychotic symptoms	Percent hitting, past month/year (number of cases in parentheses)		Percent fighting, past 5 years (number of cases in parentheses)		Percent using a weapon past 5 years (number of cases in parentheses)	
Low (scale score = 0–2)						
Patients/former patients	4.9	(144)	15.2	(66)	1.4	(69)
Never-treated community controls	3.4	(237)	11.0	(109)	2.7	(110)
Medium–low (scale score = 1–2)						
Patients/former patients	10.2	(88)	16.3	(49)	11.8	(51)
Never-treated community controls	7.5	(106)	14.8	(54)	1.9	(54)
Medium–high (scale score = 8–15)						
Patients/former patients	19.4	(67)	26.8	(41)	17.5	(40)
Never-treated community controls	8.8	(34)	38.9	(18)	5.6	(18)
High (scale score = 16+)						
Patients/former patients	24.6	(65)	57.1	(35)	14.3	(35)
Never-treated community controls	12.5	(8)	25.0	(4)	0.0	(4)

trolled for these psychotic symptoms. Relatively large patient-community differences are more common at high symptom levels on the other-psychotic-symptoms scale than for the threat/control-override scale.

To this point we have supported one of our hypotheses. The threat/control-override psychotic symptoms are strongly associated with violent behaviors and largely explain the association between mental patient status and violence. But are the threat/control-override symptoms the crucial ones that our principle of rationality-within-irrationality suggests? Given the strong association between the other psychotic symptom scale and violence, it is by no means obvious that the threat/control-override symptoms are dominant.

Threat/Control-Override Symptoms Versus Other Psychotic Symptoms

Based on the principle of rationality-within-irrationality, we hypothesized that the only reason the other psychotic symptoms are associated with violence is because they are correlated with threat/control-override symptoms. Thus we expect little or no association between other psychotic symptoms and violence when threat/control-override symptoms are controlled. In contrast, we hypothesized that threat/control-override symptoms are directly related to violent behaviors and thus should remain significant even when other psychotic symptoms are held constant. To test this hypothesis we employ logistic re-

Table 5. Effects of patient status, psychotic symptoms, and control variables on hitting

Predictor Variables	Regression coefficients (standard error)			
	Equation 1	Equation 2	Equation 3	Equation 4
Patient/former patient (1)	.935***	.402	.383	.337
vs. community control (0)	(.280)	(.307)	(.309)	(.325)
One-year (1) vs. one-month (0)	.215	.333	.296	.196
time frame	(.264)	(.276)	(.279)	(.290)
Threat/control-override psychotic	—	.241***	.188*	.166*
symptom scale		(.043)	(.077)	(.081)
Other psychotic symptoms scale	—	—	.023	.004
			(.028)	(.030)
Age (in years)	—	—	—	−.018
				(.013)
Sex (female = 1, male = 0)	—	—	—	.159
				(.304)
Education (in years)	—	—	—	−.179***
				(.049)
African American	—	—	—	.299
				(.385)
Hispanic	—	—	—	−.011
				(.414)
Crowne-Marlowe	—	—	—	−2.380**
				(.802)
Census tract homicide rate	—	—	—	.002
				(.007)
Chi-square (d.f.)	13.04(2)	44.51(3)	45.21(4)	69.09(11)

Note: $N = 750$.
* $p < .05$.   ** $p < .01$.   *** $p < .001$.

gression and examine the effects of each psychotic symptom scale while controlling for the other.

Tables 5, 6 and 7 show four logistic equations for each of the three indicators of violence. The first equation includes only a dummy variable for patient status (current/former patient = 1; never-treated community control = 0). The second equation adds the three-item threat/control-override symptom scale. The third analysis adds the ten-item other psychotic symptom scale. The fourth and final equation adds the full battery of control variables used in the Link, Andrews, and Cullen (1992) study.

The results presented in tables 5, 6, and 7 show the same pattern. In each case the first equation shows a significant effect for the dummy variable representing current or former patient status versus never-treated community control. The second equation in each table shows that the effect of the threat/control-override scale is highly significant and renders the patient status variable nonsignificant. When the scale of other psychotic symptoms is added in

Table 6. Effects of patient status, psychotic symptoms, and control variables on fighting

Predictor Variables	Regression coefficients (standard error)			
	Equation 1	Equation 2	Equation 3	Equation 4
Patient/former patient (1)	.660*	.179	.123	−.025
vs. community control (0)	(.264)	(.291)	(.295)	(.325)
Threat/control-override psychotic	—	.238***	.189*	.258**
symptom scale		(.053)	(.086)	(.093)
Other psychotic symptoms scale	—	—	.039	.021
			(.029)	(.032)
Age (in years)	—	—	—	−.038**
				(.014)
Sex (female = 1, male = 0)	—	—	—	−.987**
				(.309)
Education (in years)	—	—	—	.010
				(.051)
African American	—	—	—	.559
				(.397)
Hispanic	—	—	—	.208
				(.421)
Crowne-Marlowe	—	—	—	.186
				(.771)
Census tract homicide rate	—	—	—	.019**
				(.007)
Chi-square (d.f.)	6.456(1)	37.41(2)	39.50(3)	73.63(10)

Note: $N = 376$.
* $p < .05$.   ** $p < .01$.   *** $p < .001$.

the third equation, it is never significant. By contrast, the threat/control-override scale remains a significant predictor even when other psychotic symptoms are held constant. Finally the fourth equation shows that this pattern of significance for the threat/control-override symptoms and nonsignificance for other psychotic symptoms persists when controls for other potential determinants of violent behavior are included.

A Check Using More Detailed Treatment Groups

Recall that the data allow the use of more detailed classification of patients into first-treatment contact, repeat-treatment contact, and former patient groups. Analyses like those presented in tables 4, 5, and 6 using these more detailed patient groupings lead to the same conclusions as analyses with the combined patient group. Entering the threat/control-override symptoms into an equation with the detailed patient groups renders the contribution of the patient status variables nonsignificant. Furthermore the pattern of significance

Table 7. Effects of patient status, psychotic symptoms, and control variables on weapon use

Predictor Variables	Regression coefficients (standard error)			
	Equation 1	Equation 2	Equation 3	Equation 4
Patient/former patient (1)	1.363**	.834	.880	.676
vs. community control (0)	(.514)	(.546)	(.548)	(.585)
Threat/control-override psychotic	—	.265***	.367**	.398**
symptom scale		(.069)	(.126)	(.146)
Other psychotic symptoms scale	—	—	−.041	−.082
			(.042)	(.052)
Age (in years)	—	—	—	−.001
				(.021)
Sex (female = 1, male = 0)	—	—	—	−.286
				(.489)
Education (in years)	—	—	—	−.174*
				(.080)
African American	—	—	—	.225
				(.587)
Hispanic	—	—	—	−.175
				(.686)
Crowne-Marlowe	—	—	—	−3.346*
				(1.329)
Census tract homicide rate	—	—	—	.021*
				(.010)
Chi-square (d.f.)	8.57(1)	22.86(2)	23.80(3)	39.42(10)

Note: N = 381.
* $p < .05$.   ** $p < .01$.   *** $p < .001$.

for the threat/control override and nonsignificance for other psychotic symptoms (with threat/control-override symptoms held constant) remains using the detailed patient groupings.

Discussion

We began this paper by raising the issue of whether current or former mental patients are more likely to be violent than nonpatient controls. We observed that the preponderance of evidence from recent research suggests that the mentally ill are somewhat more likely to be violent and that efforts to explain the association as spurious have largely failed. Our specific starting point was a previous report showing that differences in rates of recently occurring violent behavior between patient groups and community controls could be explained using a 13-item psychotic symptoms scale (Link, Andrews, and Cullen 1992). This finding explicitly linked an aspect of mental illness with higher rates of violence—something that had not been done in previous patient-community comparisons. But why should psychotic experiences be associated with violent behaviors, and are all psychotic symptoms associated with elevated rates?

We proposed that there is some specificity in the relationship between violence and psychotic symptoms and that violence is more likely when psychotic symptoms cause a person to feel personally threatened or involve the intrusion of thoughts that can override self-controls. Our results lend support to this proposal. Out of thirteen measured psychotic symptoms, the three that involved threat or control-override predicted rates of relatively recent violent behaviors even controlling for a scale composed of the other ten. Moreover, the three threat/control-override symptoms accounted for differences between patient groups and community controls. In contrast the scale of other psychotic symptoms was not significantly associated with rates of violence when the threat/control-override symptom scale was held constant.

The results of this study must be considered preliminary. Not only are our results based on data from a single urban community but, more importantly, we did not set out to test an a priori hypothesis linking specific psychotic symptoms with violent behavior. Indeed the theoretical ideas motivating the original research focused on factors that might explain the association between mental illness and violence as spurious. It was only when these efforts failed that we began to consider mechanisms linking forms of mental illness with violence. The post hoc quality of our theorizing coupled with the geographic restrictiveness of the sample indicate the need for replication. Nevertheless, within the context of these limitations, our results speak to a number of concerns.

First, while not confirmatory, our results support a plausible explanation for the observed association between psychotic symptoms and violence, thereby increasing confidence of a causal connection between the two. In a general way, we become more confident that a causal explanation is valid if we find support for derivative hypotheses. Here we started with a scale of psychotic symptoms that accounted for patient-community differences in violence, made more refined predictions based on the rationality-within-irrationality principle about which symptoms in the scale might account for the pattern, and provided evidence to substantiate our hypothesis. In addition, our tests help with two issues of causal inference left ambiguous in previous epidemiological studies, which relied on retrospective self-report data. With retrospective data causal order cannot be definitely determined; violence may cause psychotic symptoms rather than the reverse. With self-report data differences in willingness to report undesirable behavior may account for the association between violence and psychotic symptoms since both are socially undesirable. Neither of these alternative explanations, however, makes the same prediction about the association between specific psychotic symptoms and violence made by the principle of rationality-within-rationality. If violence causes psychotic symptoms rather than vice versa, there is no reason to believe that it causes threat/control-override symptoms more than other psychotic experiences. Similarly, most of the psychotic symptoms are socially undesirable; consequently, there is little reason to believe that the threat/control-override symptoms are more strongly related to violence than the rest. Since our results are consistent with the rationality-within-irrationality hypotheses, they cast doubt on these alternative explanations and thereby support a causal relationship between mental illness and violence, if only by default.

Our results also clarify why psychotic symptoms explain elevated rates of violence among current and former mental patients. People enter mental health treatment for a wide variety of problems. Some do so because they are experiencing psychotic symptoms. When these symptoms cause people to feel threatened or override their self-controls, physical fights, weapon use, and other forms of violence are more likely. It is because some psychotic symptoms have these potent effects that mental patient groups have elevated rates of violent behaviors.

In a very limited way our results also inform predictions about who is more likely to be violent in treatment or other settings. Threat/control-override symptoms are likely to be better predictors of violence than other psychotic symptoms alone. We emphasize, however, both the dangers and limitations associated with predicting individual behavior. Not only do symptom scales miss all the potent environmental and individual sources of violent behavior that have nothing to do with mental illness, but their association with violence—both in an absolute sense and compared with other known causes and correlates of violence—is also modest. For the most part, most respondents in our study who experienced threat/control-override psychotic symptoms had not engaged in recent violent behavior, just as most members of other "high risk" groups (e.g., men, young adults, economically disadvantaged individuals) had not done so. As a result we view these symptoms only as an "internal opportunity structure" that makes violence more or less likely, not as an accurate predictor of individual behavior.

Finally, our results and their theoretical underpinnings challenge the unfortunate stereotyping of mental patients. Most mental patients do not experience the specific psychotic symptoms we identified as risks for violent behavior. Relating to persons as if they represent a violence threat simply because of their history of illness or hospitalization represents a grave personal injustice, one that can compromise their life chances (Link 1987; Link et al. 1987; Link et al. 1989). In addition, for individuals who experience such symptoms and engage in subsequent violence, our perspective makes the connection between symptoms and violence more comprehensible. Once one accepts that psychotic symptoms are experienced as real, one can better understand (without condoning) the emergence of violent responses on the part of individuals who fear imminent harm or experience "external" forces as overriding their personal control. This understanding sharply contrasts with media images of methodical, calculating, and clever mentally ill people wreaking havoc on unsuspecting and innocent victims, an image that produces almost unbridled opprobrium on the part of the audience and legitimizes coercive, even violent, reactions to the perpetrator (for an analysis of media portrayals of mentally ill persons see Gerbner et al. 1981). In short, by specifying who among the mentally ill is likely to be violent and why they are likely to be so, we hope to challenge such stereotypes about mental illness and violence and temper public responses to individuals who are more likely to be victims of their illness than victimizers.

As we have indicated our results need to be replicated and extended by future research. If such research supports our general conclusions, an evidence-guided approach to public education might be possible in which people are taught the specific conditions under which people with mental illness are likely to be violent and what should be done when those conditions are evident. If people with psychotic symptoms are offered appropriate and acceptable pharmacological (Davis 1975) and psychosocial treatments (e.g., Falloon et al. 1982; McFarlane 1990) violence might be prevented and disastrous situations for both potential victims and the mentally ill themselves avoided. Indeed, it would represent an ironic twist if at some future point intervention efforts focusing on the treatment of psychotic symptoms became so successful and acceptable to patients and their families that we could confidently assert that the mentally ill are no more dangerous than other people.

Acknowledgments

This research was supported by NIMH grant number MH43610. Arrest data were obtained from the New York State Division of Criminal Justice Services in the form of criminal history records which were computerized and then destroyed. The Division of Criminal Justice Services bears no responsibility for errors in the methods of this study nor is it responsible for the conclusions drawn from it. We thank John Monahan and Henry Steadman for helpful comments.

References

Crowne, D. P., and D. Marlowe. 1960. A new scale of social desirability independent of psychopathology. *Journal of Consulting and Clinical Psychology* 24:349–54.
Davis, J. 1975. Overview: Maintenance therapy in psychiatry. I: Schizophrenia. *American Journal of Psychiatry* 132:1237–45.
Dohrenwend, B. P., P. Shrout, G. Egri, and F. Mendelsohn. 1980. Measures of nonspecific psychological distress and other dimensions of psychopathology in the general population. *Archives of General Psychiatry* 37:1229–36.

Dohrenwend, B. P., P. Shrout, B. Link, J. Martin, and A. Skodal. 1986. Overview and initial results from a risk factor study of depression and schizophrenia. In J. E. Barret and R. M. Rose, eds., *Mental Disorders in the Community,* 184–215. New York: Guilford.

Falloon, I., J. L. Boyd, C. W. McGill, J. Razani, H. B. Moss, and A. Gilderman. 1982. Family management in the prevention of exacerbations of schizophrenia. *New England Journal of Medicine* 306:1437–40.

Link, B. 1987. Understanding labeling effects in the area of mental disorders: An empirical assessment of the effects of expectations of rejection. *American Sociological Review* 52:96–112.

Link, B. G., H. A. Andrews, and F. T. Cullen. 1992. The violent and illegal behavior of mental patients reconsidered. *American Sociological Review* 57:275–92.

Link, B. G., F. T. Cullen, J. Frank, and J. F. Wozniak. 1987. The social rejection of former mental patients: Understanding why labels matter. *American Journal of Sociology* 92:1461–1500.

Link, B. G., F. T. Cullen, E. Struening, P. Shrout, and B. P. Dohrenwend. 1989. A modified labeling theory approach to mental disorders: An empirical assessment. *American Sociological Review* 54:400–423.

Link, B., R. Moore, S. Schwartz, E. Struening, and A. Stueve. 1992. Does the American public show evidence of compassion fatigue concerning homelessness? Paper Presented at the American Public Health Association meetings, Washington, D.C.

McFarlane, W. 1990. Multiple family groups and the treatment of schizophrenia. In M. Herz, S. Keith, and J. Docherty, eds., *Handbook of schizophrenia.* Vol. 4, *Psychosocial treatment of schizophrenia.* New York: Elsevier.

Melick, M. E., H. J. Steadman, and J. Cocozza. 1979. The medicalization of criminal behavior among mental patients. *Journal of Health and Social Behavior* 20: 228–37.

Monahan, J. 1973. The psychiatrization of criminal behavior: A reply. *Hospital and Community Psychiatry* 24:105–7.

———. 1992. Mental disorder and violent behavior: Attitudes and evidence. *American Psychologist* 47 :511–21.

Monahan, J., and H. Steadman. 1983. Crime and mental disorder: An epidemiological approach. In M. Tonry and N. Morris, eds., *Crime and justice: An annual review of research,* 145–89. Chicago: University of Chicago Press.

National Mental Health Association. 1987. Stigma: A lack of awareness and understanding. Alexandria, Va.: National Mental Health Association.

Rabkin, J. 1979. Criminal behavior of discharged mental patients. *Psychological Bulletin* 86:1–27.

Shrout, P., M. Lyons, B. P. Dohrenwend, A. Skodol, M. Solomon, and F. Kass. 1988. Changing time frames on symptom inventories: Effects on the Psychiatric Epidemiology Research Interview. *Journal of Consulting and Clinical Psychology* 56:267–72.

Sosowsky, L. 1986. More on crime among the mentally ill. *American Journal of Psychiatry* 143:1325.

Steadman, H. J., J. J. Cocozza, and M. E. Melick. 1978. Explaining the increased arrest rate among mental patients: The changing clientele of state hospitals. *American Journal of Psychiatry* 135:816–20.

Swanson, J. W., C. E. Holzer, V. K. Ganju, and R. T. Jono. 1990. Violence and psychiatric disorder in the community: Evidence from the Epidemiologic Catchment Area surveys. *Hospital and Community Psychiatry* 41:761–70.

Teplin, L. 1983. The criminalization of the mentally ill: Speculation in search of data. *Psychological Bulletin* 94:54–67.

———. 1984. Criminalizing mental disorder: The comparative arrest rate of the mentally ill. *American Psychologist* 39:794–803.

———. 1985. The criminality of the mentally ill: A dangerous misconception. *American Journal of Psychiatry* 142:593–99.

Torrey, E. F. 1988. *Nowhere to go*. New York: Harper and Row.

7 Delusions and Violence

PAMELA J. TAYLOR, PHILIPPA GARETY, ALEC BUCHANAN, ALISON REED,
SIMON WESSELY, KATARZYNA RAY, GRAHAM DUNN, AND DON GRUBIN

Research can be found to support any of the three principal hypotheses on an association between violence and schizophrenia—that people with schizophrenia are more likely, as likely, or less likely than the general population to be violent (Taylor 1982). These hypotheses could probably be equally well applied to other forms of psychosis, but schizophrenia is generally more commonly implicated than the others and is more frequently specifically addressed. Much of the apparent dissonance in findings of risk can be attributed to sampling differences between studies. Evaluation of the nature of the relationship between violence and psychosis seems at least as promising as broad-sweep prevalence studies as a means of establishing the presence or absence of a more-than-chance association between the phenomena. Further, indications of group tendencies to display or contain violence based on prevalence studies alone are of limited help in practical management. An understanding of the nature of the relationship and the development of a simple means of evaluating its important elements are vital to the identification of risk in any individual case. This chapter will review the research evidence for an association between violence and delusions, considered likely mediators of any direct effect. It will comment on substantive and methodological issues that arise in measuring delusions in this context and describe the development of a new instrument to measure reliably the theoretically relevant dimensions of delusional experiences. First, however, brief consideration will be given to what it means to call a belief "delusional."

The Nature of Delusions

A delusion is widely held to be a pathological belief, but neither the concept of belief nor the definition of a core pathology are straightforward. Most definitions of belief require such elements as "trust" or "mental conviction," that is, acceptance of something as true or actual without necessarily the evidence that it is so. While some have argued that, in relation to pathology, it is not so much the nature and quality of the belief that is outside normal limits as

161

the process of reaching that state, it must be acknowledged that the range of processes accepted as normal is considerable. From a strictly Popperian viewpoint, if a person says, "water boils at 100 degrees centigrade at sea level under ordinary conditions of pressure," this must be regarded as a belief, because it is not possible to prove that this will always be the case in the future, only that it has been shown to be true under test conditions in the past. Nevertheless, the process of arriving at such a belief through observations and testing of observations is definable and demonstrable, and the evidence accumulated to support it is considerable. Where a belief is testable in this way, pathology may be relatively easy to define as deviation from an accepted route of testing the belief or from the body of knowledge thus derived. By contrast, belief in a deity, a characteristic not only widely regarded as normal but even required by many societies, is so defined that it is not testable under any known scientific conditions and may even require of its adherents that they accept the existence of a god as a truth without question or testing. The point at which the unquestioning acceptance of an idea becomes pathological is accordingly more difficult to define, limited as it has to be by collective social opinion rather than standards of knowledge. Indeed, to add to the confusion, the mere fact that a belief is widely shared does not make it "normal." Mackay (1869) described not only the spread of ill-founded beliefs through whole communities, often in the face of contrary evidence, but also the fact that members of those communities, individually or collectively, often acted on them. He even called these false beliefs "popular delusions" and their effect "the madness of crowds."

Other qualities of beliefs which have been held as characteristic of delusions, are, similarly, not pathognomonic. In relation to *falsity* of a belief, Mullen and Maack (1985) described just one of a number in their series of patients with pathological jealousy whose central hypothesis about the infidelity of his spouse proved correct, while the nature of the belief was undoubtedly pathological because of the route by which he had acquired it. *Bizarreness* or improbability of belief is similarly an inconsistent finding. What clinician has not had to attempt to care for a patient who sees his world disrupted only by petty persecutions? *Fixity* of belief has been advanced as another standard for pathology, and yet many political or religious beliefs which are regarded as normal are not conspicuous for their flexibility and changeability. Conversely, Garety (1985) has demonstrated that delusions are not invariably fixed. Sacks, Carpenter, and Strauss (1974) and Rudden, Gilmore, and Frances (1982), among others, have also emphasized that absolute conviction is not an essential component of delusions, and this has been taken into account in some interview schedules, such as the Present State Examination (PSE; Wing, Cooper, and Sartorius 1974). *Distress* accompanies only some beliefs, and, to make matters more complicated, disorders of affect such as incongruity or flatness are often pronounced in association with those beliefs which healthy people would regard as the most intensely disturbing. Another feature which appears to be commonly associated with beliefs generally regarded as abnormal is *egocentricity* or profound personal *idiosyncrasy*. Not only is the belief not shared by any one else from the sufferer's culture, but often the belief is of such great personal significance that the individual feels, and is, completely isolated by it. Nevertheless, real shared pathology occasionally occurs between close family members, for example the folie à deux of a mother and child or between siblings.

Perhaps Kraupl Taylor (1979) has made the most useful distinction between "normal delusions," which he defined as beliefs which are held to be false because held by a political opponent or someone of another culture or religion, and "psychotic delusions," which he suggested are based on an absolute conviction of the truth of a proposition which is idiosyncratic, incorrigible, ego-involved and often preoccupying. Oltmanns (1988) has offered a list of eight defining characteristics of delusions, which include conviction, preoccupation, and personal reference, but he stressed that these features may be more or less obvious. If these definitions are taken as emphasizing that no one characteristic of a belief is of overriding importance in rendering it pathological, then there seems to be a consensus emerging that delusions are complex, multidimensional phenomena (see also Kendler, Glazer, and Morganston 1983; Garety and Hemsley 1987).

Psychosis and Violence

Monahan and Steadman (1983) emphasized the almost insuperable problems in epidemiological approaches to an understanding of possible links between psychosis and violence, in that *true* disorder and *true* crime rates had not then been measured simultaneously in any study and that, to achieve this, one would require not only huge community samples but highly reliable and valid measures of the target behaviors. Swanson et al. (1990) have perhaps come closest to this ideal in the Epidemiologic Catchment Area project, which suggests that people with schizophrenia, as defined by a DSM III, Axis 1 diagnosis, are four to six times more likely to report engaging in some form of violence than people without illness. The rate depends on whether they have a relatively pure form of schizophrenia (the lower risk) or schizophrenia with an additional diagnosis. The report is unclear on the relative risk of violence among people with other psychotic illnesses. Although it initially asserts that people with affective disorders, including manic-depressive psychosis, do not have lower rates of assaultive behaviors than those with other diagnoses, including schizophrenia, it does seem that those with affective psychosis were at lower risk of repeated episodes of violence, of assaulting strangers, or of using weapons. Overall, it was concluded that those with affective disorders only had a relatively low rate of violence (3.4%) which was not substantially different from that of people without illness (2.05%) but well below that of those with schizophrenia alone (8.4%). Even this community self-report survey, however, may have been susceptible to differential reporting of violence, a suggestion being that the rates of violence in the healthy sample seem low, and that people with psychotic illnesses are much less likely to dissemble about their violence than those without. This would result in an exaggeration of the frequency of association between psychosis and violence.

Link, Andrews, and Cullen (1992) were rather more rigorous in their inquiry into violent and offending behavior, while pursuing a different approach to minimizing bias in sampling. They derived samples of "treated" patients, identified by contact with one hospital, and of never-treated community residents, as a comparison group, within a defined area of New York City. Both official criminal statistics and interview-elicited information about offending behavior not treated as criminal was considered and thus something as close as possible to true violence rates was measured simultaneously with something approaching true psychosis rates. All patient groups showed higher offending and violence rates than the never-treated community residents, but the relationships between the various measures of violent behavior and repeat-contact patient status were almost invariably very significant, while strong relationships were less likely in the other patient groups (first-contact and former patients).

Two of us (Wessely and Taylor 1991) have argued that longitudinal studies based on the criminal career model may be the best way forward in the process of clarifying relationships, but that more reliable methods of defining and measuring key illness factors and violent or destructive behaviors would also be essential. Lindqvist and Allebeck (1990) took such a view of offending and found that, over a 15-year period, while the rate of recorded criminal offenses was remarkably similar between men with schizophrenia compared with those without, the rate of violent offenses was four times higher among the former. Women with schizophrenia were at greater risk of committing any offense. In an English sample of interviewed pretrial male prisoners, for whom a wealth of independent data were also available, it has been demonstrated that, while criminal behavior overall seems as likely to precede as to follow the apparent onset of a psychotic illness among men, violent behavior, whether designated criminal or not, almost invariably follows it (Taylor 1993). This work was based on a sample identified by recognized criminality. In a subsequent analysis of data from the Camberwell Register of a representative English community sample Wessely (1992) has confirmed that the recording of personal violence and criminal damage rises after the onset of illness among both men and women with schizophrenia, but not the recording of other criminal activities. Their criminal careers thus appear very different from those of controls. Hodgins (1992) was able to take advantage of perhaps the least biased sampling of all—an entire birth cohort for a major European city, Stockholm—although study was confined to criminal and mental health records. This follows a Scandinavian tradition; she was able to cite an important study in Danish (Ortmann 1981) of the 1953 birth cohort of Copenhagen, which suggested that mental disorder serious enough to result in hospital admission was associated with a significantly higher risk of having been convicted of an offense, regardless of offense category. In the Swedish sample of 7,039 women and 7,362 men, surviving and in Stockholm for 30 years, there was a very significant relationship between psychosis and each category of offense tested, including violence, both among men and women. This was also, however, true for mental handicap among the men and substance abuse for the men and women. In contrast to subjects without mental disorder, socioeconomic status of the family bore no relationship to criminality among those with psychosis or mental handicap.

Delusions and Violence

Delusions are probably the most widely experienced of the positive symptoms among people with schizophrenia, with around 90% of patients experiencing them at some time during their illness career (Lucas, Sainsbury, and Collins 1962; Taylor, Dalton, and Fleminger 1982). They also occur commonly in other psychotic illnesses. Assuming that psychosis and violence are associated at greater than chance levels, delusions, therefore, are also likely to be widely prevalent among people who are violent and psychotic on a chance basis alone. There is evidence, however, that among people with psychosis the violent may be more likely than a nonviolent group to have experienced delusions at some crisis in their history, such as hospital admission. Hafner and Boker ([1973] 1982) compared people with a psychotic illness who had been homicidal with psychotic inpatients who had not been violent and found a significant difference in the prevalence of delusions between the two groups, even though they were common in both. Among those with schizophrenia 89% had been deluded at the time of the killing or attempted killing compared with 76% of the nonviolent patients at the time of inquiry. The proportions for those with an affective psychosis were 56% and 26% respectively.

The excessive association between violence and delusions has also been shown through the indirect evidence that the paranoid subtype of schizophrenia, paranoid states, or delusional disorders, all characterised by the prominence of delusional symptomatology, are generally cited as being more commonly associated with violence than other psychotic diagnoses (e.g., Tardiff and Sweillam 1980; Planansky and Johnston 1977). These studies, however, did not take account of the relative frequencies of the subtypes of illness in a psychotic population. Those that did provide mixed evidence of subtype association (Shader et al. 1977; Rofman, Askinazi, and Fant 1980). Among a second English series of pretrial male prisoners what almost amounted to a gradation of the influence of delusions was found, in that men whose schizophrenia had followed an almost exclusively delusional course were very significantly more likely to have been seriously violent than those whose delusions had been associated with other symptoms (Robertson and Taylor, 1993). The latter had, in turn, been more violent than those who had shown no more than transient delusions.

Most studies that have attempted to explore the possibility of a direct causal relationship between delusions and violence have depended on the study of case records. They generally, however, focus on homicides, where records include reports for the courts, so that it is likely that the recording clinicians did consider causal links. These studies have suggested that between 25% (Gibbens 1958; Wolfgang 1958; McKnight et al. 1966) and 40% (Lanzkron 1963; Petersson and Gudjonsson 1981) of the mentally abnormal, not necessarily all psychotic, were motivated by delusions. Hafner and Boker ([1973] 1982) also limited themselves to the review of such case records, but analyzed the delusional influence more extensively. While a specific delusion appeared directly relevant to offending only in a minority of cases, they described 70% of the people with schizophrenia as being in a delusional relationship with their victim, for example perceiving the victim as an enemy. In the first of the two English series of pretrial prisoners, and the first study to use research interviews to elucidate illness relationships with criminal violence, all but nine of the 121 psychotic men were symptomatic at the time of their offending. Nevertheless, an apparently direct influence from delusions on offending generally was found in only 40% of cases. A significant, specific association between delusional motivation and serious violent offending was, however, established (Taylor 1985). An important finding in this study was that no person without a psychosis attempted a delusional explanation of his behavior, rather giving the lie to a common suggestion that people are likely to fake symptoms of illness to excuse their behavior. Other kinds of beliefs may be important, but no one has systematically evaluated the role of normal beliefs in violence. Patterns of religious conflict through the history of many parts of the world would suggest this to be a not unimportant area for exploration.

An interview study of patients selected for being in a first episode of schizophrenia, rather than for having offended or been violent, also confirmed the importance of delusions. Twenty percent of patients (52 of 253) in a first episode of illness, but having been ill for anything from a few days to ten years, had behaved in a way that was threatening to the life of others (Johnstone et al. 1986). The most important illness characteristics associated with such threat were length of illness, which for the delusional may reflect growing conviction in and intrusiveness of the beliefs, and the presence of delusions of being poisoned (Humphreys et al. 1992).

Of the many possible characteristics of delusions it is not known which, if any, may result in action on the belief. Of particular interest here is the possibility that certain characteristics increase the risk of violent actions. Taylor (unpublished data) found that strength of conviction and certain kinds of belief content, such as that of the presence of spiritual or physical control by outside agencies, were significantly associated with delusional drive to criminal, mostly violent criminal, acts. It follows that reliable and valid measures not only of such beliefs themselves, but also of their characteristics, will be fundamental to risk evaluation among people with a psychotic illness.

Reliable and Valid Measurement of Delusions

One difficulty in the evaluation of delusions is that little has been recorded of their natural history, and in particular the rate of fluctuation over time either of the delusions or of their impact on the sufferer. Brett-Jones, Garety, and Hemsley (1987) studied longitudinally nine deluded subjects and found considerable fluctuations in different aspects of their delusions. Thus, although a finding of congruence of ratings taken on different interview occasions might lend support to the test-retest reliability of a scale, significant dissonance between occasions would be harder to interpret. It could suggest poor reliability of the scale, but it might be at least as likely to indicate real change in mental state, particularly as most delusional subjects, once identified, would soon be under treatment. One approach to dealing with this problem is to try and time a pair of interviews such that the repeat interview would be distanced enough from the first to allow subjects to be thoroughly rested and to be distracted from its format, but not so widely separated that significant, real change in delusional symptomatology would be probable. Patients suffering from the disorders known to show more rapid cycling would be avoided for purposes of evaluation of the scale.

The evaluation of interrater reliability similarly poses difficulties, in that people with psychosis may be particularly distractable, or suspicious of aids to the development of a new schedule such as the presence of a second interviewer or recording equipment. Work with previous, more general standardized mental state schedules, however, suggests that sufficient numbers of patients can be found to cooperate with one or more of these procedures to enable such evaluation. This is of crucial importance because in psychiatry and psychology each interviewer is, essentially, his own tool. Standardized interview schedules, such as the PSE, then require training in the use of the technique to ensure that each interviewer acquires and maintains reliability in recording the data.

The concept of validity of a delusion might well be considered as almost delusional in itself. A delusion is a subjective experience, and so, almost by definition, there can be no full standard of truth independent of what the patient says. This is no different from the position with respect to "normal" beliefs, which are similarly not subject to ordinary standards of proof. Nevertheless, phenomena approaching validity may be measurable, and in particular an attainable target seems a measure of the consistency with which the subject presents his accounts of his beliefs under simple repetition, through accounts given in relation to different methods of eliciting the belief, and under challenge to his belief. Observations of various kinds of activity apparently associated with the belief may also add weight to the likelihood of its existence or understanding of its nature. The interviewer may notice congruent actions during the interview, for example searching and suspicious actions on the part of someone who claims to be being watched or persecuted. Evidence from people who know the subject well in his everyday life may be particularly important, since there is less risk that in these circumstances the subject will have initiated or maintained actions merely to lend verisimilitude to his stories. The absence of other explanations for certain kinds of action may also yield indirect evidence. An apparent absence of actions may not, however, call the beliefs into question, but may rather reflect poor observation on the part of the observer, good concealment on the part of a patient trying to cover his disturbance, or simply a belief that does not seem to the patient to require action.

Development and Testing of the Maudsley Assessment of Delusions Schedule

An instrument for the reliable and valid assessment of delusional experiences and their possible consequences was created and tested at the Institute of Psychiatry of the University of London. A lengthy interview process was first developed, from the evaluation of which key items were selected for a schedule for practical clinical use.

The original interview allowed the subject a variety of methods of expressing his experience of his beliefs and the determination of the general mental context. The development was dependent not only on the joint efforts of the present authors, but also on advice from and discussion with a number of others experienced in the field. The full interview package included the opportunity for the patient to give a wholly spontaneous account of his beliefs and also elicited standard, detailed accounts during a structured question-and-answer session with the research interviewer. This was followed by a full, structured mental state examination (the PSE) and skeleton cognitive testing. The latter was done because some attributes of beliefs, such as the capacity to seek relevant evidence or the degree of systematization, are almost certainly related to the intelligence of the subject. In addition, for some patients, a semistructured telephone interview was conducted with relatives or staff in close contact with the patient about the patient's day-to-day behavior over the same time period as that covered by the interview with the patient.

The spontaneous account of beliefs is an important starting point for both the original, extended Maudsley Assessment of Delusions Schedule (MADS) and the brief form for clinical use. Only simple prompting questions are used, such as, "Tell me about some of your beliefs." The dangers of introducing interviewer bias are thus minimized, and the patient's verbatim account can be recorded and used as a form of indirect validity check on the material subsequently extracted and recorded in standardized form in the structured part of the interview. For those unable to respond to wholly open questions, progression to the use of the delusions content subsection of the PSE provides an alternative entry into the patient's beliefs. Comparable sections of other structured mental state examinations could probably serve the same purpose. The subject is then asked to choose from the beliefs he has described the one that he regards as most important to him. The more detailed questioning is focused on that belief. The time addressed is the month prior to the interview, on the grounds that recall for events over a longer period is likely to be significantly less accurate, and over a shorter period much less useful (Rutter and Brown 1966; Wing, Cooper, and Sartorius 1974). There is no reason why other beliefs—normal or abnormal—should not be evaluated by the same process if the patient will tolerate an extension of the interview, but, using the MADS, one belief should be explored in its entirety before proceeding to the next.

The original version of the schedule borrowed heavily from the work already undertaken by Garety (1985, 1990) and Brett-Jones, Garety, and Hemsley (1987) for the sections on belief formation and maintenance, together with some aspects of conviction. An item for rating the extent of preoccupation with beliefs and one for rating their systematization were adopted from the PSE (Wing et al. 1974). New rating systems were developed to cover the affective impact of the belief, the idiosyncrasy of the beliefs, the subject's account of the manner or degree in which he had acted on them, and the quality and degree of insight. A brief interview schedule for rating relative or staff observer accounts of the patients' behavior was developed and tested separately by Wessely et al. (in press). The feasibility of conducting the full interview package was checked before proceeding to a trial of the MADS.

Evaluation of the Maudsley Assessment Delusions Schedule (MADS)

Sample

All psychotic patients admitted to the Bethlem Royal and Maudsley Hospital over six months, and to the nearby Dulwich Hospital over the latter part of that time, were identified by the principal researchers (Buchanan and Reed). Any of these patients who had been in hospital for longer than one week and who were said to have had, throughout that time, delusions which were not congruent with a primary mood disorder were considered for inclusion. Patients whose only delusion was entirely congruent with mood and those who had a strong history of recent consumption of drugs of abuse, including alcohol, were excluded from the study only because of the probability that such patients were particularly likely to have rapidly fluctuant mental states which would increase the problems in interpreting differences between test-retest ratings made at interviews even days apart. No prescribed medications, however, were withheld from the patients during the study as this was regarded as unethical. Thus, it was not possible to exclude entirely the complicating factor that the patients included were at various, if relatively early, stages of active, specific treatment for their illness. Only consenting patients from clinical teams who were fully supportive of their participation in the study took part, and only those showing at least one full delusion according to PSE criteria (Wing, Cooper, and Sartorius 1974) at a preliminary interview were retained for the study.

The sample finally comprised 83 patients between the ages of 17 and 66, the mean age being 33. There were slightly more (56%) male than female patients. Diagnoses were mostly made on the basis of computer-derived syndromes recorded during the PSE, from data analyzed using the CATEGO program (Wing, Cooper, and Sartorius 1974). For the 80% of subjects for whom a full PSE was completed, the majority (62%) had schizophrenia; the next most common diagnosis was affective psychosis (26%), while a very small proportion had a pure paranoid psychosis (9%) or some other form of psychotic illness (3%). For the 20% of subjects who could not tolerate the complete interview package the clinical diagnoses were of schizophrenia. Just 13% of the samples as a whole were in a stable marriage or cohabitation, while nearly two-thirds had never formed such a relationship. Nearly one-third were in recognized employment or full-time education, so for such a patient group they were unremarkable in their levels of gross social adjustment.

Interviews

All prospective subjects were told that they were being asked to participate in a study of beliefs and would be asked to talk to a researcher and answer some questions on three occasions. They were reassured that anything that they said would be held in confidence. Separate oral consents were taken by the researcher for each interview and for approaching a relative, and written consent was obtained to examine the relevant case records.

At the first interview, before either the open inquiry about beliefs or the structured recordings began, some basic demographic data were collected, aimed in part at helping to establish rapport. The extended version of the MADS was then completed by one of the researchers, allocated to the patient in random order. No other interviewing was attempted on the first occasion, since the entire interview package could take two to three hours, and it was thought that the chances of completing second and third interviews would be maximized by not exhausting the patient on the first occasion. Twenty-five first interviews were rated independently by the other researcher, who was present in the same room as a silent observer. The two sets of ratings formed the basis for the interrater reliabilities calculated subsequently.

The second interview took place three to five days after the first. The extended MADS was repeated, followed by the full Present State Examination, the National Adult Reading Test (NART; Nelson 1982), and the digit-symbol test from the Wechsler Adult Intelligence Scale-Revised (WAIS-R; Wechsler 1981). All elements of the interview were completed on the same day, but not necessarily at the same sitting. This flexibility ensured maximum data collection while minimizing potential distress in restless or "persecuted" patients. For the 14 patients who, during this process, indicated that they no longer wished to continue with the work, interviewing was terminated, with resultant gaps in CATEGO classification. The first and second interview ratings were used to calculate the test-retest reliability.

Where possible a third interview was completed at discharge from hospital or six months after the second, whichever came first. The extended MADS alone was conducted by one of the researchers on this occasion. The goal had been to apply a statistical model derived from the work of Heise (1969) and Wiley and Wiley (1970)—the three way panel design—to assist in the separation of reliability from stability or change. Unfortunately data from the third interview could not be used because of full recovery in most cases and in one a change in the principal belief.

The data analyzed comprised ratings from 79 completed first interviews, 25 of which were rated by both researchers (time 1), and 58 second interviews rated by a single researcher. Agreement between raters on individual questionnaire items at time 1 was assessed from the use of the chance converted agreement index, kappa, using either the weighted or unweighted forms (Dunn 1989). The marginal distributions of the ratings were also examined as a check against bias of one rater as opposed to the other. Agreement between test and retest was investigated in exactly the same way. In this latter case a change in the marginal distributions of the ratings might be indicative of change in the patient's delusional state (i.e., improvement or deterioration).

Results

Performance on the NART provided an assessment of premorbid intelligence, while the results of the digit-symbol component of the WAIS-R provided a more objective assessment of attention and concentration than possible from clinical impression alone. The calculated mean full-scale IQ equivalent from the NART was above average (109) and contrasted with the results on the digit-symbol test which gave a mean scale score of 5, well below average. In general, however, a low score on this subtest was not associated with difficulty in completing the schedule.

The kappa coefficients for interrater reliability showed a generally good level of agreement between the two researchers on most questions, and where this was not the case questions were dropped from the schedule. It is worth noting that two items which seemed particularly important, given the principal purpose of this schedule, had to be abandoned for this reason. The questions "Have you harmed anyone in any other way?" and "Are you planning to do anything to anyone?" (both following on from questions about loss of temper and hitting someone, in the section on acting on the belief) did not lead to reliable responses (kappas of 0.04 and 0, respectively). Most patients started to become rather agitated at this point in the questioning and appeared to regard the extended questioning in this area as threatening and intrusive, which may have accounted for the poor reliability. All of the interrater reliability kappas for the items retained for the final version exceeded 0.6; the mean kappa was 0.82.

Fifty-eight patients completed the second interview using the extended MADS, and provided the data for the test-retest reliability evaluation. More often than not levels of agreement on items between the interviews were lower than those of the interrater agreement, although 80% were above 0.5 and 50% above 0.6. The mean was 0.63. Although modest kappas could be due to lack of precision in the interviewing or rating, this seemed unlikely in the view of the high interrater reliabilities. The first interview had invariably taken place with newly admitted, floridly psychotic patients and there had undoubtedly been real changes in mental state, even in the short time between interview occasions. It was thought that the lower kappas reflected real change rather than poor reliability of the instrument, even though there was considerable overlap in the time period (one month) for which questions were being asked. At the second interview the experience of the immediately previous 3 to 5 days, perhaps not surprisingly, seemed to have more impact on the patient's responses than the 23 to 25 days before that. The level of certainty with which the patients adhered to their beliefs provides a good example of the patterns of these influences, which largely accounted for the relatively low kappa of 0.56 (see table 1). At the time of the first interview, it had been possible to rate all but four patients, and the confidence with which those ratings were made was likely to have been well founded, since the interrater reliability was high (0.84). By the time of the second interview, there seemed to be lessening pathology. Only two people who had expressed grave doubts about their belief (rating 0 or 1) became more confident in it, while 11 people were expressing less confidence than at the first interview.

The number of people refusing to complete a second MADS did affect the

Table 1. Conviction about belief: Variation and consistency between interviews

			\<Second interview\>						
			0	1	2	3	4	9	Totals
First interview	Doubts belief (\<40% certain)	0	1	1					2
	Some doubts (40–69%)	1	1	2	1			2	6
	Quite certain (70–88%)	2		1	2		2	1	6
	Almost certain (90–99%)	3		3		4		6	13
	Absolutely certain (100%)	4	3	1		2	34	12	52
	Unrated[a]	9						4	4
	Totals		5	8	3	5	36	25	83

Note: Test-retest kappa = 0.56.

[a] All but two of the unrated patients, who were too thought disordered to rate, refused to complete one or more times of the extended MADS.

reliability, but this was an interesting problem in itself. Fourteen patients could not or would not cooperate at all with a second interview, but eleven of these patients refused principally and explicitly on the grounds that they had only just answered the questions, three to five days beforehand, although they were prepared to answer the questions new to them in the full PSE and cognitive assessment. For 74% of those patients who claimed a definite level of conviction at both interviews there was full agreement on the ratings between them. It was largely the failure to get commitment to a second interview which reduced overall agreement to 57%.

Belief maintenance factors, on the whole, were well sustained, the exception being that confrontation directed at the belief seemed to have a very different impact between sessions, which would fit with the hint that degree of conviction was probably diminishing. The patient's feelings about the belief had changed little between sessions but in some cases the activity level apparently had. The one item in the latter group of ratings that might have been expected to show both reliability and stability—knowing the person harmed—did yield a sound test-retest kappa (0.73). Otherwise the more general the question about activity the greater the reliability or stability in response between interviews. Ratings appeared relatively consistent in relation to patients trying to protect themselves (0.73) but more specific actions, like moving away from the source of persecution (0.43) were much less consistent between sessions and may have reflected the fact that these would be much more intermittent activities.

Answers to the questions about communicating beliefs to others (talking

Table 2. Talking to others about the principal belief

			Second interview[a]			
			0	1	2	Totals
First interview	Never	0	**10**		3	13
	Less than once per week	1	1	**7**	7	15
	Often	2	4	1	**25**	30
	Totals		15	8	35	58

Note: Test-retest kappa = 0.55.
[a]Twenty-five patients unratable at second interview (see table 1).

to, 0.55, and writing to, 0.45) again seemed to reflect change between interviews rather than poor reliability, although it has to be said that comparatively few patients claimed writing at all. Table 2 shows that for those who could be rated at both interviews, 10 (35%) of those who at first interview said that either they had not talked to anyone about their belief, or they had done so less than once a week, were often talking more freely by the time of the second interview, but only 4 (11%) of those frequently talking had ceased to do so. Again, this seems to indicate a group tendency towards improvement.

Once the most reliable items had been selected from the original MADS on the basis of a kappa coefficient of interrater reliability of 0.6 or more, further analysis was performed to test for overlap or covariance of items within the scale. This resulted in further reduction in the length of the instrument by just three items, to the form presented here. One item, for example, "Have you tried to escape what is happening?" covaried strongly with "Have you tried to stop x happening?" and so the former was omitted. In such pairs the item with the better interrater reliability was retained. Although such covariation provided some indirect evidence of validity, as hoped, we were impressed by the remaining sizeable range of discrete markers of the attributes and impact of delusions.

Relating the Informant Interviews

Fifty-nine informants were traced and interviewed (by Wessely), with the interviewer and informants blind to the characteristics of the patient as elicited at the patient interview. Most of the informants were relatives, but a few were social workers or hostel workers. All had been in regular, quite frequent contact with the subjects. No overall association was found between self and informant ratings of action on delusions (chi-square = 1.21; DF = 2; p = .55). There was an inverse relationship between patient and informant reporting of association between some specific delusions (e.g., delusions of catastrophe) and some actions (Wessely et al., in press). The actions the patients reported, however, fell into three main classes on the basis of latent class analysis, namely action which was aggressive to self or others (9 cases), defensive action (13 cases), which usually meant some kind of withdrawal, and either no action or a single, generally unobtrusive action (33 and 28 cases, respectively; Wessely et al., in press). The dissonances between patient and informant reporting had mainly to do with the patients stopping activities in which they had previously engaged, like meeting friends, watching TV, or even eating. In these circumstances the informants often failed to report the delusions, failed to report the activity (or withdrawal of it), or both. The informants were untrained observers, but the patients may also have attempted to conceal their behavior from any nonclinical or nonneutral figure. There was closer congruence between patient and informant reporting of aggressive acting and persecutory drive, both of which seemed readily apparent as intrusive and different from usual. The informant interviews were conducted in isolation from the patient interviews in the hope that they would provide a form of indirect validation, but in many cases they appeared to reflect better the likely true differences in individual experience of a phenomenon viewed from different participator perspectives than a distortion of the accuracy in reporting of either party.

The Resultant Patient Interview

Multiple characteristics of delusions can be reliably rated among a majority of acutely ill psychotic patients. The extent to which the attention and concentration of this series of patients seemed to have been influenced by their illness emphasized its severity in most cases. It was, nevertheless, striking that, while nearly 20% of the consenting sample were unable to complete a full PSE, all but two patients, who were very thought disordered, were able to complete even the extended version of the MADS at least once. Perhaps the selection of the belief that the patient regarded as most important as the subject of evaluation was a factor in encouraging compliance. In this sample, none was unable to choose a belief for assessment. Refusals to participate in the study at all might have been kept lower if the patient could have been asked to make less of a commitment to work, as would have been the case with the final MADS, which takes at most 15 minutes to complete, although it was our impression that a subgroup of very paranoid patients will resist compliance with any formal evaluation.

The testing of the extended MADS confirmed the importance, inferred from the previous literature, and measurability of the principal descriptors of delusions. These were conviction, belief maintenance factors, affective impact of belief, preoccupation, systematization of belief, insight, and action on belief. In some areas, such as conviction in belief, it proved possible to rely on a single clarifying question, whereas with others, such as belief maintenance or affective consequences of the belief, questions about several distinct aspects of the dimension had to be retained in order to build up a complete picture of the interaction between the patient, the belief, and the environment.

The concept of "dimensions" of delusions has been employed by others in the literature, and there is some empirical support for it (Kendler, Glazer, and Morganston 1983; Harrow, Rattenbury, and Stoll 1988). Garety and Hemsley (1987) found few significant correlations between individual characteristics of delusions, but a principal-components analysis yielded four clusters of variables: belief strength, preoccupation, distress, and reassurance seeking. The dimensions particularly associated with acting were elucidated further in the MADS study reported here (Buchanan et al., in press). Acting on the delusion was associated with being aware of and having actively sought "evidence" that supported the belief together with, paradoxically, some reduction in the conviction with which the belief was held on direct challenge. Acting was also associated with a range of affective changes (e.g., increase in fear or anxiety) which the patient attributed to the belief.

The choice of the delusion to be rated remains something of a dilemma, particularly if the instrument is to be used for a specific purpose—for example, as an aid to measuring the risk of violence. Our preference remains to allow the patient to choose the delusion for rating on the basis of its importance for him. Most patients seem able to do that, and it seems logical to suppose that, insofar as pathological beliefs have implications for other sorts of behavior, the delusion that the patient rates as most important will be likely to hold the most important consequences for him, and probably for others, without prejudicing investigation on the basis of other target characteristics. Asking a patient to select a delusion for evaluation on grounds that it had already made him act violently or that he thought it would could lead to a misleadingly biased selection of samples for research or, particularly if this were the sole belief studied, to missing data of potential clinical importance. In the case of studies comparing violent and nonviolent patients the selection of delusions on one criterion for the violent group (apparent relationship to past violent behavior) and on a totally different criterion for the nonviolent group (importance) could render the results invalid. Given, too, that there is still no resolution of the question as to whether delusions that influence action do so directly or indirectly, again to select for apparent association with violence gives potential for bias. Persecutory delusions, for example, associated with an attack on a presumed persecutor, might indeed be construed as having a direct relationship with the violent action. They may be interpreted by both patient and an independent observer as driving him to act. Delusions may, however, also enable action, effectively weakening the resistance of the patient to normal social controls that would have protected all concerned in an otherwise provocative situation. A delusion that an outside force is totally in control of the patient's actions may drive actions or may simply provide the background or permission for acting on some other delusion, such as one of persecution, on a normal belief, or on actual external provocation. In the first English pretrial prisoner study, passivity delusions were the delusions most frequently associated with apparent delusional drive to criminal, usually violent acting, but they were less often the belief to which the man attributed his actions (Taylor, unpublished data).

Applications of the Scale

Ideas of risk prediction and the attendant possibilities of prevention are so attractive and theoretically plausible that it is tempting to adopt as a substantive clinical tool any new instrument which purports to be able to evaluate an aspect of risk. The MADS has been developed as a research tool, and at this stage clinical application may be premature. Nevertheless any aid to the objective and systematic measurement of mental state and its impact is an advance over the use of clinical impression alone as the basis for the management of patients.

The association between delusions and violent acting appears to be stronger than would be expected by chance, but that still leaves a majority of deluded patients who, even if they act on their delusions, rarely do so violently. Only 9 (11%) of the 83 general psychiatry patients so far studied using this schedule had acted at all violently, even towards themselves, but only one 28-day period was studied. Sixty percent had apparently acted in some way at least once in that time on a belief (Wessely et al., in press). The work which has established statistical links between delusions and violent acting is based on only a handful of case record reviews and two interview-based studies (Taylor 1985; Robertson and Taylor, 1993) and would bear replication. The importance of an apparent dissonance between the content of delusions which seem most associated with acting in general (Wessely et al., in press) and that associated with violent acting in particular (Taylor, unpublished data, see above) is unclear. It may reflect a genuine marker in the content of delusions that lead to violent acting or may simply be evidence of the obvious—that no information should be accepted as uniformly applicable on the basis of one study with one sample.

Whatever else previous work has shown, it seems clear that it points to a complex relationship between thinking, feeling, and activity, with some external factors also influencing events. The MADS will enable the systematic evaluation of a core group of those factors and, perhaps most importantly, it will enable their evaluation over time. Remarkably little seems to be known about the course of psychotic illnesses in ordinary psychiatric practice, except in the most general terms, such as whether they tend to lead to overall deterioration in social function or the need for admission or readmission to hospital. Where acute episodes of psychosis resolve, there is little indication of whether recurrence involves repetition of a more or less complete pattern of the earlier episode, the repetition of key symptoms in the episode, or the emergence of completely new patterns. An attempt, in relation to the first pretrial prisoner study, to examine retrospectively the recurrence rates of a selection of symptoms apparently related to violence proved fruitless. The quality of existing records was sufficiently variable to render impossible a reasonable estimate of the historical details of symptomatology. Thus, a prospective study of the course of specific symptoms and their characteristics would be necessary and not merely an ideal.

A longitudinal prospective study would also enable evaluation of the impact of treatment, not only on some quality which seems to be associated with the general well-being of the patient, but specifically on individual symptoms, in particular delusions, hallucinations, and their associated characteristics. The development and evaluation of the MADS also confirmed the potential importance of hallucinatory drive (Reed et al., in preparation). Even the most specific and consistently credited treatments for psychosis, predominantly neuroleptic medications, do not necessarily have a uniform effect on all aspects of the illness. Among the positive symptoms of psychosis, some systematized delusions in particular may be peculiarly resistant to these drugs, and yet the patients nevertheless change sufficiently to be restored safely to ordinary social life in the community outside hospital. In one case in treatment with one of us, for example, a woman had nearly killed a prominent businessman on account of her delusion that not only was he her lover, but also that at that time he was interfering adversely in her life because of his consequent jealousy. A range of neuroleptic medication administered in substantial doses, and by different routes, over many years, wholly failed to shift even fractionally her conviction that this man wanted to be her lover. Various aspects of her treatment, however, completely changed the emotional impact for her of this belief, and she has not, during treatment, found or experienced any direct evidence of his continuing passion and certainly not of his interference. An intelligent woman, she dismissed with contempt the notion that her belief about the man is part of an illness, even though, as she said, she might have been able to secure her release from hospital more easily if she had been prepared to say so. Differential insight appeared such, however, that she nevertheless complied fully with treatment for several years. During that time, her relationship with treating staff was transformed from active hostility to a courteous partnership in her care. The apparently differential impact of treatment on various characteristics of her beliefs and their impact, in turn, on her behavior need further, prospective exploration, not only in her case, but also in a group of similar patients. Her progress may be unique, but it may rather illustrate a more general situation in which an instrument that can tease out the elements and impact of pathological beliefs and measure them independently could be extremely useful.

In relation to violent acting among people with psychosis, it would appear that there is time to measure the development of the illness and its potential dangers. Walker and McCabe (1973), Hafner and Boker ([1973] 1982), Humphreys et al. (1992) and Taylor (1993) have all indicated substantial delays between the onset of a psychotic illness and serious violence. In the first Brixton pretrial study, of the 121 psychotic men interviewed in detail just one gave a clear description of an autochthonous delusion leading rapidly to a seriously violent offense. Not only the illness but also the delusional systems had been present in almost all cases over a long period of time. The MADS could, even should, be used to monitor critical developmental patterns of the characteristics of symptoms which may trigger violence, but as models for testing, not yet as markers for clinical practice.

Acknowledgments

We are extremely grateful to Doctors John Cutting, Graham Robertson, and Robert Sharrock and Professor John Gunn of the Institute of Psychiatry and Bethlem Royal and Maudsley Hospital, for all their assistance in the development and preliminary discussion of the scale, and to Denise Formosa for preparing the manuscript. Support for the development of the MADS was provided by the John D. and Catherine T. MacArthur Foundation Research Network on Mental Health and the Law.

References

Brett-Jones, J., P. Garety, and D. Hemsley. 1987. Measuring delusional experiences: A method and its application. *British Journal of Clinical Psychology* 26:257–65.

Buchanan, A., A. Reed, S. Wessley, P. Garety, P. J. Taylor, D. Grubin, and G. Dunn. In press. The phenomenological correlates of acting on delusions. *British Journal of Psychiatry.*

Dunn, G. 1989. *Design and analysis of reliability studies: The statistical evaluation of measurement error.* London: Edward Arnold.

Garety, P. 1985. Delusions: Problems in definition and measurement. *British Journal of Medical Psychology* 58:25–34.

Garety, P. 1990. Reasoning, rationality and delusion: Studies in the concepts, characteristics and rationality of delusions. Unpublished Ph.D. manuscript, University of London.

Garety, P. A., and D. R. Hemsley. 1987. Characteristics of delusional experience. *European Archive of Psychiatry and Neurological Sciences* 236:294–98.

Gibbens, T. C. N. 1958. Sane and insane homicide. *Journal of Criminal Law, Criminology and Police Science* 49:110–15.

Hafner, H., and W. Boker. [1973] 1982. *Crimes of Violence by Mentally Abnormal Offenders*. Trans. Helen Marshall. Cambridge: Cambridge University Press.

Harrow, M., F. Rattenbury, and F. Stoll. 1988. Schizophrenic delusions: An analysis of their persistence, of related premorbid ideas, and of three major dimensions. In T. F. Oltmanns and B. A. Maher, eds., *Delusional beliefs*. New York: Wiley.

Heise, D. R. 1969. Separating reliability and stability in test-retest correlation. *American Sociological Review* 34:93–101.

Hodgins, S. 1992. Mental disorder, intellectual deficiency, and crime. *Archives of General Psychiatry* 49:476–83.

Humphreys, M. S., E. C. Johnstone, J. F. MacMillan, and P. J. Taylor. 1992. Dangerous behaviour preceding first admissions for schizophrenia. *British Journal of Psychiatry* 161:501–5.

Johnstone, E. C., T. J. Crow, A. L. Johnson, and J. F. MacMillan. 1986. The Northwick Park study of first episodes of schizophrenia. 1: Presentation of the illness and problems relating to admission. *British Journal of Psychiatry* 148:115–20.

Kendler, K. S., W. M. Glazer, and H. Morganston. 1983. Dimensions of delusional experience. *American Journal of Psychiatry* 140:466–69.

Kraupl Taylor, F. 1979. *Psychopathology: Its causes and symptoms*. Romney Marsh, U.K.: Quartermain House.

Lanzkron, J. 1963. Murder and insanity: A survey. *American Journal of Psychiatry* 119:754–58.

Lindqvist, P., and P. Allebeck. 1990. Schizophrenia and crime. *British Journal of Psychiatry* 157:345–50.

Link, B. G., H. Andrews, and F. T. Cullen. 1992. The violent and illegal behavior of mental patients reconsidered. *American Sociological Review* 57:275–92.

Lucas, C., P. Sainsbury, and J. Collins. 1962. A social and clinical study of delusions in schizophrenia. *Journal of Mental Science* 108:747–58.

Mackay, C. 1869. *Memoirs of extraordinary popular delusions and the madness of crowds*. London: George Routledge and Sons.

McKnight, C. K., J. W. Mohr, R. E. Quinsey, and J. Erochko. 1966. Mental illness and homicide. *Canadian Psychiatric Association Journal* 1:91–98.

Monahan, J., and H. J. Steadman. 1983. Crime and mental disorder: An epidemiological approach. In M. Tonry and N. Morris, eds., *Crime and justice: An annual review of research*, 145–89. Chicago: University of Chicago Press.

Mullen, P. E., and L. H. Maack. 1985. *Jealousy, pathological jealousy and aggression*. In D. P. Farrington and J. Gunn, eds., *Aggression and Dangerousness*, 103–26. London: Wiley.

Nelson, H. 1982. *National Adult Reading Test*. Henley, U.K.: NFER-Nelson.

Oltmanns, T. F. 1988. Approaches to the definition and study of delusions. In T. F. Oltmanns and B. A. Maher, eds., *Delusional beliefs*. New York: J. Wiley and Sons.

Ortmann, J. 1981. Psykisk ofvigelse og kriminel adfaerd en under sogelse af 11533 maend fodt i 1953 i det metopolitane omrade koberhaun. Copenhagen, Denmark: Rapport til Justitsministeriet Direktoratet for kriminal forsorgen, Forksningsrapport No. 17.

Petersson, H., and G. H. Gudjonsson. 1981. Psychiatric aspects of homicide. *Acta Psychiatrica Scandinavica* 64:363–72.

Planansky, K., and R. Johnston. 1977. Homicidal aggression in schizophrenic men. *Acta Psychiatrica Scandinavica* 55:65–73.

Reed, A., A. Buchanan, P. J. Taylor, S. Wessely, P. Garety, and G. Dunn. In preparation. Acting on hallucinations.

Robertson, G., and P. J. Taylor. 1993. The presence of delusions and violence among remanded male prisoners with schizophrenia. In Psychosis, violence and crime. Chap. 8 of J. Gunn and P. J. Taylor, eds., *Forensic psychiatry: Clinical, ethical and legal issues,* 338–39. Oxford: Heinemann-Butterworth.

Rofman, E. S., C. Askinazi, and E. Fant. 1980. The prediction of dangerous behavior in emergency civil commitment. *American Journal of Psychiatry* 137:1061–1064.

Rudden, M., M. Gilmore, and A. Frances. 1982. Delusions: When to confront the facts of life. *American Journal of Psychiatry* 139:929–32.

Rutter, M., and G. Brown. 1966. The reliability and validity of measures of family life and relationships in families containing a psychiatric patient. *Social Psychiatry* 1:38–53.

Sacks, M. H., W. T. Carpenter, and J. S. Strauss. 1974. Recovery from delusions. *Archives of General Psychiatry* 30:117–20.

Shader, R. I., A. H. Jackson, J. S. Harmatz, and P. S. Appelbaum. 1977. Patterns of violent behavior among schizophrenic in patients. *Diseases of the Nervous System* 38:13–16.

Swanson, J. W., C. E. Holzer, V. K. Ganju, and R. T. Jono. 1990. Violence and psychiatric disorder in the community: Evidence from the Epidemiologic Catchment Area surveys. *Hospital and Community Psychiatry* 41:761–70.

Tardiff, K., and A. Sweillam. 1980. Assault, suicide and mental illness. *Archives of General Psychiatry* 37:164–69.

Taylor, P. J. 1982. Schizophrenia and violence. In J. Gunn and D. P. Farrington, eds., *Abnormal offenders, delinquency and the criminal justice system.* Chichester: John Wiley and Sons.

———. 1985. Motives for offending among violent and psychotic men. *British Journal of Psychiatry* 147:491–498.

———. 1993. Schizophrenia and crime: Distinctive patterns in association. In S. Hodgins, ed., *Crime and mental disorder,* 63–85. Newbury Park, Calif.: Sage Publications.

Taylor, P. J., R. Dalton, and J. J. Fleminger. 1982. Handedness and schizophrenic symptoms. *British Journal of Medical Psychology* 55:287–91.

Walker, N., and S. McCabe. 1973. *Crime and insanity in England.* Vol. 2, *New solutions and new problems.* Edinburgh: Edinburgh University Press.

Wechsler, D. 1981. *The Wechsler Adult Intelligence Scale.* New York: Harcourt Brace Jovanovich.

Wessely, S. 1992. The criminal careers of people in one London borough with and without schizophrenia. Presentation to the Winter Workshop on Schizophrenia, Badgastein, Austria, 1 February.

Wessely, S., A. Buchanan, A. Reed, B. Everitt, P. Garety, J. Cutting, and P. J. Taylor. In press. Acting on delusions. *British Journal of Psychiatry.*

Wessely, S., and P. J. Taylor. 1991. Madness and crime: Criminology versus psychiatry. *Criminal Behaviour and Mental Health* 1:193–228.

Wiley, D. E., and J. A. Wiley. 1970. The estimation of measurement error in panel dates. *American Sociology Review* 35:112–17.

Wing, J. K., J. E. Cooper, and N. Sartorius. 1974. *The measurement and classification of psychiatric symptoms.* Cambridge: Cambridge University Press.

Wolfgang, M. I. 1958. *Patterns in criminal homicide.* London: Oxford University Press.

8 Hallucinations and Violence

Dale E. McNiel

Assaultive behavior by persons who are suffering from hallucinations represents a dramatic example of the co-occurrence of mental disorder and violence. Psychiatric textbooks note that patients with disorders such as schizophrenia can be "driven to homicide often for very unpredictable and bizarre reasons based on hallucinations" (Kaplan and Sadock 1988, 261). Clinical lore suggests that the presence of hallucinations that command a patient to behave in an aggressive manner is an especially ominous precursor to violence. Despite the intuitive plausibility of such clinical beliefs, only limited empirical research has been conducted on the topic, much of that within the last ten years.

This chapter will first review the prevalence of hallucinatory experiences, along with the types of mental states and disorders in which they occur. After presentation of pertinent background theory, quantitative studies concerning the association of hallucinations and violent behavior among different subgroups of the mentally disordered will be reviewed. Finally, implications for assessment of the risk of violence of current research and theory about hallucinations will be discussed, along with promising directions for further research.

The DSM III-R defines the term "hallucination" as follows:

> a sensory perception without external stimulation of the relevant sensory organ. A hallucination has the immediate sense of reality of a true perception, although in some instances the source of the hallucination may be perceived as within the body. . . . There may or may not be a delusional interpretation of the hallucinatory experience. For example, one person with auditory hallucinations may recognize that he or she is having a false sensory experience whereas another may be convinced that the source of the sensory experience has an independent physical reality." (American Psychiatric Association 1987, 398)

183

Conventionally, the term hallucination is not used to describe the false perceptions that occur while dreaming, while falling asleep, or when awakening. Similarly, hallucinations are distinguished from illusions, in which an external stimulus is misperceived or misinterpreted. Hallucinations have been described in auditory, visual, tactile, gustatory, olfactory, and other somatic modalities.

Hallucinations per se do not have specific diagnostic significance. Transient hallucinatory experiences are reported by roughly 10–15% of people without mental disorder (Slade and Bentall 1988; Stevenson 1983). During grief reactions, for example, it is not uncommon for individuals to experience auditory or visual hallucinations of the deceased. Sometimes referred to as pseudohallucinations, the initial experience is usually quickly recognized by the individual as not being based in reality. Hallucinatory experiences can also be induced by prolonged isolation and sensory deprivation, sleep deprivation or fatigue, food or water deprivation, or life-threatening stress.

Hallucinations in Psychiatric Disorders

Hallucinations occur in a heterogeneous group of psychiatric disorders, particularly schizophrenia, major mood disorders (e.g., bipolar disorder and major depression), personality disorders, and dissociative disorders. Epidemiologic studies (e.g., Goodwin, Anderson, and Rosenthal 1971) suggest that hallucinations per se are not diagnostic of a specific disorder.

Schizophrenia is often associated with hallucinations. For example, Andreasen and Flaum (1991) described the base rate of hallucinations in two samples of schizophrenic patients: in one sample of 111 patients, 50% had prominent hallucinations; in another sample of 55 patients, 35% had prominent hallucinations. Fenton and McGlashan (1991) reported that 66% of a sample of 187 schizophrenic patients had hallucinations. Although the most common hallucinations in schizophrenia are auditory, many schizophrenic patients also experience hallucinations in other sensory modalities, such as vision, touch, or taste. For example, Small, Small, and Anderson (1966) reported that a total of 76% of a sample of 50 schizophrenic patients experienced hallucinations in various sensory modalities: auditory (66%), tactile (42%), olfactory (38%), and visual (30%). Eighteen patients described hallucinations in only one modality (14 auditory, 3 tactile, and 1 visual); 20 reported hallucinations in more than one modality.

Schizophrenic patients often report hallucinations of voices familiar to the patient that make insulting remarks and may command the patient to do certain things (Small, Small, and Anderson 1966). Hearing voices that speak directly to the patient or comment on his or her ongoing behavior are common hallucinations. For example, Andreasen (1990) reported that of 111 schizophrenic patients 22% heard voices commenting on their behavior, and 21% heard voices conversing.

Mood disorders, such as bipolar disorder and major depressive disorder, in their more severe forms can be associated with hallucinations (American Psychiatric Association 1987). A recent review of the world literature indicated that roughly 20% of bipolar patients have hallucinations while manic or depressed (Goodwin and Jamison 1990). Unipolar depressives are less likely to have hallucinations than bipolar patients. Auditory hallucinations are the most common type in patients with mood disorders. For example, Goodwin, Anderson, and Rosenthal (1971) reported that of 28 hallucinating patients with primary affective disorder, 82% heard voices, 14% had other auditory hallucinations, 72% had visual hallucinations, 25% had tactile hallucinations, and 18% had olfactory hallucinations. Sixty-eight percent of the patients reported hallucinations in more than one sensory modality. The content of hallucinations in such patients is often mood-congruent: depressed persons may have hallucinations with themes of guilt, personal inadequacy, disease, death, nihilism, or deserved punishment (American Psychiatric Association 1987), for example, hearing voices berating them for their shortcomings or sins. Similarly, a manic patient may hear God's voice telling him or her that he or she is on a special mission. However, a subgroup of patients with a full affective syndrome (manic or depressive) have hallucinations which have content unrelated to grandiose or depressive themes (Kendler 1991).

Patients with personality disorders, particularly borderline personality disorder, are occasionally subject to hallucinations, which are usually transient and occur during brief psychotic regressions (American Psychiatric Association 1987). In fact, the American Psychiatric Association's Task Force on DSM IV has recommended including "transient, stress-related severe dissociative symptoms or paranoid ideation" as one of the criteria for the diagnosis of borderline personality disorder (American Psychiatric Association 1991). Various types of hallucinations have also been reported in dissociative disorders such as multiple personality disorder; for example, one or more of the personalities may report having talked with or done things with one or more of the other personalities. Putnam (1987) reports that the majority of multiple personality disorder patients experience auditory or visual hallucinations. Consistent with this conclusion, Ross et al. (1990) found that 89 of a sample of 102 multiple personality disorder patients reported hearing voices.

Hallucinations in Substance Abuse

Inpatient alcohol treatment units have reported that up to 22% of admissions have a history of hallucinations (Schuckit 1982). Hallucinations are associated with two syndromes related to alcohol: alcohol withdrawal delirium and alcoholic hallucinosis (Asaad 1990; Schuckit 1982). Visual hallucinations can be a feature of alcohol withdrawal when accompanied by delirium tremens (alcohol withdrawal delirium). Delirium tremens usually begins on the second or third day of abstinence following many years of heavy drinking, and is characterized by clouding of consciousness, disorientation, agitation, and autonomic hyperactivity. Visual hallucinations predominate, commonly involving rats, snakes, and other small animals, and are accompanied by intense anxiety. Tactile hallucinations (e.g., of small animals crawling on the skin) also often occur.

Alcoholic hallucinosis is a state in which vivid and persistent hallucinations develop shortly after cessation or reduction of heavy alcohol ingestion in a patient with alcohol dependence (Surawicz 1980). Alcoholic hallucinosis usually involves auditory hallucinations occurring in the context of a clear sensorium. Frequently the hallucinations are of a persecutory or threatening nature and may command the patient to do things against his or her will. Alcoholic hallucinosis usually only lasts a few hours or days, but can become a chronic condition.

Hallucinations induced by drug abuse often are visual, with vivid images and colors. Psychedelic drugs such as LSD, peyote, and psilocybin are known to induce hallucinations, as are phencyclidine (PCP), cocaine, and amphetamines, though the specific manifestations vary widely depending on the person, dose, mood, social setting, and physical condition of the individual (Siegel and West 1975; Slade and Bentall 1988; Asaad and Shapiro 1986). Hallucinations also occur in up to 75% of patients experiencing acute abstinence syndromes associated with abrupt withdrawal from agents such as barbiturates, benzodiazepines, chloral hydrate, paraldehyde, meprobromate, methaqualone, opioid compounds, and cocaine (Lipowski 1980).

Hallucinations in Other Disorders

Temporal lobe lesions, especially those associated with seizure disorders, are often accompanied by hallucinations (especially olfactory and visual hallucinations; Cummings 1985). For example, Currie et al. (1971) reported that 17% of a sample of 514 partial seizure disorder patients had hallucinations. Numerous other neurological conditions also have been associated with hallucinations, including occipital and temporoparietal lesions, dementia, delirium, head trauma, cerebrovascular diseases, space-occupying lesions, and central nervous system infections (Cummings and Miller 1987; Lishman 1987; Strub and Black 1988). For example, hallucinations have been reported in 40% to 70% of patients with delirium, such as the acute confusional states produced by various medical illnesses (Lipowski 1980). Hallucinations associated with focal lesions in the visual pathways in the temporal, parietal, or occipital lobes can produce "release" hallucinations, usually consisting of well-formed images which may be altered by opening or closing the eyes

(Cummings and Miller 1987). Ictal hallucinations, which occur as expressions of seizure activity, are brief stereotyped visual experiences; ictal hallucinations resulting from temporal lobe foci produce formed hallucinations and visual recollections of past experiences, whereas occipital seizure foci lesions tend to produce unformed hallucinations such as flashes, lights, and colors (Cummings and Miller 1987). Both release and ictal visual hallucinations are more frequently associated with right-sided than left-sided focal lesions, possibly because of the more specialized functions of the right cerebral hemisphere in visual-spatial information processing.

Hallucinations also have been reported as a side-effect of numerous medications such as antidepressants (e.g., amitriptyline), beta-andrenergic blocking agents (e.g., propranolol), and anticholinergic agents (e.g., benztropine) (Asaad 1990; Cummings 1985).

Hallucinations have also been associated with acquired deafness and eye diseases, phenomena usually explained on the basis of sensory deprivation (Asaad and Shapiro 1986; Cummings 1985). Similarly, persons who have had limbs amputated may have hallucinations of the missing limbs, i.e., phantom limb syndrome. In one study of 73 soldiers who were seen within six months of traumatic limb amputations, all had phantom limb sensations and 67 had experienced phantom limb pains (Carlen et al. 1978).

Theories of Hallucinations

Numerous theoretical explanations of hallucinations have been proposed (Asaad 1990; Horowitz 1975; Siegel and West 1975; Slade and Bentall 1988). However, development of a comprehensive theory of hallucinations has been limited by evidence of multiple etiological influences on hallucinatory phenomena.

West (1975) proposed a "perceptual release" theory of hallucinations. The theory assumes that life experiences affect the brain so as to leave permanent neural traces or engrams, which provide the substrate for memory, thought, and fantasy. West suggested that conscious awareness is regulated through a general arousal process mediated by the ascending midbrain reticular activating system. The brain is constantly bombarded by sensory impulses from inside and outside of the body, most of which are selectively filtered out of awareness. According to the model, hallucinations occur when the level of sensory input is insufficient to organize the filtering mechanisms but when enough arousal remains for conscious awareness to be maintained (e.g., during the excessive affect during functional psychosis, faulty synaptic transmission during toxic states, or prolonged sensory deprivation). This state allows the emergence of earlier perceptual "traces" or engrams into consciousness, which may be experienced as fantasies, dreams, illusions, or hallucinations.

When the level of arousal is high enough, the perceptual traces are experienced as hallucinations.

Slade and Bentall (1988) proposed a five-factor model of hallucinations, based on the concept of a failure of reality discrimination, i.e., hallucinators mistake their own internal mental or private events for external or public events. The five factors in the model are (a) stress-induced arousal, (b) predisposing factors (e.g., limited cognitive ability and a tendency to make over-rapid judgments about the sources of one's perceptions), (c) the extent and clarity of environmental stimulation, (d) reinforcement (e.g., when hallucinations are followed by a reduction in arousal or express an idea or intention which involves an important psychological concern that has been disowned by the conscious mind of the patient), and (e) expectancy (e.g., perceptual sets that lead hallucinators to interpret ambiguous events as real).

Asaad (1990) proposed a theory of hallucinations based on the failure of a central screening mechanism that controls the flow of stimuli from the external environment and the brain and that performs the function of excluding extraneous stimuli that are not relevant to attentiveness. The hypothesized site for the screening mechanism is the reticular formation at the brain stem level. The screening mechanism can be impaired under certain pathological or physiological conditions in which specific neurotransmitter systems (e.g., catecholamine, indolamine, and cholinergic receptor sites) play a role. This system may be affected by hallucinogenic drugs, various pharmacologic agents, neurotransmitter changes associated with functional psychoses, stress, sleep or food deprivation, or various neurologic conditions. Asaad suggests that the content of hallucinations is related to previous life experience and unconscious material.

These models share the view that both biological and environmental factors influence hallucinatory phenomena, as well as the view that hallucinations are associated with an impaired capacity to discriminate between personal experience and consensual reality. Each model attempts to explain the efficacy of antipsychotic medication in reducing hallucinations in terms of influence on the hypothesized biological mechanisms that set the conditions for hallucinations. Consequently, while not specifically addressing the issue of violence risk, these models imply the potential relevance of medication compliance and treatment of comorbid psychotic symptomatology (that impairs reality discrimination) in reducing the risk of violence in patients whose hallucinations have been associated with aggressive behavior.

Evaluating the Relationship between Hallucinations and Violence

Violent behavior by mentally disturbed persons is a function of an interaction of diverse personal, situational, and clinician factors (Brizer and Crowner

1989; Krakowski, Volavka, and Brizer 1986; Monahan 1981; Mulvey and Lidz 1984). Personal factors include clinical variables such as diagnosis (Krakowski, Volavka, and Brizer 1986; Rossi et al. 1986), acute symptomatology (Beck, White, and Gage 1991; Lowenstein, Binder, and McNiel 1990), and course of illness (Krakowski, Jaeger, and Volavka 1988); personal history (e.g., previous violence, substance abuse, being raised in a violent family; Monahan 1981); and demographic variables such as age (Kalunian, Binder, and McNiel 1990; Swanson et al. 1990) and gender (Binder and McNiel 1990; Tardiff and Koenigsberg 1985). Situational factors include family environment (Binder and McNeil 1986; Klassen and O'Conner 1988), availability of potential victims, availability of weapons (McNiel and Binder 1987), and whether the patient is in the community or the hospital (Binder and McNiel 1988). Clinician factors include the accuracy of the clinician in identifying a patient's level of risk for violence (McNiel and Binder 1991; Poythress 1990) and the nature of the clinical intervention undertaken (e.g., hospitalization, civil commitment, psychotropic medication, warning intended victims, etc.; Beck 1985; McNiel and Binder 1986). Each of these factors must be considered when evaluating the relationship between hallucinations and violence.

Most research on hallucinations and violence has used samples of patients who are being evaluated for psychiatric hospital admission or have been admitted to an inpatient setting. Study of hallucinations and violence in this context permits detailed examination of psychopathology and comprehensive evaluation of the occurrence of aggressive behavior because patients can be observed continuously. Efforts to study the relationship of hallucinations and violence in the community are complicated by the difficulty in attaining a valid index of violent behavior, since any one source of data (e.g., arrest rates, self-reports, reports of family or friends) may fail to identify violent acts that have occurred. A related complication is that the co-occurrence of hallucinations and violence in the community in itself often results in the patient being considered for hospital admission; both hallucinations and violence are among the better predictors of the decision to admit patients to the hospital (Beck, White, and Gage 1991; Friedman 1983; Marson, McGovern, and Pomp 1988; McNiel et al. 1992).

The question of generalizability of findings concerning hallucinations and violence obtained in one setting to other settings is an important issue about which the final answers are not currently available. For example, the situational precipitants of assaultive behavior in the community (availability of potential victims, alcohol and drugs, and weapons) differ from those in the hospital (the frustrations inherent in confinement and setting of limits by staff). A potentially important factor which may affect the relationship between community and hospital violence is the course of illness, particularly as it is affected by psychotropic medication. The few studies that have followed the same patients across community and hospital settings have yielded results compatible with this hypothesis. That is, violent behavior just before admission and during the early phase of hospitalization appears to be correlated (Beck and Bonnar 1988; McNiel, Binder, and Greenfield 1988), and psychopathology appears related to violence in both contexts (Beck, White, and Gage 1991; McNiel, Binder, and Greenfield 1988). However, violent behavior during hospitalization has not been shown to be a good predictor of violence in the community after release (Steadman 1981). McNiel, Binder, and Greenfield (1988) suggested that patients who are hospitalized after violent acts are at risk for continued violence in the hospital until their most acute symptoms are reduced by treatment, such as psychotropic medication, whereas patients who have received extensive treatment may not be as prone to violence related to their psychopathology after release. In any event, because of the potential importance of this issue, the following review will identify the setting in which each study of hallucinations and violence was conducted.

Quantitative Studies of Hallucinations and Violence

Several quantitative studies of hallucinations and violence have been conducted. Most of these have used samples of civilly committed or voluntary psychiatric patients hospitalized on a short-term basis. Typically hallucinations are rated based on a standardized scale covering a range of symptomatology, such as the Brief Psychiatric Rating Scale (BPRS; Overall and Gorham 1962) or the Nurses' Observation Scale for Inpatient Evaluation (NOSIE; Honigfeld and Klett 1965). On the BPRS, the clinician uses data obtained in a semistructured interview to rate the patient on 18 symptom scales ranging from 0, not present, to 6, extremely severe. The Hallucinatory Behavior scale of the BPRS concerns "perceptions without normal external stimulus correspondence." The interviewer rates only those experiences which are reported to have occurred within the last week and which are described as distinctly different from the thought and imagery processes of most people. On the NOSIE, nursing staff rate the frequency of each of 80 behaviors within the last three days on a scale ranging from 1, never, to 4, always. Within the Manifest Psychosis scale of the NOSIE are several items concerning hallucinations, such as "Hears things that are not there" and "Sees things that are not there."

Lowenstein, Binder, and McNiel (1990) compared ratings of symptoms on the BPRS at the time of admission with the occurrence of physical assaults during the first week of hospitalization for a diagnostically heterogeneous group of 127 inpatients. Twenty-seven percent had schizophrenic disorders, 15% had manic disorders, 15% had organic psychotic conditions, 18% had affective psychoses other than manic disorders, and 25% had other diagnoses. Hallucinatory behavior was significantly higher in patients who later physically attacked others during hospitalization (mean ± SD = 2.00 ± 2.09, mild) than in nonviolent patients (mean ± SD = 1.20 ± 1.81, very mild). The association between hallucinations and assaults occurred in the context of a general tendency for other positive symptoms of psychosis to be associated with violence. Specifically, patients who became physically assaultive had been rated higher on these factor-based subscales of the BPRS: thinking disturbance, hostile-suspiciousness, and agitation-excitement.

Similar findings have been reported by Yesavage and colleagues among patients admitted to a Veterans Administration hospital. For example, Werner et al. (1984) rated 40 male patients with the BPRS at the time of admission, then evaluated whether the patients became assaultive during the first week of hospitalization. Of the 40 patients 72.5% had a schizophrenic diagnosis, 10% had manic-depressive disorder, and 17.5% had other diagnoses. Hallucinatory behavior had a significant correlation ($r = .37$) with assaultive inpatient behavior.

Yesavage et al. (1981) studied inpatient behavior of 26 male patients, of whom 25 had schizophrenic diagnoses. Although ratings of hallucinatory behavior on the BPRS at the time of admission had a nonsignificant zero-order correlation with later assaults in the hospital ($r = .29, p < .07$), in a multiple regression equation hallucinatory behavior in combination with grandiosity did predict assaultiveness at the $p < .05$ level of significance. In addition, hallucinatory behavior had the highest correlation of any of the 18 BPRS scales with number of days on the ward on which an assault occurred ($r = .57, p < .001$).

Using a sample of 40 male patients with bipolar affective disorder, Yesavage (1983) reported that scores on a "psychosis" factor (which included hallucinatory behavior, conceptual disorganization, delusions, and grandiosity) derived from BPRS ratings at admission correlated significantly ($r = .32, p < .05$) with physical assaults during the first week of hospitalization. The psychosis factor also entered significantly in a regression equation that combined various predictors of assault.

On the other hand, Yesavage and colleagues have also published results in which they did not find a significant relationship between hallucinations and violence in a group of 80 inpatients, of whom 70% had schizophrenic diagnoses, 11% had manic-depressive diagnoses, and 19% had other diagnoses (Yesavage et al. 1982).

Janofsky, Spears, and Neubauer (1988) reported that the presence of hallucinations at the time of hospital admission was a significant predictor of battery incidents during the first week of hospitalization for 47 patients on a voluntary, university-affiliated inpatient unit. Their sample included diagnoses of schizophrenia (17%); depression (21%); bipolar disorder, manic or mixed (23%); adjustment disorder (17%); and other (22%).

Using the NOSIE, Tardiff and Sweillam (1982) reported a higher rate of violence by patients with hallucinations among a diagnostically heterogeneous group of chronic inpatients; 68% had schizophrenic diagnoses, 20% had psychotic organic brain syndrome, 6% had depression, and 6% had other disorders. Assaultive patients also manifested more severe impairment in other psychotic symptoms such as delusions, bizarre habits, inappropriate affect, and agitation.

Overall, studies based on quantitative clinical ratings of psychotic patients generally have shown a significant positive relationship between hallucinations and violent behavior. Typically, this association has been in the context of correlations between violence and other positive psychotic symptoms such as thinking disturbance and conceptual disorganization. These conclusions have been supported by studies using different methods, for example, a review of violent incidents in several British psychiatric hospitals (Noble and Roger 1989) and by studies conducted with other categories of patients, such as persons suffering from alcoholism and seizure disorders. For example, Schuckit (1982) reported that 22% of a sample of 220 consecutive male patients admitted to an alcohol treatment program at a Veterans Administration hospital had a history of hallucinations, and another 19% had other psychotic symptoms such as delusions. Of the patients with a history of psychosis 34% reported having injured someone and 15% had used a weapon, compared to 15% and 6%, respectively, of the alcoholic patients without a history of psychosis. Similarly, some research suggests that violence in patients with temporal lobe seizures is more common among the subgroup of such patients who have hallucinatory and paranoid symptoms (Lewis et al. 1982; Treiman and Delgado-Escueta 1983).

Significance of Command Hallucinations

A dimension of hallucinatory behavior typically considered important in evaluating a patient's risk of violence is whether or not the hallucinations command the patient to act in a certain manner such as to behave in a violent way. Hellerstein, Frosch, and Koenigsberg (1987) reviewed the charts of 789 patients admitted to a university-based hospital, and found that 151 patients had auditory hallucinations. Fifty-eight (35%) of the hallucinating patients heard commands. The content of the command hallucinations for the 58 patients was: suicide (51%), homicide (5%), nonlethal injury of self or others (12%), nonviolent acts (14%), and unspecified (17%). There was no significant difference in the proportion of patients with assaultive acts leading to admission between patients with and without auditory hallucinations or between those with and without command hallucinations. Hallucinating patients were more likely to be put in seclusion rooms than nonhallucinating patients, suggesting an overall correlation between hallucinations and aggressive inpatient behavior. However, there was no significant difference between patients with command and noncommand hallucinations in likelihood of being secluded. The authors concluded that the prognostic significance of command hallucinations was not confirmed. Hellerstein, Frosch, and Koenigsberg (1987) speculated that most patients ignore the commands but that there may be subgroups of patients who are at risk for violence if command hallucinations occur (e.g., patients who have acted violently in the past in response to command hallucinations or patients with previous impulsive or violent behavior). The study leaves unclear whether command hallucinations per se are particularly significant, compared with the presence of any acute psychotic symptoms such as delusions, unusual perceptions, or any kind of hallucinations.

Junginger (1990) attempted to identify which of 44 inpatients and outpatients with command hallucinations were most likely to comply with the instructions of their hallucinations. Patients who reported hallucination-related delusions (i.e., delusional beliefs for which the patient offered as evidence aspects of his or her auditory hallucinations) and could identify the voices were more likely to comply with command hallucinations, a relationship that was not affected by whether or not the commands were related to "dangerous" content (i.e., pertaining to self-harm or harm to others). Eight of 20 subjects who experienced command hallucinations with content involving harm to self or others reported that they had complied with the commands, as did 12 of 31 patients who experienced commands with "harmless" content. Although raising interesting possibilities, the relevance of this study for assessing the risk of violence by patients with command hallucinations is limited by such methodological problems as a vague definition of violence, reliance on patients' self-reports of violence, and a small sample.

Goodwin, Anderson, and Rosenthal (1971) interviewed 117 hallucinating inpatients from several diagnostic groups, and found that 42 reported hearing voices that attempted to influence them in certain ways. The authors reported that patients generally ignored hallucinatory commands or suggestions. None acknowledged having committed destructive or antisocial acts because of the voices.

Studies of prisoners with hallucinations have shown that command hallucinations (e.g., the patient being commanded by God to kill someone) can result in violent behavior. Taylor (1985) described a sample of 121 psychotic male prisoners who showed active psychotic symptoms at the time of committing a criminal offense; the criminal behavior of 23 of the prisoners could be attributed directly to their psychotic symptoms. Five of the patients blamed their behavior on hallucinations, although none had committed severe violent behavior. Two of the patients said their voices instructed them to break windows or carry a knife. Three patients damaged property or became assaultive in efforts to escape their voices.

Rogers and colleagues have studied patients in forensic hospitals who report command hallucinations. Rogers (1986) reported that 5.8% of a sample of 385 persons being evaluated for insanity had committed their offense in response to command hallucinations; these patients represented 43% of the forensically referred persons he saw with auditory hallucinations.

Rogers et al. (1990), describing 65 psychotic inpatients on a forensic assessment unit, reported that research interviewers identified twice as many patients with command hallucinations as did clinical staff. Research interviewers identified 38% of the 65 patients as having command hallucinations, 37% as having noncommand hallucinations, and 25% as not having hallucinations. Command hallucinations were associated with guilt and self-reproach. Eighty percent of patients who reported command hallucinations said that they had recently obeyed them. Fifty-six percent ($N = 14$) of patients with command hallucinations had at least one experience of responding to a command hallucination with unquestioning obedience and 44% responded with obedience on a frequent basis. However, there was no significant association between command hallucinations and assaultive behavior. Command hallucinations showed more aggressive and self-punishing content than did noncommand hallucinations, and patients experiencing command hallucinations displayed more helplessness and dependency on the hallucinations and greater reliance on the hallucinations for advice than did patients with noncommand hallucinations.

In sum, studies of hallucinating patients have failed to show a clear relationship between assaultive behavior and whether or not the hallucinations involve commands. Studies with systematic sampling techniques suggest that most patients with violent command hallucinations do not comply with them. Although a subgroup of patients may behave in a violent manner based on their command hallucinations, research has yet to identify how they differ from others with command hallucinations.

Integration: Implications for Assessment of the Risk of Violence

Research over the past ten years has identified a positive relationship between hallucinations and violent behavior. However, the relationship is not a simple one and is affected by a range of variables:

Personal Variables

The nature of the disorder underlying hallucinations is important. Most research documenting assaultive behavior in conjunction with hallucinations has been conducted with patients with major mental disorders such as schizophrenia, bipolar disorder, and organic psychotic conditions. Although hallucinations have been reported in patients with other disorders associated with violence (e.g., certain seizure disorders), less research has been done to document an association between hallucinations and violence in such disorders (cf. Trimble 1991).

The course of illness is also known to affect the relationship between psychopathology and violence (Monahan 1988). For example, most studies documenting associations between hallucinations and violence have evaluated patients during acute episodes of illness, such as the period just before or after hospital admission. As patients are stabilized with treatment, hallucinations may be less useful indicators of violence risk. Empirical support for this formulation comes from a study of 44 patients admitted to a special state hospital unit for violent patients (Krakowski, Jaeger, and Volavka 1988). The authors found a significant correlation ($r = .47$) between violence and thought disturbance (defined as the hallucinatory behavior, conceptual disorganization, and unusual thought content items of the BPRS) during the first half of patients' stay on the unit, but found no significant association between thought disturbance and violence during the final half of the patients' stay.

Associations between hallucinations and violence have been reported in the context of other personal characteristics that are correlated with violence, such as conceptual disorganization and unusual thought content, history of violence, history of substance abuse, and younger age. Although such variables do not explain the relationship between hallucinations and violence, they are relevant. For example, if a patient has a history of behaving violently in response to hallucinations, the risk of assault is obviously higher than would be the case with only the knowledge that the patient is hallucinating.

Situational Variables

The setting that the patient is in may affect whether hallucinations will be associated with violence. For example, Krakowski, Volavka, and Brizer (1986) reviewed several studies suggesting that patients with paranoid schizophrenia are more likely to be violent outside the hospital setting, but are not especially violent in hospital settings following an initial period of stabilization. Tardiff (1984) has presented data supporting similar conclusions. It is possible that such an interaction between psychopathology and situational variables reflects differential responsiveness of paranoid schizophrenic patients to pharmacological treatment, a tendency of paranoid schizophrenic patients to be noncompliant with outpatient treatment, a differential response to the external structure imposed by the inpatient setting, or the differential availability of persons who are the focus of paranoid patients' delusions. In any event, all of these factors could moderate the relationship between hallucinations and violence. Yesavage (1984) has shown that lower serum levels of the antipsychotic thiothixene are associated with higher rates of inpatient assault and higher levels of hallucinatory behavior, delusions, and grandiosity. Hence, it appears plausible that noncompliance with medication treatment could affect the association of hallucinations and violence in the outpatient setting. Data from a recent study of 133 schizophrenic outpatients (Bartels et al. 1991) are compatible with this hypothesis. Patients who were higher in "characteristic hostility" (a variable defined as ranging from 1, "no hostility," to 5, "assaultiveness with potential or actual harm") were higher in medication noncompliance (Kendall's tau-c $= .25$, $p < .001$) and higher in symptoms such as hallucinations and delusions (Kendall's tau-c $= .28$, $p < .001$).

Clinician Variables

Because clinicians have a legal and ethical responsibility to intervene when they believe a patient is at risk for violence, variables which may have an association with violence outside the treatment setting may not appear significantly related to violence in the treatment context. For example, some studies have failed to identify correlations between hostility and inpatient violence, possibly because clinicians intervened to prevent violence in hostile patients perceived as at risk (Werner et al. 1984). Similarly, when a patient says that he or she is hearing voices telling him or her to kill someone, many clinicians would interpret this communication as constituting a threat, invoking a duty to protect the potential victim by actions such as hospitalization, additional medication, or issuing a warning (Beck 1985). Such preventive clinical interventions could attenuate any correlations observed between command hallucinations and violence.

Research on forensic samples has suggested a higher association between command hallucinations and violence than has been reported in other samples. Whether this is due to an actual overrepresentation of patients with command hallucinations among violent forensic mental patients or whether violent patients perceive more benefit for malingering such symptoms within a forensic context is not clear at this time (cf. Resnick 1988).

Future Research Directions

Further research is needed to identify the subgroups of patients for whom hallucinations are most closely associated with violence. To advance knowledge about hallucinations and violence, future research needs to simultaneously assess pertinent personal, situational, and clinician variables over time. Personal variables should include course of illness, as the frequency and intensity of hallucinations experienced by a given patient typically vary over time. It is possible that hallucinations have a greater influence on a patient's risk of violence during episodes of acute exacerbation of his or her disorder as opposed to periods of relative remission. Similarly, the covariation of hallucinations and other comorbid conditions should be considered. Existing studies suggest that it is not just hallucinations, but hallucinations along with other manifestations of acute psychosis, such as impaired reality testing, delusions, and poor judgment that increase the risk of violence. More generally, research needs to evaluate whether the most useful level of analysis is the symptom (e.g., hallucinations) or the diagnosis (e.g., schizophrenia), or whether the relative importance of a symptom such as hallucinations in increasing the risk of violence varies depending on a patient's diagnosis (e.g., does the presence of hallucinations have different implications for the risk of violence in a schizophrenic patient than in a manic patient?). Future research should also evaluate whether the strategies used by patients for coping with their hallucinations affects the likelihood of violence. Previous research has identified a variety of techniques patients use to cope with their hallucinations, such as changes in physical activity (e.g., walking, running, inactivity, lying down), changes in posture, engaging in leisure activities (e.g., hobbies, reading, and television), increasing interpersonal contact, distraction or suppression (e.g., ignoring the voices, thinking distracting thoughts), going to sleep, taking extra doses of prescribed medication, and using nonprescribed drugs or alcohol (Carr 1988; Faloon and Talbott 1989). It is possible that the effectiveness of strategies used by patients to cope with their hallucinations could affect their risk of violence. Future research on hallucinations and violence should evaluate the potential relevance of features of hallucinations in addition to presence versus absence and command versus noncommand content. Areas of possible study include other aspects of content, vividness, loudness, duration and frequency, continuousness or intermittence, perception of single or multiple voices, location of voices inside or outside of the head, tone of voice of hallucinations, patient's insight into the unreality of voices, belief that others could hear the voices, familiarity versus unfamiliarity of the person speaking in the hallucination, whether or not the patient converses with the voices, patient's ability to put the hallucinations outside of his or her mind, the relationship of the hallucinations to delusions, the patient's reaction to the hallucinations, strategies used to diminish the hallucinations, and efforts to not obey any commands given by the voices (Resnick 1988).

Future research is also needed on the influence of situational variables on the relationship between hallucinations and violence. For example, the same group of patients could be followed before, during, and after hospital admission to monitor how hallucinations relate to violent behavior. This type of research is needed with samples of both criminal and civil patients. Similarly, it could be useful to assess whether the ways family caregivers cope with potentially violent behavior could have a differential outcome depending on whether or not the patient is actively hallucinating. Some research suggests that family interactions characterized by calming the patient and increasing the distance between patient and family may be more adaptive with potentially violent psychotic patients than interactions that involve assertion of limits and restriction of other family members' own behavior to avoid confrontation with the patient (Swann and Levitt 1988).

Future research in this area needs also to address clinician factors. Research is needed concerning the manner in which clinicians use information about hallucinations in their assessment of patients' risk of violence. Some evidence suggests that hallucinations may have a stronger association with assaultive behavior than they do with clinicians' assessments of risk of violence (Werner, Rose, and Yesavage 1983). Confirmation of this finding could suggest ways of improving clinical assessments of potential for violence. Finally, given evidence that both hallucinations and assaultive behavior are inversely related to treatment with antipsychotic medication (Yesavage 1984), research to identify actors influencing psychotic patients' potential for medication compliance may be of use in evaluating the risk of violence based on hallucinations.

In summary, existing research suggests that hallucinations may be related to violence as part of a presentation of acute psychosis, along with impaired reality testing and poor judgment. Just as threats of violence by acutely psychotic patients serve as cues of increased risk of aggression (not necessarily limited to the threatened victim; McNiel and Binder 1989), hallucinatory experiences, when they occur in the context of other personal and situational correlates of violence, can indicate further increased risk of violent behavior.

References

American Psychiatric Association. 1987. *Diagnostic and statistical manual of mental disorders*. 3d ed., rev. (DSM III-R). Washington, D.C.: American Psychiatric Association.

American Psychiatric Association, Task Force on DSM IV. 1991. *DSM IV options book: Work in progress*. Washington, D.C.: American Psychiatric Association.

Andreasen, N. C. 1990. Positive and negative symptoms: Historical and conceptual aspects. In N. C. Andreasen, ed., *Modern problems of psychopharmacology: Positive and negative syndromes and symptoms*. Vol. 24. Basel, Switzerland: S. Karger, A. G.

Andreasen, N. C., and M. Flaum. 1991. Schizophrenia: The characteristic symptoms. *Schizophrenia Bulletin* 17:27–49.

Asaad, G. 1990. *Hallucinations in clinical psychiatry*. New York: Brunner/Mazel.

Asaad, G., and B. Shapiro. 1986. Hallucinations: Theoretical and clinical overview. *American Journal of Psychiatry* 143:1088–97.

Bartels, S. J., R. E. Drake, M. A. Wallach, and D. H. Freeman. 1991. Characteristic hostility in schizophrenic outpatients. *Schizophrenia Bulletin* 17:163–71.

Beck, J. C., ed. 1985. *The potentially violent patient and the Tarasoff decision in psychiatric practice.* Washington, D.C.: American Psychiatric Press.

Beck, J. C., and J. Bonnar. 1988. Emergency civil commitment: Predicting hospital violence from behavior in the community. *Journal of Psychiatry and Law* 16:379–88.

Beck, J. C., K. A. White, and B. Gage. 1991. Emergency psychiatric assessment of violence. *American Journal of Psychiatry* 148:1562–65.

Binder, R. L., and D. E. McNiel. 1986. Victims and families of violent psychiatric patients. *Bulletin of the American Academy of Psychiatry and the Law* 14:131–39.

———. 1988. Effects of diagnosis and context on dangerousness. *American Journal of Psychiatry* 145:728–32.

———. 1990. The relationship of gender to violent behavior in acutely disturbed psychiatric patients. *Journal of Clinical Psychiatry* 51:110–14.

Brizer, D. A., and M. L. Crowner, eds. 1989. *Current approaches to the prediction of violence.* Washington, D.C.: American Psychiatric Press.

Carlen, P. L., P. D. Wall, H. Nadvorna, and T. Steinbach. 1978. Phantom limbs and related phenomena in recent traumatic amputations. *Neurology* 28:211–17.

Carr, V. 1988. Patients' techniques for coping with schizophrenia: An exploration study. *British Journal of Medical Psychology* 61:339–52.

Cummings, J. L. 1985. *Clinical neuropsychiatry.* New York: Grune and Stratton.

Cummings, J. L., and B. L. Miller. 1987. Visual hallucinations: Clinical occurrence and use in differential diagnosis. *Western Journal of Medicine* 146:46–51.

Currie, S., K. W. G. Heathfield, R. A. Henson, and D. F. Scott. 1971. Clinical course and prognosis of temporal lobe epilepsy. *Brain* 94:173–90.

Faloon, I. R., and R. E. Talbott. 1989. Persistent auditory hallucinations: Coping mechanisms and implications for management. *Psychological Medicine* 11:329–39.

Fenton, W. S., and T. H. McGlashan. 1991. Natural history of schizophrenia subtypes. II: Positive and negative symptoms and long-term course. *Archives of General Psychiatry* 48:978–86.

Friedman, R. S. 1983. Hospital treatment of psychiatric emergencies. *Psychiatric Clinics of North America* 6:293–303.

Goodwin, D. W., P. Anderson, and R. Rosenthal. 1971. Clinical significance of hallucinations in psychiatric disorders. *Archives of General Psychiatry* 24:76–80.

Goodwin, F. K., and K. R. Jamison. 1990. *Manic-depressive illness.* New York: Oxford University Press.

Hellerstein, D., W. Frosch, and H. W. Koenigsberg. 1987. The clinical significance of command hallucinations. *American Journal of Psychiatry* 144:219–21.

Honigfeld, G., and C. J. Klett. 1965. The Nurses' Observation Scale for Inpatient Evaluation. *Journal of Clinical Psychology* 21:65–71.

Horowitz, M. J. 1975. Hallucinations: An information processing approach. In R. K. Siegel and L. J. West, eds., *Hallucinations: Behavior, experience, and theory.* New York: John Wiley and Sons.

Janofsky, J. S., S. Spears, and D. N. Neubauer. 1988. Psychiatrists' accuracy in predicting violent behavior on an inpatient unit. *Hospital and Community Psychiatry* 39:1090–94.

Junginger, J. 1990. Predicting compliance with command hallucinations. *American Journal of Psychiatry* 147:245–47.

Kalunian, D. A., R. L. Binder, and D. E. McNiel. 1990. Violence by geriatric patients who need psychiatric hospitalization. *Journal of Clinical Psychiatry* 51:340–43.

Kaplan, H. I., and B. J. Sadock. 1988. *Synopsis of psychiatry: Behavioral sciences, clinical psychiatry.* 5th ed. Baltimore: Williams and Wilkins.

Kendler, K. S. 1991. Mood-incongruent affective illness: A historical and empirical review. *Archives of General Psychiatry* 48:362–70.

Klassen, D., and W. O'Connor. 1988. A prospective study of predictors of violence in adult male mental patients. *Law and Human Behavior* 12:143–48.

Krakowski, M., J. Jaeger, and J. Volavka. 1988. Violence and psychopathology: A longitudinal study. *Comprehensive Psychiatry* 29:174–81.

Krakowski, M., J. Volavka, and D. Brizer. 1986. Psychopathology and violence: A review of the literature. *Comprehensive Psychiatry* 27:131–48.

Lewis, D. O., T. H. Pincus, S. S. Shanok, and G. H. Glaser. 1982. Psychomotor epilepsy and violence in a group of incarcerated adolescent boys. *American Journal of Psychiatry* 139:882–87.

Lipowski, Z. J. 1980. *Delirium: Acute brain failure in man.* Springfield, Ill.: Charles C. Thomas.

Lishman, W. A. 1987. *Organic psychiatry.* 2d ed. Boston: Blackwell Scientific Publications.

Lowenstein, M., R. L. Binder, and D. E. McNiel. 1990. The relationship between admission symptoms and hospital assaults. *Hospital and Community Psychiatry* 41:311–13.

Marson, D. C., M. P. McGovern, and H. C. Pomp. 1988. Psychiatric decision making in the emergency room. *American Journal of Psychiatry* 145:918–25.

McNiel, D. E., and R. L. Binder. 1986. Violence, civil commitment and hospitalization. *Journal of Nervous and Mental Disease* 174:107–11.

———. 1987. Patients who bring weapons to the psychiatric emergency room. *Journal of Clinical Psychiatry* 48:230–33.

———. 1989. Relationship between preadmission threats and later violent behavior by acute psychiatric inpatients. *Hospital and Community Psychiatry* 40:605–8.

———. 1991. Clinical assessment of the risk of violence among psychiatric inpatients. *American Journal of Psychiatry* 148:1317–21.

McNiel, D. E., R. L. Binder, and T. K. Greenfield. 1988. Predictors of violence in civilly committed acute psychiatric patients. *American Journal of Psychiatry* 145:965–70.

McNiel, D. E., R. S. Myers, H. Zeiner, H. L. Wolfe, and C. Hatcher. 1992. The role of violence in decision-making about hospitalization from the psychiatric emergency room. *American Journal of Psychiatry* 142:207–12.

Monahan, J. 1981. *The clinical prediction of violent behavior.* DHHS Publication ADM 89-92. Rockville, Md.: National Institute of Mental Health.

———. 1988. Risk assessment of violence among the mentally disordered: Generating useful knowledge. *International Journal of Law and Psychiatry* 11:249–57.

Mulvey, E., and C. Lidz. 1984. Clinical considerations in the prediction of dangerousness in mental patients. *Clinical Psychology Review* 4:379–401.

Noble, P., and S. Roger. 1989. Violence by psychiatric inpatients. *British Journal of Psychiatry* 155:384–90.

Overall, J., and D. R. Gorham. 1962. The Brief Psychiatric Rating Scale. *Psychological Reports* 10:799–812.

Poythress, N. G. 1990. Avoiding negligent release: Contemporary clinical and risk management strategies. *American Journal of Psychiatry* 147:994–97.

Putnam, F. W. 1987. *Diagnosis and treatment of multiple personality disorder.* New York: Guilford Press.

Resnick, P. J. 1988. Malingered psychosis. In R. Rogers, ed., *Clinical assessment of malingering and deception.* New York: Guilford.

Rogers, R. 1986. *Conducting insanity evaluations.* New York: Van Nostrand Reinhold.

Rogers, R., J. R. Gillis, R. E. Turner, and T. Frise-Smith. 1990. The clinical presentation of command hallucinations in a forensic population. *American Journal of Psychiatry* 147:1304–7.

Ross, C. A., S. D. Miller, P. Reagor, L. Bjornson, G. A. Fraser, and G. Anderson. 1990. Schneiderian symptoms in multiple personality disorder and schizophrenia. *Comprehensive Psychiatry* 31:111–18.

Rossi, A. M., M. Jacobs, J. Monteleone, R. Olsen, R. W. Surber, E. L. Winkler, and A. Wommack. 1986. Characteristics of psychiatric patients who engage in assaultive or other fear-inducing behaviors. *Journal of Nervous and Mental Disease* 174:154–60.

Schuckit, M. A. 1982. The history of psychotic symptoms in alcoholics. *Journal of Clinical Psychiatry* 43:53–57.

Siegel, R. K., and L. J. West, eds. 1975. *Hallucinations: Behavior, experience, and theory.* New York: John Wiley and Sons.

Slade, P. D., and R. P. Bentall. 1988. *Sensory deception: A scientific analysis of hallucination.* Baltimore: Johns Hopkins University Press.

Small, I. F., I. G. Small, and J. M. Andersen. 1966. Clinical characteristics of hallucinations in schizophrenia. *Diseases of the Nervous System* 27:349–53.

Steadman, H. J. 1981. Special problems in the prediction of violence among the mentally ill. In T. K. Hays, T. K. Roberts, and K. S. Solway, eds., *Violence and the violent individual.* New York: Spectrum.

Stevenson, I. 1983. Do we need a new word to supplement "hallucinations"? *American Journal of Psychiatry* 140:1609–11.

Strub, R. L., and F. W. Black. 1988. *Neurobehavioral disorders: A clinical approach.* Philadelphia: F. A. Davis.

Surawicz, F. G. 1980. Alcoholic hallucinosis: A missed diagnosis. *Canadian Journal of Psychiatry* 25:57–63.

Swann, R. W., and M. Levitt. 1988. Patterns of adjustment to violence in families of the mentally ill. *Journal of Interpersonal Violence* 3:42–54.

Swanson, J. W., C. E. Holzer, V. K. Ganju, and R. T. Jono. 1990. Violence and psychiatric disorder in the community: Evidence from the Epidemiologic Catchment Area surveys. *Hospital and Community Psychiatry* 41:761–70.

Tardiff, K. 1984. Research on violence. In J. A. Talbott, ed., *The chronic mental patient five years later.* San Francisco: Grune and Stratton.

Tardiff, K., and H. W. Koenigsberg. 1985. Assaultive behavior among psychiatric outpatients. *American Journal of Psychiatry* 142:960–63.

Tardiff, K., and A. Sweillam. 1982. Assaultive behavior among chronic inpatients. *American Journal of Psychiatry* 139:212–15.

Taylor, P. J. 1985. Motives for offending among violent and psychotic men. *British Journal of Psychiatry* 147:491–98.

Treimen, D. M., and A. V. Delgado-Escueta. 1983. Violence and epilepsy: A critical review. In T. A. Pedley and B. J. Meldrum, eds., *Recent advances in epilepsy.* New York: Churchill Livingston.

Trimble, M. R. 1991. *The psychoses of epilepsy.* New York: Raven Press.

Werner, P. D., T. L. Rose, and J. A. Yesavage. 1983. Reliability, accuracy, and decision-making strategy in clinical predictions of imminent dangerousness. *Journal of Consulting and Clinical Psychology* 51:815–25.

Werner, P. D., P. D. Rose, J. A. Yesavage, and K. Seeman. 1984. Psychiatrists' judgements of dangerousness on an acute care unit. *American Journal of Psychiatry* 141:263–66.

West, L. J. 1975. A clinical and theoretical overview of hallucinatory phenomena. In R. K. Siegel and L. J. West, eds., *Hallucinations: Behavior, experience, and theory.* New York: John Wiley and Sons.

Yesavage, J. A. 1983. Bipolar illness: Correlates of dangerous inpatient behavior. *British Journal of Psychiatry* 143:554–57.

———. 1984. Correlates of dangerous behavior by schizophrenics in hospital. *Journal of Psychiatric Research* 18:225–31.

Yesavage, J. A., P. D. Werner, J. M. T. Becker, C. Holman, and M. Mills. 1981. Inpatient evaluation of aggression in psychiatric patients. *Journal of Nervous and Mental Disease* 169:299–302.

Yesavage, J. A., P. D. Werner, J. M. T. Becker, and M. Mills. 1982. Short-term civil commitment and the violent patient. *American Journal of Psychiatry* 139:1145–49.

9 Personality Disorders and Violence

Thomas A. Widiger and Timothy J. Trull

Persons with personality disorders have long been considered to constitute a considerable proportion of the violent mentally disordered (Krakowski, Volavka, and Brizer 1986). Litwack and Schlesinger suggested in their overview that "repetitive violence is more likely to stem from relatively enduring personality traits" than from momentary crises and other difficult to predict events (Litwack and Schlesinger 1987, 211). Violent behavior is in fact a defining feature for two of the personality disorders included in the American Psychiatric Association's (APA) revised third edition of the *Diagnostic and Statistical Manual of Mental Disorders* (DSM III-R; American Psychiatric Association 1987): the borderline and the antisocial (Reid and Balis 1987). Antagonistic, hostile traits are evident in eight of the personality disorders (paranoid, antisocial, borderline, histrionic, narcissistic, passive-aggressive, schizotypal, and obsessive-compulsive), whereas complementary traits of agreeableness are prominent in just one—the dependent personality disorder (Widiger et al., in press). One would expect that persons who are excessively compliant, trusting, altruistic, and softhearted (i.e., those with dependent personality disorder) would be unlikely to engage in aggressive, violent behavior. A personality disorder diagnosis proposed for DSM III-R and DSM IV, the self-defeating, is said to predispose a person to become a victim of abuse and violence (Widiger and Frances 1989).

Surprisingly, systematic research on violent, aggressive tendencies among the mentally disordered has rarely considered disorders of personality, and there are no systematic studies on how personality disorders might inhibit aggressive, violent behavior. The dearth of research is perhaps understandable, given the inadequacies of the APA nomenclature for personality disorder pathology. In this chapter, we will discuss two of the DSM III-R personality disorders for which there is some relevant literature (the borderline and the antisocial) and a third proposed for DSM III-R and DSM IV (the sadistic personality disorder). Our discussion will emphasize issues that hinder the utility and validity of these diagnoses as risk factors for violent behavior. We will then offer an alternative model for the classification of personality functioning that might prove to be more useful in this area of research.

Borderline Personality Disorder

One of the diagnostic criteria for DSM III-R borderline personality disorder (BPD) is "inappropriate, intense anger or lack of control of anger, e.g., frequent displays of temper, constant anger, recurrent physical fights" (American Psychiatric Association 1987, 347). This criterion is often observed in borderline patients (Gunderson, Zanarini, and Kisiel, in press), and the clinical literature contains many anecdotal descriptions of violent rages (Kernberg 1984). It is not surprising then that there would be speculation that spouse abuse and other violent behaviors would at times be attributable to borderline personality disorder (e.g., Hamberger and Hastings 1988).

History of sexual and physical abuse. Consistent with this speculation is the observation that a significant proportion of BPD patients have a history of childhood sexual or physical abuse. Childhood abuse is correlated with abusive behavior as an adult, whether this is transmitted biogenetically (DiLalla and Gottesman 1991) or through parent-child interactions (Pollock et al. 1990; Widom 1989). For example, among 29 patients in one study who reported early sexual abuse BPD was the most frequently diagnosed personality disorder (59% of the sample reported some type of abuse prior to age 16, and only two of the subjects with BPD were without a history of childhood sexual abuse (Bryer et al. 1987). Brown and Anderson (1991) sampled over one thousand psychiatric inpatients from a military tertiary-care medical center (59% male). Overall, 18% reported a history of either physical or sexual abuse, 7% reported just physical abuse, and 7% reported just sexual abuse. Only 3% of the nonabused group received an adult diagnosis of BPD, whereas BPD was diagnosed in 19% of the physically abused, 21% of the sexually abused, and 29% of those who experienced both forms of abuse. Similar results are reported by Barnard and Hirsch (1985), Briere and Zaidi (1989), Herman (1986), and Swelt, Surrey, and Cohen (1990).

A number of studies have also examined the prevalence of abuse and violence in well-defined samples of BPD patients (diagnosed with semistructured interviews) and compared these rates to those of non-BPD patients. For example, Links et al. (1988) compared rates of physical and sexual abuse in consecutively admitted patients with a diagnosis of BPD with rates for those who exhibited only a subset of the BPD diagnostic traits. Twenty-nine percent of the BPD patients reported physical abuse and 26% reported sexual abuse; corresponding figures for the comparison group were significantly lower (9% and 12%, respectively).

Zanarini et al. (1989) compared abuse histories of BPD ($N = 50$), antisocial ($N = 29$), and dysthymic ($N = 26$) outpatients (the dysthymic patients met the criteria for personality disorders other than BPD or antisocial). The prevalence of any type of abuse (i.e., verbal, physical, or sexual) was significantly higher in the BPD (80%) than in the dysthymic (50%) or antisocial (38%) groups. The prevalence of sexual abuse in the BPD group (26%) was also significantly higher than that reported for the antisocial (7%) or dysthymic (4%) groups. There were no significant differences with respect to history of physical abuse.

Herman, Perry, and van der Kolk (1989) reported that a significantly higher proportion of their borderline subjects ($N = 21$) reported a history of some type of trauma (81%), physical abuse (71%), sexual abuse (67%), and witnessing domestic violence (62%) than their two comparison groups of subjects with just BPD traits ($N = 11$) or without any BPD symptoms ($N = 23$). No significant findings were obtained for antisocial or schizotypal personality disorder diagnoses. Shearer et al. (1990) assessed the frequency and correlates of childhood sexual and physical abuse histories in a sample of female BPD inpatients. Forty percent reported a history of sexual abuse, 28% reported a history of incest, 25% reported a history of physical abuse with injury, and 18% were categorized in the worst abuse group involving severe abuse of prolonged duration or with multiple perpetrators. Ludolph et al. (1990) reported that 52% of 27 BPD subjects had a history of physical abuse and 52% had a history of sexual abuse. The corresponding figures for non-BPD subjects were 26% and 19%, respectively. Ogata et al. (1990) compared the childhood histories of 24 BPD inpatients and 18 non-BPD depressed inpatients. The proportion of BPD subjects who reported sexual abuse was significantly higher than that of the depressed subjects (71% vs. 22%). However, the proportion of subjects reporting physical abuse was not significantly different between the BPD and depressed groups (42% vs. 33%). Finally, Byrne et al. (1990) compared BPD ($N = 15$) and schizophrenic ($N = 14$) patients. A history of childhood sexual abuse was significantly more prevalent in the BPD subjects (87% vs. 29%), as was a history of childhood physical abuse resulting in the need for hospital treatment (33% vs. 7%).

In sum, research on victims of abuse and on patients with borderline personality disorder have consistently demonstrated an association of childhood abuse with adult BPD. To the extent that violent abuse provides a risk factor for adult violent behavior, one would then expect that a diagnosis of BPD would itself suggest some risk for violent behavior. Clinical anecdotes of borderline patients have also described the occurrence of impulsive, violent anger. However, it should be emphasized that the studies of childhood abuse and BPD have not assessed whether this abusive history is related to violent, aggressive acts towards others. The focus has instead been on self-destructive, suicidal behaviors of borderlines (i.e., violent acts toward oneself).

Serotonin studies. More direct support is provided by serotonin studies on BPD, impulsivity, and aggression (Coccaro 1989). Brown et al. (1982) examined the relationship between levels of cerebral-spinal fluid (CSF) 5-HIAA (a serotonin metabolite) and history of aggression and suicidal behavior in 12 male subjects diagnosed with BPD (without a history of affective or schizophrenic disorder, medical disorder, organic brain syndrome, or heavy drug abuse). Subjects were male active-duty military inpatients. All subjects were free of medication, drugs, or alcohol for ten days prior to the lumbar puncture. Each subject's history was evaluated for severity of aggression. In addition, all subjects completed the Buss-Durkee Hostility Inventory (BDHI; Buss and Durkee 1957) and the MMPI. Levels of CSF 5-HIAA were negatively correlated with the MMPI psychopathic deviate scores ($r = .77$, $p < .004$) and with history of aggression ($r = .53$, $p < .08$). No significant differences were found with the BDHI.

Linnoila et al. (1983) examined levels of CSF 5-HIAA in a sample of 36 male violent offenders, all of whom had committed or attempted to commit murder. Subjects were grouped according to the nature of their acts: impulsive offenders who acted without provocation or premeditation and nonimpulsive offenders who acted with premeditation. Among the 27 impulsive offenders, 20 received a diagnosis of "explosive" personality and 7 a diagnosis of antisocial personality; all 27, however, also met the criteria for borderline personality disorder. The nonimpulsive group consisted of nine subjects with paranoid or passive-aggressive personality disorder. The results indicated that the impulsive violent offenders had significantly lower CSF 5-HIAA concentrations than did the nonimpulsive offenders.

Coccaro et al. (1989) assessed the serotonergic functioning of mood disordered ($N = 25$), personality disordered ($N = 20$), and normal ($N = 18$) subjects by evaluating the prolactin responses to flenfluramine challenge. Flenfluramine is a serotonin-releasing, 5-HT uptake-inhibiting agent (i.e., a 5-HT agonist). Reduced prolactin response to flenfluramine (PRL) would suggest lower levels of serotonin or inhibition of serotonergic effects. Subjects were medically healthy male veterans with no history of schizophrenia; the personality disorder subjects had no history of mania. The results indicated that the BPD patients ($N = 8$) had significantly lower peak PRL values than did those with non-BPD personality disorders and normal controls. Among all subjects, peak PRL levels were significantly lower in those who had attempted suicide versus those who had not (independent of level of depression). An inverse relation was also found between peak PRL values and with clinician-rated aggression ($r = .38$, $p < .01$) and self-rated motor aggression ($r = .27$, $p < .05$). In contrast, peak PRL levels were not significantly related to nonaggressive impulsivity measures (e.g., sensation-seeking). Further analyses indicated that the BDHI scores for assault and irritability accounted for more than half of the variance in peak PRL levels. The authors concluded that reduced PRL levels in personality disordered patients (especially those with BPD) appeared to be related to impulsivity/aggression and suicidal behavior. More recent work by this research team (e.g., Coccaro, Garbriel, and Siever 1990) has further suggested that reduced sensitivity of $5\text{-}HT_{1a}$ receptors may be implicated in impulsive, aggressive personality disordered patients. Fluoxetine is a 5-HT uptake inhibitor and therefore has the net effect of enhancing central 5-HT activity. Recent studies have suggested that fluoxetine may be effective in reducing impulsive, aggressive behavior in patients with BPD (Coccaro et al. 1990; Markovitz et al. 1991).

Siever and Davis (1991) have recently offered a compelling neurochemical model for personality disorders. They suggest that the serotonergic system mediates behavioral inhibition. Lesions of the serotonergic system result in a diminished capacity to suppress punished behavior and a concomitant increase in unmodulated aggressive behaviors. A similar diminution of serotonergic function may be associated with the disinhibition of impulsive and aggressive behaviors in patients with personality disorders, particularly the borderline and antisocial. However, it is important to note that this neurochemical model for impulsivity/aggression was presented by Siever and Davis in a general critique of the DSM III-R categorical taxonomy. They suggest that it may be more fruitful to consider more fundamental dimensions (i.e., cognitive/perceptual organization, affective instability, anxiety/inhibition, and impulsivity/aggression) that underly all of the personality disorders. "Impulsivity/aggression does not define a single personality disorder but, rather, a dimension of behavior and related defenses that can occur in a range of personality disorders" (Siever and Davis 1991, 1650). Siever and Davis therefore suggest researchers concerned with the correlates of personality disorder pathology should assess the dimension of impulsivity/aggressivity rather than the more global diagnoses of BPD and antisocial personality disorder. We will return to this issue below.

BPD and violent behavior. There have been only two empirical studies (that we could identify) concerned with violent behavior in borderline patients. Neither provided particularly compelling results. Snyder, Pitts, and Pokorny (1986) reviewed the psychiatric charts and psychological test sources of 4,800 VA hospital inpatients. From the medical records and an initial history questionnaire, they assessed the presence or absence of recent use of physical violence both within and outside of the hospital and the presence of borderline symptomatology. A significant association between BPD trait scores and the recent use of violence was obtained for both within and outside the hospital.

Stone (1990) followed over 200 DSM III BPD patients over a number of years subsequent to index psychiatric hospitalization between 1963 and 1976. Data regarding diagnostic features and abuse were based on a review of the subjects' psychiatric records. Twenty-three (11%) of the BPD patients were victims of parental abuse, and 26% ($N = 6$) of the abused borderlines were perpetrators of abuse. This rate was not significantly higher than that for some of the other diagnostic groups examined (e.g., schizophrenia, schizoaffective and bipolar mood disorder). Stone suggested that a stronger association than that between being abused and being an abuser would be found between being abused and developing a more general impulsivity, manifesting itself through promiscuity, criminal activity, substance abuse, and similar behaviors.

In sum, there have been only two empirical studies on the disposition of borderline patients toward violent behavior. More direct support is perhaps obtained from the studies concerned with serotonin and impulsive aggressivity. A diagnosis of BPD does not itself suggest violent, aggressive behavior towards others. It does suggest violent, destructive acts towards oneself and an impulsivity and anger that may at times result in violent acts towards others.

Antisocial Personality Disorder

One of the specific criteria for DSM III-R antisocial personality disorder (APD) is a history of repeated physical fights and assaults (American Psychiatric Association 1987). The criminal and aggressive tendencies associated with APD are well documented (Sutker, Bugg, and West 1993), but little has been written specifically on violent tendencies.

Robins, Tipp, and Przybeck (1991) reported that 85% of the 628 persons diagnosed with APD in the NIMH Epidemiologic Catchment Area program had a history of (unspecified) violence. Brownstone and Swaminath (1989) reported an association between a history of violent crime and personality disorders in a sample of 91 female inmates of a psychiatric forensic unit. Approximately equal numbers were given diagnoses of histrionic and of antisocial personality disorder; the female antisocial inmates were characterized as being more unstable and impulsive than the prototypic male antisocial. Bland and Orn (1986) suggested, on the basis of an epidemiologic study of 1200 randomly selected residents of a large Canadian city, that the diagnosis of APD provided a significant risk factor for violent behavior toward a spouse or child, particularly when combined with an alcohol or depressed mood disorder. Just under half of the subjects with APD were involved in violent behavior, but 80% to 93% were involved with violent acts when alcoholism was combined with depression or APD. Hall and Proctor (1987) reviewed the records from the period 1970 to 1980 of 342 nonpsychotic male sexual offenders at a state hospital. Sexual offenders against children reoffended sexually against children, and sexual offenders against adults reoffended against adults. However, those who offended against adults also engaged in a variety of nonsexual offenses. Hall and Proctor concluded that "the involvement of adult rapists in nonsexual criminal activity suggests that adult rape is symptomatic of a more generalized pattern of antisocial behavior" (Hall and Proctor 1987, 112). Hall (1988) subsequently provided a more detailed actuarial analysis of these data and again confirmed that antisocial behavior, as well as other past violent behaviors, provided optimal validity for predicting recidivism in sexual offenses.

Heilbrun (1990) recently replicated his prior findings that antisocial traits (as measured by a combined score on the Psychopathic Deviate scale of the MMPI and the Socialization scale of the California Psychological Inventory) were associated with severity of criminal acts when combined with low intelligence. Subjects were 275 men within the Georgia penal system, all of whom had been convicted of at least one violent crime. The severity of the violence was classified into three levels: high severity (murder), intermediate severity (rape and robbery), and low severity (assault, manslaughter, and child molestation). The three groups obtained different scores on measures of psychopathy and intelligence. Heilbrun concluded that "these results, especially when considered in light of earlier findings . . . support the contention that criminal dangerousness can be predicted from antisocial personality combined with low intelligence" (Heilbrun 1990, 146). These findings are consistent with those of earlier studies by Heilbrun and his colleagues (Heilbrun 1979, 1982; Heilbrun and Gottfried 1988; Heilbrun and Heilbrun 1985). The protective effect of high IQ has been replicated in studies by Kandel et al. (1988) and White, Moffitt, and Silva (1989). Wilson and Herrnstein (1985) suggested that a low IQ contributes to a present-oriented cognitive style that helps foster irresponsible and exploitative behavior, but an equally likely explanation is that "a high IQ [might] protect an at-risk child against delinquent outcome by increasing the probability of academic success and hence encouraging attachment to the school, a crucial socializing agent" (White, Moffitt, and Silva 1989, 723).

Much of the really informative research on antisocial personality traits and violent behavior has involved Hare's (1991) construct of psychopathy, developed as an alternative to the DSM III-R APD diagnosis (Hare, Hart, and Harpur 1991). For example, Hare and McPherson (1984) reported that 104 criminal psychopaths assessed by the Psychopathy Checklist (PCL) were significantly more likely than 139 other criminals to have engaged in physical violence and other forms of aggressive behavior, including verbal abuse, threats, and intimidation. Global ratings of violence correlated ($r = .46$) with the PCL. Persons obtaining high scores on the PCL were more likely to have had a history of assault, kidnapping, vandalism, or fighting; persons obtaining medium or high scores were more likely to have a history of robbery or the possession of a weapon. There were no significant differences, however, with respect to the most severe violence—murder or rape. In prison, the psychopaths were more likely to display verbal abuse, verbal threats, irritation, belligerence, and fighting.

Harpur and Hare (1991) provided a more detailed analysis of these data. They found that a combination of the two major factors of the PCL (discussed in more detail below) provided more predictive power than either factor alone. The full regression equation accounted for between 6% and 26% of the variance in the dependent measures. Harpur and Hare had predicted that psychopathy would be less highly correlated with alcohol-related violence (since psychopathic violence is presumably more instrumental than emotional or impulsive) but the reverse was found. Low IQ combined with high psychopathy produced the greatest number of convictions for crimes of violence, but high IQ combined with psychopathy was predictive of weapons-related behavior. The authors speculated that psychopaths with high IQ considered the greater advantages and opportunities to be gained through the use of weapons.

Rice, Harris, and Quinsey (1990) followed 54 rapists released from a maximum security hospital. PCL-Revised scores (PCL-R; Hare 1991) correlated with postrelease sexual offenses ($r = .31$) and other violent offenses ($r = .35$). A combination of the PCL-R score and a penile plethysmography measure of sexual arousal predicted postrelease outcome for 77% of the rapists (28% of those released committed a sexual offense and 43% committed some other violent offense).

Williamson, Hare, and Wong (1987) compared the offenses committed by 55 psychopathic and 46 nonpsychopathic inmates (identified through police reports). Most of the murders and assaults by the nonpsychopaths occurred during domestic disputes or periods of apparently intense emotionality; this did not occur nearly as often with the psychopaths. The victims of the psychopaths were more likely to be male and unknown to them. The authors concluded that the violence committed by the psychopaths typically had revenge or retribution as the motive or occurred during a period of heavy drinking and was more cold and calculated, lacking the emotionality common among the nonpsychopaths.

Harris, Rice, and Cormier (1991) followed up 169 male patients released from a forensic psychiatric unit, most with a prior history of violent offenses. Forty percent met their criteria for a "violent failure" (i.e., incurred a new charge for a criminal offense against a person or were returned to prison for a violent behavior against a person). This violent recidivism was related to a history of aggressive and antisocial behavior in childhood, adult criminality, and misbehavior during the inpatient program. Of the 52 psychopaths (diagnosed as such with a lower cutoff score than recommended by Hare [1991]), 40 (77%) failed violently, compared to only 24 of the 114 nonpsychopaths (21%). In addition, the PCL improved the prediction of violent recidivism beyond that which was predicted by a set of criminal history variables (previous violent offenses, admissions to corrections, previous criminal convictions, and convictions history). The presence of any DSM III personality disorder, in particular APD, was also predictive of violent recidivism, DSM III APD correctly identifying 67% of the cases. The authors emphasized that neither of the latter measures were as successful as the PCL (which obtained a 78% overall accuracy), but it should be noted that the assessment of the DSM III personality disorders was not nearly as rigorous as the assessment of psychopathy.

Discussion. The research on APD and psychopathy suggests that the presence of these personality disorders increases the likelihood that a person will at some time engage in a violent act. However, this does not imply that one can predict their occurrence within any given period. Violence is unlikely to be predictable in the absence of an established pattern of violent behavior (Hall 1990; Mulvey and Lidz 1984; Pollock 1990). Some studies have found DSM III-R APD and especially PCL-R psychopathy to be predictive of violent behavior even when controlled for past history of violent behavior (e.g., Hare and McPherson 1984; Harris, Rice, and Cormier 1991), but these studies were confined to populations in which most (if not all) of the subjects had a prior history of violent behavior. The findings may not generalize to more diverse populations.

It is no small achievement to identify which violent offenders are most likely to continue to be violent in the future (Monahan 1984, 1988). The PCL-R may be quite useful in the context of evaluations for discharge or parole following criminal convictions. Within the restricted range of these populations, the incremental validity provided by the PCL-R is impressive. However, clinicians should not infer from this research that the PCL-R is generally useful in predicting violent behaviors, particularly in persons with no known history of aggressive acts (Pollock, McBain, and Webster 1989).

One interpretation of the findings of Harpur and Hare (1991) is that the personality trait of psychopathy is a moderator variable that interacts with aggressivity. Psychopathy or APD, in the presence of a history of aggressive behavior, increases the likelihood of continued aggressive behavior despite the intervention of a prison term or clinical treatment (Harris, Rice, Cormier 1991). Psychopathy, as formulated by the PCL-R, includes traits that would contribute to a failure to inhibit aggression (e.g., lack of empathy, failure to accept responsibility for one's own actions, shallow affect, lack of remorse or guilt, poor behavior controls, and impulsivity). These traits contribute to a disposition to engage in a variety of antisocial, manipulative, and irresponsible behaviors, violence being only one among many possible manifestations. For psychopathy to be predictive of violent behavior in particular, one might need to verify the presence of violent acts in the past.

Future research may also determine which aspect of psychopathy provides the incremental, predictive validity in the context of a history of aggressive behavior. Psychopathy is a rather broad construct assessed by the presence of a combination of twenty items—glibness or superficial charm, grandiose sense of self-worth, need for stimulation and proneness to boredom, pathological lying, conning or manipulative behavior, lack of remorse or guilt, shallow affect, callous lack of empathy, parasitic lifestyle, poor behavior controls, promiscuous sexual behavior, early behavior problems, lack of realistic long-term goals, impulsivity, irresponsibility, failure to accept responsibility for one's own actions, many short-term marital relationships, juvenile delinquency, revocation of conditional release, and criminal versatility. With such an extensive set of indicators it is not at all clear on what basis the PCL-R is predicting violent behavior. Prior studies have controlled for past history of violent acts (by excluding the poor behavior control and adult criminal behavior items) but it remains unclear whether lack of empathy, juvenile delinquency, or impulsivity provides the primary predictive power.

Harpur, Hare, and Hakstian (1989) have identified two correlated factors in the PCL. Factor 1 is defined largely by the relatively broader traits of psychopathy (e.g., egocentricity, grandiosity, callousness, lack of empathy or remorse, and manipulativeness). Hare (1991) describes this factor as representing a selfish, callous, and remorseless use of others. Factor 2 includes the more behaviorally based measures of social deviance and is identified with a chronically unstable and antisocial lifestyle. The second factor is more highly related to disruptive behavior in prison, drug and alcohol problems, and DSM III-R APD, and the first factor to personality measures of dominance, Machiavellianism, and low empathy (Hare 1991). In their reanalysis of the Hare and McPherson (1984) data, Harpur and Hare (1991) found that the interaction of these two factors accounted for a significant increase in the variance of most of the violence dependent measures, but it was the second factor that provided much of the unique variance. The first factor rarely provided any unique information. An analysis at the item level of the second factor would then be particularly informative.

It may also be the case that different aspects of psychopathy will relate to different violent acts occurring under different circumstances. Violence comes in many forms—murder, assault, fights, rape, spouse abuse—and even one general form of violence will have a variety of causes. This has been the emphasis of Prentky and Knight (1991) in their effort to differentiate among different types of rape and of rapists. "Offenders with widely varying family and developmental experiences, psychological profiles, psychiatric diagnoses, and criminal histories have been treated as a cohesive, homogeneous group by virtue of the presence of sexual coercion in their offenses" (Prentky and Knight 1991, 643). It may be the case that a more precise characterization of the personality traits associated with rape and a more precise prediction of rape will be obtained by a more precise measure of the relevant facets of psychopathy that are involved.

For example, a variety of studies have reported associations between APD and rape (e.g., Hall 1988; Malamuth 1989) and psychopathy and rape (e.g., Rice, Harris, and Quinsey 1990). Prentky and Knight concluded on the basis of their own findings and the prior research that an antisocial-criminality dimension "evidence[s] by far the strongest linkage with particular developmental antecedents, the greatest cross-temporal stability, and the most wide-ranging predictive potency among rapists. . . . The fact that this dimension has emerged as an important discriminator across . . . widely divergent samples suggests that it is a powerful theoretical component of rape" (Prentky and Knight 1991, 649, 655). In comparison, alcohol served primarily as a disinhibitor of the prior inclination, consistent with other studies that have found that premorbid personality traits were more important in predicting aggressive, violent behavior during drug states (e.g., phencyclidine intoxication) than the drug itself (Geffner and Rosenbaum 1990; McCardle and Fishbein 1989). Prentky and Knight, however, characterized this dimension as "life-style impulsivity" rather than APD or psychopathy. They acknowledged that impulsivity may represent only one component of a larger nosologic entity (e.g., psychopathy), but they suggested that impulsivity may provide the unique etiologic characteristic that interacts with other personality traits (e.g., aggressivity) and situational variables to produce episodes of rape.

Sadistic Personality Disorder

Aggression has been recognized as a fundamental trait of personality throughout the history of personality theory and assessment. A personality trait is essentially a summary statement of the frequency of acts that are prototypic exemplars of the trait (Buss and Craik 1983). Aggression as a personality trait has been implicated in research on violent tendencies (Prentky and Knight 1991) and, to the extent that past aggressive behavior is the best predictor of future aggressive behavior (Hall 1990; Klassen and O'Connor 1988; Pollock 1990), one would expect that aggression as a personality trait should receive substantial consideration. Jaffe, Babor, and Fishbein (1987), for example, reported that "histories of early aggression account for a greater proportion of variance in aggression and anger [among their sample of] alcoholics and that, once the groups were adjusted for levels of childhood aggression, there is no significant relationship between the diagnosis of antisocial personality disorder and the likelihood of aggressive behavior while drinking" (Jaffe, Barbor, and Fishbein 1987, 216).

As we indicated above, aggressive tendencies are a feature of DSM III-R diagnoses of BPD and APD (American Psychiatric Association 1987) and of Hare's (1991) construct of psychopathy, but they are neither necessary nor fundamental features for any of these personality disorders. Aggressive acts are represented explicitly in only one of the ten criteria for APD (irritability and aggressiveness as indicated by repeated physical fights or assaults, including spouse or child beating) and indirectly in one item (failure to conform to social norms with respect to lawful behavior, including the destruction of property, harrassment, murder, or rape, but also theft, embezzlement, counterfeiting, and other crimes). The PCL-R resembles DSM III-R APD in this respect, as only one of the 20 PCL-R items explicitly concerns aggressive behavior (i.e., poor behavior controls, as indicated by being short-tempered, angry, abusive, aggressive, or violent) and another item has the potential to include hostile, aggressive acts (i.e., criminal versatility).

It is then apparent that one could receive a diagnosis of APD or psychopathy without having any history of aggressive or violent tendencies. A sadistic personality disorder (SPD) diagnosis was proposed for DSM III-R (American Psychiatric Association 1987; Widiger et al. 1988) and is currently being considered for DSM IV (Fiester and Gay, in press). This diagnosis might provide more utility and validity with respect to predicting violent behavior than either APD, BPD, or psychopathy. The SPD proposal was in fact developed on behalf of requests by forensic psychiatrists who found APD (and psychopathy) to be inadequate in its description and understanding of abusive and violent patients. "During the development of DSM-III-R, psychiatrists who evaluated patients in forensic settings suggested the need for a diagnosis of sadistic personality disorder to describe individuals who demonstrated a long-standing maladaptive pattern of cruel, demeaning, and aggressive behavior toward others but whose personality disturbance was not adequately described by any of the existing DSM-III personality disorders" (Spitzer et al. 1991, 875).

SPD is defined as "a pervasive pattern of cruel, demeaning, and aggressive behavior" (American Psychiatric Association 1987, 571). The diagnostic criteria include such items as (a) the use of physical cruelty or violence for the purpose of establishing dominance in a relationship (e.g., not merely for the purpose of theft); (b) a fascination with violence, weapons, martial arts, injury, or torture; (c) treating or disciplining others unusually harshly; (d) taking pleasure in the psychological or physical suffering of others (including animals); and (e) getting others to do what he or she wants through terror or intimidation (American Psychiatric Association 1987). It is apparent that a person who has displayed these tendencies since late childhood would be likely to engage in violent, aggressive acts in the future.

The concept of a sadistic personality disorder does have precedents within the psychoanalytic, psychiatric, and psychological literature (Widiger et al. 1988). Millon's (1981) influential taxonomy of personality disorders included an "aggressive personality syndrome" that placed less emphasis on criminality than the DSM III-R and more emphasis on aggressive hostility than Hare's (1991) construct of psychopathy. Millon, for example, described these aggressive persons as temperamentally hostile, intimidating, malicious, explosively angry, domineering, and humiliating, with "an irascible temper that flares quickly into argument and attack, as evidenced in frequent verbally abusive and physically cruel behaviors" (Millon 1981, 182). In a recent revision of his taxonomy, Millon (1986) explicitly distinguished between the antisocial and the aggressive. The antisocial is irresponsible and hedonistic whereas the aggressive is vicious, brutal, argumentative, and threatening.

SPD was recommended for inclusion in DSM III-R by the Personality Disorders Advisory Committee (Work Group 1985). However, it was not included due to the absence of empirical support and the controversy generated by the complementary proposal for a masochistic personality disorder (Widiger and Frances 1989). Since the publication of DSM III-R, Dr. Spitzer and his colleagues have attempted to generate empirical data to support the proposal. Gay and Fiester (1990) reported that 12 of 235 child-abusing adults met the proposed criteria for SPD, and 10 of these persons failed to meet the criteria for APD (or any other personality disorder diagnosis). Spitzer et al. (1991) surveyed 279 forensic psychiatrists to document support. Fifty-two percent of the respondents reported that they had seen patients who would meet the diagnostic criteria. Seventy-five percent of the 787 purported SPD cases evaluated over the past year were also said to meet the DSM III-R criteria for APD but 73% of the respondents felt that the SPD diagnosis still contained unique and useful information.

The diagnosis is unlikely to receive formal recognition in DSM IV (Pincus et al. 1992). The threshold for the addition of a new diagnosis to the official nomenclature of the APA is higher for DSM IV than was the case for DSM III or DSM III-R, particularly for diagnoses that have the potential for misuse and negative social repercussions. The survey by Spitzer et al. (1991) also indicated that 66% of the respondents believed that SPD had considerable potential for being misused (e.g., to mitigate criminal responsibility for abusive acts). Only 11% of the respondents said that SPD was likely to be very useful and should be included, 44% said it could be useful but should be included only if there is research to document its incremental validity over current personality disorder diagnoses, and 45% felt that it was of limited value and had inadequate data to justify its inclusion in DSM IV. A review of the literature solicited by the DSM IV Personality Disorders Work Group could not find any current or published studies on the concurrent or predictive validity of the proposed criteria set (Fiester and Gay, in press). The proposal has in fact received little attention within the clinical and empirical literature since its appearance in the 1985 draft of DSM III-R.

Discussion

A diagnosis of DSM III-R borderline or antisocial personality disorder does provide a risk factor for violent, aggressive behavior. However, neither diagnosis in the absence of a history of violent, aggressive behavior is likely to indicate a risk with substantial clinical or social significance. Hare's alternative to the DSM III-R, psychopathy as assessed by the PCL-R, provides a considerable improvement over DSM III-R APD in a variety of ways (Hare,

Hart, and Harpur 1991), including possibly the prediction of violent behavior (Harris, Rice, and Cormier 1991), but this diagnosis suffers from comparable limitations.

Violent behavior results from a complex interaction among a variety of social, clinical, personality, and environmental factors whose relative importance varies across situations and time. The complexity of this interaction raises the issue of the extent to which one should conceive violent behavior as resulting from a personality disorder rather than a situational, environmental, or other factor. Only the proposed diagnosis of sadistic personality explicitly suggests a disposition toward aggressive, violent behavior. The antisocial and borderline personality disorders may provide an absence of inhibition against violent acts but do not require a disposition for violent acts.

It will be important in future research to carefully disentangle the interactive factors that contribute to a specific violent act. For example, one of the current controversies in personality disorder research is the differentiation of a personality disorder from an Axis I disorder, such as brief reactive psychosis, substance abuse, or paranoid (delusional) disorder (Widiger and Shea 1991). It will be difficult to determine whether a violent act by a person with antisocial personality disorder who is using cocaine or PCP is due to the effects of the substance use disorder or the personality disorder. In the absence of a history of violent, aggressive behavior prior to the drug usage the unique and interactive effects will be difficult to isolate. Even if violent behavior occurs only when under the influence of a substance, the substance use may itself be a manifestation or effect of the personality disorder (or the substance may be acting simply as a disinhibitor of premorbid aggressive tendencies). On the other hand, a substance use disorder can contribute to the development, maintenance, and escalation of antisocial behaviors. In any case, the complexity of the interaction and confusion of personality and Axis I disorders does suggest the need for longitudinal research that can trace their mutual development and interaction across time. It is unlikely that their effects will be adequately differentiated with cross-sectional studies (Widiger 1993).

The current trend in modeling personality for the understanding and prediction of violent behavior is toward the development of interactive, multifactorial models (e.g., Heilbrun 1990; Malamuth 1986; Prentky and Knight 1991). It is likely that the DSM III-R personality disorder taxonomy will be inadequate for these models for at least three reasons. First, DSM III-R is a dichotomous model that imposes arbitrary categorical distinctions between the presence and absence of a disorder that may have little relationship to the predictability of violent behavior. Second, the diagnostic categories are substantially heterogeneous with respect to the personality variables that are most likely to be predictive of violent behavior. Third, DSM III-R does not provide a comprehensive model of personality dysfunction. Each of these limitations will be discussed in turn.

Arbitrary Categorical Distinctions

A disorder of personality is defined in DSM III-R as occurring "when personality traits are inflexible and maladaptive and cause either significant functional impairment or subjective distress" (American Psychiatric Association 1987, 335). This is an adequate definition of a personality disorder but the thresholds for the DSM III-R and Hare's categorical delineation of psychopathy bear little resemblance to this definition.

For example, the DSM III-R criteria for APA require any four of ten criteria since the age of 15, but the presence of just the one criterion of a history of being "irritable and aggressive, as indicated by repeated physical fights or assaults (not required by one's job or to defend someone or oneself), including spouse or child beating" (American Psychiatric Association 1987, 345) would suggest the presence of a maladaptive personality trait predisposing the person toward violent acts (Jaffe, Babor, and Fishbein 1987). In contrast, the presence of four of the other criteria may have little predictive validity for violent behavior (e.g., inability to sustain consistent work behavior, failure to honor financial obligations, failure to plan ahead, and never sustaining a totally monogamous relationship).

There is no reason to assume that the threshold of four of ten criteria for a diagnosis of APD provides the optimal threshold for distinguishing persons who are more rather than less likely to engage in violent acts. More consideration was given to the selection of a score of 30 on the PCL-R for the diagnosis of psychopathy (Hare 1991), but some researchers have preferred to use different thresholds (e.g., Harris, Rice, and Cormier 1991). Hare (1991) has acknowledged that a quantitative score (e.g., the number of PCLR criteria met by the subject), used in many of the studies considered above, has superior psychometric properties. Researchers who are considering the role of DSM III-R personality disorders in predicting violent behavior are also advised to use a quantitative score (e.g., the number of personality disorder criteria) rather than the categorical diagnoses.

Heterogeneity of Cases

The authors of DSM III-R recognized that monothetic criteria sets (in which all of the criteria are required) are overly restrictive and inconsistent with the heterogeneity among persons with the respective personality disorders (Spitzer 1987). The monothetic criteria sets that were used for some personality disorders in DSM III described only prototypic cases that rarely appeared in actual clinical practice (Livesley 1985). Persons with the respective personality disorders will share only a subset of the defining features, resembling the prototype to varying degrees.

The diagnostic criteria for all of the DSM III-R personality disorders were therefore polythetic: a set of optional criteria are provided, only a subset of which are required (Widiger et al. 1988). However, recognition of the heterogeneity among the persons with the respective diagnoses does not actually resolve the problem of the heterogeneity. The polythetic format still makes categorical, black-and-white distinctions that fail to appreciate the complexity that actually exists. There are 93 different ways to meet the DSM III-R criteria for BPD and 149,495,616 different ways to meet the DSM III-R criteria for APD (only 848 different combinations if one does not count the different ways to meet the subcriteria for the conduct disorder and parental irresponsibility items). One would not need to distinguish between all 149,495,616 different combinations to provide a useful description, but it is evident that not all antisocial persons are alike with respect to their antisocial symptomatology and that some of these differences can be of considerable importance to clinical practice and empirical research (Hare, Hart, and Harpur 1991; Harpur, Hare, and Hakstian 1989).

For example, impulsivity, hostility, and aggressivity are characteristic of both APD and BPD (Siever and Davis 1991), contributing to their substantial comorbidity (Widiger and Rogers 1989). And, not only do persons with these respective personality disorders differ with respect to their degree of impulsivity, hostility, and aggressivity, but persons who share a BPD or an APD diagnosis also vary substantially with respect to these traits.

Comprehensive Coverage

The DSM III-R does not purport to provide a comprehensive set of all the personality disorders, nor is there a clear rationale for how many personality disorders exist or should be included within the nomenclature. "It seems likely [that] an optimal number falls somewhere between the extremes of Fourier's 810 and Hippocrates' four, but it is not clear just where. For some purposes just a few categories may be most desirable, while for others finer distinctions may be necessary" (Frances and Widiger 1986, 247). Frances and Widiger described the DSM III personality disorder nomenclature as "a fairly heterogeneous hodgepodge of disorders with origins in many different historical sources" (Frances and Widiger 1986, 244). The narcissistic and borderline diagnoses were derived from a psychoanalytic perspective, the antisocial from a neo-Kraepelinian, the schizotypal from a biogenetic, and the avoidant from a social learning model.

In addition, the DSM III-R is not simply a scientific document that provides an extensional definition of personality disorders by listing all known cases in a manner comparable to the periodic table of elements (Widiger and Trull 1991). It is a document that must be sensitive to a variety of clinical, forensic, professional, international, and public health issues (Frances et al. 1990). As a result, a diagnosis such as sadistic personality disorder will not be included because of potential negative social repercussions. We are not suggesting that DSM IV should include SPD, but we are suggesting that as a result of the need to be responsive to a variety of pragmatic, social, professional, and clinical issues the DSM III-R and DSM IV may not provide the optimal nomenclature for identifying and clarifying the role of maladaptive personality traits in the development of violent behavior.

Recommendations

Hamberger and Hastings recently reviewed the literature on male spouse abusers and concluded that "many of these profiles comprise characteristics consistent with DSM III criteria for personality disorders" (Hamberger and Hastings 1988, 763). Their review was helpful in highlighting and illustrating the role that personality disorders (particularly APD and BPD) may play in spouse abuse. Many of the persons who abuse their spouses will meet the DSM III-R criteria for antisocial or borderline personality disorder, and research on the aggressive correlates of these personality disorders would support their construct validity. However, reliance on the DSM III-R nomenclature to understand and to make predictions regarding spouse abuse may be unnecessarily handicapping and procrustean. The personality traits that are most important and useful in understanding spouse abuse are only partially or indirectly represented in the DSM III-R diagnostic constructs (e.g., impulsivity, hostility, aggression, and lack of empathy).

An alternative nomenclature that may be of particular use in this area of research is the five-factor model of personality (Digman 1990). This nomenclature is appealing for a variety of reasons. First, it is a dimensional model and therefore does not impose arbitrary categorical distinctions; second, it includes personality constructs that are likely to be of particular importance in the understanding and prediction of violent behavior; and third, it is an empirically derived nomenclature that provides a more comprehensive description of the major personality traits.

The initial derivation of the five-factor model was based on the compelling rationale that the most important and fundamental traits of personality would be identified through an empirical (lexical) analysis of the natural language. The importance of a trait would be indicated by the number of terms that describe the trait and the structure of these traits would be identified by the relationship among these terms. Many such lexical analyses have been conducted and the findings have consistently supported the five-factor model (Digman 1990; John 1990). The five factors have obtained excellent temporal stability (Costa and McCrae 1988) and have been replicated across other languages and ratings by self, peers, spouses, and other observers (Costa and

McCrae 1992). The five factors have also been successful in subsuming and accounting for the traits included within other models of personality (John 1990) and personality disorders (Costa and McCrae 1992; Trull, in press). In sum, to the extent that personality disorders are inflexible and maladaptive variants of personality traits, a comprehensive and empirically based nomenclature of personality would provide a compelling alternative to the DSM III-R personality disorder nomenclature.

McCrae and Costa (1990) identify the five factors as neuroticism, extraversion versus introversion, openness to experience, agreeableness versus antagonism, and conscientiousness. Each of these factors has been broken down into six facets (Costa, McCrae, and Dye 1991): neuroticism into anxiety, hostility, depression, self-consciousness, impulsivity, and vulnerability; antagonism (vs. agreeableness) into suspiciousness (vs. trust), manipulativeness (vs. straightforwardness), exploitation (vs. altruism), aggressive opposition (vs. compliance), arrogance (vs. modesty), and tough-mindedness (vs. tender-mindedness). Aggressive personality traits may thus be represented directly by respective facets of antagonism and neuroticism. Support for this hypothesis is provided in a study by Costa, McCrae, and Dye (1991) in which they administered the revised NEO Personality Inventory (NEO-PIR) and the BDHI to 394 community subjects. The BDHI assault and verbal hostility subscales correlated substantially with NEO-PIR antagonistic manipulation, and BDHI suspicion correlated with NEO-PIR suspicion. The hostility facet of neuroticism could provide additional clarification of the tendency to display impulsive, explosive outbursts of dyscontrolled anger and rage as opposed to the more calculated, instrumental manipulation and ruthlessness of antagonism, comparable to the distinctions made between expressive and instrumental aggression (Hazelwood and Burgess 1987) or nonstrategic and strategic violence (Felson and Krohn 1990). The additional factors and facets of the five-factor model provide the potential to clarify and distinguish the respective roles of other personality traits considered within the literature that are not explicitly or specifically emphasized by a personality disorder diagnosis (e.g., Lisak and Roth 1988), including the impulsivity facet of neuroticism, low empathy (tough-mindedness), the interpersonal coldness facet of introversion, and the exploitation facet of antagonism. And, finally, the facets of agreeableness (e.g., compliance, altruism, and tender-mindedness) would provide a measure of a disposition against violent, aggressive behavior. In sum, researchers who are attempting to develop a multifactorial model of violent behavior that includes personality dispositions (along with situational variables, Axis I disorders, substance use, and other contributing factors) would be advised to consider the five-factor model as a viable alternative to the DSM III-R personality disorder nomenclature.

References

American Psychiatric Association. 1987. *Diagnostic and statistical manual of mental disorders.* 3d ed., rev. (DSM III-R). Washington, D.C.: American Psychiatric Association.

Asberg, M., D. Schalling, L. Traskman-Bendz, and A. Wagner. 1987. Psychobiology of suicide, impulsivity, and related phenomena. In H. Y. Meltzer, ed., *Psychopharmacology: Third generation of progress,* 655–88. New York: Raven Press.

Barnard, C. P., and C. Hirsch. 1985. Borderline personality and victims of incest. *Psychological Reports* 57:715–18.

Bland, R., and H. Orn. 1986. Family violence and psychiatric disorder. *Canadian Journal of Psychiatry* 31:129–37.

Briere, J., and L. Y. Zaidi. 1989. Sexual abuse histories in sequelae in female psychiatric emergency room patients. *American Journal of Psychiatry* 146:1602–6.

Brown, G. L., M. H. Ebert, P. F. Goyer, D. C. Jimerson, W. Klein, W. E. Bunney, and F. K. Goodwin. 1982. Aggression, suicide, and serotonin: Relationships to CSF amine metabolites. *American Journal of Psychiatry* 139:741–46.

Brown, G. R., and B. Anderson. 1991. Psychiatric morbidity in adult inpatients with childhood histories of sexual and physical abuse. *American Journal of Psychiatry* 148:55–61.

Brownstone, D. Y., and R. S. Swaminath. 1989. Violent behavior and psychiatric diagnosis in female offenders. *Canadian Journal of Psychiatry* 34:190–94.

Bryer, J. B., B. A. Nelson, J. B. Miller, and P. A. Krol. 1987. Childhood sexual and physical abuse as factors in adult psychiatric illness. *American Journal of Psychiatry* 144:1426–30.

Buss, D. M., and K. H. Craik. 1983. The act frequency approach to personality. *Psychological Review* 90:105–26.

Buss, A. H., and A. Durkee. 1957. An inventory for assessing different kinds of hostility. *Journal of Consulting Psychology* 21:343–49.

Byrne, C. P., V. R. Velamoor, Z. Z. Cernovsky, L. Cortesse, and S. Losztyn. 1990. A comparison of borderline and schizophrenic patients for childhood life events and parent-child relationships. *Canadian Journal of Psychiatry* 35:590–95.

Coccaro, E. F. 1989. Central serotonin and impulsive aggression. *British Journal of Psychiatry* 155:52–62.

Coccaro, E. F., E. S. Astill, J. L. Hubert, and A. G. Schut. 1990. Fluoxetine treatment of impulsive aggression in DSM-III-R personality disordered patients. *Journal of Clinical Psychopharmacology* 10:373–75.

Coccaro, E. F., S. Gabriel, and L. J. Siever. 1990. Buspirone challenge: Preliminary evidence for a role for central 5-HT$_{1a}$ receptor function in impulsive aggressive behavior in humans. *Psychopharmacology Bulletin* 26:393–405.

Coccaro, E. F., L. J. Siever, H. M. Klar, G. Maurer, K. Cochrane, T. B. Cooper, R. C. Mohs, and K. L. Davis. 1989. Serotonergic studies in patients with affective and personality disorders. *Archives of General Psychiatry* 46:587–99.

Coons, P. M., E. S. Bowman, T. A. Pellow, and P. Schneider. 1989. Post-traumatic aspects of the treatment of victims of sexual abuse and treatment. *Psychiatric Clinics of North America* 12:325–34.

Costa, P. T., and R. R. McCrae. 1988. Personality in adulthood: A six-year longitudinal study of self-reports and spouse ratings on the NEO Personality Inventory. *Journal of Personality and Social Psychology* 54:853–63.

———. 1992. The five-factor model of personality and its relevance to personality disorders. *Journal of Personality Disorders* 4:343–59.

Costa, P. T., R. R. McCrae, and D. A. Dye. 1991. Facet scales for agreeableness and conscientiousness: A revision of the NEO Personality Inventory. *Personality and Individual Differences* 12:887–98.

Digman, J. M. 1990. Personality structure: Emergence of the five-factor model. *Annual Review of Psychology* 41:417–40.

DiLalla, L. F., and I. I. Gottesman. 1991. Biological and genetic contributors to violence—Widom's untold tale. *Psychological Bulletin* 10:125–29.

Felson, R. B., and M. Krohn. 1990. Motives for rape. *Journal of Research in Crime and Delinquency* 27:222–42.

Fiester, S. J., and M. Gay. In press. Sadistic personality disorder: A review of data and recommendations for DSM-IV. *Journal of Personality Disorders*.

Frances, A. J., H. A. Pincus, T. A. Widiger, W. W. Davis, and M. B. First. 1990. DSM-IV: Work in progress. *American Journal of Psychiatry* 147:1439–48.

Frances, A. J., and T. A. Widiger. 1986. The classification of personality disorders: An overview of problems and solutions. In A. J. Frances and R. E. Hales, eds., *Psychiatry Update,* 5:240–57. Washington, D.C.: American Psychiatric Press.

Gardner, D. L., P. B. Lucas, and R. W. Cowdry. 1990. CSF metabolites in borderline personality disorder compared with normal controls. *Biological Psychiatry* 28:247–54.

Gay, M., and S. Fiester. 1990. Sadistic personality disorder. In J. O. Cavenar, R. Michels, and A. M. Cooper, eds., *Psychiatry.* Vol. 1. Philadelphia: J. P. Lippincott.

Geffner, R., and A. Rosenbaum. 1990. Characteristics and treatment of batterers. *Behavioral Sciences and the Law* 8:131–40.

Gunderson, J. G., M. C. Zanarini, and C. L. Kisiel. In press. Borderline personality disorder: A review of data on DSM-III-R descriptions. *Journal of Personality Disorders*.

Hall, G. C. N. 1988. Criminal behavior as a function of clinical and actuarial variables in a sexual offender population. *Journal of Consulting and Clinical Psychology* 56:773–75.

———. 1990. Prediction of sexual aggression. *Clinical Psychology Review* 10:229–45.

Hall, G. C. N., and W. C. Proctor. 1987. Criminological predictors of recidivism in a sexual offender population. *Journal of Consulting and Clinical Psychology* 55:111–12.

Hamberger, L. K., and J. H. Hastings. 1988. Characteristics of male spouse abusers consistent with personality disorders. *Hospital and Community Psychiatry* 39:763–70.

Hare, R. D. 1991. *The Hare Psychopathy Checklist—Revised.* Toronto: Multi-Health Systems.

Hare, R. D., S. D. Hart, and T. J. Harpur. 1991. Psychopathy and the DSM-IV criteria for antisocial personality disorder. *Journal of Abnormal Psychology* 100: 391–98.

Hare, R. D., and L. M. McPherson. 1984. Violent and aggressive behavior by criminal psychopaths. *International Journal of Law and Psychiatry* 7:35–50.

Harpur, T. J., and R. D. Hare. 1991. Psychopathy and violent behavior: Two factors are better than one. Paper presented at the 99th annual meeting of the American Psychological Association, August, San Francisco.

Harpur, T. J., R. D. Hare, and A. R. Hakstian. 1989. Two-factor conceptualization of psychopathy: Construct validity and assessment implications. *Psychological Assessment: A Journal of Consulting and Clinical Psychology* 1:6–17.

Harris, G. T., M. E. Rice, and C. A. Cormier. 1991. Psychopathy and violent recidivism. *Law and Human Behavior* 15:625–37.

Hazelwood, R. R., and A. W. Burgess. 1987. The behavioral-oriented interview of rape victims: The key to profiling. In R. R. Hazelwood and A. W. Burgess, eds., *Practical aspects of rape investigation: A multidisciplinary approach,* 151–68. New York: Elsevier.

Heilbrun, A. B. 1979. Psychopathy and violent crime. *Journal of Consulting and Clinical Psychology* 47:509–16.

———. 1982. Cognitive models of criminal violence based upon intelligence and psychopathy levels. *Journal of Consulting and Clinical Psychology* 50:546–57.

———. 1990. The measurement of criminal dangerousness as a personality construct: Further validation of a research index. *Journal of Personality Assessment* 54: 141–48.

Heilbrun, A. B., and D. M. Gottfried. 1988. Antisociality and dangerousness in women before and after the women's movement. *Psychological Reports* 62:37–38.

Heilbrun, A. B., and M. R. Heilbrun. 1985. Psychopathy and dangerousness: Comparison, integration and extension of two psychopathic typologies. *British Journal of Clinical Psychology* 24:181–95.

Herman, J. L. 1986. Histories of violence in an outpatient population: An exploratory study. *American Journal of Orthopsychiatry* 56:137–41.

Herman, J. L., J. C. Perry, and B. A. van der Kolk. 1989. Childhood trauma in borderline personality disorder. *American Journal of Psychiatry* 146:490–95.

Jaffe, J. H., T. F. Babor, and D. H. Fishbein. 1987. Alcoholics, aggression, and antisocial personality. *Journal of Studies on Alcohol* 49:211–18.

John, O. P. 1990. The "big five" factor taxonomy: Dimensions of personality in the natural language and in questionnaires. In L. A. Pervin, ed., *Handbook of personality: Theory and research,* 66–100. New York: Guilford.

Kandel, E., S. A. Mednick, L. Kirkegaard-Sorenson, B. Hutchings, J. Knop, R. Rosenberg, and F. Schulsinger. 1988. IQ as a protective factor for subjects at high risk for antisocial behavior. *Journal of Consulting and Clinical Psychology* 56: 22–226.

Kernberg, O. F. 1984. *Severe personality disorders.* New Haven, Conn.: Yale University Press.

Klassen, D., and W. A. O'Connor. 1988. A prospective study of predictors of violence in adult male mental health admissions. *Law and Human Behavior* 12:143–58.

Krakowski, M., J. Volavka, and D. Brizer. 1986. Psychopathology and violence: A review of the literature. Comprehensive Psychiatry 27:131–48.

Links, P. S., M. Steiner, D. R. Offord, and A. Eppel. 1988. Characteristics of borderline personality disorder: A Canadian study. Canadian Journal of Psychiatry 33:336–54.

Linnoila, M., M. Virkkunen, M. Scheinin, A. Nuutila, R. Rimon, and F. K. Goodwin. 1983. Low cerebrospinal fluid 5-hydroxyindoleacetic acid concentration differentiates impulsive from nonimpulsive violent behavior. Life Sciences 33: 2609–14.

Lisak, P., and S. Roth. 1988. Motivational factors in nonincarcerated sexually aggressive men. Journal of Personality and Social Psychology 55:795–802.

Litwack, T. R., and L. B. Schlesinger. 1987. Assessing and predicting violence: Research, law, and applications. In I. B. Weiner and A. K. Hess, eds., Handbook of forensic psychology, 205–57. New York: Wiley.

Livesley, W. J. 1985. The classification of personality disorder. I. The choice of category concept. Canadian Journal of Psychiatry 30:353–58.

Ludolph, P. S., D. Westen, B. Misle, A. Jackson, J. Wixon, and F. C. Wiss. 1990. The borderline diagnosis in adolescents: Symptoms and developmental history. American Journal of Psychiatry 147:470–76.

Malamuth, N. M. 1986. Predictors of naturalistic sexual aggression. Journal of Personality and Social Psychology 50:953–62.

———. 1989. The Attraction to Sexual Aggression Scale: Part 2. Journal of Sex Research 26:324–54.

Markovitz, P. J., J. R. Calabrese, S. C. Schultz, and H. Y. Meltzer. 1991. Fluoxetine in the treatment of borderline and schizotypal personality disorders. American Journal of Psychiatry 148:1064–67.

McCardle, L., and D. H. Fishbein. 1989. The self-reported effects of PCP on human aggression. Addictive Behaviors 14:465–72.

McCrae, R. R., and P. T. Costa. 1990. Personality in adulthood. New York: Guilford.

Millon, T. 1981. Disorders of personality. DSM-III: Axis II. New York: Wiley.

———. 1986. Personality prototypes and their diagnostic criteria. In T. Millon and G. Klerman, eds., Contemporary directions in psychopathology, 671–712. New York: Guilford.

Monahan, J. 1984. The prediction of violent behavior: Toward a second generation of theory and policy. American Journal of Psychiatry 141:10–15.

———. 1988. Risk assessment of violence among the mentally disordered: Generating useful knowledge. International Journal of Law and Psychiatry 11:249–57.

Mulvey, E. P., and C. W. Lidz. 1984. Clinical considerations in the prediction of dangerousness in mental patients. Clinical Psychology Review 4:379–401.

Ogata, S. N., K. R. Silk, S. Goodrich, N. E. Lohr, D. Weston, and E. M. Hill. 1990. Childhood sexual and physical abuse in adult patients with borderline personality disorder. American Journal of Psychiatry 147:1008–13.

Pincus, H. A., A. J. Frances, W. W. Davis, M. B. First, and T. A. Widiger. 1992. DSM-IV and new diagnostic categories: Holding the line on proliferation. American Journal of Psychiatry 149:112–17.

Pollock, N. L. 1990. Accounting for predictions of dangerousness. *International Journal of Law and Psychiatry* 13:207–15.

Pollock, N. L., I. McBain, and C. D. Webster. 1989. Clinical decision making and the assessment of dangerousness. In K. Howells and C. Hollins, eds., *Clinical approaches to aggression and violence,* 89–115. New York: John Wiley.

Pollock, V. E., J. Briere, L. Schneider, J. Knop, S. A. Mednick, and D. W. Goodwin. 1990. Childhood antecedents of antisocial behavior: Parental alcoholism and physical abusiveness. *Journal of Consulting and Clinical Psychology* 147:1290–93.

Prentky, R. A., and R. A. Knight. 1991. Identifying critical dimensions for discriminating among rapists. *Journal of Consulting and Clinical Psychology* 59:643–61.

Reid, W. H., and G. U. Balis. 1987. Evaluation of the violent patient. In R. E. Hales and A. J. Frances, eds., *Psychiatry update,* 6:491–509. Washington, D.C.: American Psychiatric Press.

Rice, M. E., G. T. Harris, and V. L. Quinsey. 1990. A follow-up of rapists assessed in a maximum security psychiatric facility. *Journal of Interpersonal Violence* 4: 435–48.

Robins, L. N., and J. Helzer. 1986. Diagnosis and clinical assessment: The current state of psychiatric diagnosis. *Annual Review of Psychology* 37:409–32.

Robins, L. N., J. Tipp, and T. Przybeck. 1991. Antisocial personality. In L. N. Robins and D. Regier, eds., *Psychiatric disorders in America,* 258–90. New York: Free Press.

Schacht, T. 1985. DSM-III and the politics of truth. *American Psychologist* 40: 513–21.

Shearer, S. L., C. P. Peters, M. S. Quaytman, and R. L. Ogden. 1990. Frequency and correlates of childhood sexual and physical abuse histories in adult female borderline inpatients. *American Journal of Psychiatry* 147:214–16.

Shearer, S. L., C. P. Peters, M. S. Quaytman, and B. E. Wadman. 1988. Intent and lethality of suicide attempts among female borderline inpatients. *American Journal of Psychiatry* 145:1424–27.

Siever, L. J., and K. L. Davis. 1991. A psychobiological perspective on the personality disorders. *American Journal of Psychiatry* 148:1647–58.

Snyder, S., W. M. Pitts, and A. D. Pokorny. 1986. Selected behavioral features of patients with borderline personality traits. *Suicide and Life-Threatening Behavior* 16:28–39.

Spitzer, R. L. 1987. Nosology. In A. Skodol and R. L. Spitzer, eds., *An annotated bibliography of DSM-III,* 3–11. Washington, D.C.: American Psychiatric Press.

Spitzer, R. L., S. Fiester, M. Gay, and B. Pfohl. 1991. Results of a survey of forensic psychiatrists on the validity of the sadistic personality disorder diagnosis. *American Journal of Psychiatry* 148:875–79.

Stone, M. H. 1990. Abuse and abusiveness in borderline personality disorder. In P. S. Links, ed., *Family environment and borderline personality disorder,* 131–48. Washington, D.C.: American Psychiatric Press.

Sutker, P. B., F. Bugg, and J. A. West. 1993. Antisocial personality disorder. In P. B. Sutker and H. Adams, eds., *Comprehensive handbook of psychopathology.* 2d ed., 337–69. New York: Plenum.

Swelt, C., J. Surrey, and C. Cohen. 1990. Sexual and physical abuse histories and psychiatric symptoms among male psychiatric outpatients. *American Journal of Psychiatry* 147:632–36.

Trull, T. J. In press. DSM-III-R personality disorders and the five-factor model of personality: An empirical comparison. *Journal of Abnormal Psychology.*

White, J. L., T. E. Moffitt, and P. Silva. 1989. A prospective replication of the protective effects of IQ in subjects at high risk for juvenile delinquency. *Journal of Consulting and Clinical Psychology* 57:719–24.

Widiger, T. A. 1993. Assessment issues. In M. H. Klein, D. Kupfer, and M. J. Shea, eds., *Personality and depression,* 77–118. Chicago: University of Chicago Press.

Widiger, T. A., and A. J. Frances. 1989. Controversies concerning the self-defeating personality disorder. In R. Curtis, ed., *Self-defeating behaviors,* 289–309. New York: Plenum.

Widiger, T. A., A. J. Frances, R. J. Spitzer, and J. B. W. Williams. 1988. The DSM-III-R personality disorders: An overview. *American Journal of Psychiatry* 145: 786–95.

Widiger, T. A., and J. Rogers. 1989. Prevalence and comorbidity of personality disorders. *Psychiatric Annals* 19:132–36.

Widiger, T. A., and T. Shea. 1991. Differentiation of Axis I and Axis II disorders. *Journal of Abnormal Psychology* 100:399–406.

Widiger, T. A., and T. J. Trull. 1991. Diagnosis and clinical assessment. *Annual Review of Psychology* 42:109–33.

Widiger, T. A., T. J. Trull, P. T. Costa, R. R. McCrae, J. Clarkin, and C. Sanderson. In press. Describing the DSM-III-R and DSM-IV personality disorders from the perspective of the five-factor model. In P. T. Costa and T. A. Widiger, eds., *Personality disorders and the five factor model.* Washington, D.C.: American Psychological Association.

Widom, C. S. 1988. The cycle of violence. *Science* 244 (14 April): 160–66.

Williamson, S., R. D. Hare, and S. Wong. 1987. Violence: Criminal psychopaths and their victims. *Canadian Journal of Behavioral Science* 19:454–62.

Wilson, J. Q., and R. J. Herrnstein. 1984. *Crime and human nature.* New York: Simon and Schuster.

Work Group to Revise DSM-III-R. 1985. *Draft of DSM-III-R.* Washington, D.C.: American Psychiatric Association.

Zanarini, M. C., J. G. Gunderson, M. F. Marino, E. O. Schwartz, and F. R. Frankenburg. 1989. Childhood experiences of borderline patients. *Comprehensive Psychiatry* 30:18–25.

Part III
Historical and Contextual Factors

"Historical" risk factors refer to events that have been experienced in the past that may predispose a person to act violently. "Contextual" risk factors refer to aspects of the current environment that may be conducive to the occurrence of violent behavior.

Deidre Klassen and William O'Connor address the ways in which the interaction between a person's life history and demographic characteristics can lead to violence. They consider factors that can lead people to acquire violent tendencies, such as modeling; factors that can moderate the occurrence of violence, such as parental supervision; factors that can predispose toward violence, such as cognitive impairment; and factors that can affect the acceptability of violence, such as group norms. They speculate on how the interaction among these classes of variables can affect the type and level of violence that is observed.

Sue Estroff and Catherine Zimmer consider contextual variables that influence violent behavior. Based on a large study of patients with severe, persistent mental disorder, they find that the composition of a person's social network—including the presence or absence of mental health professionals—and the types of emotional and instrumental support available to the person affect both the likelihood of violence and the typical victims of violence.

10 Demographic and Case History Variables in Risk Assessment

DEIDRE KLASSEN AND WILLIAM A. O'CONNOR

In this chapter we explore the relationship between demographic and case history variables, on the one hand, and violent behavior, on the other. Before considering prior research findings, however, let us point out four explicit assumptions that guide our efforts:

1. Violence as a dependent measure may be viewed as continuously distributed in the population studied.
2. Violence may be heterogeneous; it may be legitimate to study the different types of violence or patterns of violent behavior.
3. Independent or predictor variables may also be distributed in the population studied.
4. Predictors or markers of risk may be interactive; the contribution of some variables may depend on interaction with other predisposing, moderating, or direct contributor variables.

These assumptions suggest some very interesting questions where risk assessment is concerned. First, if a continuum or several continua of violent behaviors are distributed in the general population, then how is violent behavior at the high-rate end of the distribution acquired? Is violence learned and reinforced as a frequent or high-probability behavior over time for some individuals? Are certain immediate, contemporaneous situations likely to produce a high rate (or intensity) of violent response in all or most of the population? What are the processes which determine baseline risk?

Second, if predictors are distributed and interactive, are there processes which are not unique to violence but which vary from time to time in individuals and therefore moderate the occurrence of violence, "state" variables which increase or decrease baseline risk? In practical terms, what suppresses or escalates violence in persons who are at risk? What triggers the behavior?

Third, are there particular conditions or characteristics of persons at risk

229

which are stable over time, such as traits, which are also not unique to violence but which increase predisposition or vulnerability to violent patterns of response? Are certain individuals more at risk or more likely to learn violence or to not learn alternative or suppressing behaviors?

Fourth, certain demographic factors, including gender, age, socioeconomic and educational level, and race, are associated with arrests for violent crimes. But these same variables have been treated and conceptualized very differently outside of the area of violence prediction. Intelligence tests are normed differentially by these variables, as are many personality tests. Heaton, Grant, and Matthews (1991) have recently normed a wide range of indicators of brain damage by gender, age, and education level, demonstrating improved accuracy of "predictions" of central nervous system dysfunction. In this research strategy, demographic variables are neither independent nor dependent measures, but are used to improve the accuracy of measures.

Social learning theories involving aggression, assumed to be distributed, provide a model. Bandura (1983) organized these findings under three headings: origins of aggression, instigators of aggression, and regulators of aggression. Interestingly only three origins or direct causal mechanisms are proposed: observational learning, reinforced performance, and structural determinants. A longer list of instigators was proposed; these appear similar to the elusive situational variables frequently discussed in risk assessment research. The most extensive list is organized under the heading of regulators. Goldstein (1989), in a similar review, describes both long-term and immediate causes of aggression, including physical predisposition (which subsumes demographic variables, such as gender, *and* trait measures, such as temperament), moderators, such as self-control and alternate prosocial values and behaviors, and what again might be viewed as direct acquisition mechanisms, such as parental and peer modeling.

From this perspective, how might we view demographic and case history findings in risk assessment research? First, we might view high base rate risk as involving: (*a*) acquisition of violent behavior patterns, e.g., evidence for modeling, rehearsal, and reinforcement, and (*b*) contemporaneous risk factors. Second, we might consider moderators including (*a*) antecedent childhood and adolescent processes and (*b*) contemporary processes such as the role of stress, support, and structure, as well as mental illness. Third, we might consider possible predisposing variables, including (*a*) vulnerability factors, such as cognitive impairment, and (*b*) contemporary predisposers, such as substance abuse. We might then consider whether some stable demographics might be used as subgroup norms rather than predictors, allowing more accurate prediction of risk for specific target groups. We will use this four-part framework to organize our review of relevant studies.

Prior Findings

Acquisition of Violent Behavior

Antecedent Risk Markers

A wide range of studies in diverse areas is supportive of the view that learning is a direct major contributor to the occurrence of violent behavior. Modeling is one of several mechanisms by which this learning may occur. Bandura's (1973) review of experimental studies of children's physical aggression after viewing physically aggressive role models is strongly supportive of this view. Prospective studies extending this effect into adulthood are fewer in number but are suggestive. For example, McCord (1979) found a link between parental aggression for a group of boys in a delinquency prevention program and criminal convictions when the boys were followed into adulthood up to age 40.

The literature on viewing violent TV programs and aggression later in life is also supportive of the effects of modeling. The first longitudinal study documenting this effect was that of Lefkowitz et al. (1977), which found a relationship between preference for violent TV shows at grade 3 and aggression at grade 13, but in boys only. Since that time additional studies across various cultures have found a relationship between childhood TV viewing and aggression in adulthood. Turner, Hess, and Peterson-Lewis (1986, 51) have summarized these studies and concluded that the "balance of findings are consistent with the hypothesis that television produced a long-term increase in the aggressive behavior of boys but not of girls." Huesmann (1986), in a review, concluded that TV viewing appeared to interact with violent family role models in producing adult aggression. In addition, violent family role models may interact with other factors in producing aggression (Fantuzzo et al. 1991).

A larger number of studies have used adult recollections to measure modeling for violence in childhood. Although these are weaker support from a methodological standpoint, the findings are consistent with results of longitudinal studies. These studies have used various measures of subjects' observations of parental violence as the independent variable. In a study of 62 habitually violent males, Bach-y-Rita and Veno (1974) found that 53% reported that their parents had engaged in physical conflict; however, there was no control group. More-violent juvenile offenders more frequently reported witnessing extreme violence than did less-violent offenders (Lewis et al. 1979). Similarly, a greater proportion of abusive husbands said they had witnessed parental spouse abuse than did control subjects (Rosenbaum and O'Leary 1981). In a national sample of married or cohabiting adults, severe marital aggression was correlated with reports of seeing a parent hit the other parent (Kalmuss 1984). Three studies of male mental patients found that subjects' reports of parents fighting with persons outside the family were correlated with violence prior to admission and in-hospital assaults (Yesavage et al. 1983), with subsequent arrest or readmission for violence within six months (Klassen and O'Connor 1988a), and with subsequent arrest or readmission for violence within one year (Klassen and O'Connor 1988b). In the last study, the effect occurred for both schizophrenic and nonschizophrenic patients.

Modeling may also occur when the child is the target of violence. Being abused as a child has also been found to differentiate between more-violent and less-violent male juvenile offenders (Lewis et al. 1979) and abusive husbands and controls (Hershon and Rosenbaum 1991; Rosenbaum and O'Leary 1981). Parental hitting of a teenage child was correlated with severe marital violence (Kalmuss 1984). Being injured by a sibling before age 15 was predictive of subsequent violence in a sample of male psychiatric patients (Klassen and O'Connor 1988a), and being injured by an adult before age 15 was predictive for violence in both schizophrenic and nonschizophrenic male patients (Klassen and O'Connor 1988b). Severe discipline administered by the father (Yesavage et al. 1983) and severity of childhood discipline (Yesavage 1984) were correlated with in-hospital violence in male schizophrenic patients. In one of the few studies of violence in an all-female sample, Climent et al. (1973) found that severe punishment by parents differentiated violent and nonviolent women prisoners.

Widom (1989) has conducted a thorough review of the literature on the relationship between child abuse or neglect and adult violence, and concluded that methodological weakness creates some doubt about the strength of the evidence. However, from a standpoint of risk assessment, if persons who report childhood abuse are found to be more violent in the future, it is still an important risk factor that should be included in studies in this area.

When we consider these studies of modeling from a risk perspective, note that while many studies involve a dichotomous independent variable, the actual wording of the variable (e.g., "extreme" violence, "severe" punishment or abuse, or "severe" violence, injury, or discipline) implies a continuum. This is critical from a research perspective in terms of measurement and also important when we consider the frequency with which violence is likely to be modeled for children. Violence on television and in the home have been suggested as relatively commonplace occurrences. Considering these phenomena as continuous suggests that there may be some proportional relationship between the risk factor and subsequent violence.

Exposure to violent role models is not the only component of learning associated with subsequent violence. The literature suggests that rehearsal and reinforcement also play important roles. Studies of early problematic youth behaviors associated with crime and violence later in life are suggestive of the role of rehearsal of violent and antisocial behavior. Loeber and Dishion (1983), in reviewing early predictors of male delinquency, cited early youth behavior problems, early youth aggression, later youth aggression, and antisocial behavior as consistent predictors of subsequent delinquency. The review by Justice et al. (1974) of childhood predictors of adult violence identifies fighting, temper tantrums, school problems, and truancy. In a similar vein, aggression in grade 3 was found to be related to aggression in grade 13 (Lefkowitz et al. 1977) and prior assaultiveness to more recent assaultiveness in children (Pfeffer, Plutchik, and Mizruchi 1983). Other relevant variables that have been noted are the triad of enuresis, firesetting, and cruelty to animals (Hellman and Blackman 1966).

Rehearsal during adolescence may be particularly critical in the development of adult violence. There is a large group of studies correlating crime and violence during adolescence with crime and violence in adulthood. Presence of a juvenile record is predictive of adult violence in male mental patients (Steadman and Cocozza 1974; Cocozza and Steadman 1974; Klassen and O'Connor 1988a). Further, the earlier the arrest, the more likely are future crime and violence (State of Michigan 1978; Thornberry and Jacoby 1979; Petersilia 1980). The seriousness of juvenile crime has also been correlated with the probability of violent criminal recidivism (State of Michigan 1978; Petersilia 1980), as has prior juvenile violence (Wenk, Robison, and Smith 1972). It appears that the earlier this rehearsal occurs, the greater the likelihood that the behavior will persist into adulthood.

Studies correlating adult crime and violence with future crime and violence may demonstrate a consistency of learned violent behaviors. The samples in these studies variously include offenders, patient-offenders, and patients. Predictor variables are obtained both from official records and self-reports. Specific predictive measures evaluated have included number of prior arrests (Cocozza and Steadman 1974), number of prior convictions (Gilmore and Walkey 1981), prior incarcerations (Steadman and Cocozza 1974; Tardiff and Sweillam 1980; Sepejak et al. 1983), arrests for disturbing the peace (Klassen and O'Connor 1988a), previous arrests for violent crime (Thornberry and Jacoby 1979; Steadman and Morrissey 1982; Klassen and O'Connor 1988a; Quinsey et al. 1975; Convit et al. 1988; State of Michigan 1978; Shore, Filson, and Johnson 1988), seriousness of prior offenses (Thornberry and Jacoby 1979; Cocozza and Steadman 1974; Quinsey and MacGuire 1986), commission of sex crimes (Quinsey and MacGuire 1986), history of weapons possession (State of Michigan 1978), and self-reports of violent incidents (Klassen and O'Connor 1988a, 1988b; Hall 1978). Based on the findings to date it appears that virtually any measure of past offending can be expected to predict future violence.

Studies of hospitalizations associated with violence have consistently shown a positive association when both criterion and predictor measures were assault occurring in the community (Rossi et al. 1986; Klassen and O'Connor 1987 1989). However, of four studies that examined the relationship between community violence and in-hospital violence, two found a significant relationship (Werner et al. 1983; Yesavage 1984) and two did not (Quinsey and MacGuire 1986; Rofman, Askinazi, and Font 1980). Differences in context may suggest some specificity in the learning of violence.

Rehearsal alone would not be sufficient for learning violence. Reinforcement of aggressive and violent behaviors is also required. Unfortunately, the previously cited studies do not examine this process.

A review of the learning literature is beyond the scope of this chapter; however, a few citations may be instructive here. Bandura (1965) found that children who observed a model who was either rewarded for aggression or suffered no consequences spontaneously performed a greater amount and variety of aggressive actions than children who saw the model punished. Whether aggressive responses acquired through modeling are retained or lost with the passage of time depends in part on the extent to which rehearsal memory aids are employed (Bandura 1973).

An example of the role of reinforcement in children's learning of aggressive behavior is seen in a study by Patterson, Littman, and Bricker (1967). Children in nursery school were observed and aggressive acts and consequences measured. The highest degree of aggressive response was found in those children who encountered positive reinforcers (such as whining and crying by the victim) compared to children exposed to potential punishers (counterattacks) or neutral responses (being ignored). These effects have also been seen in animal studies.

The effects of intermittent schedules of reinforcement are well known (Ferster and Skinner 1957). Partial reinforcement effects and resistance to extinction have also been documented in regard to aggressive behavior (Geen and Pigg 1970). Inconsistency of reinforcement is likely to produce a higher rate of aggression that is more difficult to extinguish.

Longitudinal studies on the role of rehearsal and reinforcement of violent behavior appear to be lacking in the literature. There are, however, excellent examples of empirical and theoretical work on the development of antisocial and high-risk children, such as that by Patterson and his associates (Patterson, DeBaryshe, and Ramsey 1989; Patterson and Bank 1985; Patterson 1986). The Patterson, DeBaryshe, and Ramsey (1989) model is based on their own empirical findings and other literature in the area. In this model disrupted family management practices are the immediate direct contributor to antisocial behavior. (Other factors, such as family stressors, lead to these disrupted management practices.) In such a situation, the parent administers consequences following aggressive behavior only intermittently. In addition, naturally occurring consequences of aggressive behavior will, on at least some occasions, reinforce the behavior.

Contemporaneous Risk Markers

If there are antecedent processes associated with baseline risk, we should then ask if there are contemporaneous variables which increase risk in the general population or across a wide range of baseline risk. This is an area which has not been well integrated in prediction models or in risk assessment. Milgram's (1974) shock experiments readily come to mind. Berkowitz and Rawlings (1963) suggest that violence is more likely to occur when the victim seems to deserve an aggressive response, i.e., when it seems justified. Berkowitz (1989) has also suggested that observing violence may lower restraints, what has been termed trivialization of aggression. Attribution theory may hold great promise in assessing risk and understanding the processes involved in the immediate situation (e.g., Berkowitz 1989; Zillman 1978).

General cultural or subcultural norms also may contribute to the incidence and occurrence of violence. Membership in certain types of peer groups can greatly increase violence across a wide range of individuals with varying levels of baseline risk. Nazis, for instance, felt tremendous pride when their kill rate surpassed other camps' rates (Lanzmann 1985). Similarly, gangs often compile scrapbooks about their violent acts (Short 1968); members are heavily reinforced for their violence, gaining both respect within the gang community and individual self-esteem.

More specific factors within the immediate situation might be considered direct contributors toward aggression and violence. Specifically, provocations or threats by the eventual victim have been shown to play a role in homicides and assaults. Two very interesting studies examined the interactions between offender and victim preceding a violent crime. Luckenbill (1977) studied 70 homicides and found that the typical sequence involved the victim issuing an offensive move, the offender retaliating with a challenge, a tacit agreement favoring the use of violence, and the death of the victim. In the Felson and Steadman (1983) study, official data from 153 incidents of homicide and assault were studied. Systematic patterns were noted in the interchanges. Typically the incident began with identity attacks followed by attempts and failures to influence the antagonist. Threats were then made and verbal conflict ended in physical attack. Aggressive action by the victim increased the likelihood that the victim would be killed.

A somewhat related finding is that being the victim of a violent crime increases the individual's risk of becoming violent (cf. Singer 1986). This is especially true if there is an "absence of justice" for the perpetrator of the original violent crime. Novaco's (1989) work in the area of anger and provocation presented in this volume is also clearly relevant.

The presence of weapons dramatically increases the lethality of a violent encounter. The United States has the highest homicide rate for males, more than five times higher than that of the second-ranking country (Fingerhut and Kleinman 1990). Three-quarters of these homicides resulted from the use of firearms. Zimring (1991) reviewed more than 16,000 violent assaults from Chicago police records and found that an assault with a gun was five times more likely to result in a fatality than an attack with a knife, but attacks with knives were equally likely to damage a part of the body where injury can cause death and were more likely to result in multiple wounds. The greater death rate for assaults with guns seems to stem from their greater lethality as a weapon, what is described as an instrumentality effect.

Moderating Variables

Having begun by identifying variables which may have some direct link to violence, we must now consider a second class of variables, those which may increase or decrease the probability of violence where contributors (modeling, learning, or others) have produced a high baseline "propensity" for violent behavior.

For example, a number of childhood factors other than violence in the home have been found to be associated with later violent behavior. Some are variables relating to parental caregiving, such as parental nurturance, a rating of how well parents provided for needs (Lefkowitz et al. 1977; Klassen and O'Connor 1988a), and parental supervision (McCord 1979). A longer exposure to poor supervision increases the probability of delinquency (Loeber 1990). Parental loss, whether due to death, separation, or divorce, has often been found to be a correlate of violence and of psychopathology. Parental loss variables studied include parental separation (Pfeffer, Plutchik, and Mizruchi 1983), not living with both parents until age 16 (Quinsey et al. 1975), not living with natural parents (Gilmore and Walkey 1981; Klassen and O'Connor 1987), seeing mother once a year or less before age 15 (Klassen and O'Connor 1988b), loss of mother before age 10 (Climent et al. 1973), mean age at time of paternal loss (Climent et al. 1973), mean age at time of maternal loss (Climent et al. 1973), and death of father before age 15 (Klassen and O'Connor 1988a). Finally, disruptions in the family environment from parental psychiatric hospitalization or drug and alcohol abuse (Convit et al. 1988) and arrests of parents (Loeber and Dishion 1983) have been correlated with adult violence and juvenile delinquency respectively. What these variables appear to have in common is the possible disruption of adequate bonding or socialization during childhood. A relationship between lack of bonding in childhood and lack of empathy in adulthood is believed to exist. Persons who lack empathy for others lack an important deterrent to aggression against others.

We consider these to be indirect measures of the probability that bonding might have been disrupted. The occurrence of one or more of these events does not necessarily indicate a lack of bonding. Loss of a parent early in life may not lead to psychopathology or violence if other close bonds are available. For example, Breier et al. (1988) found that type of parental loss did not predict pathology; rather, factors such as poor quality of home life after the loss, particularly a nonsupportive relationship with the remaining parent, were related to adult psychopathology.

These types of variables seem highly amenable to scaling efforts. A list of possible disruptions of bonding could be compiled and perhaps weighted. These types of problems are not unusual in the childhoods of psychiatric patient populations, and adequate distributions could be obtained.

Moderators of different types may also be discovered. Impulsiveness appears to us to fit well here. The chapter by Barratt in this volume addresses the relationship between impulsivity and aggression.

Contemporaneous Moderators

We should also consider contemporaneous moderators, generally termed situational variables. This area is not well developed at present. Because situational variables are, by definition, factors that change over time, they are more difficult to study than stable predictors. There is virtually universal agreement that situational factors play an important role (Monahan 1981; Cohen, Groth, and Siegel 1978; Moos 1973). A lengthy list of individual situational risk factors exists in the literature; however, they have not often been incorporated into a coherent overall assessment of risk factors. In a prior research project, we mounted such an effort, but the findings regarding situational factors were, as we stated, disappointing (Klassen and O'Connor 1989). Ongoing research of this type which appears very promising includes the Risk Assessment Project of the MacArthur Foundation Research Network on Mental Health and the Law (Monahan 1990), a study of conditional prediction by Lidz and Mulvey (Lidz 1987), and our own work (Klassen 1989).

In examining lists of situational correlates of violence, it appears that most of the findings can be subsumed under the constructs of stress, support, and structure. In all of these areas, however, there are both positive and negative findings.

Stress, measured by life events scores, has been found in some studies to be related to the occurrence of crime (Masuda, Cutler, and Holmes 1978) and violence (Levinson and Ramsay 1979). However, others have found no relationship with violence in a sample of subjects (Klassen and O'Connor 1987). Steadman and Ribner (1982) found a relationship between high life stress and violence in a sample of mental patients but not in a sample of the general population. Specific individual life events that have been identified as correlated with violence include breakup of a relationship or work problems (Hall 1978), unwanted pregnancy (Garbarino 1977; Gelles 1975), recent death in family (Daniel et al. 1983), work life events (Barling and Rosenbaum 1986), low income (Straus, Gelles, and Steinmetz 1980), number of children in family (Straus, Gelles, and Steinmetz 1980), and crowded physical environment (Booth and Edwards 1976; Garbarino 1977). Unemployment is a frequently studied stressor that has been shown to be correlated with crime and violence in some studies (Sviridoff and Thompson 1979; Loeber and Dishion 1983; Straus, Gelles, and Steinmetz 1980; Klassen and O'Connor 1989) and uncorrelated in others (Rossi et al. 1985; Sepejak et al. 1983). Other, more subjective measures of stress have also been found to be related to violence: feeling let down by family members (Klassen and O'Connor 1988b), being dissatisfied with relatives (Klassen and O'Connor 1987), and a score called family satisfaction, which includes stressor items (Klassen and O'Connor 1989).

Social support has often been identified as a negative correlate of crime and violence on the basis of individual predictor variables presumed to be reflective of social support. Unmarried persons, for example, presumed to lack an important source of support, are found to have higher rates of violence (Klassen and O'Connor 1988a; State of Michigan 1978; Tardiff and Sweillam 1980; Rossi et al. 1986; Tardiff and Koenigsberg 1985) and criminal recidivism (Waller 1974). Other negative correlates which seem closely tied to the social support construct are intimate relationship scores (Klassen and O'Connor 1989), cohesiveness of the family network (Davies 1969), and compatibility of parents (Davies 1969). Social isolation, which may indicate a lack of social support, has been related to child abuse (Daniel, Hampton, and Newberger 1983; Garbarino 1977). The most interesting recent work on social support and violence has been done by Estroff (1990), whose work is represented in this volume.

Structure appears to be a useful construct for addressing situational factors and risk of violence. It has not received the same degree of attention as stress and support; i.e., there are no existing structure scales, whereas there are stress and support scales. Following Barker (1968) we conceive structure as essentially the degree to which a setting exerts control over its occupants. Most of the evidence regarding such relationships comes from studies of inpatient violence. In a study of treatment outcome in chronic patients, Klass, Growe, and Strizich (1977) found that violent episodes resulting in injury were lower in programs that emphasized organization than in programs that emphasized anger and aggression. Patients treated in programs that were high in structure and low in aggression spent longer periods of time out of the hospital. Moos and Schwartz (1972) also found that programs high in structure were most successful in keeping long-term patients in the community.

Morrison (1989), in a study of interactions between nursing staff and patients, found that inconsistency in social expectation by nurses correlated with violence on hospital wards. Drummond, Sparr, and Gordon (1989) described a program that was effective in reducing violence in a treatment setting that essentially consisted of flagging high-risk patients and imposing more structure on them. Probably the best evidence that structure prevents violent behavior comes from a study by Katz and Kirkland (1990). They found that violence was more frequent and more extreme in wards in which staff functions were not clear and events such as activities or meetings were unpredictable. In contrast, violence was less extreme in wards with strong leadership, structured staff roles, and standardized predictable events.

Mental illness as another type of moderator presents interesting conceptual problems. While clinical factors are addressed elsewhere in this volume, a brief discussion is relevant for our purposes. The evidence can be viewed as suggesting that at least some aspects of mental illness may be direct contributors to the occurrence of violent incidents. But at the present time it appears that diagnosis alone is not a reliable risk marker. Different studies have identified many different diagnoses with high risk, for example, schizophrenia (Binder and McNiel 1988; Craig 1982), personality disorder (Tardiff and Sweillam 1982; Tardiff and Koenigsberg 1985), organic brain syndrome (Craig 1982), antisocial personality (Farrington 1989), and substance abuse (Zitrin et al. 1976).

Krakowski, Volavka, and Brizev (1986) have found some order in these diverse findings. They point out that various psychoses in their acute phase are associated with an increased risk of violence and that apparent differences in propensity for violence between persons with different diagnoses may partly reflect assessment of violence at different times during the course of the illness. From this perspective, symptoms may moderate violent responses, interacting with high baseline risk.

Where symptoms have been directly measured, diverse types of symptoms have been correlated with violence, for example, homicidal ideation (Hedlund et al. 1973), hostility (Menzies, Webster, and Sepejak 1985), paranoia (Yesavage 1983), command hallucinations (Shore, Filson, and Johnson 1988), thought disorder (Tanke and Yesavage 1985), hallucinatory behavior (Yesavage et al. 1981), and motor retardation (Werner et al. 1983). Many of these findings and symptoms are typical of schizophrenia, and a schizophrenic symptom score has been linked to inpatient violence (Yesavage 1984).

A recent study by Link, Cullen, and Andrews (1990) beautifully demonstrates a moderating relationship between the occurrence of psychotic symptomatology and violent behavior. They found that patients were more frequently violent than a never-treated community sample, even when controlling for a large number of other variables. They then controlled for current psychotic symptomatology and found that differences between patients and the community sample disappeared. Further, the presence of psychotic symptoms predicted violence in the community sample. Monahan (1991), reviewing this and several other studies, concluded that mental illness is associated with violence. This would imply that psychotic symptoms are a moderating variable in the occurrence of violence.

It may be, then, that some types of mental disorder may be closely and directly linked to violence, as when specific delusional content can be linked to specific acts of violence (see Taylor 1986). We might also speculate that command hallucinations can have a direct link to violence.

But it seems likely that many mental illness "predictors" may moderate rather than predicting directly: the loss of control and organization and the disinhibition which may occur with increased symptoms, particularly in manic or depressed patients, may lead to violence in individuals where violence has been modeled or rehearsed and is relatively high in the response hierarchy. It is also possible to consider that some of the mentally ill may be predisposed or vulnerable because of chronic impairment, e.g., in cognitive functioning; this might apply to chronic undifferentiated schizophrenics and certain other categories.

Predisposing Variables

A third major class of variables can be considered using a conceptual approach which involves some arbitrary judgments. If moderators regulate some aspect of the criterion variable, violence, we might assume or hypothesize a type of variable which predisposes to violence but is not in the strictest sense a regulator. Our concept of predisposing variables is similar to that of Lewis et al. (1985, 1989), who suggested that central nervous system dysfunction may make individuals vulnerable to violence as a pattern of behavior.

A number of studies have identified cognitive deficits as correlates of violence and crime. Low IQ has been found to be significantly associated with the occurrence of delinquency (Wolfgang, Figlio, and Sellin 1972; Hirschi and Hindelang 1977) and violence (Lewis et al. 1979; Holland, Beckett, and Levi 1981; Quinsey and MacGuire 1986; Klassen and O'Connor 1987). However, at least two studies failed to establish this association (Pfeffer, Plutchik, and Mizruchi 1983; Black and Spinks 1985). Similarly, retardation has been correlated with delinquency (Wolfgang, Figlio, and Sellin 1972) and violent behavior (Hedlund et al. 1973; Pfeffer, Plutchik, and Mizruchi 1983; Klassen and O'Connor 1988b; Tardiff and Sweillam 1980; Tardiff and Koenigsberg 1985). Other studies have lumped together a variety of cognitive problems and found an association with violence. Krakowski et al. (1989) found that neurological impairment was more common in persistently violent patients than less violent patients. In a comparison of adolescent homicide offenders and controls, Busch et al. (1990) found that killers were more likely to have had severe educational difficulties or to have a low IQ. These results were replicated in a second study (Zagar et al. 1990). Neurological impairment was also found to differentiate children who later committed murder from a control group (Lewis et al. 1985).

There is evidence that these cognitive impairments are most likely to be important in interaction with other factors, and it is this evidence that leads us to categorize cognitive deficits as predisposing. In the Lewis et al. (1985) study of children who later murdered, a combination of five risk factors (psychosis, neurological problems, abuse, mental illness in family, and commission of serious violence as a juvenile) were present in 75% of the subjects. In a later study, Lewis et al. (1989) found that a combination of intrinsic vulnerabilities (cognitive impairment, psychosis, or neurological dysfunction) and abusive family environment showed interaction effects. Similarly, Hughes et al. (1991) found that medical, family, and scholastic problems interacted in predicting the number and type of offenses committed by urban delinquents.

Contemporaneous Risk Markers

We should also consider the possibility of variables which are contemporaneous and predisposing. One possible example is alcohol or drug intoxication. Particular substances, PCP and crack being obvious examples, may exert a powerful influence. It is well known by police officers, for example, than an individual on PCP may be relatively docile unless suddenly touched or restrained; the response to touch or restraint may be extraordinarily violent.

Generally, the published literature on alcohol and drug use shows alcohol or drug use to increase the probability of violence. Alcohol use has been linked to violent crime and domestic violence (Collins et al. 1980) and to criminal recidivism (Wenk, Robison, and Smith 1972). Alcohol and drug use has been associated with self-reported disputes (Steadman 1982) and criminal careers (Petersilia 1980). Drug use has frequently been found to be associated with delinquency (Loeber and Dishion 1983), and in investigations of specific drugs, opiate abuse has been found to be a consistent predictor of criminal recidivism (Prichard 1977), and recent amphetamine use has been linked to violence (Klassen and O'Connor 1988b).

In a recent metaanalysis of the experimental literature on alcohol use and aggressive behavior, Bushman and Cooper (1990) concluded that the consumption of alcohol can increase aggressive behavior. It is unknown to what extent aggressive behavior measured in the laboratory generalizes to aggressive and violent behavior in real world settings.

There do exist studies showing no relationship between drug use and violence (e.g., Klassen and O'Connor 1987). In addition, at least two studies found a negative correlation between alcohol use and violence (Tardiff and Koenigsberg 1985; Menzies, Webster, and Sepejak 1985).

Considering violence as a heterogeneous phenomenon might shed some light on these discrepancies. Some crimes and violence are instrumental in nature, such as burglaries or robberies committed in order to support a drug habit. In such circumstances drug use might be considered a direct contributor. However, alcohol and drug use may be predisposing when the violence is more spontaneous in nature. In addition, in populations with large proportions of chronically mentally ill persons, the occurrence of psychotic symptoms may be the most prominent moderating factor present, and drug and alcohol use effects might not be noted, depending on the distribution of diagnoses in the study sample.

Demographic Variables and Norms

Specific demographic variables are strongly associated with arrests for violent crime: gender, age, socioeconomic status, and race. But in other areas of behavioral research, these variables are used to establish subpopulation norms, not as predictors. Notice that if a raw test score or a frequency cutoff were used to classify high and low intelligence or memory, we might conclude that IQ and memory increase from childhood, peak somewhere between the ages of 20 and 40, and then decline; intelligence would appear to be "predicted" by age. Gender would be associated with visual, motor, and strength measures of brain damage. Education level and socioeconomic status are correlated with a wide range of cognitive measures and can produce artifacts, e.g., differences by ethnicity. But if we group subjects by another demographic indicator, inpatient status, these differences are less pronounced and less reliable. Studies of mixed gender psychiatric patient populations have found males to be disproportionately violent when the criterion measure is violence occurring in the community (Hedlund et al. 1973; Rossi et al. 1986; Tardiff and Sweillam 1980; Craig 1982). Three studies of in-hospital violence report no sex differences (Tardiff and Sweillam 1982; Karson and Bigelow 1987) or females as more violent (Fotrell 1980). One study which included dangerous behavior in the community (as well as in institutions) found no gender differences (Sepejak et al. 1983). More recently, in the MacArthur Risk Assessment study, self-reports of recent violence in the community were approximately equal for males and females (Steadman et al. 1991). Some studies of domestic violence have found that women are more likely to be physically aggressive than men (O'Leary et al. 1989).

Most studies of patients and patient-offenders have found differences on the basis of age, whether the criterion measure is in-hospital violence (Barnard et al. 1984; Fotrell 1980; Harris and Varney 1986; Karson and Bigelow 1987; Steadman and Cocozza 1974) or violence in the community (Black and Spinks 1985; Cocozza and Steadman 1974; Klassen and O'Connor 1988a; Quinsey and MacGuire 1986; Steadman and Cocozza 1974; Tardiff and Sweillam 1980, 1982; Thornberry and Jacoby 1979). On the other hand, several studies have found no age differences in community violence (Rossi et al. 1986; Hall 1978; Klassen and O'Connor 1989) or dangerous behavior in both hospital and community (Sepejak et al. 1983). The MacArthur study found that patients under age 40 were disproportionately violent in the community (Steadman et al., in press).

Studies of patients and patient-offenders have not uniformly correlated incidence of violence with race. Klassen and O'Connor (1989) have found racial differences in some patient samples. Rossi et al. (1986) found an overall difference, but not when controlling for diagnosis. Similarly, Tardiff and Sweillam (1980) found no racial differences when controlling for education. Three studies found no overall differences on the basis of race (Thornberry and Jacoby 1979; Craig 1982; Klassen and O'Connor 1987).

Lower education or occupational status have been associated with greater risk of violence in a number of studies of patient populations (Tardiff and Sweillam 1980; Quinsey et al. 1975; Harris and Varney 1986). But a similar number of studies found no differences (Thornberry and Jacoby 1979; Barnard et al. 1984; Black and Spinks 1985; Rossi et al. 1986; Hall 1978). Also, conflicting results have been found in different samples drawn from the same facility (Klassen and O'Connor 1989). It is impossible to draw any firm conclusions from the evidence in patient populations. It is quite possible that patients of low socioeconomic status are more frequently violent, but this would not be detected since virtually all studies of patient samples consist predominantly of persons from lower social classes.

We should consider the possibility of viewing demographic differences as norms under certain conditions, e.g., if these result from a greater exposure to conditions or factors that actually increase risk for violence. There are more violent male role models in the media, and aggression and violence by boys are probably more frequently reinforced. Blacks and persons of lower socioeconomic status may be disproportionately exposed to violent group norms, as suggested by Wolfgang and Ferracuti's (1967) subculture of violence theory. Age differences are not so readily explicable. We anticipate that when differential exposure to the true factors that produce violence has been controlled for, demographic differences will disappear or at least be greatly attenuated.

Implications for Future Research

Four basic directions for future research are suggested: (1) risk management research, (2) studies which identify the type of violence or risk, (3) studies which evaluate the degree of risk, and (4) studies which evaluate the contribution of multiple determinants of risk and violence.

Research findings are persistently and powerfully shaped by the questions asked and the methods used to answer them. Notice, for example, that the criterion variable, violence, has often been measured as a dichotomy, e.g., violence occurs or does not occur. This definition of violence can lead to the assumption that any marker of membership in the violent group, such as arrests for violent crimes, can be selected as the criterion measure. A meta-theory in which violence is categorical can then lead easily, if illogically, to a second assumption: that violence is a homogeneous or unitary construct, that violence is violence.

Suppose that an alternate set of assumptions or metatheory were explicitly selected in which violence may be a distributed variable in the general population, and in which violence may be heterogeneous, i.e., different types of violence may be studied. A change in definition of the criterion or dependent measure might then produce a considerable change in the demographic and case history variables yielded by research. For example, violence might well *not* be considered a low–base rate phenomenon if behaviors such as child abuse, domestic violence, and sexual aggression were considered.

We might also reconsider assumptions from a risk assessment perspective where the independent variable is concerned. As is the case with dependent variables, independent variables have frequently been treated as dichotomous. Dichotomizing variables which are essentially continuous yields a less sensitive measure of risk.

Risk Management

When we approach the practical issue of risk management, we are concerned with what may increase and especially with what may decrease some dimension of violent outcome. A continuous dependent measure, that is, a scaled criterion measure or a number of scales of violent outcome, would allow the use of baseline deviation designs. These types of research designs are particularly applicable in areas such as treatment outcome. We can select different scales depending on the question asked; for some questions, the frequency of violent events may be particularly critical, while in other areas of research, we may wish to weight a scale to consider lethality or some other aspect of the violence. It may be particularly beneficial, for certain questions, to measure aggression on the part of the subject independent of its effects.

Such an approach is frequently utilized in program evaluation studies, particularly in mental health settings. We know relatively little about how to treat or manage violent patients in a mental health facility with predictable results. In this regard, the state of the art with respect to violence is very much analogous to the medical field of oncology a decade ago. The problem is serious and admittedly we cannot demonstrate effective outcomes of specific treatment or management techniques. But effective treatment and management techniques and programs to deliver services develop only with repeated treatment outcome and program evaluation studies. If the results of demographic and case history studies to date allow us to identify certain groups at risk, e.g., individuals admitted for violence or individuals with a history of prior violence, then progress in the area of risk management depends on the use of a scale which is not dichotomous, so that changes can be assessed, and of quasi-experimental and naturalistic designs, which have been well demonstrated in many other areas of mental health research: repeated measures designs, for example, as well as multiple baseline and reversal designs.

Types of Risk

If we also consider the possibility that violence may be heterogeneous, then multiple comparison group designs become an obvious method by which to answer a set of very relevant questions. We can study the possibility that different subpopulations present different types of risk. We can begin to address questions as to the differences between individuals who are frequently violent toward a specific class of victims, subgroups which are more likely to engage in violence of a particular type, such as sexual assault, and the like. This again becomes particularly relevant in the area of risk management in a mental health population. Different types of aggression present different risks and may necessitate different management techniques.

This area is also potentially fruitful in studying the origins, causes, or processes involved in violence, conceptualized as a learned behavior. Are there some individuals for whom violence is modeled and subsequently rehearsed in ways which are specific and independent of those behaviors which identify an individual as mentally ill? Are there, on the other hand, processes by which mental illness, viewed as a learned behavior, does not involve any component of violence? In other words, when we study the association between violence and mental illness, it is possible that violence is modeled under certain conditions as part of a more general pattern which includes learned aspects of mental illness. Perhaps some individuals learn violence in a very discreet and instrumental fashion which is highly independent of mental health status, while other persons learn violence in the context of disorganized, poorly controlled, pathological interactions.

If this is so, we can also begin to ask questions, in a multiple comparison group approach, as to the specificity of learning. For example, does modeled violence by males toward females without modeling of peer violence and without rehearsal in the peer community lead in a very specific fashion to domestic violence, while modeling which extends to the peer and community subgroups and involves rehearsals in these contexts leads to community violence? Are there other subgroups for whom the modeling and rehearsing of criminal behavior increases the risk of violence only as a subcomponent of aggressive and antisocial behavior patterns?

Some of the research to date suggests very general factors such as impulsivity and poor cognitive controls associated with violent behavior. But there are also intriguing suggestions that the process may at times be highly focused and highly specific. We might wonder, for example, how it is that serial killers seem to select with such specificity and predictability a class of victims with so much in common. How is it that some individuals appear to engage in random violence, while others may only pick prostitutes or blonde coeds or adolescent males? If we approach future research by considering the possibility that there are different types of violence, we might even hypothesize that some violence patterns are very nonspecific and based on generalized aggression, while others are highly focused, learned patterns of behavior. The specificity of sexual assault, for example, is an intriguing area for future study.

Heterogeneity of patterns of violence might also be studied with respect to predisposing and moderating variables. It would be logical to consider, in the obvious absence of a large body of empirical support, the possibility that certain predisposing variables such as neurological impairment may be associated with generalized violence under conditions of high stress or conflict, while different patterns of violence might be precipitated by moderating variables such as loss. We note that early bonding failure and a history of loss are generally associated with violence, and that certain patterns of violent behavior appear to be precipitated by the recent loss of a relationship, job, or significant source of life support. The profiles of mass murderers described by law enforcement agencies might provide the possibility of studying a group of individuals who may not have an extensive history of prior mental health contact or an extensive history of prior violence, but for whom loss, in combination with an as yet unidentified direct contributor, is a powerful moderator which leads to violent outcome rather than suicide, hospitalization for depression, or other decompensation reactions.

Degree of Risk

If both the criterion measure and the predictor can be adequately scaled, then research can be designed beyond the nominal level to answer a practical and critical question: As the intensity or some other dimension of the independent variable increases, does some aspect of risk increase proportionately? Can we determine, for example, whether the probability or intensity of violent outcome will increase in relation to the intensity of increased symptomatology? If variables such as stress or the loss of support are predictive of violence, does their degree or intensity associate with more frequent, more lethal, or more generalized risk?

In the study of managing violence in populations with mental disorder, we are unlikely to produce useful results with binary or categorical predictors and outcome measures. If we approach violence in a manner consistent with other mental health research, we can ask some practical and very useful questions, such as whether increased therapeutic dosage levels for particular medications do in fact reduce some aspect of violent outcome. Does increased structure in environmental placement proportionately or differentially reduce risk? What is the relationship between length of treatment and risk?

This again generates critical questions as to the processes by which violence develops. We might consider the possibility that violence is modeled to some degree in the childhood history of an overwhelming percentage of the general population. Does modeling of more violent behavior increase some dimension of subsequent risk? Studies of aggression would suggest a relationship but would also suggest that the observed consequences of violent behavior are a critical component in future aggression. When approached in this fashion, we can consider an enormous number of potentially useful studies to determine whether an increased level or weight of the predictor is associated with increased risk; does more severe neglect, with a hypothesized failure in bonding and development of empathy, progressively impair moderating variables which may inhibit future violence?

Interaction Effects

Finally, the interaction of multiple determinants of risk and violence presents the greatest challenges for research design and analysis. Ultimately, however, this approach is likely to generate the most substantive and powerful results. We have, in fact, identified a good many demographic and case history variables which are associated with violence. These variables, however, clearly are more prevalent in the general population than is violence if violence is measured by a narrowly defined and dichotomous marker such as arrests or readmissions. We are forced by this observation to consider the possibility that violence is a special case of aggression defined as aggression in which the effect involves injury to the victim, the injury is caused in an illegal manner (self-defense is not considered violence), and the perpetrator is clearly identified (e.g., arrested). We might consider the possibility that some apparent predictors of violence—low IQ, low socioeconomic status, prior arrests—may in fact be strongly associated with being arrested or admitted to a mental health facility because of violence; we might wonder if bright educated individuals who engage in crimes which are difficult to prosecute (e.g., acquaintance rape) are underrepresented demographically.

The use of multiple comparison group or multiple predictor designs is one approach to this series of questions. So long as the criterion variable is narrowly defined and poorly scaled, we will continue to have difficulties obtaining a sufficient sample for such complex analysis. However, it seems very reasonable to reject the hypothesis that there is one, unique cause for violent behavior; if we reject this premise, then the effective study of violence will require consideration of the interactions of different variables or classes of variables. Even with the severe limitations in scaling and design, research to date suggests that there are different patterns of violent behavior that arise or may be predicted from the interaction of several variables and quite probably from the interaction of direct contributors such as learning with both long-term and immediate or situational moderators.

Theory and Policy

It is admittedly premature to propose an explicit theory in which predis-posing, moderating, and direct causal variables interact with proportional and differential effects to produce specified patterns and degrees of risk. But the alternative metatheory in which independent and dependent variables are both dichotomous does not appear fruitful. Nor does it make sense to avoid an explicit theory and to describe as "markers" a list of demographic and case history variables that are identified on the basis of frequency statistics in violent-nonviolent group comparisons but that also occur frequently in the general population. A variable associated by frequency with violence but gen-erally distributed—being male, for example—does not provide an adequate basis for assessing risk in any individual clinical situation. It does not tell us that all males will be violent or that all females will be nonviolent. What, then, do we know from demographic and case history studies to date?

First, we know that an adequate design will be necessary and that certain types of variables are likely to be fruitful in terms of future research. The frequency and consistency with which certain variables are reported, whether or not they are adequately conceptualized as predisposing, moderating, and directly causal, can give direction to future study. What is critical is the evi-dence that certain variables consistently correlate or associate; they may not identify the specific causes or mechanisms by which violence occurs, but they suggest that key variables could be identified which individually or in com-bination account for a substantial proportion of the variance in predicting well-scaled violent outcome.

Second, there is at least inferential evidence that violence is not a unique phenomenon isolated from the body of behavioral research and theory. There is a considerable body of research suggesting the mechanisms by which be-havior is learned; research on prior violence suggests that these mechanisms are worth future study. Studies of aggression may in fact provide a more general framework if violence is a special case of aggression defined by out-come. We can, then, test theoretical statements about how behaviors, includ-ing violence, are acquired or learned, if we can develop working definitions of violence.

Third, the accumulating body of knowledge promises to be applicable in a service delivery setting. For decades, service providers have conceptualized three levels of prevention—primary, secondary, and tertiary. If there are fixed and predisposing variables which establish a baseline of risk, identification of these variables implies the possibility of prevention. Linking, for example, physiological conditions affecting the central nervous system to violence risk would indicate an area in which prevention of the underlying condition affects incidence of violence in the general population. Prevention is also possible where moderators are concerned; we have enough evidence to suspect that neglect and abuse in childhood are associated with the incidence of violence. Further, identifying specific mechanisms in the acquisition of violent behavior and specific precipitating or situational variables will also allow preventive intervention. Access to weapons, for example, is clearly an area in which prevention is hotly disputed on a political if not an empirical level.

Management of risk is also clearly an area in which our results to date suggest cause for optimism. For effective management, we must refine the assessment of baseline or long-term risk and clearly identify variables which increase or decrease baseline probability. If violence is adequately defined and measured, program evaluation and treatment outcome research lies easily within our grasp both methodologically and analytically. We have often approached violence as if we must know its precise causes and cures before program evaluation and outcome research can begin. This position has not led to progress in any other area of health or mental health research. We stay frozen in the assumption that an effective treatment for violence has not yet been demonstrated. This may be yet another example of the paralyzing effects of a dichotomous mindset. Existing knowledge could certainly be applied to evaluation of experimental management and intervention techniques which, with even modest predictive effects, would lead to progressive refinement of intervention in the clinical and service delivery setting.

Fourth, it may be time to reconsider the relationship between violence and mental illness, beyond the categorical question of whether they are or are not related. We can consider the possibility, for example, that certain conditions may be predisposing to both violent behavior and behaviors associated with specific processes in mental illness. This is a critical distinction, for it removes the pejorative and premature inference that mental illness somehow causes violence. We can explore, for example, whether conditions of neglect and impairment from early childhood may increase the risk of vulnerability of individuals to stress, mental illness, violent response, and other patterns of unsuccessful adaptation.

We may also explore whether mental illness, not as a generic category, but as a specific impairment of functioning can serve as a moderator where violent responses are concerned. Research on the relationship of symptomatic status and violent outcome is subject to various interpretations, but it is legitimate to consider the possibility that general impairment in functioning is a moderator variable only for those individuals where other combinations of circumstance and causal factors are present. Whether a combination of behaviors including violence and those associated with mental illness may be conjointly modeled is a similarly intriguing question. We may discover that the link between mental illness and violence, when it is not identified on a frequency association basis alone, involves such discreet contributors as shared predispositions, shared moderators, and also more direct linkages, as in the case of individuals with command hallucinations or delusions leading to specific violent acts. We would certainly consider the possibility that the link between depression and violence is less direct than that between delusions and violence and that low IQ is not appropriately conceptualized as a cause of violence but may be differentially associated depending on early socialization.

Certain policy implications are evident; patient advocacy groups have good reason to resist the essentially unsupported presumption that all mentally ill persons are likely to be violent or that mental illness causes violence. But other significant policy implications extend well beyond the scope of this chapter. The traditional metatheoretical position directs research on the assumption that the violent are a small, discrete group entirely different from the rest of us, thus segregating both the violent individual and the violent process from general social process. The rest of us, then, are dichotomously, categorically nonviolent and need not consider aggression in our society. We need not consider prenatal and neonatal health risks, socialization and education of children, stressors and supports in the general population, and issues of mental health and optimal functioning common to us all, and we need not consider prevention or treatment. We may fail to consider proactively how we socialize around aggression, sexuality, or the capacity to manage stress, intimacy, or the general fabric of our lives. Thus, we have separated violence research from the body of our knowledge about human behavior. In 1969 Hartman published an article entitled "The Key Jingler," which focused on the attempt to reorganize state hospital mental health systems. The author pointed out an important function of the locked ward which had not been considered: Locks require keys, and keys clearly tell us who is not mentally ill.

Acknowledgments

Preparation of this paper was supported by the John D. and Catherine T. MacArthur Foundation Research Network on Mental Health and the Law. We would like to thank Lisa M. Johnson for her comments and suggestions on an earlier draft of this chapter.

References

Bach-y-Rita, G., and A. Veno. 1974. Habitual violence: A profile of 62 men. *American Journal of Psychiatry* 131:1015–17.

Bandura, A. 1965. Influence of models' reinforcement contingencies on the acquisition of imitative responses. *Journal of Personality and Social Psychology* 1:589–95.

————. 1973. *Aggression: A social learning analysis.* Englewood Cliffs, N.J.: Prentice Hall.

————. 1983. Psychological mechanisms of aggression. In R. G. Geen and E. I. Donnerstein, eds., *Aggression: Theoretical and empirical reviews. I: Theoretical and methodological issues.* New York: Academic Press.

Barker, R. 1968. *Ecological psychology.* Stanford: Stanford University Press.

Barling, J., and A. Rosenbaum. 1986. Work stressors and wife abuse. *Journal of Applied Psychology* 71:346–48.

Barnard, G. W., L. Robbins, G. Newman, and F. Carrera. 1984. A study of violence within a forensic treatment facility. *Bulletin of the American Academy of Psychiatry and the Law* 12:339–48.

Berkowitz, L. 1989. Frustration-aggression hypothesis: Examination and reformulation. *Psychological Bulletin* 106:59–73.

Berkowitz, L., and E. Rawlings. 1963. Effects of film violence on inhibitions against subsequent aggression. *Journal of Abnormal and Social Psychology* 66:401–12.

Binder, R., and D. E. McNiel. 1988. Effects of diagnosis and context on dangerousness. *American Journal of Psychiatry* 145:728–32.

Black, T., and P. Spinks. 1985. Predicting outcomes of mentally disordered and dangerous offenders. In D. P. Farrington and R. Tarling, eds., *Prediction in criminology.* New York: State University of New York Press.

Booth, A., and J. N. Edwards. 1976. Crowding and family relations. *American Sociological Review* 41:308–21.

Breier, A., J. R. Kelsoe, P. D. Kirwin, S. A. Beller, O. M. Wolkowitz, and D. Pickar. 1988. Early parental loss and development of adult psychopathology. *Archives of General Psychiatry* 45:987–993.

Busch, K. D., R. Zagar, J. R. Hughes, J. Arbit, and R. E. Bussell. 1990. Adolescents who kill. *Journal of Clinical Psychology* 46:472–85.

Bushman, B. J., and H. M. Cooper. 1990. Effects of alcohol on human aggression: An integrative research review. *Psychological Bulletin* 107:341–54.

Climent, C. E., A. Rollins, F. R. Ervin, and R. Plutchik. 1973. Epidemiological studies of women prisoners. I: Medical and psychiatric variables related to violent behavior. *American Journal of Psychiatry* 130:985–90.

Cocozza, J. J., and H. J. Steadman. 1974. Some refinements in the measurement of prediction of violent behavior. *American Journal of Psychiatry* 131:1012–14.

Cohen, M. L., A. N. Groth, and R. Siegel. 1978. The clinical prediction of dangerousness. *Crime and Delinquency* 24:28–39.

Collins, J. J., L. L. Guess, J. R. Williams, and C. J. Hamilton. 1980. A research agenda to address the relationship between alcoholism and assaultive criminal behavior. Submitted to the Center for the Study of Crime and Criminal Behavior, National Institute of Justice.

Convit, A., J. Jaeger, S. Lin, M. Meisner, and J. Volavka. 1988. Predicting assaultiveness in psychiatric inpatients: A pilot study. *Hospital and Community Psychiatry* 39:429–34.

Craig, T. J. 1982. An epidemiologic study of problems associated with violence among psychiatric inpatients. *American Journal of Psychiatry* 139:1262–66.

Daniel, J. H., R. L. Hampton, and E. H. Newberger. 1983. Child abuse and accidents in black families: A controlled comparative study. *American Journal of Orthopsychiatry* 54:654–53.

Davies, M. 1969. *Probationers in their social environment*. London: Her Majesty's Stationery Office.

Drummond, D. J., L. F. Sparr, and G. H. Gordon. 1989. Hospital violence reduction among high-risk patients. *Journal of the American Medical Association* 261:2531–34.

Estroff, S. 1990. Social networks and violence among persons with severe, persistent mental illnesses: An exploratory analysis. Paper presented at Risk Special Studies Meeting, MacArthur Foundation Program of Research on Mental Health and the Law. September, Pittsburgh, Penn.

Fantuzzo, J. W., L. M. DePaola, L. Lambert, T. Martino, G. Anderson, and S. Sutton. 1991. Effects of interparental violence on the psychological adjustment and competencies of young children. *Journal of Consulting and Clinical Psychology* 59:258–65.

Farrington, D. P. 1989. Early predictors of adolescent aggression and adult violence. *Violence and Victims* 4(2):79–100.

Felson, R. B., and H. J. Steadman. 1983. Situational factors in disputes leading to criminal violence. *Criminology* 21:59–74.

Ferster, C. B., and B. F. Skinner. 1957. *Schedules of reinforcement*. New York: Appleton Century-Crofts.

Fingerhut, L. A., and J. C. Kleinman. 1990. International and interstate comparisons of homicide among young males. *Journal of the American Medical Association* 263:3292–95.

Fotrell, E. 1980. A study of violent behavior among patients in psychiatric hospitals. *British Journal of Psychiatry* 136:216–21.

Garbarino, J. 1977. The human ecology of child maltreatment: A conceptual model for research. *Journal of Marriage and the Family* 39:721–35.

Geen, R. G., and R. Pigg. 1970. Acquisition of an aggressive response and its generalization to verbal behavior. *Journal of Personality and Social Behavior* 15:165–70.

Gelles, R. J. 1975. Violence and pregnancy: A note on the extent of the problem and needed services. *Family Coordinator* 24:81–86.

Gilmore, D. R., and F. H. Walkey. 1981. Identifying violent offenders using a video measure of personal distance. *Journal of Consulting and Clinical Psychology* 49:287–91.

Goldstein, A. P. 1989. Aggression reduction: Some vital steps. In J. Groebel and R. A. Hinde, eds., *Aggression and war: Their biological and social bases*. Cambridge: Cambridge University Press.

Hall, H. V. 1978. *Violence prediction: Guidelines for the forensic practitioner*. Springfield, Ill.: Charles C. Thomas.

Harris, G., and G. W. Varney. 1986. A ten-year study of assaults and assaulters on a maximum security psychiatric unit. *Journal of Interpersonal Violence* 1:173–91.

Hartman, C. 1969. The key jingler. *Community Mental Health Journal* 5:199–205.

Heaton, R. K., I. Grant, and C. G. Matthews. 1991. Comprehensive norms for an expanded Halstead-Reitan Battery: Demographic corrections, research findings, and clinical applications. Odessa, Fla.: Psychological Assessment Resources.

Hedlund, J. L., I. W. Sletten, H. Altman, and R. C. Evenson. 1973. Prediction of patients who are dangerous to others. *Journal of Clinical Psychology* 29:443–47.

Hellman, D. S., and N. Blackman. 1966. Enuresis, fire-setting and cruelty to animals: A triad predictive of adult crime. *American Journal of Psychiatry* 122:1431–35.

Hershon, M., and A. Rosenbaum. 1991. Over- vs. undercontrolled hostility: Application of the construct to classification of maritally violent men. *Violence and Victims* 6(2):151–58.

Hirschi, T., and M. J. Hindelang. 1977. Intelligence and delinquency: A revisionist review. *American Sociological Review* 42:571–87.

Holland, T. R., G. E. Beckett, and M. Levi. 1981. Intelligence, personality and criminal violence: A multivariate analysis. *Journal of Consulting and Clinical Psychology* 49:106–11.

Huesmann, L. R. 1986. Psychological processes promoting the relationship between exposure to media violence and aggressive behavior by the viewer. *Journal of Social Issues* 42:125–39.

Hughes, J. R., R. Zagar, R. B. Sylvies, J. Arbit, and K. G. Busch. 1991. Medical, family, and scholastic conditions in urban delinquents. *Journal of Clinical Psychology* 47:448–64.

Justice, B., R. Justice, and L. A. Kraft. 1974. Early warning signs of violence: Is a triad enough? *American Journal of Psychiatry* 131:457–59.

Kalmuss, D. 1984. The intergenerational transmission of marital aggression. *Journal of Marriage and the Family* February, 11–19.

Karson, C., and L. B. Bigelow. 1987. Violent behavior in schizophrenic inpatients. *Journal of Nervous and Mental Disease* 175:161–64.

Katz, P., and F. R. Kirkland. 1990. Violence and social structure on mental hospital wards. *Psychiatry* 53:262–77.

Klass, D., G. Growe, and M. Strizich. 1977. Ward treatment milieu and post-hospital functioning. *Archives of General Psychiatry* 34:1047–52.

Klassen, D. 1989. Violence risk assessment in mental patients. Grant application, National Institute of Mental Health.

Klassen, D., and W. A. O'Connor. 1987. Predicting violence in mental patients. Paper presented at the annual meeting of the American Public Health Association. October.

———. 1988a. A prospective study of predictors of violence in adult male mental health admissions. *Law and Human Behavior* 12:143–58.

———. 1988b. Predicting violence in schizophrenic and non-schizophrenic patients. *Journal of Community Psychology* 16:217–27.

———. 1989. Assessing the risk of violence in released mental patients: A cross-validation study. *Psychological Assessment: A Journal of Consulting and Clinical Psychology* 1(2):75–81.

Krakowski, M., J. Volavka, and D. Brizev. 1986. Psychopathology and violence: A review of the literature. *Comprehensive Psychiatry* 27:131–48.

Krakowski, M. I., A. Convit, J. Jaeger, L. Shang, and J. Volavka. 1989. Inpatient violence: State and trait. *Journal of Psychiatric Research* 23:57–64.

Lanzmann, C. 1985. *Shoah.* Documentary film, color, 570 min. France: Les Films Aleph and Historia Films, with the assistance of the French Ministry of Culture.

Lefkowitz, M., L. Eron, L. Walder, and L. Huesmann. 1977. *Growing up to be violent.* New York: Pergamon.

Levinson, R. M., and G. Ramsay. 1979. Dangerousness, stress, and mental health evaluations. *Journal of Health and Social Behavior* 20:178–87.

Lewis, D. O., S. S. Shanok, J. H. Pincus, and G. H. Glaser. 1979. Violent juvenile delinquents. *Journal of Child Psychiatry* 18:307–19.

Lewis, D. O., E. Moy, L. D. Jackson, R. Aaronson, N. Restifo, S. Serra, and A. Simos. 1985. Biopsychological characteristics of children who later murder: A prospective study. *American Journal of Psychiatry* 142:1161–67.

Lewis, D. O., R. Lovely, C. Yeager, and D. Della Femina. 1989. Toward a theory of the genesis of violence: A follow-up study of delinquents. *Journal of the American Academy of Child and Adolescent Psychiatry* 28:431–36.

Lidz, C. W. 1987. Conditional prediction in the management of dangerousness. Grant application, National Institute of Mental Health.

Link, B., F. Cullen, and H. Andrews. 1990. Violent and illegal behavior of current and former mental patients compared to community controls. Paper presented at the meeting of the Society for the Study of Social Problems. August.

Loeber, R. 1990. Development and risk factors of juvenile antisocial behavior and delinquency. *Clinical Psychology Review* 10:1–41.

Loeber, R., and T. Dishion. 1983. Early predictors of male delinquency: A review. *Psychological Bulletin* 94:68–99.

Luckenbill, D. F. 1977. Criminal homicide as a situated transaction. *Social Problems* 25:176–86.

Masuda, M., D. L. Cutler, and T. H. Holmes. 1978. Life events and prisoners. *Archives of General Psychiatry* 35:197–203.

McCord, J. 1979. Some child-rearing antecedents of criminal behavior in adult men. *Journal of Personality and Social Psychology* 37:1477–86.

Menzies, R. J., C. D. Webster, and D. Sepejak. 1985. The dimensions of dangerousness: Evaluating the accuracy of psychometric predictions of violence among forensic patients. *Law and Human Behavior* 9:49–70.

Milgram, S. 1974. *Obedience to authority: An experimental view.* New York: Harper and Row.

Monahan, J. 1981. *The clinical prediction of violent behavior.* Washington, D.C.: U.S. Government Printing Office.

———. 1990. Violence risk assessment project. Grant application, MacArthur Foundation Research Network on Mental Health and the Law.

———. 1991. Mental disorder and violent behavior: Attitudes and evidence. 1990 Distinguished Contribution to Research in Public Policy Award Address. Presented at the American Psychological Association Convention. August.

Moos, R. 1973. Conceptualizations of human environments. *American Psychologist* 28:652–65.

Moos, R. H., and J. Schwartz. 1972. Treatment environment and treatment outcome. *Journal of Nervous and Mental Disease* 154:264–75.

Morrison, E. F. 1989. Theoretical modeling to predict violence in hospitalized psychiatric patients. *Research in Nursing and Health* 12:31–40.

Novaco, R. 1989. The assessment of anger as violence risk. Paper presented at the MacArthur Foundation Program of Research on Mental Health and the Law, Study Group Meeting on Risk. January, Palm Beach, Fla.

O'Leary, K. D., J. Barling, I. Arias, A. Rosenbaum, J. Malone, and A. Tyree. 1989. Prevalence and stability of physical aggression between spouses: A longitudinal analysis. *Journal of Consulting and Clinical Psychology* 57:263–68.

Patterson, G. R. 1986. Performance models for antisocial boys. *American Psychologist* 41:432–44.

Patterson, G. R., and L. Bank. 1985. Bootstrapping your way in the nomological thicket. *Behavior Assessment* 8:49–73.

Patterson, G. R., B. D. DeBaryshe, and E. Ramsay. 1989. A developmental perspective on antisocial behavior. *American Psychologist* 44:329–35.

Patterson, G. R., R. A. Littman, and W. Bricker. 1967. Assertive behavior in children: A step toward a theory of aggression. *Monographs of the Society for Research in Child Development* 32(5), no. 113.

Petersilia, J. 1980. Criminal career research: A review of the recent evidence. In N. Morris and M. Tonry, eds., *Crime and justice: An annual review of research.* Vol. 2. Chicago: University of Chicago Press.

Pfeffer, C. R., R. Plutchik, and M. S. Mizruchi. 1983. Predictions of assaultiveness in latency age children. *American Journal of Psychiatry* 140:31–35.

Prichard, D. 1977. Stable predictions of recidivism. *Journal Supplement Abstract Service* 7:72.

Quinsey, V. L., and A. MacGuire. 1986. Maximum security psychiatric patients. *Journal of Interpersonal Violence* 1:143–71.

Quinsey, V. L., A. Warneford, M. Pruesse, and N. Link. 1975. Rebased Oak Ridge patients: A follow-up study of review board discharges. *British Journal of Criminology* 15:264–70.

Rofman, E. S., C. Askinazi, and E. Fant. 1980. The prediction of dangerous behavior in emergency civil commitment. *American Journal of Psychiatry* 137:1061–64.

Rosenbaum, A., and K. D. O'Leary. 1981. Marital violence: Characteristics of abusive couples. *Journal of Consulting and Clinical Psychology* 49:63–71.

Rossi, A. M., M. Jacobs, M. Monteleone, R. Olsen, R. W. Surber, E. L. Winkler, and A. Womak. 1985. Violent or fear-inducing behavior associated with hospital admissions. *Hospital and Community Psychiatry* 36:643–47.

Rossi, A. M., M. Jacobs, M. Monteleone, R. Olser, R. W. Surber, E. L. Winkler, and A. Wommack. 1986. Characteristics of psychiatric patients who engage in assaultive or other fear-inducing behavior. *Journal of Nervous and Mental Disease* 174:154–60.

Sepejak, D., R. J. Menzies, C. D. Webster, and F. A. S. Jensen. 1983. Clinical predictions of dangerousness: Two-year follow-up of 408 pretrial forensic cases. *Bulletin of the American Academy of Psychiatry and the Law* 11:171–81.

Shore, D., C. R. Filson, and W. E. Johnson. 1988. Violent crime arrests and paranoid schizophrenia: The White House case studies. *Schizophrenia Bulletin* 14(2): 279–81.

Short, J. F., Jr., ed. 1968. *Gang delinquency and delinquent subcultures.* New York: Harper and Row.

Singer, S. I. 1986. Victims of serious violence and their criminal behavior: Subcultural theory and beyond. *Violence and Victims* 1:61–70.

State of Michigan Department of Corrections. 1978. Summary of parolee risk study. Unpublished manuscript.

Steadman, H. J. 1982. A situational approach to violence. *International Journal of Law and Psychiatry* 5:171–86.

Steadman, H. J., and J. J. Cocozza. 1974. *Careers of the criminally insane.* Lexington, Mass.: Lexington Books.

Steadman, H. J., J. Monahan, P. S. Appelbaum, T. Grisso, E. P. Mulvey, L. H. Roth, P. C. Robbins, and D. Klassen. In press. Designing a new generation of risk assessment research. In J. Monahan and H. J. Steadman, eds., *Violence and mental disorder: Developments in risk assessment.* Chicago: University of Chicago Press.

Steadman, H. J., J. Monahan, P. C. Robbins, P. Applebaum, T. Grisso, D. Klassen, E. Mulvey, and L. Roth. 1991. From dangerousness to risk assessment: Implications for appropriate research strategies. Paper presented at the NATO Conference on Crime and Mental Disorder, Tuscany, Italy. August.

Steadman, H. J., and J. P. Morrissey. 1982. Predicting violent behavior: A note on a cross-validation study. *Social Forces* 61:475–83.

Steadman, H. J., and S. A. Ribner. 1982. Life stress and violence among ex-mental patients. *Social Science and Medicine* 16:1641–47.

Straus, M. A., R. J. Gelles, and S. K. Steinmetz. 1980. *Behind closed doors.* Garden City, N.Y.: Anchor.

Sviridoff, M., and J. W. Thompson. 1979. *Linkage between employment and crime: A qualitative study of Rikers releases.* New York: Vera Institute of Justice.

Tanke, E. D., and J. A. Yesavage. 1985. Characteristics of assaultive patients who do and do not provide visible cues of potential violence. *American Journal of Psychiatry* 142:1409–13.

Tardiff, K., and H. W. Koenigsberg. 1985. Assaultive behavior among psychiatric outpatients. *American Journal of Psychiatry* 142:960–63.

Tardiff, K., and A. Sweillam. 1980. Assault, suicide, and mental illness. *American Journal of Psychiatry* 37:164–69.

———. 1982. Assaultive behavior among chronic inpatients. *American Journal of Psychiatry* 139:212–15.

Taylor, P. J. 1986. The risk of violence in psychotics. *Integrative Psychiatry* 4: 12–24.

Thornberry, T. P., and J. E. Jacoby. 1979. *The chronically insane.* Chicago: University of Chicago Press.

Turner, C. W., B. W. Hess, and S. Peterson-Lewis. 1986. *Journal of Social Issues* 42:51–73.

Waller, I. 1974. *Men released from prison.* Toronto: University of Toronto Press.

Wenk, E. A., J. O. Robison, and G. W. Smith. 1972. Can violence be predicted? *Crime and Delinquency* 18:393–402.

Werner, P. D., T. L. Rose, and J. A. Yesavage. 1983. Reliability, accuracy and decision making strategy in clinical predictions of imminent dangerousness. *Journal of Clinical and Consulting Psychology* 51:815–25.

Werner, P. D., J. A. Yesavage, J. Becker, D. W. Brunsting, and J. S. Isaacs. 1983. Hostile words and assaultive behavior on an acute inpatient psychiatric unit. *Journal of Nervous and Mental Disease* 171:385–87.

Widom, C. S. 1989. Does violence beget violence? A critical examination of the literature. *Psychological Bulletin* 106:3–28.

Wolfgang, M. E., and F. Ferracuti. 1967. *The subculture of violence.* London: Tavistock.

Wolfgang, M., R. Figlio, and T. Sellin. 1972. *Delinquency in a birth cohort.* Chicago: University of Chicago Press.

Yesavage, J. A. 1983. Inpatient violence and the schizophrenic patient. *Acta Psychiatrica Scandinavica* 67:353–57.

———. 1984. Correlates of dangerous behavior by schizophrenics in hospitals. *Journal of Psychiatric Research* 18:225–3.

Yesavage, J. A., J. M. T. Becker, P. D. Werner, M. J. Patton, K. Seeman, D. W. Brunsting, and M. J. Mills. 1983. Family conflict, psychopathology, and dangerous behavior by schizophrenic inpatients. Psychiatry Research 8:271–80.

Yesavage, J. A., P. D. Werner, J. Becker, C. Holman, and M. Mills. 1981. Inpatient evaluation of aggression in psychiatric patients. *Journal of Nervous and Mental Diseases* 169:299–302.

Zagar, R., J. Arbit, R. Sylvies, K. G. Busch, and J. R. Hughes. 1990. Homicidal adolescents: A replication. *Psychological Reports* 67:1235–42.

Zillman, D. 1978. Attribution and misattribution of excitatory reactions. In J. H. Harvey, ed., *New directions in attribution research.* Vol. 2. Hillsdale, N.J.: Erlbaum.

Zimring, F. E. 1991. Firearms, violence, and public policy. *Scientific American* November, 48–54.

Zitrin, A., A. S. Hardesty, E. I. Burdock, and A. K. Drossman. 1976. Crime and violence among mental patients. *American Journal of Psychiatry* 133:142–49.

11 Social Networks, Social Support, and Violence among Persons with Severe, Persistent Mental Illness

SUE E. ESTROFF AND CATHERINE ZIMMER

The following headlines and stories appeared in Cincinnati area newspapers as the Ohio Department of Mental Health proceeded with plans to consolidate two underutilized psychiatric hospitals:

> Cop-Killer is walk away from Lewis Center [the hospital to remain open] (*Valley Courier,* March 7, 1990)
>
> Danger Looms Heavily in Valley Communities (*Valley Courier,* March 21, 1990)
>
> [The] councilwoman said the Lewis Center is not ready for more patients because security is poor. She said residents in Elmwood Place—a mile or so from the hospital—already are fearful of the patients. A resolution passed by Elmwood officials says residents and others are at risk from patients who walk away from the Lewis Center. It also cites an instance in which an Elmwood officer was left permanently disabled after a former Lewis patient stabbed him. (*Cincinnati Post,* April 6, 1990)

Violent incidents involving persons with psychiatric disorders fuel a perceived need for their confinement, and psychiatric hospitals represent, actually and symbolically, the capacity to confine. In this chapter, we interrogate an underlying rationale and largely unexamined assumption of confinement because of dangerousness to others: that diagnosed persons engage in and incite violence primarily because they are mentally ill, independent of the actions of others who are not diagnosed or confined, and of social context and interpersonal situation. Here we examine whether and how the web of relationships and quality of ties with others—social networks and social supports—may be related to violent acts and threats made by people diagnosed with mental illness.

Empirical, Conceptual, and Methodological Background

As a prelude to the investigation reported here, Estroff and Morrissey (1989) reviewed existing findings about the influence of social networks and social

259

support on the risk for violence among persons with serious psychiatric disorders. They concluded that so little pertinent research had been conducted that it was not possible to say with any confidence how or even if the nature and structure of social relations were related to violent behavior among the target population.

Prior conceptual and empirical work on the interrelations between chronically ill and disabled persons and their social networks and supports (see Rook 1984; Rook and Pietromonaco 1987; Revenson et al. 1991) suggested that social networks and support might (a) influence violence directly or indirectly and (b) contribute to or prevent the occurrence of violence by and among persons with mental illnesses. For example, living with unrelated adults in a group home might be more threatening to an individual than living at home with relatives; thus the group home social network might evoke violent behaviors that the home setting would not. On the other hand, an individual living in a household where there were long-standing family disputes might more likely be involved in violence in that setting than in another with no history of conflict or ongoing hostile relationships. A spouse might intervene directly to prevent an act of violence or might provide a trusting atmosphere which would indirectly reduce the occurrence of threatening behaviors.

In other words, social support characteristics and actions by social network members might either constitute risk factors for violence by creating the opportunity or need for violence or serve to prevent or decrease the opportunity and need for threatening or assaultive behaviors.

A few investigations touch on these direct and indirect, and causal and preventive, influences of social networks and social support on violence outside of hospital settings by persons with mental illnesses. Family and household composition and climate, employment status, relations with friends, and past substance abuse, violence, and disorder by and around the patient were explored by Hill (1982), Splane et al. (1982), Klassen and O'Connor (1988a), and Hiday and Scheid-Cook (1987). Chaotic, violent family environments where there was alcohol or substance abuse, an ongoing history of conflict among family members, and a controlling atmosphere were associated with violence by patients in at least one of these studies. Parents, especially mothers, were the relatives most likely to live with patients as primary caretakers or instrumental supporters and, not surprisingly, were the most frequent initiators of commitment petitions for dangerous behavior (see also Cook 1988). These findings are suggestive but inconclusive as to how social networks and support figure in the occurrence of violence in the community.

Much of the research on violence among this population suffers from a narrow and socially uninformed focus on the behavior and characteristics of patients alone, ignoring influences from the interpersonal situations within which the violence occurs. For example, the targets of violence are seldom identified, nor is the nature and duration of their relationship with the patient described in any detail. While patient characteristics such as age, social race,[1] gender, marital status, education, and employment are typically thought of as social factors and are reported almost universally (e.g., Nicholson 1986), they demonstrate very little about social experience or relationships.

Similarly, a biographical dimension is absent from most investigations. Patients whose violent behavior is at issue are typically described as ahistorical, socially and interpersonally decontextualized subjects, devoid of life histories apart from their psychiatric or legal careers. Relations with others, past or present, that were wounding or threatening are seldom considered (see Jacobson 1989; Jacobson and Richardson 1987; Post et al. 1980). It is hardly surprising that such an incomplete and impoverished view has contributed to the inability to predict, accurately assess, or understand the risk for violence among the target population (Brooks 1984; Monahan 1988).

Inattention to contextual contributions to violence may also perpetuate the current stalemate over whether or why people with psychiatric disorders are at increased risk for engaging in violence towards others and whether clinical or demographic characteristics more accurately predict risk for violence (e.g., Monahan and Steadman 1983; Monahan 1992; Rossi et al. 1986). In the view taken here, risk for violence is best assessed by investigating *what kinds of persons, in what kinds of situations, at what phase of their lives and illnesses,* are likely to engage in dangerous behaviors (see Monahan and Klassen 1982; Klassen and O'Connor 1988a).

The interdisciplinary perspective and multiple methods required to address these issues no doubt contribute to the paucity of such work. Lack of communication between researchers from different disciplines or with differing perspectives studying violence and mental illness, bemoaned by many (Hiday 1988; Monahan 1988), is epitomized in the study of social networks and social support. Violence toward persons was not discussed in any of the relevant social network/social support literature reviewed (e.g., Beels 1981; Hammer 1986; Sokolovsky et al. 1978), nor were there any references to social network and support findings in the investigations of violence and mental illness surveyed (e.g., Sepejak et al. 1983; Tardiff and Koenigsberg 1985).

There are some basic incompatibilities between the methodological requirements of social network/social support research and customary investigations of violence. Social network and support protocols are time-consuming, require face to face interviews, and are most accurate when the time referent is the present and when repeated elicitation and contact with the informant increases trust and the accuracy of the information. In contrast, nearly all the studies of violence we reviewed relied exclusively on archival data in the form

---

1. We use the term "social race" to underscore the social and political nature of the category of race (Omi and Winant 1986) and to make a distinction between race as a social category based on physiognomy, and ethnicity, which is derived from cultural rather than anatomical sources.

of hospital charts and court records, with a few exceptions that involved face to face interviews with patients or their families (see Hiday 1988 for a comprehensive review). Treated samples, or persons who were involuntarily committed as dangerous to others or charged with violent crimes, form the bulk of the research base. Cross-sectional and retrospective time frames predominate, with longitudinal or prospective investigations a rarity.

In order to address some of these shortcomings, an exploratory analysis was conducted among a cohort of persons with severe, persistent mental illnesses, who were followed for 32 months in an ongoing study of if and how they became disability income recipients.[2]

Research Questions

This investigation aimed to explore correlations and causal links between the social networks and social support of the cohort and violence they committed toward others during an 18-month period. We asked the following specific research questions:

1. Who was violent toward other persons? In particular, were baseline social networks and social supports related in any ways to who was violent?
2. Towards whom were they violent? Who were the targets?

Who Was Violent Toward Other Persons?

To determine who was violent toward other persons we investigated *social and demographic* characteristics such as age, gender and social race, and marital status; *clinical* factors such as diagnosis and severity and type of symptoms; *prior violence* committed by the patient or toward the patient in childhood or in the present social network; and *social network and social support* variables such as household composition, size and composition of the social network, and quality of relations with network members. The goal was to compile a comprehensive description of persons in the sample who had committed a violent act or threat and to compare them to those who had not. These data were then used in bivariate and multivariate analyses to identify differences between those who were violent and those who were not and to model who would be violent.

Our focus was on investigating the influence of social network and social support variables as a means to developing a multicausal, contextualized

2. The larger study investigates processes of disablement among persons with severe, persistent mental illnesses, focusing on the application for Supplemental Security Income (SSI) and Social Security Disability Income (SSDI) as a critical juncture in a career of chronicity. The study compares people who do and do not apply for or receive SSI and SSDI, examining how or if receipt signals a transition to a disabled identity.

view of violence among the target population. First, we explored the nature and structure of the cohort's social networks and support to characterize accurately their intimate and social relationships and daily living environments. Next, we examined whether specific characteristics of their networks, in terms of size, composition, and nature and degree of instrumental dependence, were related to whether a person had been violent during the study period. The nature and quality of relationships with those in the social network were examined, giving particular attention to focal relationships—those with spouses, children, siblings, and parents. We were especially concerned with whether household composition had any influence on whether a person was seen to be or was violent and toward whom. That is, was proximity and intensity of contact with certain types or numbers of persons a corollary of reported violent threats or acts.

Toward Whom Were Violent Acts Directed?

Another goal was to identify factors that contributed to being at risk for being a target and to explore whether any of our instruments elicited information that might reliably signal such risk. We investigated whether the respondent and target lived in the same household and whether the target was related or unrelated (and, if related, how), known or unknown, or identified previously in the social network. The respondent's relationship with the target was explored using the SASB psychological scale (Benjamin 1974); we noted whether the respondent named the target as an instrumental helper, how the target was described in the social network elicitation, and whether the target was named in response to questions about especially problematic relationships. We were also interested in whether particular types of people were targets of repeated or single episodes of violence and whether they had ever been identified as perpetrators of violence toward the respondent or as having psychiatric or substance abuse problems themselves.

Methodology

Sampling and Data Collection

The subjects in this investigation were 169 individuals with severe, persistent mental illnesses, who were recruited from four hospitals—two state psychiatric facilities, a university hospital, and a general hospital psychiatric unit. Six interviews, all but the last face-to-face, were conducted over a 32-month period. With the patients' consent, significant others or family members were interviewed once separately, producing 59 Significant Other Interviews (SOINT). The analysis reported here covers the first 18 months of the study period.

We recruited individuals early in the course of their illness who were likely eligible for disability income (i.e., were impoverished and unemployed) and who had major, enduring psychiatric disorders. Patients on forensic units were not screened for study admission, nor did we recruit from among forensic admissions to adult psychiatric units or individuals with confirmed patterns of very violent behavior.[3] The cohort may thus underrepresent persons with violent histories in an inpatient psychiatric setting, but might likewise be representative of the patient population in community settings in general.

Measurement of Variables

There were four data sources for this analysis: (1) baseline to time 3 interview data covering an 18-month period; (2) chart abstracts derived from review of the medical records of all study participants, from the four psychiatric hospitals in which they were initially recruited and to which they were admitted during the study; (3) arrest records from courts in the five counties of residence of study participants; and (4) content analysis of transcripts of respondent and SOINT interviews. Table 1 presents the univariate distributions of all study variables.

Measuring Violence

A violent act was defined as an arrest or criminal charge and adjudication for assault and battery, manslaughter, or murder; a danger-to-others (DTO) commitment which specified that the respondent hit, hit with an object or weapon, sexually assaulted, or threatened with an object or weapon another person; or a confirmed report of a violent act by the respondent. There were 39 acts of violence committed by 23 persons. An object or weapon was used in 41% (16 acts), while the remainder included hitting (19 acts) and 4 sexual assaults (no rapes). A threat was defined as an arrest or criminal charge and adjudication for communicating threats or threatening conduct, a DTO commitment specifying vague ideation or verbal threat towards another person, or a confirmed report of other threatening behaviors. There were 75 threats of violence toward persons made by 52 individuals in the study. Over half, 53.3%, involved threats made to or about specific people, while the remainder were vague ideation regarding harm to others.

Using these definitions, 157 study participants[4] were assigned to one of three groups based on their behavior during the 18-month study period: those who engaged in no reported violent behavior toward a person ($N = 101$;

---

3. This was because the study required follow-up interviews in community settings. We did not wish the project staff to jeopardize their well-being in any way, as they worked alone and away from potential assistance should a problem arise.

4. Due to missing data for 12 respondents, the sample size for the analysis is 157.

64.3% of the sample), those who made violent threats only ($N = 33$; 21.0%), and those who engaged in violent acts ($N = 23$; 14.6%). Within the third group, 4 people had committed a violent act only and 19 had both threatened violence and committed a violent act.

Measuring Explanatory Variables

Social and demographic variables. The youngest participants were 18 years old and the oldest was 56, with an average age of 28.57 years. We cross-classified participants on race and gender and found 19.4% of the sample to be African American men, 30.3% white men, 9.7% African American women, and 40.6% white women. For multivariate analysis, African American men were the reference category. As expected, a small portion of the sample was married—about 10%.

We derived the socioeconomic status (SES) index using the Hollingshead and Redlich (1958) two-factor (education and occupation) method for respondent's parents if the respondent did not have an occupation and lived in the parental home, or for the respondent if he or she had an occupation. Respondents fell into five groups, with SES 1 the highest group and SES 5 the lowest. The majority of the respondents were ranked in SES 4 and SES 5 (52.3%); SES 5 was the reference category.

A respondent was classified as having worked if he or she reported being employed for a period longer than two weeks during the year prior to the baseline interview. Just over 80% were classified as working, but stable gainful work histories were uncommon.

Clinical variables. Diagnosis was based on review of the most recent DSM III-R discharge diagnosis, the admitting or working diagnosis for the baseline hospitalization, and the discharge diagnosis for the baseline hospitalization. In the rare event that there were discrepancies among these, the most frequent diagnosis was assigned. We classified diagnoses into four categories: schizophrenias (39.5%), affective disorders (33.1%), personality disorders (17.2%), and other diagnoses (10.2%). For multivariate analysis, there were two diagnostic categories: schizophrenia and all other diagnoses.

Hospitalizations prior to baseline ranged from 1 to 10, with an average of 2.78 for the sample. Mental health center use was classified into seven categories, measured by the actual number of visits recorded in the mental health center files. A large portion of the sample did not use mental health center services at all (41.4%), but a small number of these used private psychiatric services instead. Another sizable group (30.6%) used mental health center services regularly, at rates of 1 to 3.5 visits per month.

Study participants were classified as having comorbidity (18.5%) if they had received a secondary diagnosis of alcohol or substance abuse or dependence in the hospital chart or a diagnosis plus self-reported interference with functioning due to alcohol or substance abuse or dependence.

Table 1. Descriptive statistics for study variables

Name	Mean	Percentage Distribution	
Violence		64.3%	No threat or act
		21.0	Violent threat(s) only
		14.6	Violent act
Demographic variables			
Age	28.57 years		
Race/gender		19.4%	African American men
		30.3	White men
		9.7	African American women
		40.6	White women
Marital status		9.9%	Married
		90.1	Not married
SES index		12.3%	SES 1
		17.4	SES 2
		18.1	SES 3
		31.0	SES 4
		21.3	SES 5
Work status		80.3%	Worked
		19.7	Did not work
Clinical variables			
Diagnosis		39.5%	Schizophrenias
		33.1	Affective disorders
		17.2	Personality disorders
		10.2	Other
Previous hospitalizations	2.78 times		
Mental health center use		41.4%	No visits
		5.0	1–3 visits ever
		7.6	Less than 1 visit/month
		15.3	1–2 visits/month
		15.3	2–3.5 visits/month
		8.9	3.5–5 visits/month
		6.4	5+ visits/month
Comorbidity		18.5%	Yes
		81.5	No
PERI items:			
Confused thinking	2.03		
False beliefs and perceptions	1.15		
Perception of hostility	1.81		
Schizoid personality	2.20		
BPRS total score	12.88		
Previous violence variables			
Prior violent behavior		41.4%	Yes
		58.6	No
Childhood network abuse		31.8%	Yes
		68.2	No
Adult network problems		67.5%	Yes
		32.5	No

Table 1. *continued*

Social network variables			
Network size	11.86 people		
Composition		62.73%	Relatives
		28.15	Friends
		9.12	MH professionals
Instrumental support		57.25%	Relatives
		23.76	Friends
		19.00	MH professionals
Symmetry of support	.67		
SASB Attack 1	− .57		
SASB Attack 2	− .57		
Residence type		17.2%	Alone
		69.5	With family
		13.2	With unrelated person(s)
Living situation		13.9%	Partner
		86.1	No partner

Note: Sample size ranges from 148 to 157 due to missing data for some items.

Severity and type of symptoms were measured with two instruments. First, we used scores from four Psychiatric Epidemiology Research Interview subscales (PERI; Dohrenwend and Shrout 1981; Shrout, Dohrenwend and Levav 1986) that assess primary psychotic processes: Confused Thinking (thought disorder), False Beliefs and Perceptions (hallucinations), Perception of Hostility (paranoia and threatening environment), and Schizoid Personality (isolation). The subscales each have a potential range from 0 to 4 with higher scores indicating more severe symptoms. The highest mean score in our sample was 2.20 for Schizoid Personality; the lowest was 1.15 for False Beliefs and Perceptions.

The second symptom measure was the sum of eight symptom constructs from the Brief Psychiatric Rating Scale (BPRS) checklist (Overall and Gorham 1962). These were conceptual disorganization, excitement, motor retardation, blunted affect, tension, mannerisms and posturing, uncooperativeness, and emotional withdrawal. At the end of the baseline interview, each interviewer rated the respondent on these dimensions, providing an independent assessment of severity of symptoms. The range for each item is from 1 to 7, and a higher score indicates greater severity. The mean BPRS total score was 12.88.

Previous violence variables. To investigate how a history of violence by or toward the respondent affected subsequent violent behavior, we included three dummy variables. First, evidence of prior violent behavior by the respondent was collected, including court records of arrests or charges for violent crimes, previous DTO commitments (from the hospital chart), positive response to a prior violence question on the PERI Anti-Social History subscale, and self-reported violence toward another person; 41.4% of the respondents had behaved violently prior to the study. Second, childhood network abuse was measured by information about childhood physical or sexual abuse from hospital charts or from self-report during the interview. About 32% of the sample reported being abused as children, despite there being no specific questions on this topic in our interview. Third, current physical or sexual abuse by, substance abuse by, or mental illness of a partner, relative, or household member were classified as adult network problems. Experiences with violence in the environment were common, reported by 67.5% of the respondents.

Social network variables. Network size was elicited throughout the baseline interview, and there was no limit to the number of potential listings. All individuals mentioned by respondents (other than casual references) were included in the network. Network size ranged from 1 to 31, with an average of about 12 people.

Social network composition was determined by examining the relationship of the individuals listed in the network to the respondent. We categorized all network members as relatives, friends, or mental health or service professionals. Overall, 62.73% were relatives, 28.15% friends, and 9.12% mental health or service professionals.

Instrumental support, or help in daily living and problem solving, was assessed by asking who helps with domestic tasks such as shopping and budgeting, who helps in times of material need, and whether there is material reciprocity between the respondent and their most important others. Each person named in response to these questions was considered to be an instrumental supporter, and was classified by the type of relationship with the respondent. The average breakdown of instrumental supporters was 57.25% relatives, 23.76% friends, and 19.00% mental health or service professionals. The reciprocity of support, which we call symmetry, is the percentage of relationships within which the respondents lend and give material resources to their most significant network members who lend and give material resources to them. Symmetry occurred on average for 67% of relationships.

The Structural Analysis of Social Behavior (SASB) scale (Benjamin 1974, 1979, 1989) requires the respondent to choose another person with whom they rate their own behavior and the other's behavior in relation to themselves. Study participants identified their most significant other, usually a parent or spouse, as the referent for the scale. Over half ($N = 70$; 55%) of the sample rated their mothers, with an additional 11% rating parents as a unit. Spouses were rated by 15 respondents. Significant others who were interviewed completed the same scale in relation to the respondent, producing 42 matched sets of ratings. Sixteen individuals who became targets of violence were rated by respondents as their significant others at baseline.

The structure of the SASB is based on a two-axis model of relationships: a submission-autonomy dimension, and an affiliation-attack dimension. The scale yields Attack 1 and Attack 2 coefficients, which have been rigorously established psychometrically. Attack 1 coefficients are ratings of the significant other in transitive action toward the respondent. Attack 2 coefficients are the respondents' ratings of themselves in intransitive relation to the other. Lower coefficients indicate less hostile, more friendly sentiments, higher coefficients, i.e., closer to zero, indicate more hostile sentiments. The average for both coefficients was − .57 in this sample.

Among the cohort, 17.2% of the respondents lived alone, 69.5% lived with family, and the remaining 13.2% lived with unrelated others. In the multivariate analysis, the last two categories were coded as dummy variables with living alone as the reference category. Living situation measures whether the respondent lived with a spouse or an adult cohabitant.

Analytic Techniques

Both qualitative and quantitative methods were used to answer the two major research questions. For the question concerning who was violent, the techniques included text analysis of patient and significant other interviews, simple descriptive statistics, bivariate analysis of the relationships between the explanatory variables and violence, and multivariate analysis of these same relationships. The dependent variable, violence, is categorical with three levels (violent act, violent threat, and no violence). Explanatory variables are categorical and continuous. The bivariate and multivariate analysis techniques reflect these levels of measurement. For categorical explanatory variables, a chi-square test of independence was used to assess the significance of bivariate relationships, and logistic regression for polytomous dependent variables was used to test multivariate relationships (Aldrich and Nelson 1984). For continuous explanatory variables, logistic regression for polytomous variables was used to analyze both bivariate and multivariate relationships. The small sample we have for analysis, especially in a multivariate context, makes our findings of statistical significance conservative. To study the targets of violence, the focus of our second research question, we use descriptive statistics.

Findings

Who Was Violent Toward Other Persons?[5]

As noted above, 56 persons in the sample, or about one-third (35.6%), engaged in threats or acts directed at other persons during the 18-month period.

---

5. In the following discussion, the referent condition is always reported violence, or violence of which we were aware. Undoubtedly there is an unknown amount and type of violence that we did not identify, but for ease of prose, we will not modify each statement in this regard.

Twenty-three (14.6%) committed a violent act, and 33 (21.0%) made a violent threat only. Nineteen individuals (12.1%) committed both an act and a threat. Five (3.2%) of the 19 had criminal charges for violent incidents, only one of which was for a violent act (assault and battery). All of those charged were male, four of the five were white, and only two were incarcerated following conviction.

Content Analysis of Interview Transcripts

The nature and incidence of violence involving psychiatric patients in community and family settings is a controversial subject, difficult to inform with data. Unreported incidents, different versions of who did what to whom, and other logistical obstacles to data collection make any assessment of the extent of such violence tentative at best (see Hiday 1990; Klassen and O'Connor 1988b). A recent investigation conducted among members of the National Alliance for the Mentally Ill (NAMI) sheds some light on the experiences of this admittedly select group of families (Skinner, Steinwachs, and Kasper 1991). Among one cohort ($N = 465$) of families in that study, 40% reported placating their mentally ill family member to avoid upsetting them or out of fear of inciting violence. During the past year, 11% reported that physical harm was done to a "family member or anyone else," and 19% indicated that physical harm was threatened. While these data are intriguing, they tell us little of the nature of the violence, the participants and precipitants, and the means by which families accommodate and cope with these behaviors. We also lack comparable data for the general population, and so have no basis for assessing whether or in what ways the incidence and patterns of violence in these families are distinct.

The primary purpose of our investigation was not to determine the extent of violence in respondent families, but we did collect pertinent information from relatives, patients, and archival sources. An analysis of the 84 semi-structured, in-depth interviews with respondents at time 2 and 59 SOINT interviews yielded information regarding the incidence and dynamics of violence within the networks of the respondent that was not found in the hospital or court records. Four individuals who were not otherwise identified in the investigation were found to have been violent based on these interviews, which, it is important to stress, contained no direct questions regarding violence.[6]

The excerpts below illustrate several recurrent themes that emerged from

---

6. Patient respondents were less likely than their significant others to mention violence in their interviews, but 5 voluntarily reported committing violent acts. More importantly, 11 respondents discussed being victims of violence. Fifteen significant others mentioned the violence of the respondent, and 10 reported that the respondent had been victimized as adults or children. In addition, 4 significant others discussed their own violence toward the respondent and other family members.

these interviews. Many of the respondents, especially women, reported living in threatening environments, highly charged with conflict. These discussions are remarkable for their similarity to descriptions by women in general of being abused and sometimes abusive (see Carmen, Rieker, and Mills 1984; Craine et al. 1988). Some respondents explained to us that their violence toward themselves was a means of coping with hostile sentiments toward others. Men were more likely to deny being intentionally violent or to express bewilderment at being perceived as threatening by others. These interviews make clear that violence seldom happens unilaterally, and that hostility and violence from others is not uncommon in the personal histories and current social networks of the respondents (Rose 1991; Rose, Peabody, and Stratigeas 1991).

Some family members, particularly parents, described substantial accommodation over an extended period to the violence and threatening behaviors of their family member. The families we interviewed also described extensive attempts to placate, explain away, or deny actual violent behavior, and living with intense intimidation and fear of potential violence (see Lawson 1986).

Threatening adult networks and abuse of respondents. Women reported violence not only at the hands of spouses and boyfriends, but also at the hands of their parents. D., who had been living at home with her father reported:

> Well, not only was he—sometimes he'd get drunk and, and was abusive—hit me and stuff like that—but it was almost like I became a hermit. Yeah, he didn't want me to work. He wanted me to stay at home all the time and he wanted me to cook dinner or go out to dinner with him every night. And he didn't want me to go—out after 9:00 and when you're almost 27, you really want to go out on a date or something and he wouldn't—didn't like it.

This respondent did not commit an act of violence against others. Instead, she made a nearly lethal suicide attempt.

In another family, childhood violence was seen as the cause of the patient's mental illness. N.'s mother described emotional abuse by his father as the cause of N.'s problems:

> Like I said, my husband was a alcoholic, and he drank, and he'd run us out of the house, in cold weather. We's all, what you say, scared of him till he calmed down. He'd go to bed and go to sleep, you know, we'd ease back in the house, them two boys and my mother. And I think that's beared on his mind alot.

Like the woman above, N. made various suicide attempts and did not engage in violence towards his family.

Although one female respondent never mentioned incest or being abused as a child, her history reveals both. She married a man who was previously her foster parent, and he reported that:

Her father tied her to the bed and raped her and beat her, and did all kinds of things to her, and, until she got pregnant with our first child, none of this surfaced. She'd always deny it every time it came up. She would deny it ever happened.

Respondent denial, bewilderment, and explaining away. Many patients in the study, particularly men, did not perceive themselves to be threatening or violent, expressing surprise and bewilderment at the response of others, and contesting their confinement for being dangerous. After an altercation with his mother (over groceries) in which he "accidentally" pushed her and she fell down, a young African American male respondent, G., described his subsequent "trouble" with the police in equally innocent terms:

A police officer came to my house and the police officer was like listening to everything my mother had to say. . . . I said, "Police, please listen to my side too." So he thought I was disrespecting my mama because I cursed. So he came towards me like he was going to hit me and I touched his uniform. You can't touch a police uniform in Durham. I didn't know that though. . . . The other big—big, big black guy came in and he said, "Arrest this man for assaulting me." And my mama said, "That's wrong." You know, she got on my side then, "Get up off my son." And she was trying to help me get the police up. You know, she going to help me now. And they threw me down . . . they threw me down and slid my head across the floor and put his knee in my back. And I wouldn't let them handcuff me. See, I was trying to get up saying, "I'm sorry. I didn't mean to cuss you." And they threw me in the car. They took my head and threw me in the car. I said, "Ya'll some mean police officers."

Perhaps the most striking example of explaining away came from a female respondent who related the following:

A few months ago I tried to kill my mama with a butcher knife. She didn't want me talking to my boyfriend on the telephone and so I run up there to the drawer and I said, "I ought to kill you." I went and got the butcher knife and tried to cut her throat and my son, he grabbed the knife away from me. But it wasn't reported or nothing to the law or nothing like that. We just let it go. We been getting along. . . . Ever since that happened, we've been getting along better now.

Family accommodation, denial, placation, and intimidation. K., described here by his mother, spent 8 years "in and out of institutions—one institution or another since he was about 12. Mostly, I'd say he's been in an institution more than he's been in a noninstitution setting." As K. grew older, he threatened and assaulted his father and other family members:

He was completely like out of control, you know, he really was. . . . It was very, very scary. In fact, for I'd say two or three years, like when we'd go to bed at night, and this is when his sister was living at home, too, and she was a little bit older than K. But we would go to bed at night, and everyone of us afraid that if K. came in home during the middle of the night, that he would kill us. And we lived like that for about three years.

Other families had similar fears. Q.'s mother said:

He knows I'm afraid of him. I try to pretend I'm not. He's a big guy and he—I don't like violence. . . . I'm past violence and screaming and yelling and—it upsets me, more than I wish it does, but it hasn't gotten bad and I shouldn't have said it out loud, but I dread what could happen.

Accounts from other families were equally compelling. Family members in S.'s household were too frightened even to sleep, as his mother reported:

He got real angry about me taking him for help. And then that's when he started saying stuff like he was going to destroy us and destroy the house. And I coped with it as long as I could, and I got to the place I couldn't deal with it any longer. I told him he couldn't stay with me anymore. 'Cause we used to take turns sleeping at night. We'd have to set up, and I'd sleep, then my daughter would sleep a little while, then my 12-year-old. But at that time he was about 10. And we would let him take the first staying awake time, while we catch a nap. And it was real rough.

S. assaulted his sister, injuring her so that she could not walk for two weeks, and on several occasions he attacked his father, who, because of rheumatoid arthritis, could not defend himself. He had also broken out all of the windows in his father's car. As a result, the family is still afraid, even though S. no longer lives with them:

Rarely do we be in the house with the doors open. So we more or less shuts up in the house all the time there. 'Cause we do not want him to walk in without knocking. And that gives you a little chance of bracing yourself for him. But when he's in there, everybody's watching him, keeping their eyes on him. You have to watch him cause he'll take your stuff, you know, take stuff. And he'll think that's what he's supposed to do. And we're all nervous, you know.

Some families accommodated violence by denying its occurrence, developing an almost dismissive whimsy. An example was provided by P.'s spouse, who explained after describing a violent incident with her husband:

P. wasn't going to hurt me. P. would die for me. I, you know, I didn't have any thoughts that he was going to hurt me. And he

> was just irritated, and he finally just went on out of the house. And I just got up, you know, cause he probably didn't even shove me. He probably just pushed me, and I just got off balance and fell down. And uh, but he was just real hostile towards all of us.

This was the conclusion to an incident of escalating violence which began when his wife, annoyed by P., hit him:

> I said, "P., I do not want to be here with you because you are not acting yourself. You're acting very hostile, and you're acting like you want to do bodily harm to people." . . . I hit him. I hit him when I'm angry like that, you know, just like pushing him and stuff like that. Like, "Get out of my face."

Nuclear families constitute the core of social networks, and provide the overwhelming majority of instrumental and affective support among the cohort. These interviews substantially reinforced our view that the emotional quality and historical dimensions of an individual's social networks and social support influenced whether he or she was threatening or violent and toward whom. Childhood abuse, threatening behavior from others, long-term disputes, fearful parents, and descriptions of familial violence and conflict pervade these narratives. Biographical and current contextual influences on violence are difficult to quantify but provide essential clues to the causes and meanings of menacing behaviors. The complex dynamics illustrated in the content analysis inform the quantitative analyses that follow.

Social and Demographic Characteristics

Table 2 reports bivariate relationships between study variables and violence during the study period. Race-gender is the only demographic variable significantly related to violence. African American men were by far the most likely to have committed a violent act (30%), compared to 20% of African American women, 15% of white men, and 6% of white women. The pattern for threatening is somewhat different. African American men were still the most likely to threaten (40%), followed in this case by African American women (20%), white women (18%), and white men (15%). Age, marital status, SES, and work status were not related significantly to violence·when tested individually.

Clinical Characteristics

Individuals with a diagnosis of schizophrenia were much more likely to have threatened or acted than individuals in the other diagnostic groups (34 of 62; 55%). This was in stark contrast to those diagnosed with affective disorders, among whom 14 of 52 (27%) engaged in violent behaviors. When diagnosis was broken down into DSM III-R classifications within the schizophrenias, there was a nearly even distribution of violence among paranoid, schizophren-

Table 2. Bivariate relationships between explanatory variables and violence

Name	Chi-square	Degrees of freedom
Demographic variables		
Age	1.380	2
Race/gender	21.475***	6
Marital status	2.322	2
SES index	12.797	8
Work status	0.557	2
Clinical variables		
Diagnosis	20.007***	6
Previous hospitalizations	3.180	2
Mental health center use	14.496	12
Comorbidity	1.514	2
PERI Items:		
Confused thinking	13.470***	2
False beliefs and perceptions	5.610*	2
Perception of hostility	3.430	2
Schizoid personality	4.070	2
BPRS total score	4.600*	2
Previous violence variables		
Prior violent behavior	2.729	2
Childhood network abuse	6.065**	2
Adult network problems	3.134	2
Social network variables		
Network size	3.140	2
Composition:		
% Relatives	7.490**	2
% Friends	2.800	2
% MH professionals	6.370**	2
Instrumental support:		
% Relatives	4.070	2
% Friends	0.600	2
% MH professionals	3.810	2
Symmetry of support	1.630	2
SASB Attack 1	1.360	2
SASB Attack 2	1.490	2
Residence type	1.575	4
Living situation	3.042	2

Note: Sample size ranges from 148 to 157 due to missing data on some items.
  $* p < .10.$ $** p < .05.$ $*** p < .01.$

iform, and schizoaffective disorders. Among those with disorders of mood and affect, all but two violent persons were in the bipolar, manic category.

The co-occurrence of schizophrenia with violent behavior toward others was also reflected in the relationship between diagnosis and type of commitment, which was statistically significant. Individuals diagnosed with schizophrenia were heavily represented in the DTO *and* danger-to-self commitment group. There was a similarly strong association between diagnoses other than schizophrenia and danger-to-self only commitments during the study period. In other words, people diagnosed with schizophrenia were perceived by others, i.e., those who initiated and enacted commitments, to be dangerous to others more often than individuals with all other diagnoses, who were more likely to be seen as harmful to themselves.

Race and gender had a strong relationship to a diagnosis of schizophrenia. Of African American men, 77% had this diagnosis, whereas 60% of African American women, 49% of white men, and 11% of white women were categorized similarly. The earlier finding that race and gender affected violence is confounded with the relationship of diagnosis to violence. The multivariate analysis below will help sort out the separate effects of these explanatory variables.

Type and severity of primary symptoms were related to who was violent in a rather interesting manner when analyzed independently. Individuals who reported a higher degree of confused thinking (trouble concentrating and remembering things) were significantly *less* likely to be violent, while those who reported more false beliefs and perceptions (visual and auditory hallucinations, thought insertion and broadcasting) were *more* likely to be assaultive toward others, but less likely to threaten others. BPRS ratings by interviewers of degree of impairment were related to violence in the expected direction; as impairment increased, violence of both types was more likely. Apparently, individuals whose concentration was impaired were unable or unlikely to be organized enough to be assaultive or menacing to others, while those who were beset by disturbing thoughts and experiences of vulnerability to outside influences were more likely to respond by acting out. The two other symptom scales, perceived hostility and schizoid personality, were not significantly related to violence.

Neither previous hospitalizations nor amount of outpatient psychiatric service use at mental health centers significantly distinguished among the three violence categories. However, as we discuss later, listing a mental health professional in one's social network differentiated between those who had been violent and those who had not. Respondents who were diagnosed as having comorbidity were no more likely than those who were not to be violent in this sample.

Previous Violence Experiences

Study participants who experienced physical or sexual abuse as children were significantly less likely to threaten or act violently. Only 8% of those abused committed a violent act versus 18% of those who were not abused. Similarly, only 14% of those who were abused threatened others, compared to 24% of those who were not abused. Prior violence was not predictive of subsequent violence in this sample. Having a partner, relative, or household member who abused them, had substance abuse problems, or was mentally ill had no significant relationship to violent acts or threats.

Social Network Characteristics

Size and composition of network. Network composition differed between those who were violent and those who were not. Individuals with networks composed of a higher percentage of relatives and those with a lower percentage of mental health professionals were more likely to be violent. None of the other social network characteristics were significantly related to violence by themselves.

Table 3 illustrates that different diagnostic groups had significantly different network characteristics: network size, percentage who were relatives and friends, sources of instrumental support, and type of residence. In particular, individuals with a diagnosis of schizophrenia were more likely to live with family and had smaller networks that were more heavily concentrated among kin than those of any other diagnostic group. Friends comprised about 19% of the networks of persons diagnosed with schizophrenia, in contrast, for example, to 35% of the networks of those in the affective disorder group.

Table 3. Bivariate relationships between diagnosis and social network variables

	Mean or percentage			
Name	Schizophrenia	Affective disorder	Personality disorder	Other
Network size*	10.31	12.42	12.00	15.81
Composition:				
% Relatives*	73.43	53.56	55.69	62.97
% Friends*	19.15	35.07	34.04	30.61
% MH Professionals	7.42	11.37	10.26	6.43
Instrumental support:				
% Relatives*	70.39	49.60	44.99	55.73
% Friends*	12.96	28.70	35.11	27.11
% MH professionals	16.65	21.69	19.89	17.16
Symmetry of support	.61	.71	.68	.74
SASB Attack 1	−.60	−.57	−.48	−.59
SASB Attack 2	−.58	−.62	−.41	−.62
Living situation:				
With partner	8.20%	20.00%	16.00%	13.33%
No partner	91.80%	80.00%	84.00%	86.67%
Residence type:*				
Alone	19.67%	14.00%	12.00%	26.67%
With family	77.05%	66.00%	56.00%	73.33%
With unrelated person(s)	3.28%	20.00%	32.00%	0.00%

*Bivariate relationship, $p < .05$.

Individuals with a diagnosis of schizophrenia also received a much larger proportion of instrumental support from relatives, and a smaller proportion from friends, than people with other diagnoses.

Social support and quality of relationships. The quality of sentiment the respondent had or perceived with important others was investigated during the interview with a series of questions about most trusted persons and persons who cared unconditionally about the respondent. Additional questions probed about decidedly negative relationships—eliciting the names of persons with whom the respondent did not get along or who did not seem to like the respondent.

In terms of these social support ratings, a very low percentage of important people in the network were described negatively. In response to the four questions about specific problematic persons, slightly less than half of the sample listed anyone, and siblings, nonrelatives, and mothers predominated as those named in these questions. Overall, none of the social support ratings of relationship quality proved to be reliable predictors of violence or identifiers of eventual targets. Due to their low yield of information relevant to violence, none of these variables were included in the multivariate analyses.

Results from the SASB proved to be associated with violence in various ways. Table 4 summarizes SASB attack coefficients for those who were not violent, for those who acted or threatened, and for the targets of violence who were rated by patient respondents. The language of the scale is primarily metaphorical with regard to hostility, referring to emotional aggression, fear, and rage, rather than to explicit physical attack. For example, one item states that the other "Murders, kills, destroys and leaves me as a useless heap," while another describes respondents themselves as, "Boiling over with rage and/or fear, I try to escape, flee, or hide from them." [7]

In interpreting these results, it is important to consider that the norms for Attack 1 (significant other rated by respondent) are at best $-.91$, at worst $-.65$, and for Attack 2 (respondent self-rated in relation to significant other) at best $-.90$, at worst $-.54$ (Benjamin 1987). (Scores closer to zero indicate more hostility and disaffiliation, while those closer to -1 indicate friendlier, more affiliative sentiments.) We did not use the best-worst form of the scale, but our whole cohort scored at or well above the norms for hostility from

---

7. The attack coefficients are derived from scale items that describe both extreme hostility and affectionate affiliation as poles along a continuum. For example, the item that states that the other "Harshly punishes and tortures me, takes revenge," is countered by "Lovingly looks after my interests and takes steps to protect me, and actively backs me up." "Neglects me, my interests, needs," is presented in the opposite as "Provides for, nurtures, takes care of me." When individuals rated themselves in relation to the other, the reciprocal description for the first item above ("Harshly punishes and tortures me . . .") is "In pain and rage, I scream and shout that they are destroying me." Similarly, "I am very tense, shaky, wary, fearful with them," is presented in the opposite as "I relax, let go, enjoy, feel wonderful about being with them."

Table 4. SASB attack coefficients and violence during study

		Mean	
Name	N	Attack 1	Attack 2
Violence (dichotomous)			
Violent	56	− .502	− .633
Not violent	101	− .610	− .534
Violence (trichotomous)			
Enact violence	23	− .458	− .672
Threaten violence	33	− .533	− .605
Not violent	101	− .610	− .534
SASB (SO) referent			
Target of violence	16	− .337*	− .550
Not target	141	− .598	− .571

Attack 1 = Respondent rating of significant other, transitive action
Attack 2 = Self-rating of response to SO, intransitive state
*Difference of means T-test significant at $p < 0.1$.

others and fearful, angry response from the respondent. The mean Attack 1 coefficient for the entire sample (− .57) exceeds the norm even when the other is rated at their worst. The mean Attack 2 coefficient (− .57) closely approximates the norm for self rated with other at their worst. Those who were violent, particularly those who engaged in violent acts and those who rated individuals who were targets of violence, scored well above the norms for Attack 1 and Attack 2.

One pattern is striking and consistent in the results. The respondents who were violent described themselves as more friendly and less hostile in demeanor or reaction than the rest of the sample, but saw their significant others as substantially more attacking. In essence, these respondents felt threatened and attacked, but did not perceive themselves to be more threatening or hostile in response than individuals who did not behave violently. The 56 persons in the cohort who made violent threats or attacks described their significant others on the Attack 1 coefficient as more hostile than did the nonviolent group (− .502 vs. − .610) but rated themselves as more affiliative and less fearful or defensive on the Attack 2 coefficient (− .633 vs. − .534). Those who engaged in violent acts rated their significant others as even more menacing (Attack 1 = − .458) than either those who threatened others (Attack 1 = − .533) or those who were not violent (Attack 1 = − .610). These differences within the violent group, and between them and the whole sample, did not reach statistical significance, except when eventual targets of violence were rated.

The 16 targets of violence who were rated by respondents were seen as markedly more attacking than the significant others of the remainder of the sample. The respondents' ratings of themselves in response were more angry and wary than those of the violent group as a whole, but not significantly more so.[8]

These findings suggest strongly that perceived threat and hostility *from* significant others are linked to violence by the respondents but are not solely predictive of violence among the sample as a whole. The respondents who were violent described focal relationships in which they experienced significant emotional danger and damage, while perceiving themselves to be less angry, defensive, or offensive in response than one would expect. Their commitment to the hospital as dangerous to others challenges this perception of themselves. Nevertheless, the SASB findings signal that threatening behavior does not happen in an emotional vacuum and that perceiving measurable danger from others is a corollary of reported violence by the patients.

It is clear that there are correlations between the social network and social support characteristics and violence among the sample, but no causal inferences are yet warranted. How these demographic, clinical, and network and relationship characteristics together contribute to violence requires further analysis.

Multivariate Analysis of Who Was Violent

We added the groups of explanatory variables successively to construct four models of violence and used logistic regression for polytomous dependent variables to estimate the effects of explanatory variables on violence. For this kind of analysis there are two response functions: the log-odds of committing a violent act rather than no violent behavior, and the log-odds of making violent threats only rather than no violent behavior. Table 5 presents the results of these analyses. Note that we transformed the log-odds coefficients into effects on the odds of violence for ease of interpretation.

Model 1 included only the social and demographic variables. Like the bivariate analysis, race-gender was the only significant factor explaining acts and threats. The odds of white men and white women committing either form of violence were significantly lower than those of African American men. African American women's odds of violence did not differ from those of African American men.

The clinical variables were added in model 2. Controlling for clinical fac-

---

8. We also examined individuals in the entire sample who scored substantially above the norms for Attack 1 and 2 to determine if higher scores on either coefficient alone would reliably predict who had been violent. It was apparent again that those who were violent perceived their significant others as very hostile, but there were many who rated themselves and their others as quite hostile who did not engage in violence. For example, in table 3 individuals with personality disorders had the highest Attack 1 and 2 coefficients, but were the least likely to engage in violent acts or threats. Women were also more likely to describe both themselves and their significant others as more attacking than men, but women were in general less likely to actually threaten or act in a violent manner.

tors, the race-gender effect disappeared. The clinical factors, especially diagnosis, appear to intervene between race-gender and violence. That is, race-gender affects diagnosis and, in turn, diagnosis affects violence. Those with schizophrenia had 10 times greater odds of acting violently than those with other diagnoses. However, their odds of making violent threats did not differ from others. Previous hospitalizations affected the odds of both kinds of violence similarly. An additional previous hospitalization increased the odds of violent acts and violent threats by 1.68 and 1.56 times respectively.

Symptomatology was related to violence in complex ways. First, as in the bivariate analysis, individuals became less likely to act or threaten as their thinking was reported to be more confused. Perceptions of hostility from unidentified others increased the odds of threatening 5.7 times but did not affect the odds of acting violently. As individuals became more withdrawn and isolated, the odds of threatening were substantially reduced by a factor of 0.135. These schizoidal personality traits did not affect acting, however.

Next, in model 3, we added previous violence experience variables. Here childhood abuse reduced the odds of threatening others, but did not affect violent acts. The difference between married and nonmarried individuals' odds of making violent threats became significant in this model, with married people being much less likely to threaten. The effects of clinical variables remained essentially the same as in the previous model.

Finally, we added the social network variables to model 4. These variables had significant effects on the odds of making threats but none on the odds of acting violently. Controlling for all other variables, as a person's network included more people, the odds of their making violent threats increased. As the percentage of relatives in the network increased, so did the odds of making a threat.

The effects of the SASB coefficients were in the expected directions. The more threatened the respondent felt by a significant other, the higher the odds of making threats; the less threatening respondents felt they were, the lower their odds of making threats. In contrast to the results of the bivariate analyses, living with unrelated persons was related to violent threats. Those who lived with people not related to them were more likely to make violent threats than those who lived alone.

The pattern that emerges here diverges from the findings of some previous studies (e.g., Hiday and Scheid-Cook 1987, 1989; Swanson et al. 1990) and confirms results from others (e.g., Lindsey, Paul, and Mariotto 1989; Rossi et al. 1986; Klassen and O'Connor 1988a). Unlike Swanson et al. (1990) we did not find that SES eliminated the association of social race with violence, but we did find a rate of violence in our sample (35.6%) similar to that of respondents with diagnoses in the Epidemiologic Catchment Area (ECA) analysis. However, comorbidity was not predictive of violence in our analysis, nor was prior violence, both of which associations were reported by

Table 5. Effect on odds of violence of demographic, clinical, previous violence, and social network variables

Name	Model 1		Model 2		Model 3		Model 4	
	Act	Threaten	Act	Threaten	Act	Threaten	Act	Threaten
Demographic variables								
Age	1.045	1.032	1.000	1.042	0.981	1.037	1.012	1.067
White men	0.225**	0.174**	1.637	0.724	1.490	0.658	2.722	3.022
African American women	0.176	0.257	3.360	0.228	3.365	0.216	19.763	0.931
White women	0.052***	0.208**	0.537	0.317	0.562	0.348	1.396	0.697
Married	1.018	0.253	1.630	0.098	3.129	0.051*	a	0.0001**
SES 1	0.393	a	0.300	a	0.332	a	0.319	a
SES 2	0.447	0.441	0.243	0.205	0.292	0.283	1.078	0.219
SES 3	0.312	0.657	0.310	0.582	0.393	0.376	2.585	0.442
SES 4	0.327	0.636	0.284	0.715	0.422	0.560	0.849	0.493
Worked	0.646	0.554	0.475	0.459	0.357	0.322	0.445	0.046*
Clinical variables								
Schizophrenias			10.144**	1.497	9.321**	0.859	28.250**	4.279
Previous hospitalizations			1.680**	1.555**	1.741**	1.688**	1.610	1.882*
MHC use			1.236	1.114	1.243	1.199	1.195	1.336
Comorbidity			1.357	0.368	1.808	0.380	13.402	0.133
PERI confused thinking			0.357**	0.421**	0.400*	0.393**	0.318	0.189*
PERI false beliefs and perceptions			0.357	1.088	0.352	0.783	0.096*	0.223
PERI perception of hostility			2.213	5.719***	1.996	8.474***	7.283*	29.447***
PERI schizoid personality			0.900	0.135***	0.906	1.108***	0.631	0.035***
BPRS total score			1.020	1.171**	1.055	1.226**	1.082	1.279*

Previous violence variables				
Prior violent behavior	1.965	1.467	2.123	1.216
Childhood network abuse	0.795	0.185*	0.607	0.051*
Adult network problems	0.326	0.886	0.326	1.058
Social network variables				
Network size			1.008	1.404**
Composition:				
% Relatives			1.058	1.097*
% MH professionals			1.051	1.199
Instrumental support:				
% Relatives			0.974	0.972
% MH professionals			0.938	0.913
Symmetry of support			8.729	0.614
SASB Attack 1			7.076	55.119**
SASB Attack 2			0.068	0.012**
Lives with partner			[a]	16.837
Residence type:				
With family			1.681	0.437
With unrelated person(s)			1.347	50.249*
Model chi-square	33.81*	88.11***	95.45***	126.78***
Degrees of freedom	22	40	46	68

Note: Results of polytomous logistic regressions are reported here as coefficients of each variable's effect on the odds of committing or threatening violence.
$N = 128$.

[a] Zero cells make the coefficient inestimable.

* $p < .10$. ** $p < .05$. *** $p < .01$.

Swanson et al. (1990). Like Rossi et al. (1986) we found that increased symptomatology and a diagnosis of schizophrenia were associated with having been violent. Similar to Lindsey, Paul, and Mariotto (1989) and Ramm (1989) we encountered complex interactions of social race with perceived dangerousness, involuntary commitment, and diagnosis, especially the association of being African American and being diagnosed with schizophrenia, which was in turn related to violence and to DTO commitment to state psychiatric hospitals. Hiday and Scheid-Cook (1987) report that more contact with friends was related to fewer commitments among their sample, but we found that larger networks increased the risks for threats resulting in a commitment.

Our findings are consistent with other results of the analysis by Swanson et al. (1990) of ECA data, particularly the association of schizophrenia with increased risk for violence among those with a diagnosis. However, our cohort differs substantially from the ECA population, and the ECA study did not differentiate between violent threats and acts. Thus, further comparisons are probably both unwise and unwarranted.

Klassen and O'Connor (1988a) report findings that both converge with and diverge from ours. They found that people who lived with parents and who were more satisfied with the parental attention they received as children were less likely to be violent. In contrast, we found that residence type was not salient in predicting who would commit a violent act and that those who were abused as children were less likely to threaten violence. In concert, we found that people who lived with unrelated persons were significantly more likely to threaten others. Again, their sample differed greatly from ours in that it was composed entirely of men who had been and were likely to be violent. We suspect that the most violent people in their sample had already been expelled from related households because of their violent behavior and that those who remained with parents were able to do so because they were less violent. Most of our sample were still at home, perhaps because they were somewhat less threatening.

Violent acts among our sample were as likely to occur in related as in unrelated households. One possible explanation is that individuals with a diagnosis of schizophrenia, who were at greater risk for committing a violent act, were allowed to remain at home despite their violence towards others, while individuals with other diagnoses, who are equally likely to threaten others, were both expected to and more able to live outside the parental home. An alternative explanation is that families and unrelated others were equally likely to report violent acts to psychiatric and legal authorities, resulting in our recognizing the person as having committed an act of violence.

The significant relationship of living in an unrelated household to violent threats may be accounted for in various ways. We suggested earlier that respondents might feel more threatened in an unrelated household and thus might actually engage in more menacing behaviors. On the other hand, the amount and type of threats could be equivalent in the two household types, but relatives might be more tolerant of violent threats than nonrelatives, thus less likely to initiate commitment or other proceedings that would result in our identification of the person as one who threatened others. Certainly, the interviews with relatives lend some credence to this interpretation. Finally, it is possible that particular types of people (i.e., men) are more frequently reported as threatening and committed on this basis, even though others may engage in similar behaviors.

Unfortunately, none of the explanations suggested above for these social network influences on violent acts and threats can be tested with our data. As Lindsey, Paul, and Mariotto (1989) have suggested, preselection factors such as those mentioned above, need to be considered when accounting for the disproportionate representation of African Americans among those committed to public psychiatric hospitals as dangerous to others (Ramm 1989). Social class influences on diagnosis (Holzer et al. 1986), and the influence of social race and social class on patterns of reporting and responding to violence also deserve attention (Lawson 1986).

The most prudent conclusion supported by the logistic regressions is that the persons in this cohort who committed violent acts, compared to those who threatened, differ with regard to social and interpersonal context, and thus perhaps in the opportunity or need for violent behaviors. Those who lived with others, specifically unrelated others, were more likely to threaten but not to act violently. Perceived hostility from others, especially intimate others, was strongly predictive of threatening and is confirmed by both PERI and SASB scores.

These patterns may be interpreted as clues to family coping processes that develop over time, suggesting that disruptive behavior in the household is endured up to a point, after which relationships and living arrangements change. Both duration and type of violent behaviors need to be investigated in the social network context in order to understand these sequences more fully. Similarly, we must consider the possibility that individuals with psychiatric disorders go through stages in their illnesses during which they vary with regard to violent behaviors. Thus, our findings may represent individuals at different stages of both social network coping and psychiatric disorder.

Who Were the Targets of Violence?

There were 87 persons who were targets of violence by the patients during the study period. Forty-six (53%) of the targets were relatives, and 41 (47%) were unrelated to the respondents. Looked at in another way, 77% of the targets were known to the respondent, while 23% were either unidentified in the charts or unknown to the respondent. Among relatives, mothers accounted for 28% of the targets (15% of all targets), followed by various other relatives

26% (14% of all targets), and spouses 17% (9% of all targets). As is clear in figure 1, children were very seldom targets, and none were the targets of violent acts. A much larger proportion of all spouses were targets (36%), compared to 9% of all mothers. All those who were targets repeatedly were relatives, and 7 of the 10 repeat targets were mothers. All 13 mothers who were targets lived with the respondent at baseline, in contrast to all targets, of whom 30% lived in the respondent's household at baseline.

The social network inventory was reasonably effective in identifying future targets of violence. Of the 87 targets, 32 (37%) were named by the respondent as social network members. Targets were identified in the main from commitment petitions and hospital records relating to the commitments. It is therefore possible that additional targets were actually network members, but were not identified clearly enough in the charts to make this determination. Nonetheless, all but 2 of the 13 targets of acts and threats and all of the 10 repeated targets had been listed on the baseline social network inventory.

We examined how patterns of violence among this mentally ill cohort might differ from those of the general population. The number and proportion of targets who were relatives and the type of related targets differs from the general population. This probably reflects the predominance of relatives in the social networks of the sample, and in particular the noticeably large proportion of respondents who lived as adults in households with their parents, especially mothers. Sixty-six of the households at baseline included mothers, and 42% included a parent. Fathers are notably lacking both in households

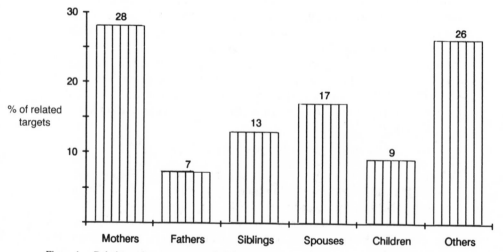

Figure 1.   Relatives who were targets of violence (%; N = 46).

and as targets, due in part to a large number of deceased fathers among the sample. There were over twice as many deceased and unavailable fathers (36) among the cohort as mothers (16). At the same time, spouses and children were comparatively rare in networks, households, and as targets, reflecting well-known characteristics of the population regarding marital status and parenthood.

In the same vein, we explored the gender of targets in relation to that of perpetrators. As in the population at large, men were much more likely to both threaten and act with violence toward women, particularly female relatives, than toward men. Sixty percent of the violent acts were male-to-female, and only 10% were male-to-male. Male-to-male threats were similarly infrequent (8% of threats), especially within families. (This may be underreported as we did not know the gender of the unknown and unidentified targets.) Men and women threatened relatives and nonrelatives in equal proportions, but when they engaged in violent acts, women were more likely than men to direct violent acts toward relatives. That is, 75% of female acts of violence were directed towards relatives, compared to 56% among the men.

This pattern coincides with that reported by Straus and Gelles (1988), who note that violence committed by women is concentrated within their nuclear families. However, the pattern differs because wife-to-husband violence is how women equal or surpass men in the population at large, and only two male spouses were targets among our cohort. We suspect that mothers (and other female relatives) are substituting for husbands as the related targets of violence by the women we studied.

One of the important ways that violence among this cohort differed from that among the overall population was the comparative predominance of relatives as targets. In particular, the pattern was distinct with regard to the type of relative, i.e., mothers. Child, albeit adult child, to parent violence seemed to be a pattern unique to this group. Not coincidentally, mothers also played a dominant role in the social networks of a substantial portion of the sample, and were, not surprisingly, second only to the respondents themselves as initiators of the commitment process.

Summary of Findings

About one-third of this cohort of people with major mental illnesses engaged in behaviors that were actually or potentially dangerous to others during an 18-month period. It is important to note that nearly twice as many threats were made than acts committed, and that very few individuals were arrested for or charged with violent crimes. Social and demographic characteristics were not significant predictors of violent acts and only slightly salient in predicting violent threats. Clinical variables proved to be the only significant predictors of who would engage in violent acts, while violent threats were influenced in various ways by the social, clinical, previous violence, and social network and support characteristics of the cohort.

Individuals with a diagnosis of schizophrenia were substantially more likely than all others to commit acts of violence toward others but no more likely to threaten others than people with other diagnoses. Perceived hostility from identified and unidentified others substantially increased the risk for violent acts and threats, but confused thinking, withdrawal, and isolation decreased the likelihood of being violent. Higher concentrations of relatives in the social network increased the odds for threatening others, as did increased size of the network. People who threatened others described their significant others as attacking and quite hostile, while perceiving themselves to be comparatively friendly toward the person. Mothers were the most frequent related targets of violence, and the most likely targets of repeated violence. The patient and family interviews corroborated these quantitative findings, revealing the reciprocal, historical, and tragic dimensions of the subject at hand.

Taken as a whole, the findings lend considerable support to our contention that interpersonal and social context, relationship quality, and subjective experience or clinical condition, as interrelated and independent factors, are important considerations in assessing risks for violence.

Conclusions

Are social networks and social supports related to violence committed by persons with mental illnesses? At this juncture, our cautious answer is in the affirmative. The findings from the varied sources and diverse methods we used cohere and support our guiding presumptions—that the structure and nature of an individual's relations with others, in combination with their subjective experiences, clinical condition, and personal histories, shed considerable light on who will be violent toward whom. Does the risk for violence reside primarily with the person with mental illness? Is confinement and treatment of the diagnosed person alone an appropriate response to violence borne of provocations and participants other than the patient? We think not.

One way to think contextually about the risk for violence is to consider that the social network represents the opportunity to engage in violence, and social support or quality of relationships the source of provocation or perceived need for such behaviors. Perhaps the most persuasive evidence in support of this view is the numerous indications in our findings that respondents who were violent felt malice and danger *from* significant others and perceived and experienced hostility within their interpersonal networks. The text analysis and two different psychological instruments confirm that *people who threatened violence felt threatened.* People who committed violent acts also perceived hostility from others in their networks, albeit to a lesser extent. Current network problems were statistically unrelated to violence, but the accounts of patients and relatives in the interview transcripts convey a somewhat different view.[9]

This issue of threat perceived by respondents deserves considerably more attention than it has received to date. If individuals with mental illnesses are living in situations which they experience as threatening, in this case mainly related households, our analytic and treatment frames need to shift. We should be assessing more carefully how fearful and victimized individuals feel (and are) in their household or social networks in order to more accurately identify high risk situations. Several recent investigations demonstrate that current domestic violence (Post et al. 1980; Carmen, Rieker, and Mills 1984) and prior sexual abuse (Craine et al. 1988) are not uncommon among psychiatric patients, but attention to these experiences by clinicians and researchers is.

We think it is a mistake to categorize people as violent or not, to conceptualize violence as a characteristic of a person without giving equal attention to the underlying or concurrent interpersonal and clinical processes and contexts. These are experienced over time and vary in their contributions to violence. For example, other family and social network members clearly engage in behaviors as menacing as those of diagnosed patients, but responses other than diagnosis and civil commitment are made. It is also possible that family and social network members reinterpret the meaning and gravity of threatening or assaultive behavior once a diagnosis of mental illness has been applied to their relative and may alter their tolerance for and responses to violence accordingly. Thus, while the patient under investigation may not have changed their behaviors after being diagnosed, those who define violence and the limits of tolerable behavior may have altered their views—initiating commitments or criminal charges at a lower threshold and higher frequency[10] (see Brooks 1984). Were we to focus only on the number and nature of the commitments or charges and attribute these to characteristics of the patient alone, the analysis would be fundamentally flawed from its inception (see Felson 1991). The intertwined processes of illness course and expression—including violence—and family response require more precise and informed investigation.

Like other investigators, we were primarily analyzing *reported* violent threats and acts. In essence, we find ourselves studying those who were reported, diagnosed, and confined—certainly not all those in the patients' networks who engaged in threatening and violent behavior. It is therefore

9. It is important to recall that the small size of the sample makes the quantitative findings quite conservative. At this early stage in understanding the complex dynamics of violence, lack of statistical significance should not be mistaken for lack of clinical or actual importance.

10. Indeed, several respondents complained that once their relatives had successfully invoked the civil commitment process, they used threats of repeating the procedure to control the patients' behavior at home after discharge.

tempting to speculate that had the patients been able or willing to report the actual and perceived violence of these others, DTO commitments might not have been a characteristic of the patients alone.

The inverse relationship of childhood trauma to violence implies that the timing of the threat or attack from others is crucial. Those who were threatened and attacked in childhood were less likely to threaten or act as adults. Some people who were harmed physically and psychologically by others subsequently harmed themselves, were unlikely to engage in threatening behaviors, and, ironically, may have responded to their abuse with the very symptoms and behaviors that result in their being diagnosed as mentally ill.

Several other findings, both substantive and methodological, deserve brief additional comment. This cohort was somewhat different from those investigated in many other inquiries into violence and mental illness. Ours was primarily an outpatient population, early in their careers with major mental illnesses, who were not, to our knowledge, markedly violent prior to recruitment. Our results may then shed some light on persons who may *become* violent, given that they have not been mentally ill for a long time and have not been excessively or criminally violent. The findings may provide a view of potential for violence among those relatively new to the mental health system.

It is clear from our investigation and some others (e.g., Cook 1988), that mothers bear not only considerable responsibility for caring for relatives with mental illness but a concurrent risk for being the targets of repeated violence by these relatives (see also Gelles and Cornell 1987). All of the mothers who were targets lived with their adult mentally ill children. A high proportion of the sample lived in a household with a parent, arguably age inappropriate as the median age of the sample was 28. Thus, the opportunities for adult-child-to-parent violence were comparatively high among the group.

Households in which a mother and adult child reside apparently are at some higher risk for violence, especially when there is no father present. It is not premature to propose some preventive intervention in these families, including teaching de-escalation and self-defense techniques to the mothers. There are very few residential services for persons with mental illnesses in the study counties, accounting in part for the large number of persons living with parents. Developing other places of residence for persons with severe, persistent mental illnesses, wherein they feel safe, might also prevent some intrafamilial violence.

Individuals who listed mental health professionals in their social networks were, on the whole, less likely to have been violent during the study. This suggests that a trained person who is involved enough with the patient to be considered a social network member may be a deterrent to violence, able to intervene should signs or precursors of violence appear. It is also possible that treatment personnel were more willing to be closely involved with individuals who were not threatening or attacking, or that those who were less likely to be violent were for other reasons more involved with treatment personnel. Nevertheless, our findings would support the assignment of intensive case managers trained in violence detection and prevention to individuals diagnosed with schizophrenia who are isolated and fearful and who live in related households or with their mothers.

We found significant differences in social network characteristics between diagnostic groups. In view of the strong association between schizophrenia and violent threats and acts, these distinctions should be investigated further. Recent investigations of social networks among this population (e.g., Hamilton et al. 1989; Holmes-Eber and Riger 1990) suggest that symptomatology and amount of time spent separated from the network in hospitals also influence social network size and composition. We need to know much more about the complicated interactions among clinical, social, and social network characteristics in relation to violence, and in relation to prognosis over time.

None of our instruments alone yielded information that proved to be a concise or reliable predictor of who would be violent. The labor-intensive nature of our data collection procedures may make such research infeasible on a large scale, but the results of our analyses suggest strongly that the breadth and diversity of the data aids considerably in understanding such a complex phenomena as violence toward others. While we did not identify many unreported incidents of violence during the study period by interviewing the patients and their relatives, we learned a great deal more about the contextual and biographical facets of the respondents' lives than we learned from hospital charts, court records, and symptom scales.

These findings recommend an interpretive stance that attends to both long- and short-term clinical and interpersonal processes related to violence and mental illness. More importantly, the results and their implications shed a rather harsh light on the conceptual and resulting methodological and analytic inadequacies of previous research into violence among persons with psychiatric disorders. We have failed to date to investigate sufficiently who else in the social network is threatening or assaultive to or around the designated patient; what and who influences the decision to make a report at all; who is reported to the authorities as dangerous but not committed and why; and how the frequency and nature of violence may differ between types of social networks and within the same network over time.

Further research questions center on the themes arising from our critique of previous work and our findings: attention to person, process, and context. Abuse experienced by individuals with psychiatric disorders, in childhood and as adults, is grossly underinvestigated (Rose 1991), mirroring and contributing to a disproportionate and misleading focus on violent persons solely as perpetrators. Equally little is known about and equally little attention is paid to their versions of how and why violence occurs. Their fears and perceptions are too often considered to be symptoms rather than legitimate concerns.

Research that addresses these issues adequately cannot rely solely on enormous data bases derived primarily from medical and court records or on the accounts or perspectives of clinicians, relatives, or patients alone. However convenient these sources may be, they cannot provide answers to the most pressing questions. A continued dearth of investigations that are face-to-face, multimethod, prospective and longitudinal, and inconclusive of all parties to the violence can only ensure that understanding and predicting violence will remain problematic.

Acknowledgments

This research was supported in part by grant number MH40314, from the National Institute of Mental Health to the first author, and a grant from the John D. and Catherine T. MacArthur Foundation Research Network on Mental Health and the Law to the first author. Dena Plemmons collected nearly all of the archival data for the project, and Julia Benoit, Linda Illingworth, Anna Johnston, William Lachicotte, and Bob Ruth collected the interview data and assisted in the analysis. Additional assistance was provided by Robert Schwartz and Christine Reed. The authors are also grateful for the clarifying commentary and questions of Virginia Hiday, Jeffrey Swanson, the editors of this volume, and members of the Research Network on Mental Health and the Law.

References

Aldrich, J. H., and F. D. Nelson. 1984. *Linear probability, logit, and probit models.* Beverly Hills, Calif.: Sage Publications.

Beels, C. 1981. Social support and schizophrenia. *Schizophrenia Bulletin* 7:58–72.

Benjamin, L. S. 1974. Structural analysis of social behavior. *Psychological Review* 8:392–425.

———. 1979. Structural analysis of differentiation failure. *Psychiatry* 42:1–23.

———. 1983. Principles of prediction using structural analysis of social behavior. In R. A. Zucker, J. Aronoff, and A. Rabin, eds., *Personality and the prediction of behavior.* New York: Academic Press.

———. 1987. SASB Short Form user's manual. Madison, Wis.: Intrex Interpersonal Institute.

———. 1989. Is chronicity a function of the relationship between the person and the auditory hallucination? *Schizophrenia Bulletin* 15:291–310.

Brooks, A. D. 1984. Defining the dangerousness of the mentally ill: Involuntary civil commitment. In M. Croft and A. Croft, eds., *Mentally abnormal offenders.* London: Balliere Tindall.

Carmen, E., P. Rieker, and T. Mills. 1984. Victims of violence and psychiatric illness. *American Journal of Psychiatry* 141:378–83.

Cook, J. A. 1988. Who 'mothers' the chronically mentally ill? *Family Relations* 3:742–49.

Craine, L., C. Henson, J. Colliver, and D. MacLean. 1988. Prevalence of a history of sexual abuse among female psychiatric patients in a state hospital system. *Hospital and Community Psychiatry* 39:300–304.

Dohrenwend, B., and P. E. Shrout. 1981. Toward the development of a two-stage procedure for case identification and classification in psychiatric epidemiology. In R. Simmons, ed., *Research in community and mental health.* Vol. 2. Greenwich, Conn.: JAI Press.

Estroff, S. E., and J. S. Morrissey. 1989. Social networks, social support and the risk for violence among persons with severe, persistent mental illnesses. Paper prepared for the MacArthur Foundation Network on Mental Health and the Law. June.

Felson, R. B. 1991. Blame analysis: Accounting for the behavior of protected groups. *American Sociologist* Spring, 5–23.

Gelles, R. 1987. Violence in the family: A review of research. In R. Gelles, ed., *Family violence.* Newbury Park, Calif.: Sage Publications.

Gelles, R., and C. Cornell. 1987. Adolescent-to-parent violence. In R. Gelles, ed., *Family violence.* Newbury Park, Calif.: Sage Publications.

Hamilton, N. G., C. Ponzoha, D. Cutler, and R. M. Weigel. 1989. Social networks and negative versus positive symptoms of schizophrenia. *Schizophrenia Bulletin* 15:625–32.

Hammer, M. 1986. The role of social networks in schizophrenia. In T. R. Norman, G. Rubinstein, and G. Burrows, eds., *Handbook of studies on schizophrenia.* Pt. 2. London: Elsevier Science Publishers.

Hiday, V. A. 1988. Civil commitment: A review of empirical research. *Behavioral Sciences and the Law* 6:15–43.

———. 1990. Dangerousness of civil commitment candidates. *Law and Human Behavior* 14:551–67.

Hiday, V. A., and T. L. Scheid-Cook. 1987. The North Carolina experience with outpatient commitment: A critical appraisal. *International Journal of Law and Psychiatry* 10:215–32.

———. 1989. A follow-up of chronic patients committed to outpatient treatment. *Hospital and Community Psychiatry* 40:52–59.

Hill, R. W. 1982. Is arson an aggressive act or a property offence? A controlled study of psychiatric referrals. *Canadian Journal of Psychiatry* 27:648–54.

Hollingshead, A., and F. Redlich. 1958. *Social class and mental illness.* New York: John Wiley and Sons.

Holmes-Eber, P., and S. Riger. 1990. Hospitalization and the composition of mental patients' social networks. *Schizophrenia Bulletin* 16:157–64.

Holzer, C. E., B. M. Shea, J. W. Swanson, P. L. Leaf, J. K. Myers, L. George, M. M. Weissman, and P. Bednarski. 1986. The increased risk for specific psychiatric disorders among persons of low socioeconomic status. *American Journal of Social Psychiatry* 6(Fall):259–71.

Jacobson, A. 1989. Physical and sexual assault histories among psychiatric outpatients. *American Journal of Psychiatry* 146:755–58.

Jacobson, A., and B. Richardson. 1987. Assault experiences of 100 psychiatric inpatients: Evidence of the need for routine inquiry. *American Journal of Psychiatry* 144:908–13.

Klassen, D., and W. A. O'Connor. 1988a. A prospective study of predictors of violence in adult male mental health admissions. *Law and Human Behavior* 12: 143–58.

———. 1988b. Crime, inpatient admissions, and violence among mental patients. *International Journal of Law and Psychiatry* 11:305–12.

Lawson, W. B. 1986. Chronic mental illness and the black family. *American Journal of Social Psychiatry* 6:57–61.

Lindsey, K. P., G. Paul, and M. J. Mariotto. 1989. Urban psychiatric commitments: Disability and dangerous behavior of black and white recent admissions. *Hospital and Community Psychiatry* 40:286–94.

Monahan, J. 1988. Risk assessment of violence among the mentally disordered: Generating useful knowledge. *International Journal of Law and Psychiatry* 11:249–57.

———. 1992. Mental disorder and violent behavior. *American Psychologist* 47: 511–21.

Monahan, J., and D. Klassen. 1982. Situational approaches to understanding and predicting violent behavior. In M. E. Wolfgang and N. A. Weiner, eds., *Criminal violence*. Beverly Hills, Calif.: Sage Publications.

Monahan, J., and H. Steadman. 1983. Crime and mental disorder: An epidemiological approach. In M. Tonry and N. Morris, eds., *Crime and justice: An annual review of research*. Chicago: University of Chicago Press.

Nicholson, R. A. 1986. Correlates of commitment status in psychiatric patients. *Psychological Bulletin* 100:241–50.

Omi, M., and H. Winant. 1986. *Racial formation in the United States: From the 1960's to the 1980's*. New York: Routledge and Kegan Paul.

Overall, J., and D. Gorham. 1962. The Brief Psychiatric Rating Scale. *Psychological Reports* 10:799–812.

Post, R., A. Willett, R. Franks, R. House, S. Back, and M. Weissberg. 1980. A preliminary report on the prevalence of domestic violence among psychiatric inpatients. *American Journal of Psychiatry* 137:974–75.

Ramm, D. 1989. Over committed. *Southern Exposure*, Fall, 13–45.

Revenson, T. A., K. M. Schiaffino, S. D. Majerovitz, and A. Gibofsky. 1991. Social support as a double-edged sword: The relation of positive and problematic support to depression among rheumatoid arthritis patients. *Social Science and Medicine* 33:807–13.

Rook, K. S. 1984. The negative side of social interaction: Impact on psychological well-being. *Journal of Personality and Social Psychology* 46:1097–1108.

Rook, K. S., and P. Pietromonaco. 1987. Close relationships: Ties that heal or ties that bind? *Advances in Personal Relationships* 1:1–35.

Rose, S. M. 1991. Another unveiling: Abuse backgrounds of psychiatric survivors and their neglect by mental health systems. In M. A. Susko, ed., *Cry of the invisible*. Baltimore: Conservatory Press.

Rose, S. M., C. G. Peabody, and B. Stratigeas. 1991. Undetected abuse among intensive case management clients. *Hospital and Community Psychiatry* 42:499–503.

Rossi, A. M., M. Jacobs, M. Monteleone, R. Olsen, R. Surber, E. Winkler, and

A. Wommack. 1986. Characteristics of psychiatric patients who engage in assaultive or other fear-inducing behaviors. *Journal of Nervous and Mental Disease* 174: 154–60.

Sepejak, D. R., J. Menzies, C. D. Webster, and F. A. S. Jensen. 1983. Clinical predictions of dangerousness: Two-year follow-up of 408 pre-trial forensic cases. *Bulletin of the American Academy of Psychiatry and the Law* 11:171–81.

Shrout, P. E., B. P. Dohrenwend, and I. Levav. 1986. A discriminant rule for screening cases of diverse diagnostic types. *Journal of Consulting and Clinical Psychology* 54:314–19.

Skinner, E., D. Steinwachs, and J. Kasper. 1991. Characteristics of consumers and family perceptions of needs for care. Paper presented at the annual meeting of the National Alliance for the Mentally Ill, July 7, San Francisco.

Sokolovsky, J. C., C. Cohen, D. Berger, and J. Geiger. 1978. Personal networks of ex-mental patients in a Manhattan SRO hotel. *Human Organization* 37:5–15.

Splane, S., J. Monahan, D. Prestholt, and H. Friedlander. 1982. Patients' perceptions of the family's role in involuntary commitment. *Hospital and Community Psychiatry* 33:569–72.

Straus, M. A., and R. J. Gelles. 1988. How violent are American families? Estimates from the National Family Violence Resurvey and other studies. In G. T. Hotaling, D. Finkelhor, J. T. Kirkpatrick, and M. A. Straus, eds., *Family abuse and its consequences*. Newbury Park, Calif.: Sage Publications.

Swanson, J. W., C. E. Holzer, V. K. Ganju, and R. T. Jono. 1990. Violence and psychiatric disorder in the community: Evidence from the ECA Studies. *Hospital and Community Psychiatry* 41:761–70.

Tardiff, K., and H. W. Koenigsberg. 1985. Assaultive behavior among psychiatric outpatients. *American Journal of Psychiatry* 142:960–63.

Designing a New Generation of Risk Assessment Research

Henry J. Steadman, John Monahan, Paul S. Appelbaum, Thomas
Grisso, Edward P. Mulvey, Loren H. Roth, Pamela Clark Robbins,
and Deidre Klassen

"Dangerousness," long "the paramount consideration in the law–mental
health system" (Stone 1975) in the United States, is now a focal concern of
mental health law throughout the world (United Nations 1991). Yet establishing a base of robust empirical knowledge to guide clinical practice and social
policy regarding dangerousness has proven remarkably elusive. Recent developments in decision theory and in public health, as well as a methodological
audit of existing studies, suggest that the next generation of research must
bear seven characteristics (Monahan and Steadman, this volume):

1. "Dangerousness" must be disaggregated into its component parts—the
   variables used to predict violence ("risk factors"), the amount and type of
   violence being predicted ("harm"), and the likelihood that harm will occur ("risk").
2. A rich array of theoretically-chosen risk factors in multiple domains must
   be chosen.
3. Harm must be scaled in terms of seriousness and assessed with multiple
   measures.
4. Risk must be treated as a probability estimate that changes over time and
   context.
5. Priority must be given to actuarial research that establishes a relationship
   between risk factors and harm.
6. Large and broadly representative samples of patients at multiple, coordinated sites must participate in the research.
7. Managing risk as well as assessing risk must be a goal of the research.

In this chapter, we illustrate how these seven methodological principles can
shape the design of a new generation of risk assessment research by describing how these principles were realized in one project—the MacArthur Risk
Assessment Study. We present the results of the field trials that preceded full-
scale research implementation, and detail the implications of those results for
the final study design.

297

Research Strategy

Informed by developments in public health and in decision theory, and responding to a thorough critique of existing research methodologies, the implications of which are summarized above, the Research Network on Mental Health and the Law of the John D. and Catherine T. MacArthur Foundation began in 1988 to plan a MacArthur Risk Assessment Study.[1] Over the course of several years, a number of fundamental decisions shaped this research initiative. A description of these decisions, and their rationale, follow.

1. We are interested in studying the relationship between violent behavior directed against others and mental disorder. We have chosen to study violence toward others by released mental patients for two reasons: (*a*) it is a fundamental issue in mental health law and policy, and (*b*) it is an important clinical and social issue, independent of its pivotal nature in formal mental health law.

We chose not to focus on violence toward one's self (although we do gather limited information on this, see below) and not to focus on samples of disordered people who have not been hospitalized. It should be clear that to select violence toward others as a focal issue in mental health law is not to disparage the significance of other issues—we concluded that the competence of disordered persons to make decisions, such as the decision to accept or to refuse treatment or to make decisions on the defense of one's criminal case, and the effects of coercive state intervention into the lives of the mentally disordered, were equally pressing questions. Violence toward others is, however, one very significant issue in mental health law and the one with which we join issue in this project.

2. There are two aspects of violent behavior toward others by mental patients that we have chosen to address: (*a*) risk assessment and (*b*) risk management.

While a study of either risk assessment or risk management would be very valuable, we have attempted to balance these two foci in our research. Risk assessment without risk management leads only to dichotomous "in-out"

1. The members of the Research Network are: the Honorable Shirley S. Abrahamson, Paul S. Appelbaum, M.D.,* Richard J. Bonnie, LL.B., Thomas Grisso, Ph.D.,* Pamela S. Hyde, J.D., John Monahan, Ph.D. (Network Director),* Stephen J. Morse, J.D., Ph.D., Edward P. Mulvey, Ph.D.,* Loren H. Roth, M.D.,* Paul Slovic, Ph.D., Henry J. Steadman, Ph.D.,* and David B. Wexler, J.D. The members of the Working Group that planned and direct the MacArthur Risk Assessment Study are indicated with an asterisk. Deidre Klassen, Ph.D., directed the Kansas City site of the field trial. William O'Connor, Ph.D., is directing the full study at that site. Carmen Cirincione and William Gardner have provided statistical consultation. Pamela Clark Robbins coordinates the overall research effort via a contract from the University of Virginia to Policy Research Associates, Inc., in Albany, New York.

judgments for institutionalization, without much relevance for clinical practice. Risk management without risk assessment, on the other hand, is not directly responsive to the concerns of mental health law, which often calls for in-out decisions. The main implication of including a risk management approach is that we plan to study relationships between dynamic, potentially alterable aspects of a patient's functioning or life situation and risk of violence over time.

A focus on these issues has opportunity costs. It precludes focusing the research on many other important aspects of the relationship between violence and mental disorder that are worthy of study. For example, it removes the focus from studying the "basic" or "fundamental" nature of any relationship between violence and mental disorder; we are not comparing the violence rates of disordered and nondisordered groups to estimate whether mental disorder per se is a risk factor for violence (see Link and Stueve, this volume; Swanson, this volume; Monahan 1992). And our decision removes the focus from studying the treatment ("risk reduction") of violence by the mentally disordered. The former would require laboratory or epidemiological methods. The latter would require randomized clinical trials of various treatment modalities. Nevertheless, we have become convinced that the approach we are taking has the highest potential payoff both for improving clinical practice and for advancing scientific understanding.

3. We have chosen to focus on one component of risk assessment and risk management: the association between given risk factors and the criterion of violent behavior toward others.

As indicated above, we concluded that it would be most useful to know what factors bear a statistically robust relationship to violent behavior before further studying the extent to which clinicians use these factors in their current practice, or the validity of the judgments that result from this practice. In addition, excellent research on the relationship between cues and judgments is already ongoing in the form of a National Institute of Mental Health–funded project directed by Charles Lidz and network member Edward Mulvey, and a great deal of research on the relationship between judgments and the criterion already exists (both described in Monahan and Steadman, this volume).

4. The ultimate goals of our research on the association between risk factors and violent behavior are (*a*) to improve the validity of clinical risk assessment, (*b*) to improve the effectiveness of clinical risk management, and (*c*) to provide information useful in reforming mental health law and policy.

If our efforts to establish robust relationships between cue or predictor variables and the criterion variable of violent behavior are successful, future research by the Network and others could address methods for training clinicians in the use of these cues, with the result that the validity of clinical risk assessments and the effectiveness of risk management would be improved. For example, if we found that cues currently in general use in clinical practice to predict violence were not in fact associated with violence, or were associated with only a certain type of violence, or that other cues not now used to predict violence were actually quite predictive, these findings might have important implications for changes in clinical evaluation of potentially violent persons. In addition, clearly establishing risk factors for future violence may have equally important implications for mental health policy. For example, statutes could be written to provide extra treatment resources to "high risk" groups (see Wiederanders 1990). Or perhaps outpatient commitment, if it were to be imposed on the basis of dangerousness to others, might be limited to groups for whom lack of compliance with medication was a key predictor of violence (see Mulvey, Geller, and Roth 1987).

5. The risk factors whose association with violence we investigate are intended to be both a reasonably comprehensive set of the risk factors that we believe actually anticipate violence among mental patients and a reasonably feasible set to assess in actual clinical practice.

One of the central problems we identified with existing risk research was that it used what we referred to as "impoverished predictor variables" (Monahan and Steadman, this volume). Each investigation tended to study only one or a few things (e.g., diagnosis, symptom severity scores, or past history). We wanted to combine risk factors in a single, comprehensive study, both to compare predictive value and to investigate potentiating interactions among predictor variables. We also wanted the set of risk factors that ultimately emerged from the research to be easily "transported" into actual clinical practice. Our goal is that the set of predictors we arrive at—hopefully a small subset of the cues we are investigating—will be useful in actual clinical practice. Also, we wished to employ factors that clinicians seemed to hold in high regard for determining risk of violence. Were these to be shown to have little relationship to subsequent violence, another set of implications for clinical practice would be clear.

It should be evident from this discussion that we have made trade-offs in our research design between "breadth" and "depth." If we did not care about being comprehensive, we could focus in depth on a more limited set of predictors. If we just wanted to study delusions and violence, for example, we could ask about even very rare delusions and use several complementary measurement instruments. Instead, we have opted for reasonable comprehensiveness—touching a number of bases—rather than exhaustive attention to any one risk factor.

6. We selected as risk factors to investigate those that have been (*a*) associated with violence in prior research, (*b*) believed to be associated with violence by experienced clinicians, or (*c*) hypothesized to be associated with violence by existing theories of violence or of mental disorder.

We are aware of the way that textbooks say variable selection is supposed to be done—by deduction from a fully articulated and validated theory. We are also aware that no such theory of violence or of mental disorder exists. Nor is it plausible to hope that the Network, or anyone else, will produce such a grand theory in the foreseeable future (see National Research Council 1993). Indeed, it may be that a single coherent theory linking each of the multiple causes of violence is not feasible. Therefore, we took a broader and more inclusive approach to variable selection.

We looked at cues that had been validated as risk factors in the existing research literature (e.g., demographic factors; Klassen and O'Connor, this volume). We looked at factors mentioned in the clinical literature or suggested by the Network members' own clinical experience as predictive of violence (e.g., delusions). And we sought cues in those "minitheories" of aggression and violence that exist (e.g., anger, psychopathy). Adequate measures seemed to exist for some cues (e.g., perceived stress). For others, we developed our own measures (e.g., Thomas Grisso devised a measure of violent fantasies and Loren Roth developed an inventory of hallucinations; see McNiel, this volume).

Finally, we concluded that there were five factors not previously studied systematically as markers of risk of violence among the mentally disordered that hold special promise to increase the validity of actuarial assessment. Those factors were social support, impulsiveness, anger control, psychopathy, and delusions. Robust measures of these five potential markers of risk were either unavailable or had not been validated in mentally disordered populations. One of the initial tasks that the Network set for itself, therefore, was to support the development of state-of-the-art instruments to measure each of these constructs.

Sue Estroff (Estroff and Zimmer, this volume) developed for us a streamlined version of her extensive instrument for measuring the affective and instrumental support received by mentally disordered persons and assessing how these indicators of social support relate to violent behavior. Since some studies (e.g., Craig 1982) have reported that treating clinicians perceive approximately one-third of hospitalized mental patients as having significant problems with the expression of anger and have suggested that these patients may be disproportionately involved in violent behavior, Raymond Novaco (this volume) developed an instrument specifically for measuring the typical anger level of mentally disordered persons and changes in that level as a result of specific provocations. Robert Hare's Psychopathy Checklist (PCL) appeared to be very promising as a predictor of violence (Harris, Rice, and Cormier 1991), but a briefer, clinical version of the PCL that was valid for disordered populations was required for our research. Therefore, Hare and his colleagues (Hart, Hare, and Forth, this volume) developed a shorter version of his PCL and pilot tested that instrument for us. The Barratt Impulsiveness Scale (BIS) is the most reliable and valid instrument available for measuring impulsivity, but this instrument was developed exclusively in nondisordered populations and many of the items were inappropriate for mentally disordered people. For our study, Ernest Barratt (this volume) developed a version of his instrument for use with mentally disordered persons. Finally, the precise characteristics of delusions that relate to violence (e.g., the type and intensity of the delusion) and how those characteristics might best be measured were unclear. Pamela Taylor and her colleagues at the University of London (Taylor et al., this volume), therefore developed and pilot tested a new and more clinically sensitive instrument to measure delusions, the Maudsley Assessment of Delusions Schedule (MADS), which was subsequently revised by Paul Appelbaum and Pamela Robbins.

7. Our chosen set of risk factors subsumes four generic "domains": (a) dispositional factors, (b) historical factors, (c) contextual factors, and (d) clinical factors.

A listing of our final set of risk factors is contained in table 1.

One domain of our variables can be thought of as "dispositional" or "individual." This would refer, for example, to the demographic factors of age, race, gender, and social class, as well as to personality variables and neurological factors (e.g., head injury).[2]

A second domain can be thought of as "historical." This would include significant events experienced by subjects in the past, e.g., family history, work history, mental hospitalization history, history of violence, and criminal and juvenile justice history.

A third domain can be thought of as "contextual." This would refer to the

2. We are aware that many believe that biological variables have great potential as markers of violence risk among the mentally disordered (Denno 1990). Cereborspinal fluid serotonin metabolite level is a leading contender for such a risk marker (Virkkunen et al. 1989). Discussions with many leading biological researchers, however, yielded the consistent conclusion that serotonin metabolite levels can only be reliably assessed in the cerebrospinal fluid of a person who has been completely medication-free for a period of at least one week. Since keeping 1,000 hospitalized patients free of psychotropic medication for a week, and performing spinal taps on each of them, was clearly infeasible, we opted for a different strategy. The Network provided support to J. John Mann, M.D., at the Western Psychiatric Institute and Clinic at the University of Pittsburgh, to supplement his ongoing NIMH-sponsored research on violence to self and biological factors, including serotonin metabolite levels. This support is allowing Dr. Mann to add the Network-developed measures of violence to others to his own measures of violence to self.

Table 1. Cue domains in the MacArthur Risk Assessment Study

1. Dispositional Factors	*History of Crime and Violence*
Demographic	Arrests
Age	Incarcerations
Gender	Self-reported Violence
Race	Violence Toward Self
Social Class	
Personality	3. Contextual Factors
Personality Style	*Perceived Stress*
Anger	*Social Support*
Impulsiveness	Living Arrangements
Psychopathy	Activities of Daily Living
Cognitive	Perceived Support
IQ	Social Networks
Neurological Impairment	*Means for Violence* (i.e., guns)
2. Historical Factors	4. Clinical Factors
Social History	*Axis I Diagnosis*
Family History	*Symptoms*
Child rearing	Delusions
Child abuse	Hallucinations
Family deviance	Symptom Severity
Work History	Violent Fantasies
Employment	*Axis II Diagnosis*
Job perceptions	*Functioning*
Educational History	*Substance Abuse*
Mental Hospitalization History	Alcohol
Prior Hospitalizations	Other Drugs
Treatment Compliance	

indices of current social supports, social networks, and stress, as well as to physical aspects of the environment, such as the presence of weapons.

A fourth and final domain can be thought of as "clinical." This would include types and symptoms of mental disorder, personality disorder (Widiger and Trull, this volume), drug and alcohol abuse, and level of functioning.

This scheme is not uncontroversial. The theoretical status of many of the variables we chose is unsettled. For example, we include both "anger control" and "psychopathy" as "dispositional" variables. If one believed that either of these factors were more in the nature of current "state" than of relatively enduring "trait" variables, then that factor could with equal justification be listed in the "clinical" domain. However, this scheme has an important virtue: it tracks both the risk assessment and risk management goals of the research. While all four of these domains are relevant to risk assessment, only two of them—the contextual and the clinical—are directly susceptible to modification for the purpose of risk management. There is nothing a clinician can do to "manage" the dispositional domain variables. The subject's age, race, gender, and basic personality structure must be taken as given. Likewise, a clinician cannot undo the past. If a patient has a history of being abused as a child, being arrested, being in a mental hospital, or being violent, there is, again, nothing a clinician can do to change this. Dispositional and historical variables are relevant to risk management only in the sense that management strategies can be conditioned on dispositional and historical variables (e.g., a given treatment may be more effective with persons of one gender than of the other, a certain environmental modification may work better with younger people than with older people). Dispositional and historical factors are not themselves candidates for direct change in order to manage risk, but existing sociological research suggests that these are the most important domains for assessing risk. For this reason, we assess dispositional and historical variables as cues only at discharge and not repeatedly as patients are followed in the community (see below).

The contextual and clinical domains, on the other hand, are not only relevant to assessing risk but are susceptible to change in direct attempts to manage risk. Contextual and clinical factors may vary "naturally," independent of clinical intervention (e.g., a patient's living arrangements may change), and disorder can be more or less acute at different times. The clinician can take advantage of these "natural" variations in managing risk (e.g., only allowing a home visit when the disorder is not acute or when the patient's parent is home) but can also intervene directly to modify these domains (e.g., providing treatment to reduce symptoms or a half-way house to augment social supports). Because contextual and clinical variables change both naturally and intentionally, we assess them not just at discharge but repeatedly while following up patients in the community.

8. Our chosen criterion variables focus on physical violence toward others in the community, categorized at two levels of seriousness.

We have chosen to concentrate on physical violence toward others rather than psychological harm or harm to property and to emphasize violence in the community after release from the hospital rather than in-hospital violence. We gather in-hospital data to be used as an independent variable in evaluating community violence. After gathering detailed information about violent incidents, we code the incidents into two levels of seriousness, depending upon whether the victim was injured or a weapon was involved. Thus, we define Level 1 violence as (a) any battery resulting in an injury, (b) any sexual battery, (c) any battery involving a weapon, and (d) any imminent threat of battery (i.e., assault) involving a weapon. Level 2 violence includes all other batteries. We do not count verbal arguments, verbal threats without a weapon present, or (more controversially) nonabusive child discipline as "violent." We also categorize incidents (e.g., throwing something, hitting with a fist) and the type of victim (e.g., spouse, child, stranger), allowing for cross-classification by seriousness and type of violence and by target.

Field Trial

Having made these strategic decisions, we were still left with several logistical and substantive questions that had to be answered empirically before a specific research design could be finalized. The logistical questions addressed in the field trial concerned our ability to recruit a sufficient number of subjects and monitor their behavior in the community and the ability of the subjects to complete our lengthy interview protocols. The substantive questions concerned the statistical adequacy of the base rates of violent behavior that we would find in the community, particularly among women and older persons, and how those base rates would be affected by the inclusion of a collateral informant for each subject.

To answer these questions, we conducted a field trial of our provisional research design from 1988 to 1990. As mentioned above, we attempted in the field trial to overcome the four methodological limitations of existing research on risk assessment described in Monahan and Steadman (this volume).

To address the cramped range of predictor variables, we administered a broad array of assessment instruments to short-term civilly hospitalized patients. The battery included four of the five specially-commissioned measures described above (the Personal Ideation Inventory-Short Form [Rattenbury et al. 1984] was used to measure delusions while the MADS was under development). It also included the Diagnostic Interview Schedule (DIS; Robins and Regier 1991), the Brief Psychiatric Rating Scale (BPRS; Overall and Klett 1972), the Global Assessment of Functioning scale (GAF; a recent revision of Endicott, Spitzer, and Fleiss 1976), and an exhaustive interview schedule that tapped psychiatric, criminal justice, family, and employment history, alcohol and drug use, child abuse history, violent fantasies, access to weapons, and a large number of other risk markers (see table 1). To address the weak criterion variables used in prior research, we measured violent behavior in the community by comprehensive face-to-face interviews with each subject and independent, collateral interviews with someone the patient named as knowledgeable about his or her behavior, at two-month intervals for up to six months after the patient's release from the hospital. To correct for restricted samples, we chose our subjects from consecutive admissions of both male and female voluntary and involuntary patients, between the ages of 18 and 64, unscreened for diagnosis (except to exclude a primary diagnosis of mental retardation). Finally, to avoid producing results that were specific to a single site, three sites were involved in the study—the Western Psychiatric Institute and Clinic at the University of Pittsburgh, the Worcester (Massachusetts) State Hospital, and the Western Missouri Mental Health Center in Kansas City.

Table 2. MacArthur risk assessment pilot study sample

Sites	Initial contact	Initial battery completed	Follow-up 1 completed	Follow-up 2 completed	Follow-up 3 completed	At least 1 follow-up
Kansas City	105	80	63	65	58	70
Worcester	109	49	39	36	NA	40
Pittsburgh	60	40	36	NA	NA	36
Total	274	169	138	101	58	146

A total of 169 subjects in the field trial completed the initial battery of risk factors. Of these 169 subjects, 146 (86%) were located for at least one follow-up interview in the community. In this follow-up interview, data on self-reported violence and treatment compliance were obtained, and the instruments to measure the "clinical" variables (see table 1) were readministered. One site (Pittsburgh) did one two-month follow-up, another (Worcester) did two two-month follow-ups, and the third (Kansas City) did three two-month follow-up interviews.

The principal results of the field trial and the conclusions we drew from them for the final design for their full-scale study are reported below.

Subject recruitment. Of the 274 patients we approached to obtain informed consent, 200 (73%) agreed to participate in the study.[3] Subjects were paid $10 to $20 (depending on the site). Of those who agreed to participate, 31 (15.5%) dropped out either prior to beginning or during the initial interview. This left a final sample of 169 persons (see table 2). The vast majority of the patients who refused either gave no reason for refusal or simply said that they were uninterested (21.6% and 32.4%, respectively), but some cited privacy (16.2%) or fear of subpoena of the research data (8.1%) as concerns. Only seven persons felt (at the time of consent) that the interview was going to be too long. The only significant difference we found between the original sample ($N = 393$) and the final sample ($N = 169$) was that males who were approached were more likely to be enrolled (55.8%) than were females (44.8%).

The demographic characteristics of the available pool of subjects and of those completing an initial interview varied by site. The sampling strategy employed for the field trial was to take every nth eligible admission to the acute care units selected. This resulted in a sample that was disproportionately

---

3. We originally sampled 393 patients as potential subjects. However, ward clinicians refused or delayed our access to 54 patients, 30 patients were discharged before they could be enrolled, 20 patients were already committed to other research projects or were otherwise unavailable, and the interviewers declined to enroll 15 patients (e.g., because a patient was too incoherent to answer questions).

white at two sites, slightly more male at the third site, and with different distributions of legal status (voluntary or involuntary) and diagnosis across sites. Our final sample was disproportionately male in Kansas City (67.5%) compared with our other two sites, where males comprised roughly half of the sample (53.1% in Worcester and 50.0% in Pittsburgh). The Worcester site subjects were almost all white (91.8%), while Kansas City had 66.3% white subjects (with random sampling) and Pittsburgh 62.5% white subjects (after oversampling for blacks). These results clearly demonstrated that we needed to use stratified sampling for the full-scale study. Otherwise, confounding of case characteristics with site would make interpretation of our data very difficult.

Initial instrument battery. Generally, the instruments contained in the initial battery were relatively easy to administer, but the total length of the interview session was unacceptably long. The time required to complete the hospital interview averaged four hours and ranged from two to ten hours over one to five interview sessions. The patients (and the interviewers) became fatigued and distracted by the length of the interview. Also, it was difficult to identify large time blocks within the active hospital routines within which the initial battery could be completed. The Diagnostic Interview Schedule (DIS) was the most time consuming and difficult instrument for the patients to complete, especially those who had multiple diagnoses or who were very symptomatic. The field study, in short, revealed that we had to eliminate some instruments and pare down the ones that remained.

Locating subjects in the community. The follow-up of subjects in the community at two-month intervals after discharge from the hospital proved to be no more difficult than we had anticipated, given the prior experience in doing community follow-ups of the study teams at two of the sites (Kansas City and Pittsburgh). While our subjects were often very difficult to locate, our staff were equally resourceful in finding them; our follow-up results reflect their efforts. Across the three sites, we have at least one follow-up on 146 of the 169 patients who completed the initial interview (86.4%). The major reason for missed follow-ups was inability to locate the subject. Very few subjects were lost because of refusal to participate in the follow-up interviews. We also found that once we had located a patient for their first community interview, our subsequent follow-up rate was over 90%. Our field trial results, therefore, strongly suggest that former patients can be successfully located and interviewed at two- to three-month intervals in the community. Our results also demonstrated how important the first contact in the community is to control attrition.

Frequency of reported violence. Our initial substantive question of the field trial data was, simply, was there "enough" violence to study? Prior research on community assaultiveness of released mental patients had generally found that between 2% and 5% had records of some type of arrest for

Table 3. Reported violence by site and instrument administration

Site	Initial battery (incidents prior to study)			Follow-up 1			Follow-up 2			Follow-up 3			All follow-ups		
	People		Incidents	People		Incidents	People		Incidents	People		Incidents	People		Incidents
	#	%	#	#	%	#	#	%	#	#	%	#	#	%	#
Kansas City	37	46.3	276	11	17.2	33	10	15.4	14	6	10.3	9	23	32.9	56
Worcester	14	28.6	20	6	15.4	8	6	16.7	14	NA	NA	NA	11	27.5	22
Pittsburgh	12	30.0	97	5	13.9	15	NA	NA	NA	NA	NA	NA	5	13.9	15
All sites	63	37.3	393	22	15.8	56	16	15.8	28	6	10.3	9	39	26.7	93

Note: Violence includes hitting with hand/fist, threatening with a weapon, or using a weapon.

violent crime during an average follow-up of one year (Steadman, Cocozza, and Melick 1978; Sosowsky 1980; Hiday 1991). Klassen and O'Connor (1988) had studied males with prior records of violence upon presentation to a community mental health center—the same one used as our Kansas City site—and found that 19% had subsequent arrests or admissions for violence over a six-month follow-up. Given that our subjects were a random cross-section of acute inpatients and had not been screened for prior violence, what rates of violence would they report? (Note that in our initial analyses of the field trial data, we have focused on self-report, rather than arrest.) The results are seen in table 3.

Across all three sites for up to three follow-up interviews (6 months) in the community, 26.7% of the subjects reported at least one violent incident. For 15.8% of the subjects the most serious incident involved hitting someone without a weapon being involved, for 5.5% it involved threatening someone with a weapon without the weapon actually being used, and for another 5.5% it involved using a weapon. In Kansas City, where all three follow-ups were attempted, 32.7% of the subjects reported at least one violent incident. When official records are added to these self-reports, the base rates of violence may be even higher. Since we have no nonpatient comparison group, any inferences regarding how rates of violence by discharged mental patients compare with rates of violence by other members of the general population are unwarranted. Our only conclusion from these data was that we did, indeed, have a sufficient number of violent incidents to study.

Violence by gender. Given the great disparity in rates of violent offending by men and women (Wilson and Herrnstein 1985; Dobash et al. 1992), we were concerned that even if the overall base rate of violence we found during follow-up was sufficient to allow for a statistical validation of our predictor variables, the observed violence would be so heavily concentrated in men that we would be able to draw no conclusions regarding the risk assessment of violence in women. Were that to be the case, we would be forced to consider limiting the sample for the full-scale research to men, as is often done in this area (e.g., Klassen and O'Connor 1988). Accordingly, the self-reports from our pilot study in which 40.8% of the subjects were women were crucial in determining the most appropriate sample for the full-scale study.

The distributions of reported violence by gender, race, and age are reported in table 4.

In fact, while a somewhat smaller proportion of women than men (34.8% vs. 39.0%) reported violence in the two months prior to their target admission, a higher proportion of women than men (32.8% vs. 22.4%) reported at least one violent incident in the community after their hospitalizations (for a similar finding, see Lidz, Mulvey, and Gardner 1993). Clearly, then, there was no reason to limit our full-scale study to male subjects.

Violence by age. Our concerns with age were analogous to those with gen-

Table 4. Initial and follow-up violence by demographic characteristics

	Initial violence (N = 169)		Follow-up violence (N = 146)	
	#	%	#	%
Sex				
Male	39	39.9	19	22.4
Female	24	34.8	20	32.8
Race				
White	43	35.0	27	25.5
African American	16	42.1	9	26.5
Age				
Under 25	17	45.9	11	37.9
25–40	38	39.2	25	29.4
Over 40	8	22.9	3	9.4

Note: Based on pooled data from all three study sites.

der. Given the great falloff in rates of violence as people age (Swanson et al. 1990), would there be an age beyond which the base rate of violence was too low, given our projected sample size, to allow for a validation of our predictor variables? As can be seen in table 4, the proportion of subjects in the field trial who reported any violent incident in any of the follow-up community interviews did indeed decrease as age increased. In the subjects over the age of 40, the proportion who reported violence was about one-third that of persons aged 25 to 40 (9.4% vs. 29.4%). Accordingly, the decision was made to concentrate on subjects between the ages of 18 and 40 years old in the full-scale study.

Using collateral informants. Finally, to provide information on how we might most accurately measure the criterion variable of interest—violence in the community—we adopted a procedure used by Lidz and Mulvey (Lidz 1987) and asked each subject to nominate the person who would best know about his or her behavior after release. We contacted these collaterals, usually family members or friends, shortly after each subject was interviewed in the community to obtain reports of any violent behavior by the released patient. The collaterals were paid the same amount as the patients. The results comparing collateral reports and subject self-reports in the field trials can be seen in table 5.

The most striking finding from these data is the number of violent incidents reported by collaterals that were not reported by the subjects themselves. Subjects reported at least one violent act during the follow-up period in 39 of the 146 cases with at least one follow-up (26.7%). If nonoverlapping self-report and collateral data were combined, we would have found a total of 49 of the 146 subjects (33.6%) to have been violent at least once during the follow-

Table 5. Self-reports and collateral reports of violence

Collateral report of subject violence	Self-report of violence					
	No		Yes		Total	
	#	%	#	%	#	%
No	97	91	27	69	124	84
Yes	10	9	12	31	22	16
Total	107	100	39	100	147	100

up—an additional 10 persons and *a 25.6% increase*. Clearly, the addition of collateral reports in the full-scale study, assuming their accuracy, would increase the base rate of community violence in the follow-up and provide us with a more complete validation of our chosen risk factors.

The field trial also provided us with information regarding the importance of appropriate collateral nomination by the subjects. Collateral selection was based solely on the subject's nomination during the initial interview in the hospital of the person who would "know the most about how you are doing after you get out of the hospital." While many of the collaterals turned out to be knowledgeable about the subjects' activities after discharge, a minority (10.7%) had contact with the subject less than several times per month. These collaterals knew very little about the subjects' lives or any violent incidents in which the subject had been involved. A preferable procedure for selecting collateral informants would be to wait until the "social support" section of the follow-up interview had been administered, see with whom the subject actually had spent the most time during the preceding two or three months, and request consent to interview that person as the collateral.

Full-Scale Study

Based on the results of our field trials, Network members made a number of final decisions that shaped the design of the full-scale study. Those decisions and their implications for the design of the study are discussed below.

1. Our criterion variables are measured by (*a*) official arrest and mental hospital records, (*b*) self-reports obtained by interviewing the subject in the community five times (every two to three months) over a one-year period after discharge from the target hospitalization, and (*c*) collateral reports obtained by interviewing informants knowledgeable about the subject's behavior in the community, also five times over a one-year period.

The limitations of relying on official records (e.g., arrest or mental hospitalization) are well known (Monahan and Steadman, this volume). Self-report, of course, is not unproblematic but is recognized as a significant improvement over the use of official records. The report of "key informants" in the community is less frequently sought in mental health research, but may go far to correct for any distortions of perception or memory, or prevarication, that may affect patient self-report.[4] We decided to use all three methods of measuring our criterion.

There is no definitive answer to the question of an optimum length of follow-up. Ultimately, duration of a follow-up is dictated both by the research questions asked and by the resources available to answer them. Our research questions have to do with the assessment of risk of violent behavior toward others in the community. The clinical and policy context in which these questions often arise, and the one in which our study takes place, is the civil hospitalization of mentally disordered persons. Since we intended our research to produce results relevant both to clinical risk assessment and risk management and to policy makers in mental health law, we had to balance a number of substantive concerns, as well as the resource allocation issue—that longer follow-ups cost more than shorter follow-ups.

On the one hand, admitting clinicians (as well as commitment statutes) tend to focus their violence assessments on the immediate future rather than the long term (Mulvey and Lidz 1988; Lidz and Mulvey 1990). This form of clinical relevance, therefore, would argue for a relatively short follow-up of no more than several months. On the other hand, many of the patients who are hospitalized on acute inpatient wards, such as those in which our research is being conducted, tend to cycle in and out of the hospital and therefore present more of an ongoing clinical management concern than a one-time treatment challenge. This form of clinical relevance—no doubt relevant to policy makers as well—would argue for a long follow-up of perhaps several years.

In addition to our desire to have our results be relevant to the clinical and policy communities, methodological considerations also played a role in our choice of follow-up period. Many of the risk factors in our clinical and contextual domains can be expected to fluctuate over time. Clinical functioning may be at its highest and symptom levels at their lowest at the time of discharge, when the patient is appropriately medicated and in a controlled setting. As the effects of medication dissipate and as some patients are noncompliant with aftercare recommendations or otherwise relapse, functioning may deteriorate and symptom levels increase. The patient's living situation and degree of social support may also vary over his or her tenure in the com-

4. Funding to support the inclusion of collateral informants in the MacArthur Risk Assessment Study has been provided by the National Institute of Mental Health, grant number R01 MH 49696.

munity. Since we want to gauge the relationship between clinical and contextual risk factors and violent behavior, a follow-up period sufficient to allow "natural" variation in these factors is necessary.

Combining these concerns for clinical and policy relevance with our methodological needs and resource constraints led us to decide on a follow-up duration of one year post-discharge from the target hospitalization.

The frequency of contact with our subjects over the one year follow-up was another decision with no obvious answer. In the field trial, we used an interval of two months between interviews, since it had appeared to work well in the prior research of Lidz and Mulvey (Lidz 1987) at one of our research sites. Every two months seemed to be sufficiently frequent to allow the subjects to be located and have them remember their participation in the research. It also seemed to be a time interval over which they could recall with apparent accuracy and detail any violent incidents that had occurred.

To further test our assumptions, we performed a small study at the Worcester field trial site. After two two-month interviews, we randomly assigned one set of subjects ($N = 20$) to a one-month, one-month, one-month, three-month interview schedule, and another set ($N = 19$) to a three-month, one-month, one-month, one-month schedule. Our questions centered both on the subjects' tolerance for more frequent contacts and the improvement or diminution of recall over one- or three-month periods. Because of the small number of subjects in this study, meaningful statistical analyses were precluded and we relied on the impressions of the research staff for guidance.

The staff found the subjects very intolerant of the imposition presented by monthly interviews. They were also concerned that a response set had developed, since the core of the interview about the frequency and details of violent incidents was the same at every administration. That response set took one of two forms. The interviewers suspected that some subjects began fabricating violent incidents so that they would have something to tell us, and others began underreporting violent incidents because they knew if they reported a violent incident, an additional set of questions would ensue and extend the interview. For these reasons, we decided against one-month interviews.

The advisability of the three-month interval was much less clear. The staff had somewhat less confidence than with the two-month interval that the subjects could clearly recall when the prior interview had been done, and, therefore, what the relevant reporting period was. Yet, the rates and types of violence reported during the three-month interval seemed to be similar to what was generated with two-month intervals, particularly for the more serious incidents. Three months was logistically attractive, since it would reduce the number of community follow-ups from six to four, which, in turn, would permit an increase in the size of the sample, thereby increasing the statistical power of the analyses we could perform. Balancing these competing substantive and resource concerns, we decided to do five interviews, with an average interval of just under two and one-half months between them, over the course of the one-year follow-up.

2. We are using both experienced clinicians and highly trained community interviewers to administer our research instruments.

Given that the field trial indicated that our initial battery of instruments took much too long to administer, shortening that battery became a methodological priority. The Diagnostic Interview Schedule was by far the longest and most difficult instrument we administered. As we rethought why we were using DIS, we recognized that it was primarily to establish an independent DSM III-R diagnosis. The particular symptom patterns in which we were most interested were all being measured by other instruments. Therefore, we sought a briefer means of establishing diagnosis. We concluded that the DSM III-R Checklist (Janca and Helzer 1990) met our needs.

The DSM III-R Checklist must be completed by a clinician, rather than by a trained nonclinical interviewer as was the case with the full DIS. Therefore, we decided to employ experienced independent clinicians to use the DSM III-R Checklist to confirm the patient's chart diagnosis and to administer those instruments requiring the greatest clinical expertise (e.g., our modification of the Maudsley Assessment of Delusions Schedule; Taylor et al., this volume). Highly trained community interviewers are able to administer the remaining instruments (e.g., the self-report measures of anger control and impulsiveness). The community interviewers also listen to an audiotape of the clinician interview done as part of the initial battery, so that they will be prepared to readminister selected clinical variables (e.g., the Brief Psychiatric Rating Scale, the Global Assessment of Functioning Scale) in the community during the follow-up interviews. Our goal in the full-scale study is to have one clinical session for the administration of the diagnostic instrument and the other interview-based symptom inventories (i.e., delusions, hallucinations, BPRS, GAF, and neurology screen) and one session with the community interviewer to complete the self-report instruments. This involves a more manageable total of two sessions in the hospital at a maximum length of one-and-a-half to two hours each.

3. Our subjects are (a) males and females, (b) between the ages of 18 and 40, (c) of white, African American, or Hispanic race or ethnicity, (d) English-speaking, (e) resident in the local area, (f) of both voluntary and involuntary admission status, (g) unscreened for prior or presenting violence, and (h) excluding only patients whose primary diagnosis is mental retardation.[5]

5. More precisely, we use the DSM III-R Checklist to screen in the following diagnoses: depression, dysthymia, mania, schizophrenia, brief reactive psychosis, schizophreniform disor-

The two principles that guided our inclusion and exclusion criteria were the desire to have as representative a sample of mental patients as possible and the necessity that the chosen sample have a sufficiently high base rate of violence during the follow-up to permit data analysis. Our choice of subjects is a straightforward attempt to balance these two principles. In our field trials, described above, females had rates of violence comparable to males, but persons over 40 had much lower rates of violence than persons under 40. Therefore females were included and people of either gender over 40 were excluded. Since race or ethnicity could be an important factor in the research, we wished to study as many racial and ethnic groupings as possible. But since the presence of groups other than whites, African Americans, and Hispanics—for example, Asian Americans—in the hospitals from which we are gathering our data is very small, any data we obtained would be uninterpretable (and therefore a waste of resources to gather).

As it is, we do not expect that the Hispanic sample will be large enough to provide a sufficient amount of follow-up violence for independent analysis. But we will at least be able to compare Hispanics and non-Hispanics on their scores on the initial in-hospital instrument. Eventually, it could be possible to prepare a Spanish-language version of our instruments. But this is clearly premature, given the enormous cost that would be involved and the fact that the instruments have not yet been validated.

Screening for prior violence in the admission incident would clearly raise the base rate of follow-up violence. But since to do so would mean that we would miss all the follow-up violence committed by people *without* prior or presenting violence, we have decided not to screen. Also, from a policy standpoint, we want to have as typical a range of patients (within the constraint of having to stratify the samples to minimize site variation) as actually presents for inpatient admission and for whom clinical risk assessments are regularly demanded.

4. We anticipate a total sample size of approximately 1,000 patients, selected from three civil mental hospitals: the Western Psychiatric Institute and Clinic in Pittsburgh, the Worcester (Massachusetts) State Hospital, and the Western Missouri Mental Health Center in Kansas City.

Given the level of follow-up violence that the field trials leads us to expect, the number of factors we wished to control for, and the problem of subject attrition over time, we concluded that a sample size of approximately 1,000 persons was necessary for meaningful analysis of our data. The chosen sites—the same ones successfully used in the field trial—represent many of

---

der, schizoaffective disorder, delusional (paranoid) disorder, atypical psychosis, psychoaffective substance dependence, psychoactive substance abuse, and adjustment disorder. The Mini–Mental State examination is also given to assess organic brain syndrome.

the settings currently providing public and private inpatient mental health care in the U.S.: a university-based medical center (WPIC, Pittsburgh), a state mental hospital (WSH, Worcester), and a metropolitan community mental health center (WMMHC, Kansas City). While the use of multiple sites makes special demands for reliability in order to pool the data for aggregate analysis, we believe we can meet this demand and the research will have substantially greater generalizability as a result.

Conclusions

We have described the MacArthur Risk Assessment Study as an illustration of how principles derived from decision theory and public health, as well as methodological critiques of the existing knowledge base, can shape the design of a new generation of risk assessment research (Monahan and Steadman, this volume). If the MacArthur Risk Assessment Study is successful in its efforts to establish robust markers of violence risk, future research might profitably address optimum methods of educating clinicians in the use of these markers. In that manner, the validity of clinical risk assessments and the effectiveness of clinical risk management could be appreciably improved. And if the study is not successful, it will stand as testimony to the intractable difficulties clinicians face in assessing the likelihood of a behavior as complex and multidetermined as violence in a population as diverse and poorly understood as the mentally disordered.

References

Cocozza, J. J., and H. J. Steadman. 1976. The failure of psychiatric predictions of dangerousness: Clear and convincing evidence. *Rutgers Law Review* 29: 1084–1101.

————. 1978. Prediction in psychiatry: An example of misplaced confidence in experts. *Social Problems* 25:265–76.

Craig, T. 1982. An epidemiologic study of problems associated with violence among psychiatric inpatients. *American Journal of Psychiatry* 139:1262–66.

Denno, D. 1990. *Biology and violence: From birth to adulthood.* Cambridge: Cambridge University Press.

Dobash, R. P., R. E. Dobash, M. Wilson, and M. Daly. 1992. The myth of sexual symmetry in marital violence. *Social Problems* 39:71–91.

Endicott, J., R. Spitzer, and J. Fleiss. 1976. The Global Assessment Scale: A procedure for measuring overall severity of psychiatric disturbance. *Archives of General Psychiatry* 33:766–71.

Felson, R. B., and H. J. Steadman. 1983. Situational factors in disputes leading to criminal violence. *Criminology* 21:59–74.

Harris, G. T., M. E. Rice, and C. A. Cormier. 1991. Psychopathy and violent recidivism. *Law and Human Behavior* 15:625–37.

Hiday, V. A. 1991. Arrest and incarceration of civil commitment candidates. *Hospital and Community Psychiatry* 42:729–34.

Janca, A., and J. Helzer. 1990. DSM-III-R Criteria Checklist. *DIS Newsletter* 7:17.

Klassen, D., and W. A. O'Connor. 1988. A prospective study of predictors of violence in adult mental health admissions. *Law and Human Behavior* 12:143–58.

Lidz, C. 1987. Conditional prediction and the management of dangerousness. Proposal submitted to the Criminal and Violent Behavior Research Branch, National Institute of Mental Health (Grant MH40030-07).

Lidz, C., and E. Mulvey. 1990. Institutional factors affecting psychiatric admission and commitment decisions. In G. Weiss, ed., *Social science perspectives on medical ethics*. Boston: Kluwer.

Lidz, C., E. Mulvey, and W. Gardner. 1993. The accuracy of predictions of violence to others. *Journal of the American Medical Association* 269:1007–11.

Monahan, J. 1988. Risk assessment of violence among the mentally disordered: Generating useful knowledge. *International Journal of Law and Psychiatry* 11:249–57.

———. 1992. Mental disorder and violent behavior: Perceptions and evidence. *American Psychologist* 47:511–21.

Monahan, J., and S. A. Shah. 1989. Dangerousness and commitment of the mentally disordered in the United States. *Schizophrenia Bulletin* 15(4):541–53.

Mulvey E., J. Geller, and L. Roth. 1987. The promise and the perils of involuntary outpatient commitment. *American Psychologist* 42:571–84.

Mulvey E., and C. Lidz. 1988. What clinicians talk about when assessing dangerousness. Paper presented at the Biennial Meeting of the American Psychology-Law Society, Miami.

National Research Council. 1993. *Understanding and preventing violence*. Washington, D.C.: National Academy Press.

Overall, J., and C. Klett. 1972. *Applied multivariate analysis*. New York: McGraw-Hill.

Rattenbury, F., M. Harrow, F. Stoll, and R. Kettering. 1984. *The Personal Ideation Inventory: An interview for assessing major dimensions of delusional thinking*. New York: Microfiche Publications.

Robins, L., and D. Regier. 1991. *Psychiatric disorders in America: The Epidemiologic Catchment Area study*. New York: Free Press.

Sosowsky, L. 1980. Explaining the increased arrest rate among mental patients: A cautionary note. *American Journal of Psychiatry* 137:1602–5.

Steadman, H. J. 1987. How well can we predict violence for adults? In F. N. Dotile and C. H. Foust, eds., *The prediction of criminal violence*. Springfield, Ill.: Charles C. Thomas.

Steadman, H. J., and J. J. Cocozza. 1974. *Careers of the criminally insane*. Lexington, Mass.: Lexington Books.

———. 1979. The dangerousness standard and psychiatry: A cross-national issue in the social control of the mentally ill. *Sociology and Social Research* 63:649–70.

Steadman, H. J., J. J. Cocozza, and M. E. Melick. 1978. Explaining the increased arrest rate among mental patients: The changing clientele of state hospitals. *American Journal of Psychiatry* 135:816–20.

Stone, A. 1975. *Mental health and the law: A system in transition*. Washington, D.C.: Government Printing Office.

Swanson, J., C. Holzer, V. Ganju, and R. Jono. 1990. Violence and psychiatric disorder in the community: Evidence from the Epidemiological Catchment Area surveys. *Hospital and Community Psychiatry* 41:761–70.

Virkkunen, M., J. DeJong, J. Bartko, F. Goodwin, and M. Linnoila. 1989. Relationship of psychobiological variables to recidivism in violent offenders and impulsive fire setters. *Archives of General Psychiatry* 46:600–3.

United Nations. 1991. Proposed Guidelines for Mental Hospitalization. New York: United Nations.

Wiederanders, M. 1990. *The effectiveness of the conditional release program.* Sacramento: California Department of Mental Health.

Wilson, J., and R. Herrnstein. 1985. *Crime and human nature.* New York: Simon and Schuster.

Index